Miles Franklin was born in 1879 in the Monaro region of New South Wales. Her first novel, *My Brilliant Career*, was published to much excitement and acclaim in 1901. She moved to Sydney in 1904; there she worked as a freelance writer and became involved in feminist and literary circles. In 1907 she moved to America, where she edited a feminist trade union magazine. She went to Europe at the beginning of the First World War, during which she served as a nurse. She returned to Australia in 1933 with an established reputation as a writer. She died in 1954.

Miles Franklin published twelve novels, many of them under pseudonyms. She also published literary criticism, autobiography and a biography of Joseph Furphy with Kate Baker. Her papers contain many unpublished novels and plays. She left her estate to establish an annual literary award for an Australian novel.

IMPRINT CLASSICS

MY
BRILLIANT
CAREER
MY CAREER GOES BUNG

MILES FRANKLIN

*Introduced
by Elizabeth Webby*

AN ANGUS & ROBERTSON BOOK

My Brilliant Career *first published in 1901*
First published in Australia in 1966 by
Angus & Robertson Publishers
A&R Classics paperback edition 1973
Reprinted 1978
Arkon paperback edition 1979
Reprinted 1979, 1980 (three times), 1981, 1982, 1983, 1984,
1985 (twice), 1986 (twice)
Eden paperback edition 1987
Reprinted 1988
My Career Goes Bung *first published in 1946*
This Imprint Classics one-volume edition published in Australia in 1990 by
Collins/Angus & Robertson Publishers Australia

Collins/Angus & Robertson Publishers Australia
Unit 4, Eden Park, 31 Waterloo Road, North Ryde
NSW 2113, Australia

William Collins Publishers Ltd
31 View Road, Glenfield, Auckland 10, New Zealand

Angus & Robertson (UK)
16 Golden Square, London W1R 4BN, United Kingdom

Copyright © Miles Franklin estate 1901, 1946, 1990

National Library of Australia
Cataloguing-in-Publication data:

Franklin, Miles, 1879–1954.
  My brilliant career; My career goes bung.

  ISBN 0 207 16642 0.

  I. Title. II. Title: My career goes bung.

A823.2

Cover painting: Waiting *by Gordon Coutts. Oil on canvas.*
Purchased 1896. Art Gallery of New South Wales.

Typeset in 10 pt Times Roman by Midland Typesetters, Victoria
Printed in Australia by Griffin Press

5   4   3   2   1
95 94 93 92 91 90

INTRODUCTION

When Stella Maria Sarah Miles Franklin began writing *My Brilliant Career* on 20 September 1898, she was eighteen years old. The book was finished in first draft just over six months later, on 25 March 1899. What, at the end of the nineteenth century, did a nineteen-year-old living in the Australian bush do with a completed manuscript? Many, no doubt, would merely have put it into a drawer and forgotten about it, but Miles Franklin was determined to achieve publication.

Initially, she sent her manuscript to the one local firm just beginning to make a name as a publisher of Australian writers, Angus & Robertson of Sydney. The accompanying letter, dated 30 March 1899 and signed 'S. M. S. Miles Franklin', began 'Herewith a yarn which I have written entitled "My Brilliant (?) Career". I would take it very kindly if you would read it and state whether or not it is fit for publication.' In what George Robertson was later to describe as 'the one *serious* mistake of our publishing department', the manuscript was returned to Franklin on 7 April.

Undaunted, Franklin sent it out again immediately, to J. F. Archibald, editor of Australia's then most famous literary magazine, the Sydney *Bulletin*. On 18 April, Alex Montgomery replied for Archibald, 'Not having time to read your ms through, I cannot pronounce upon the merits or otherwise of the plot and general handling; but from the glance I have taken of it here and there it appears to be fairly well written.' Mr Franklin was advised to send the manuscript to A. G. Stephens' literary agency, where an expert opinion could be given for a small charge.

The next to read the manuscript was, however, the person who had advised Miles Franklin to write about the local scene rather than English lords and ladies, T. J. Hebblewhite of the *Goulburn*

Post. He wrote to her on 30 July 1899 offering to go over the manuscript with her and, after revision, to send it to some literary friends in Sydney. *My Brilliant Career* was revised between 18 September and 26 November 1899, though it was Franklin who then began sending it off again. On 3 January 1900, A. G. Stephens replied to a letter from Mr M. Franklin asking to see the manuscript. But a few days earlier Franklin had received a letter from Henry Lawson, to whom she had written on 19 November. Lawson offered to read the manuscript, though he was clearly expecting the worst, 'you must give me, say, a month to get through it and see what I can do for you'. All, however, changed when he began reading *My Brilliant Career*:

> Dear 'Miles Franklin',
> Received your MS. this morning and have more than 'skimmed' through it already. Will you write and tell me who and what you really are? man or woman? and something about yourself? and will you let me keep your story till my publisher returns from England? He is somewhere on the way now. I believe that you have done a big thing.

Accordingly, Lawson again sent the manuscript to Angus & Robertson, with an accompanying letter to George Robertson praising the novel's 'truth and vividness' and comparing it to Charlotte Bronte's *Jane Eyre* and Olive Schreiner's *Story of an African Farm* (comparisons that were to be echoed by many of Franklin's first reviewers). Lawson was leaving for London on 20 April 1900 so, as no positive response had yet been received from Angus & Robetson, he wrote to Franklin on 16 April, asking if she wished him to try to place the book with an English publisher. Anticipating that some changes might be required, he asked for her 'formal permission to "place" the work as I think fit. Also some latitude in editing in case English publishers want some paragraphs "toned down".' Franklin agreed and, on arriving in London, Lawson also asked his literary agent, J. B. Pinker, to look after Franklin's novel.

Pinker soon managed to place the manuscript with William Blackwood but, as Lawson had foreseen, changes were insisted on. Blackwood wrote to Pinker on 29 January 1900:

> There are a few passages in the book which I think if allowed to stand in their present form would prejudice it with many readers, and I think it well to reserve the right to remove or tone down them after consultation with Mr Lawson. I will submit proofs of anything which I may consider injudicious on rereading the work in print.

A few years later, in January 1903, Lawson wrote to the *Bulletin*, giving his own version of the 'toning down' process:

> Note that *My Brilliant Career* was published against the judgment of Blackwood's London manager and reader, nor did William Blackwood think highly of the book. I told him that it would go in Australia; and he published it as a venture, as you may see by the cheap get-up. And I was right. I had to barrack for many religious, political, and sex-problem passages which I blushed at myself, while I was assuring him that Australians wouldn't blush—and he saw the blush and struck 'em out.

On 6 February 1900, Franklin replied to Pinker's letter of 30 January, enclosing Blackwood's offer to publish the novel, with some conditions of her own. After agreeing to the royalty offered, she requested:

> 2. Please be sure that in publication of the said MSS. the note of interrogation is not omitted from the title, thus: 'My Brilliant (?) Career'.
> 3. If convenient I would like the written mss preserved and returned to me after the publisher is done with it.
> 4. Please on no account allow 'Miss' to prefix my name on the title page as I do not wish it to be known that I'm a young girl but desire to pose as a bald-headed seer of the sterner sex.
> 5. I trust it will not be taken as presumptious (sic) on my part to say that any toning down is very, very much against

me. I have merely written a real story of what I believe, in the teeth of people's prejudices and do not look at life through the spectacles of orthodox cantists. Of course this is only my feeling regarding the matter and should Mr Blackwood consider any of the matter really unpublishable I am willing to defer to the judgment of wiser and more experienced heads and allow the cloaking of a few sentences after consultation with Mr Lawson. I am curious to know which passages are considered injudicious.

Trusting such little matters may be worthy of your attention.

But Franklin's irony and indignation were to no avail since, as Pinker informed her on 15 April, her letter reached him too late for the title to be as she wished. Also, 'It was imperative that certain passages should be omitted, and Mr Lawson and I agreed with Mr Blackwood regarding the necessity. I do not think, however, that you will find the book has lost anything that was essential to your effect.'

The sight of her toned down and interrogationless firstborn did little to mollify Franklin. On 18 September, after receiving her copies, she wrote Pinker a testy note pointing out that 'it would have been wise and fair to have allowed me to see the proofs of the story that I could have corrected the many irritating mistakes and substitutions in the matter of slang and idiom'. It was to be many more decades, with the establishment of a regular airmail service, before authors living in Australia were able to correct the proofs of works published in Britain.

Franklin's anger at the mutilation of her book and the revelation of her age and gender would not have been much assuaged by the very small amount she earned for it, despite dozens of glowing reviews in England and Australia. A. G. Stephens' *Bulletin* review of 28 September 1901 had thanked Lawson and Blackwood's for getting the novel into print, since it 'could hardly have been published in Australia with a chance of profit; the local audience which it will interest is still too scanty'. Pinker's accounts tell another story. From publication in mid-1901 until the end of 1903, only 408 copies of the six-shilling English edition of

My Brilliant Career had been sold, as against 2564 of the cheaper colonial edition which circulated in Australia. Since Franklin's royalties on the latter were a mere one and four-fifths pence a copy, her first royalty cheque, sent in July 1902, amounted to only £16 5s 6d. This pattern was maintained until Franklin withdrew *My Brilliant Career* from sale in 1910, refusing to let it be reprinted in her lifetime.

Over the alterations to her text, Franklin evidently also made her displeasure known to Lawson, since he promised to send her the corrected proofs 'which will explain and help you'. Unfortunately these, if sent, appear not to have survived. Nor, it seems, does the original manuscript, despite Franklin's repeated requests that it be returned to her. So we shall probably never be able to satisfy our curiosity as to which passages in the work were found so injudicious. It is interesting to speculate whether as much toning down would have been required if Franklin had managed to maintain the male persona she initially adopted. And just how different would the reception given to *My Brilliant Career* have been if Franklin *had* been allowed her pose as 'a bald-headed seer'? Lawson, of course, gave the game away in his prefatory comment that, 'I hadn't read three pages when I saw what you will no doubt see at once—that the story had been written by a girl.' Contemporary reviewers, and nearly all later critics, have followed Lawson in stressing Franklin's youth and gender and in reading *My Brilliant Career* as autobiography rather than fiction. Yet it is well to remember that Lawson's initial reaction had not been as certain—'man or woman?'—as he later claimed. Without the preface most readers would have assumed that 'Miles Franklin' was male. Perhaps he may even have been, as 'Mr Richardson' was a few years later with *The Getting of Wisdom*, congratulated on his remarkable insights into a young girl's mind.

My own reading of *My Brilliant Career* is based on the assumption that it is critically inept to identify Miles Franklin with Sybylla Melvyn. This identification, a commonplace in most previous criticism of the novel, was unfortunately reinforced by the film version, which ends with Sybylla sending off a package to Blackwood's and the information that this firm printed *My Brilliant Career* in 1901. My detailed account of the novel's difficult path to publication is, in part, intended to counteract the rosy romanticism of this image of authorship. There is nothing in the novel itself to suggest that Sybylla's manuscript did not end up languishing in a bottom drawer.

The distinction between Miles Franklin as author and Sybylla as narrator of *My Brilliant Career* is, I believe, clearly to be seen in Chapter 19, the episode of the picnic races. When Sybylla sees Harry Beecham escorting a beautiful woman she is obviously very jealous. Though she does not admit this directly, there are many hints: 'Somehow I was feeling very disappointed. I had expected Harold Beecham to be alone,' and, 'I don't know why I took no interest in the races. I knew nearly all the horses running . . . Of more interest to me than the races was the pair strolling at a distance. They were fit for an artist's models.' Though Sybylla acknowledges Miss Derrick's great physical attractions here, we are given a more jaundiced view of her a few pages later:

> 'By Jove, isn't she a splendid creature!' enthusiastically whispered a gentleman sitting beside me.
>
> I looked at her critically. She was very big, and in a bony stiff way was much developed in figure. She had a nice big nose, and a long well-shaped face, a thin straight mouth, and empty light eyes. If my attention had not been called to her I would not have noticed her one way or the other, but being pointed to as a beauty, I weighed her according to my idea of facial charm, and pronounced her one of the most insipid-looking people I had set eyes upon.

The pointed qualifications in the description of Miss Derrick make Sybylla's jealousy very evident here, a sign that she is more deeply involved with Harry Beecham than she cares to admit, and also a sign of her fallible status as narrator. Miles Franklin does not present us with a Sybylla we can take at face value.

Since Sybylla is purporting to be writing an autobiography rather than a novel, she frequently criticises fiction and romance conventions, claiming for her book the greater authority of non-fiction:

> This is not a romance—I have too often faced the music of life to the tune of hardship to waste time in snivelling and gushing over fancies and dreams; neither is it a novel, but simply a yarn—a *real* yarn. . . . There is no plot in this story, because there has been none in my life or in any other life which has come under my notice.

Of course, unbeknown to Sybylla, *My Brilliant Career* does have a plot, the characteristic plot of the romance: hero and heroine meet; complications arise; eventually all are resolved; marriage follows. Franklin was clearly aware of this. In her 1899 letter to Angus & Roberton she refers to her novel as 'a few pictures of Australian life with a little of that mythical commodity, love, thrown in for the benefit of young readers'. She also subverts the traditional romance plot at the end of the novel. All complications—the usual ones of financial problems and rival suitors—are resolved. Harry regains his wealth in a highly romantic way: 'some old sweetheart of Harold's father had bequeathed untold wealth to this her lost love's son'; there are even some tongue-in-cheek references to 'fiction' and 'fairy-tale'. Harry still loves Sybylla rather than her more beautiful sister—but she refuses to marry him. Apart from this major twist at the end, *My Brilliant Career* follows very closely what might be called the 'Cinderella romance plot': poor, plain, non-heroine inspires great passion in handsome, wealthy hero (also, of course, the plot of *Jane Eyre*). Just as she conceals the strength of her own attraction to him, so Sybylla will never admit the strength of Harold's love for her. In her final letter to him she dismisses his love as a fancy, 'a passing flame'. A few pages later, however, another letter, from Sybylla's grannie, reports the surprising news that Harold, who hates to travel, is distractedly touring the world. Grannie can only wonder as to Harold's sanity but the reader knows that he is behaving in the only appropriate way for a truly heartbroken lover.

Throughout *My Brilliant Career* there are also suggestions that Sybylla's attitudes to love and courtship have been influenced by her reading of popular romance fiction: when she arrives at Caddagat she is overjoyed to find a Marie Corelli novel and George du Maurier's *Trilby* (1894) on the bookshelves. At times of stress, especially stress brought on by an unwanted male proposal or suggestion, Sybylla falls back on the sort of language associated with the heroines of Victorian romance and melodrama. So, she replies to Mr McSwat's suggestion that she wishes to marry his son:

> Silence, you ignorant old creature! How dare you have the incomparable impertinence to mention my name in conjunction with that of your boor of a son. Though he were a millionaire I would think his touch contamination. You have fallen through for once if you imagine I go out at night to meet any one— I merely go away to be free for a few minutes from the suffocating atmosphere of your odious home.

Notice the amusing clash here of the Victorian high style with the Australian colloquial as Sybylla's indignation gets the better of her reading in 'You have fallen through for once . . . '.

The best example of the influence of Sybylla's reading on her attitudes to men and love can be found in Chapter 20, the episode of Harold's proposal of marriage. Here Harold's typical no-nonsense Australian approach, the complete absence of conventional romance trappings, totally confuses Sybylla:

> We stood beside the table, some distance apart, and, facing me, he said:
> 'It is no use of me making a long yarn about nothing. I'm sure you know what I want to say better than I do myself. You always are wonderfully smart at seeing through a fellow. Tell me, will it be yes or no?'
> This was an experience in love. He did not turn red or white, or yellow or green, nor did he tremble or stammer, or cry or laugh, or become fierce or passionate, or tender or anything but just himself, as I had always known him. He displayed

no more emotion than had he been inviting me to a picnic.
This was not as I had pictured a man would tell his love,
or as I had read of it, heard of it, or wished it should be.
A curious feeling—disappointment, perhaps—stole over me.
His matter-of-fact coolness flabbergasted me.

Her response is very much that of the stiff Victorian heroine:
' "Is this not rather sudden? You have given me no intimation
of your intentions," I stammered.' Sybylla is, I believe, still playing
this role when she responds to Harold's attempted kiss by hitting
him with the riding whip. As we have seen, and are meant to
have seen, throughout the novel she underestimates the strength
of Harry's feelings for her because he does not behave like a
lover in a romance—at least not until her final rejection of him,
when he goes off on his world tour.

In *The Legend of the Nineties*, Vance Palmer refers to one feature
of the 1890s Australian tradition as 'The tendency to take for
granted the values people act upon in life rather than those they
might be persuaded to accept as novel-readers.' (p. 117) *My
Brilliant Career*, along with many other novels, shows that this
sort of life/fiction opposition is too simple: the values people
act upon in life may, in fact, be derived from the novels they
have read.

Given my reading of *My Brilliant Career*, it is particularly
pleasing to be able to discuss it here alongside its sequel, *My
Career Goes Bung*. This later novel opens with a poem that
plays about with the notions of 'truth' and 'fiction' in what we
would now see as a characteristically postmodern way. In her
introductory comments, too, Franklin hints at the devastating
effect on her of the reception of her first novel as straight autobiography: 'The literalness with which *My Brilliant Career* was
taken was a shock to one of any imagination.' For Franklin,
the shock was compounded by the anger of friends and relatives
at what they took to be unflattering portraits of themselves, and
by gossip as to the identity of Harold Beecham. Little wonder
that, as Val Kent has demonstrated in her 'Alias Miles Franklin',
Franklin later became obsessively devoted to false identities and

pseudonyms. Nor that she became very dismissive of her first novel, writing in *Laughter Not for a Cage* (1956) of *My Brilliant Career* as 'a girl's story . . . conceived and tossed off on impulse in a matter of weeks. Spontaneously out of inexperience and consuming longings and discontents . . . a novel of sixteen'. Franklin's comment—belied by the actual writing and publishing history of the novel as outlined above—has unfortunately been used to reinforce critical readings of *My Brilliant Career* as autobiography rather than fiction and as a book not to be taken seriously.

My Career Goes Bung was, as Franklin notes in her introduction, a more immediate response to the debacle of *My Brilliant Career* and planned as 'a corrective'. So, for example, Sybylla Melvyn's 'real' Pa and Ma are shown to be quite different to the mother and father in *My Brilliant Career* and Sybylla now appears to be an only child. In addition, one Henry Beauchamp turns up, claiming to be the original of Harold Beecham, and so insisting that Sybylla must marry him. Sybylla herself is also portrayed as quite a different person—'her bright and illuminating self' to use Old Harris's phrase—a beauty with plenty of male suitors. Now, too, we get her opinions on motherhood, the treatment of women, the Church and the Sydney literary scene without the intervention of the editor's blue pencil. Or do we?

Though Franklin implies in her introduction to *My Career Goes Bung* that the novel remained unchanged from its first conception in 1902 to eventual publication in 1946, a very different story is told by her manuscripts. The final nine chapters of the twenty-three that make up the 1902 version of *The End of My Career*, as it was then called, are to be found among Franklin's papers in the Mitchell Library. This handwritten version was clearly the one sent to George Robertson on 10 November 1902. Franklin wished the book to be taken as a parody of *My Brilliant Career*, written by somebody else:

It is intended for a satirical skit on 'things in jinril' and takes the form of a take-off sequel to *My Brilliant Career*. The point of the idea lies in that it must not upon any account be known that I'm the perpetrator, else it would fall flat as raw pancakes, ruin the career of my other yarn, and make things less than a small medium for me.

In this version, Sybylla comes to Sydney engaged to Harold Beecham and eventually returns to the bush to marry him. While in Sydney she meets many thinly disguised writers and celebrities including 'Zither Qualey' (the poet Victor Daley); 'Violin Dadson better known as the "Barrel Organ" ' (Banjo Paterson); and 'Mr Aijee Refuseem sporting editor of "The Watch Dog" the most decorous and widely read of Australian weeklies, a journal with a pink dress and a cartoon on its face' (A. G. Stephens, then literary editor of the *Bulletin*). There is also a telling exchange with another woman writer, clearly Ethel Turner:

> 'Oh, Miss so and so, do tell me quickly: when you write books do people think it's you and tell hair lifting yarns about you and make you wish you weren't born?' . . .
> She laughed sweetly.
> 'Don't worry. I've gone through all that. Women are not only discredited with a sense of humour but in addition are not allowed an imagination in their efforts in fiction, but are supposed to draw only upon their own history.'

Franklin had already written one sequel to *My Brilliant Career*, referred to in an earlier letter to Robertson, 20 July 1902, as 'another yarn dealing with the untimely—or, in good people's ideas, the too long delayed—conclusion of that reprehensible individual, Sybylla Melvyn'. This was eventually dispatched to Pinker in London on 27 September, under the title 'On the Outside Track'. However, Pinker did not place the novel and it was eventually heavily revised to form the basis of *Cockatoos*, published under Franklin's 'Brent of Bin Bin' pseudonym in 1954. Franklin evidently felt, as she told Robertson on 4 December 1902, after he had rejected *The End of My Career*, that 'this and the other sequel would have clashed splendidly and mixed things up in rather a unique fashion.'

Robertson rightly saw that no one would be fooled: 'Your hand would certainly be recognised', he wrote on 30 November. He was also worried about publishing a novel which, because of its easily recognisable personalities, might be an instant success but have no lasting appeal. As well, he thought some of the people portrayed in the book might be upset by it, especially Mrs De Gilhooly (Mrs Crasterton in *My Career Goes Bung*), Sybylla's Sydney hostess. In this case, however, Franklin appears not to have had any particular person in mind. As with the lovely Edmée and the rest of the inhabitants of Geebung Villa, she was satirising types rather than individuals.

Franklin evidently took the rejected manuscript with her to America in 1906 and submitted a revised, typewritten version to Blackwood's in 1910. In a letter written from Chicago on 4 April, after discussing the disposal of the remaining copies of *My Brilliant Career*, she advised them:

> I have on hand the manuscript of a most inimitable sequel. Would you care to consider it? I enclose the title page and suggested foreword. It contains a story and sketches of Australian people hit off very naturally but withal safely disguised and in no way offensive. It is however purely local and would be for publication in Australia only. There would be no need for an English edition. . . . My intention was to give it to an Australian publisher when I go home in 1911 and have him bring it out as a joke at my expense, but it might go better if coming out in your style and as nearly as possible an imitation of *My Brilliant Career*.

Clearly, Franklin was still hoping that *The End of My Career*, as it was still called, would be read as parody of *My Brilliant Career* by another hand. The title page, preface, dedication, original lines, introduction and contents list survive in manuscript from the 1910 version, along with parts of Chapters 19 and 21 and the whole of the last four chapters, 26–29. A comparison between these chapter titles and those for the eventually published *My Career Goes Bung* shows a considerable degree of correspondence, suggesting that the major revision away from the specific personalities of the 1902 version to a more general satire of Sydney social and literary life had occurred by 1910. However, the typescript still ends with Sybylla's marriage to Harry Beecham; indeed, with Sybylla happy to be able to satisfy Harry's desires in life if not her own, this ending is more romantic than that of the 1902 version, which had parodied the ending of *My Brilliant Career* and then offered an epilogue in which the book was seen as a dream on the part of an elderly man.

Parody was still strongly to the fore in other sections of the 1910 typescript. The title page runs:

THE END OF MY CAREER
A STUDY IN SELF ANALYSIS
(Not Necessarily a sequel to "My Brilliant Career")
By
Miles Franklin's Understudy
With a Preface by Peter McSwat.

McSwat's preface is a direct parody of Lawson's to *My Brilliant Career*.

I haddent read three chapters when I see what any man as intelligent as myself will see at once—that the yarn must have been written by a man. No woman would have such branes for putting facts in such a plane nacheral way.

The introduction is an equally direct parody of Sybylla's to *My Brilliant Career*. The 'Original Lines' are those which, with some·modifications, appear at the opening of the 1946 edition of *My Career Goes Bung*. Comparison of the surviving portion of Chapter 21, 'A Surprise for 'Gustus—and me' with Chapter 19 of *My Career Goes Bung*, 'In Need of a Friend', shows very considerable rewriting of Gaddy's (originally 'Gustus') proposal and its aftermath.

The End of My Career was rejected by Blackwood's on 13 November 1911. Franklin, as she notes in her introduction to *My Career Goes Bung*, thought the manuscript had been lost but rediscovered it in 1936. Presumably these further revisions were made between then and 1942 when she began offering *My Career Goes Bung* to publishers. Most, as one might have expected, also wished to reprint *My Brilliant Career*, unavailable since 1910. L. L. Woolacott of the Currawong Publishing Company, for example, wrote to Franklin on 27 June 1944 proposing a combined edition of both novels. She, clearly enjoying the fact that she could now keep publishers on a string, insisted that *My Career Goes Bung* must be published before she would consider a reprint of *My Brilliant Career*. The Melbourne firm of Georgian House eventually decided to take the risk, bringing out *My Career Goes Bung* in 1946, but were still not rewarded with *My Brilliant Career*.

After Miles Franklin's death in 1954, her will was found not only to provide for an annual prize for Australian fiction but to prohibit the reprinting of *My Brilliant Career* for another decade. The first Australian edition was eventually published by Angus & Robertson in 1966. It is a nice irony—one I am sure that Miles Franklin would have appreciated—that *My Brilliant Career* and *My Career Goes Bung*, both initially rejected by Angus & Robertson, are now for the first time being brought out together by that same firm.

ELIZABETH WEBBY
University of Sydney
March, 1990

CONTENTS

MY
BRILLIANT
CAREER

PREFACE

A few months before I left Australia I got a letter from the bush signed 'Miles Franklin', saying that the writer had written a novel, but knew nothing of editors and publishers, and asking me to read and advise. Something about the letter, which was written in a strong original hand, attracted me, so I sent for the MS., and one dull afternoon I started to read it. I hadn't read three pages when I saw what you will no doubt see at once—that the story had been written by a girl. And as I went on I saw that the work was Australian—born of the bush. I don't know about the girlishly emotional parts of the book—I leave that to girl readers to judge; but the descriptions of bush life and scenery came startlingly, painfully real to me, and I know that, as far as they are concerned, the book is true to Australia—the truest I ever read.

I wrote to Miles Franklin, and she confessed that she was a girl. I saw her before leaving Sydney. She is just a little bush girl, barely twenty-one yet, and has scarcely ever been out of the bush in her life. She has lived her book, and I feel proud of it for the sake of the country I came from, where people toil and bake and suffer and are kind; where every second sun-burnt bushman is a sympathetic humorist, with the sadness of the bush deep in his eyes and a brave grin for the worst of times, and where every third bushman is a poet, with a big heart that keeps his pockets empty.

HENRY LAWSON
England, April 1901

Possum Gully, near Goulburn,
N.S. Wales, Australia, 1st March, 1899

MY DEAR FELLOW AUSTRALIANS,

Just a few lines to tell you that this story is all about myself—
for no other purpose do I write it.

I make no apologies for being egotistical. In this particular
I attempt an improvement on other autobiographies. Other autobiographies weary one with excuses for their egotism. What
matters it to you if I am egotistical? What matters it to you
though it should matter that I am egotistical?

This is not a romance—I have too often faced the music of
life to the tune of hardship to waste time in snivelling and gushing
over fancies and dreams; neither is it a novel, but simply a yarn—
a *real* yarn. Oh! as real, as really real—provided life itself is
anything beyond a heartless little chimera—it is as real in its
weariness and bitter heartache as the tall gum-trees, among which
I first saw the light, are real in their stateliness and substantiality.

My sphere in life is not congenial to me. Oh, how I hate this
living death which has swallowed all my teens, which is greedily
devouring my youth, which will sap my prime, and in which
my old age, if I am cursed with any, will be worn away! As
my life creeps on for ever through the long toil-laden days with
its agonizing monotony, narrowness, and absolute uncongeniality,
how my spirit frets and champs its unbreakable fetters—all in
vain!

1

You can dive into this story head first as it were. Do not fear encountering such trash as descriptions of beautiful sunsets and whisperings of wind. We (999 out of every 1000) can see nought in sunsets save as signs and tokens whether we may expect rain on the morrow or the contrary, so we will leave such vain and foolish imagining to those poets and painters—poor fools! Let us rejoice that we are not of their temperament!

Better be born a slave than a poet, better be born a black, better be born a cripple! For a poet must be companionless— alone! *fearfully* alone in the midst of his fellows whom he loves. Alone because his soul is as far above common mortals as common mortals are above monkeys.

There is no plot in this story, because there has been none in my life or in any other life which has come under my notice. I am one of a class, the individuals of which have not time for plots in their life, but have all they can do to get their work done without indulging in such a luxury.

MILES FRANKLIN
Australia

CHAPTER 1

I Remember, I Remember

'Boo hoo! Ow, ow; Oh! oh! Me'll die. Boo, hoo. The pain, the pain! Boo, hoo!'

'Come, come, now. Daddy's little mate isn't going to turn Turk like that, is she? I'll put some fat out of the dinner-bag on it, and tie it up in my hanky. Don't cry any more now. Hush, you must not cry! You'll make old Dart buck if you kick up a row like that.'

That is my first recollection of life. I was barely three. I can remember the majestic gum-trees surrounding us, the sun glinting on their straight white trunks, and falling on the gurgling fern-banked stream, which disappeared beneath a steep scrubby hill on our left. It was an hour past noon on a long clear summer day. We were on a distant part of the run, where my father had come to deposit salt. He had left home early in the dewy morning, carrying me in front of him on a little brown pillow which my mother had made for the purpose. We had put the lumps of rock-salt in the troughs on the other side of the creek. The stringy-bark roof of the salt-shed which protected the troughs from rain peeped out picturesquely from the musk and peppercorn shrubs by which it was densely surrounded, and was visible from where we lunched. I refilled the quart-pot in which we had boiled our tea with water from the creek, father doused our fire out with it, and then tied the quart to the D of his saddle with a piece of green hide. The green-hide bags in which the salt had been carried were hanging on the hooks of the pack-saddle which encumbered the bay pack-horse. Father's saddle and the brown pillow were on Dart, the big grey horse on which he generally carried me, and we were on the point of making tracks for home.

Preparatory to starting, father was muzzling the dogs which had just finished what lunch we had left. This process, to which

3

the dogs strongly objected, was rendered necessary by a cogent reason. Father had brought his strychnine flask with him that day, and in hopes of causing the death of a few dingoes, had put strong doses of its contents in several dead beasts which we had come across.

Whilst the dogs were being muzzled, I busied myself in plucking ferns and flowers. This disturbed a big black snake which was curled at the butt of a tree fern.

'Bitey! bitey!' I yelled, and father came to my rescue, despatching the reptile with his stock-whip. He had been smoking, and dropped his pipe on the ferns. I picked it up, and the glowing embers which fell from it burnt my dirty little fat fists. Hence the noise with which my story commences.

In all probability it was the burning of my fingers which so indelibly impressed the incident on my infantile mind. My father was accustomed to take me with him, but that is the only jaunt at the date which I remember, and that is all I remember of it. We were twelve miles from home, but how we reached there I do not know.

My father was a swell in those days—held Bruggabrong, Bin Bin East, and Bin Bin West, which three stations totalled close on 200,000 acres. Father was admitted into swelldom merely by right of his position. His pedigree included nothing beyond a grandfather. My mother, however, was a full-fledged aristocrat. She was one of the Bossiers of Caddagat, who numbered among their ancestry one of the depraved old pirates who pillaged England with William the Conqueror.

'Dick' Melvyn was as renowned for hospitality as joviality, and our comfortable, wide-veranda'ed, irregularly built, slab house in its sheltered nook amid the Timlinbilly Ranges was ever full to.overflowing. Doctors, lawyers, squatters, commercial travellers, bankers, journalists, tourists, and men of all kinds and classes crowded our well-spread board; but seldom a female face, except mother's, was to be seen there, Bruggabrong being a very out-of-the-way place.

I was both the terror and the amusement of the station. Old

boundary-riders and drovers inquire after me with interest to this day.

I knew everyone's business, and was ever in danger of publishing it at an inopportune moment.

In flowery language, selected from slang used by the station hands, and long words picked up from our visitors, I propounded unanswerable questions which brought blushes on the cheeks of even tough old wine-bibbers.

Nothing would induce me to show more respect to an appraiser of the runs than to a boundary-rider, or to a clergyman than a drover. I am the same to this day. My organ of veneration must be flatter than a pancake, because to venerate a person simply for his position I never did or will. To me the Prince of Wales will be no more than a shearer, unless when I meet him he displays some personality apart from his princeship— otherwise he can go hang.

Authentic record of the date when first I had a horse to myself has not been kept, but it must have been early, as at eight I was fit to ride anything on the place. Side-saddle, man-saddle, no-saddle, or astride were all the same to me. I rode among the musterers as gamely as any of the big sunburnt bushmen.

My mother remonstrated, opined I would be a great unwomanly tomboy. My father poohed the idea.

'Let her alone, Lucy,' he said, 'let her alone. The rubbishing conventionalities which are the curse of her sex will bother her soon enough. Let her alone!'

So, smiling and saying, 'She should have been a boy,' my mother let me alone, and I rode, and in comparison to my size made as much noise with my stock-whip as any one. Accidents had no power over me, I came unscathed out of droves of them.

Fear I knew not. Did a drunken tramp happen to kick up a row, I was always the first to confront him, and, from my majestic and roly-poly height of two feet six inches, demand what he wanted.

A digging started near us and was worked by a score of two dark-browed sons of Italy. They made mother nervous, and she averred they were not to be trusted, but I liked and trusted them. They carried me on their broad shoulders, stuffed me with lollies and made a general pet of me. Without the quiver of a nerve I swung down their deepest shafts in the big bucket on the end of a rope attached to a rough windlass, which brought up the miners and the mullock.

My brothers and sisters contracted mumps, measles, scarlatina, and whooping-cough. I rolled in the bed with them yet came off scot-free. I romped with dogs, climbed trees after birds' nests, drove the bullocks in the dray, under the instructions of Ben, our bullocky, and always accompanied my father when he went swimming in the clear, mountain, shrub-lined stream which ran deep and lone among the weird gullies, thickly carpeted with maidenhair and numberless other species of ferns.

My mother shook her head over me and trembled for my future, but father seemed to consider me nothing unusual. He was my hero, confidant, encyclopedia, mate, and even my religion till I was ten. Since then I have been religionless.

Richard Melvyn, you were a fine fellow in those days! A kind and indulgent parent, a chivalrous husband, a capital host, a man full of ambition and gentlemanliness.

Amid these scenes, and the refinements and pleasures of Caddagat, which lies a hundred miles or so farther Riverinawards, I spent the first years of my childhood.

CHAPTER 2

An Introduction to Possum Gully

I was nearly nine summers old when my father conceived the idea that he was wasting his talents by keeping them rolled up in the small napkin of an out-of-the-way place like Bruggabrong and the Bin Bin stations. Therefore he determined to take up his residence in a locality where he would have more scope for his ability.

When giving his reason for moving to my mother, he put the matter before her thus: The price of cattle and horses had fallen so of late years that it was impossible to make much of a living by breeding them. Sheep were the only profitable article to have nowadays, and it would be impossible to run them on Brugga-brong or either of the Bin Bins. The dingoes would work havoc among them in no time, and what they left the duffers would soon dispose of. As for bringing police into the matter, it would be worse than useless. They could not run the offenders to earth, and their efforts to do so would bring down upon their employer the wrath of the duffers. Result, all the fences on the station would be fired for a dead certainty, and the destruction of more than a hundred miles of heavy log fencing on rough country like Bruggabrong was no picnic to contemplate.

This was the feasible light in which father shaded his desire to leave. The fact of the matter was that the heartless harridan, discontent, had laid her claw-like hand upon him. His guests were ever assuring him he was buried and wasted in Timlinbilly's gullies. A man of his intelligence, coupled with his wonderful experience among stock, would, they averred, make a name and fortune for himself dealing or auctioneering if he only like to try. Richard Melvyn began to think so too, and desired to try. He did try.

He gave up Bruggabrong, Bin Bin East and Bin Bin West,

7

bought Possum Gully, a small farm of one thousand acres, and brought us all to live near Goulburn. Here we arrived one autumn afternoon. Father, mother, and children packed in the buggy, myself, and the one servant-girl, who had accompanied us, on horseback. The one man father had retained in his service was awaiting our arrival. He had preceded us with a bullock-drayload of furniture and belongings, which was all father had retained of his household property. Just sufficient for us to get along with, until he had time to settle and purchase more, he said. That was ten years ago, and that is the only furniture we possess yet— just enough to get along with.

My first impression of Possum Gully was bitter disappointment—an impression which time has failed to soften or wipe away.

How flat, common, and monotonous the scenery appeared after the rugged peaks of the Timlinbilly Ranges!

Our new house was a ten-roomed wooden structure, built on a barren hillside. Crooked stunted gums and stringybarks, with a thick underscrub of wild cherry, hop, and hybrid wattle, clothed the spurs which ran up from the back of the detached kitchen. Away from the front of the house were flats, bearing evidence of cultivation, but a drop of water was nowhere to be seen. Later, we discovered a few round, deep, weedy waterholes down on the flat, which in rainy weather swelled to a stream which swept all before it. Possum Gully is one of the best watered spots in the district, and in that respect has stood to its guns in the bitterest drought. Use and knowledge have taught us the full value of its fairly clear and beautifully soft water. Just then, however, coming from the mountains where every gully had its limpid creek, we turned in disgust from the idea of having to drink this water.

I felt cramped on our new run. It was only three miles wide at its broadest point. Was I always, always, always to live here, and never, never, never to go back to Bruggabrong? That was the burden of the grief with which I sobbed myself to sleep on the first night after our arrival.

Mother felt dubious of her husband's ability to make a living off a thousand acres, half of which were fit to run nothing but wallabies, but father was full of plans, and very sanguine concerning his future. He was no going to squat henlike on his place as the cockies around him did. He meant to deal in stock, making of Possum Gully merely a depot on which to run some of his bargains until reselling.

Dear, oh dear! It was terrible to think he had wasted the greater part of his life among the hills where the mail came but once a week, and where the nearest town, of 650 inhabitants, was forty-six miles distant. And the road had been impassable for vehicles. Here, only seventeen miles from a city like Goulburn, with splendid roads, mail thrice weekly, and a railway platform only eight miles away, why, man, my fortune is made! Such were the sentiments to which he gave birth out of the fullness of his hopeful heart.

Ere the diggings had broken out on Bruggabrong, our nearest neighbour, excepting, of course, boundary-riders, was seventeen miles distant. Possum Gully was a thickly populated district, and here we were surrounded by homes ranging from half a mile to two and three miles away. This was a new experience for us, and it took us some time to become accustomed to the advantage and disadvantage of the situation. Did we require an article, we found it handy, but decidedly the reverse when our neighbours borrowed from us, and, in the greater percentage of cases, failed to return the loan.

CHAPTER 3

A Lifeless Life

Possum Gully was stagnant—stagnant with the narrow stagnation prevalent in all old country places.

Its residents were principally married folk and children under sixteen. The boys, as they attained manhood, drifted outback to shear, drove, or to take up land. They found it too slow at home, and besides there was not room enough for them there when they passed childhood.

Nothing ever happened there. Time was no object, and the days slid quietly into the river of years, distinguished one from another by name alone. An occasional birth or death was a big event, and the biggest event of all was the advent of a new resident.

When such a thing occurred it was customary for all the male heads of families to pay a visit of inspection, to judge if the new-comers were worthy of admittance into the bosom of the society of the neighbourhood. Should their report prove favourable, then their wives finished the ceremony of inauguration by paying a friendly visit.

After his arrival at Possum Gully father was much away on business, and so on my mother fell the ordeal of receiving the callers, male and female.

The men were honest, good-natured, respectable, common bushmen farmers. Too friendly to pay a short call, they came and sat for hours yarning about nothing in particular. This bored my gentle mother excessively. She attempted to entertain them with conversation of current literature and subjects of the day, but her efforts fell flat. She might as well have spoken in French.

They conversed for hours and hours about dairying, interspersed with pointless anecdotes of the man who had lived there before us. I found them very tame.

After graphic descriptions of life on big stations outback, and the dashing snake yarns told by our kitchen-folk at Bruggabrong, and the anecdotes of African hunting, travel, and society life which had often formed our guests' subject of conversation, this endless fiddle-faddle of the price of farm produce and the state of crops was very fatuous.

Those men, like everyone else, only talked shop. I say nothing in condemnation of it, but merely point out that it did not then interest us, as we were not living in that shop just then.

Mrs Melvyn must have found favour in the eyes of the specimens of the lords of creation resident at Possum Gully, as all the matrons of the community hastened to call on her, and vied with each other in a display of friendliness and good-nature. They brought presents of poultry, jam, butter, and suchlike. They came at two o'clock and stayed till dark. They inventoried the furniture, gave mother cookery recipes, described minutely the unsurpassable talents of each of their children, and descanted volubly upon the best way of setting turkey hens. On taking their departure they cordially invited us all to return their visits, and begged mother to allow her children to spend a day with theirs.

We had been resident in our new quarters nearly a month when my parents received an intimation from the teacher of the public school, two miles distant, to the effect that the law demanded that they should send their children to school. It upset my mother greatly. What was she to do?

'Do! Bundle the nippers off to school as quickly as possible, of course,' said my father.

My mother objected. She proposed a governess now and a good boarding-school later on. She had heard such dreadful stories of public schools! It was terrible to be compelled to send her darlings to one; they would be ruined in a week!

'Not they,' said father. 'Run them off for a week or two, or a month at the outside. They can't come to any harm in that time. After that we will get a governess. You are in no state of health to worry about one just now, and it is utterly impossible that I can see about the matter at present. I have several specs.

on foot that I must attend to. Send the youngsters to school down here for the present.'

We went to school, and in our dainty befrilled pinafores and light shoes were regarded as great swells by the other scholars. They for the most part were the children of very poor farmers, whose farm earnings were augmented by road-work, wood-carting, or any such labour which came within their grasp. All the boys went barefooted, also a moiety of the girls. The school was situated on a wild scrubby hill, and the teacher boarded with a resident a mile from it. He was a man addicted to drink, and the parents of his scholars lived in daily expectation of seeing his dismissal from the service.

It is nearly ten years since the twins (who came next to me) and I were enrolled as pupils of the Tiger Swamp public school. My education was completed there; so was that of the twins, who are eleven months younger than I. Also my other brothers and sisters are quickly getting finishedwards; but that is the only school any of us have seen or known. There was even a time when father spoke of filling in the free forms for our attendance there. But mother—a woman's pride bears more wear than a man's—would never allow us to come to that.

All our neighbours were very friendly; but one in particular, a James Blackshaw, proved himself most desirous of being comradely with us. He was a sort of self-constituted sheik of the community. It was usual for him to take all new-comers under his wing, and with officious good-nature endeavour to make them feel at home. He called on us daily, tied his horse to the paling fence beneath the shade of a sallic-tree in the backyard, and when mother was unable to see him he was content to yarn for an hour or two with Jane Haizelip, our servant-girl.

Jane disliked Possum Gully as much as I did. Her feeling being much more defined, it was amusing to hear the flat-out opinions she expressed to Mr Blackshaw, whom, by the way, she termed 'a mooching hen of a chap'.

'I suppose, Jane, you like being here near Goulburn, better than that out-of-the-way place you came from,' he said one morning as he comfortably settled himself on an old sofa in the kitchen.

'No jolly fear. Out-of-the-way place! There was more life at Bruggabrong in a day than you crawlers 'ud see here all yer lives,' she retorted with vigour, energetically pommelling a batch of bread which she was mixing.

'Why, at Brugga it was as good as a show every week. On Saturday evening all the coves used to come in for their mail. They'd stay till Sunday evenin'. Splitters, boundary-riders, dog-trappers—every manjack of 'em. Some of us wuz always good for a toon on the concertina, and the rest would dance. We had fun to no end. A girl could have a fly round and a lark or two there I tell you; but here,' and she emitted a snort of contempt, 'there ain't one bloomin' feller to do a mash with. I'm full of the place. Only I promised to stick to the missus a while, I'd scoot tomorrer. It's the dead-and-alivest hole I ever seen.'

'You'll git used to it by and by,' said Blackshaw.

'Used to it! A person 'ud hev to be brought up onder a hen to git used to the dullness of this hole.'

'You wasn't brought up under a hen, or it must have been a big Bramer Pooter, if you were,' replied he, noting the liberal proportions of her figure as she hauled a couple of heavy pots off the fire. He did not offer to help her. Etiquette of that sort was beyond his ken.

'You oughter go out more and then you wouldn't find it so dull,' he said, after she had placed the pots on the floor.

'Go out! Where 'ud I go to, pray?'

'Drop in an' see my missus again when you git time. You're always welcome.'

'Thanks, but I had plenty of goin' to see your missus last time.'

'How's that?'

'Why, I wasn't there harf an hour wen she had to strip off her clean duds an' go an' milk. I don't think much of any of the men around here. They let the women work too hard. I never see such a tired wore-out set of women. It puts me in mind ev the time wen the black fellers made the gins do all the work.

Why, on Bruggabrong the women never had to do no outside work, only on a great pinch wen all the men were away at a fire or a muster. Down here they do everything. They do all the milkin', and pig-feedin', and poddy-rarin'. It makes me feel fit to retch. I don't know whether it's because the men is crawlers or whether it's dairyin'. I don't think much of dairyin'. It's slavin', an' delvin', an' scrapin' yer eyeballs out from mornin' to night, and nothink to show for your pains; and now you'll oblige me, Mr Blackshaw, if you'll lollop somewhere else for a minute or two. I want to sweep under that sofer.'

This had the effect of making him depart. He said good morning and went off, not sure whether he was most amused or insulted.

CHAPTER 4

A Career Which Soon Careered to an End

While mother, Jane Haizelip, and I found the days long and life slow, father was enjoying himself immensely.

He had embarked upon a lively career—that gambling trade known as dealing in stock.

When he was not away in Riverina inspecting a flock of sheep, he was attending the Homebush Fat Stock Sales, rushing away out to Bourke, or tearing off down the Shoalhaven to buy some dairy heifers.

He was a familiar figure at the Goulburn sale-yards every Wednesday, always going into town the day before and not returning till a day, and often two days, afterwards.

He was in great demand among drovers and auctioneers; and in the stock news his name was always mentioned in connection with all the principal sales in the colony.

It takes an astute, clear-headed man to keep himself off shore in stock dealing. I never yet heard of a dealer who occasionally did not temporarily, if not totally, go to the wall.

He need not necessarily be downright unscrupulous, but if he wishes to profit he must not be overburdened with niceties in the point of honour. That is where Richard Melvyn fell through. He was crippled with too many Utopian ideas of honesty, and was too soft ever to come off anything but second-best in a deal. He might as well have attempted to make his fortune by scraping a fiddle up and down Auburn Street, Goulburn. His dealing career was short and merry. His vanity to be considered a socialistic fellow, who was as ready to take a glass with a swaggie as a swell, and the lavish shouting which this principle incurred, made great inroads on his means. Losing money every time he sold a beast, wasting stamps galore on letters to endless auctioneers, frequently remaining in town half a week at a stretch, and being

15

hail-fellow to all the spongers to be found on the trail of such as he, quickly left him on the verge of bankruptcy. Some of his contemporaries say it was grog that did it all.

Had he kept clear-headed he was a smart fellow, and gave promise of doing well, but his head would not stand alcohol, and by it he was undermined in no time. In considerably less than a twelvemonth all the spare capital in his coffers from the disposal of Bruggabrong and the Bin Bins had been squandered. He had become so hard up that to pay the drovers in his last venture he was forced to sell the calves of the few milch-cows retained for household uses.

At this time it came to my father's knowledge that one of our bishops had money held in trust for the Church. On good security he was giving this out for usury, the same as condemned in the big Bible, out of which he took the text of the dry-hash sermons with which he bored his fashionable congregations in his cathedral on Sundays.

Father took advantage of this Reverend's inconsistency and mortgaged Possum Gully. With the money thus obtained he started once more and managed to make a scant livelihood and pay the interest on the bishop's loan. In four or five years he had again reached loggerheads. The price of stock had fallen so that there was nothing to be made out of dealing in them.

Richard Melvyn resolved to live as those around him—start a dairy; run it with his family, who would also rear poultry for sale.

As instruments of the dairying trade he procured fifty milch-cows, the calves of which had to be 'poddied', and a hand cream-separator.

I was in my fifteenth year when we began dairying; the twins Horace and Gertie were, as you already know, eleven months younger. Horace, had there been any one to train him, contained the makings of a splendid man; but having no one to bring him up in the way he should go, he was a churlish and trying bully, and the issue of his character doubtful.

Gertie milked thirteen cows, and I eighteen, morning and

evening. Horace and mother, between them, milked the remaining seventeen.

Among the dairying fraternity little toddlers, ere they are big enough to hold a bucket, learn to milk. Thus their hands become inured to the motion, and it does not affect them. With us it was different. Being almost full grown when we started to milk, and then plunging heavily into the exercise, it had a painful effect upon us. Our hands and arms, as far as the elbows, swelled, so that our sleep at night was often disturbed by pain.

Mother made the butter. She had to rise at two and three o'clock in the morning, in order that it would be cool and firm enough to print for market.

Jane Haizelip had left us a year previously, and we could afford no one to take her place. The heavy work told upon my gentle, refined mother. She grew thin and careworn, and often cross. My father's share of the work was to break in the wild cows, separate the milk, and take the butter into town to the grocer's establishment where we obtained our supplies.

Dick Melvyn of Bruggabrong was not recognizable in Dick Melvyn, dairy farmer and cocky of Possum Gully. The former had been a man worthy of the name. The latter was a slave of drink, careless, even dirty and bedraggled in his personal appearance. He disregarded all manners, and had become far more plebeian and common than the most miserable specimen of humanity around him. The support of his family, yet not its support. The head of his family, yet failing to fulfil the obligations demanded of one in that capacity. He seemed to lose all love and interest in his family, and grew cross and silent, utterly without pride and pluck. Formerly so kind and gentle with animals, now he was the reverse.

His cruelty to the young cows and want of patience with them I can never forget. It has often brought upon me the threat of immediate extermination for volunteering scathing and undesired opinions on his conduct.

The part of the dairying that he positively gloried in was going to town with the butter. He frequently remained in for two or three days, as often as not spending all the money he got for the butter in a drunken spree. Then he would return to curse his luck because his dairy did not pay as well as those of some of our neighbours.

The curse of Eve being upon my poor mother in those days, she was unable to follow her husband. Pride forbade her appealing to her neighbours, so on me devolved the duty of tracking my father from one pub to another and bringing him home.

Had I done justice to my mother's training I would have honoured my paternal parent in spite of all this, but I am an individual ever doing things I oughtn't at the time I shouldn't.

Coming home, often after midnight, with my drunken father talking maudlin conceited nonsense beside me, I developed curious ideas on the fifth commandment. Those journeys in the spring-cart through the soft faint starlight were conducive to thought. My father, like most men when under the influence of liquor, would allow no one but himself to handle the reins, and he was often so incapable that he would keep turning the horse round and round in the one place. It is a marvel we never met with an accident. I was not nervous, but quite content to take whatever came, and our trusty old horse fulfilled his duty, ever faithfully taking us home along the gum-tree-lined road.

My mother had taught me from the Bible that I should honour my parents, whether they were deserving of honour or not.

Dick Melvyn being my father did not blind me to the fact that he was a despicable, selfish, weak creature, and as such I despised him with the relentlessness of fifteen, which makes no allowance for human frailty and weakness. Disgust, not honour, was the feeling which possessed me when I studied the matter.

Towards mother I felt differently. A woman is but the helpless tool of man—a creature of circumstances.

Seeing my father beside me, and thinking of his infant with its mother, eating her heart out with anxiety at home, this was the reasoning which took possession of me. Among other such inexpressible thoughts I got lost, grew dizzy, and drew back appalled at the spirit which was maturing within me. It was a grim lonely one, which I vainly tried to hide in a bosom which was not big or strong enough for its comfortable habitation. It was as a climbing plant without a pole—it groped about the ground, bruised itself, and became hungry searching for something strong to which to cling. Needing a master-hand to train and prune, it was becoming rank and sour.

CHAPTER 5

Disjointed Sketches and Grumbles

It was my duty to 'rare the poddies'. This is the most godless occupation in which it has been my lot to engage. I did a great amount of thinking while feeding them—for, by the way, I am afflicted with the power of thought, which is a heavy curse. The less a person thinks and inquires regarding the why and the wherefore and the justice of things, when dragging along through life, the happier it is for him, and doubly, trebly so, for her.

Poor little calves! Slaves to the greed of man! Bereft of the mothers with which Nature has provided them, and compelled to exist on milk from the separator, often thick, sour, and icy cold.

Besides the milking I did, before I went to school every morning, for which I had to prepare myself and the younger children, and to which we had to walk two miles, I had to feed thirty calves and wash the breakfast dishes. On returning from school in the afternoon, often in a state of exhaustion from walking in the blazing sun, I had the same duties over again, and in addition boots to clean and home lessons to prepare for the morrow. I had to relinquish my piano practice for want of time.

Ah, those short, short nights of rest and long, long days of toil! It seems to me that dairying means slavery in the hands of poor people who cannot afford hired labour. I am not writing of dairy-farming, the genteel and artistic profession as eulogized in leading articles of agricultural newspapers and as taught in agricultural colleges. I am depicting practical dairying as I have lived it, and seen it lived, by dozens of families around me.

It takes a great deal of work to produce even one pound of butter fit for market. At the time I mention it was 3d. and 4d. per lb., so it was much work and small pay. It was slaving and delving from morning till night—Sundays, week-days, and holidays, all alike were work-days to us.

Hard graft is a great leveller. Household drudgery, wood-cutting, milking, and gardening soon roughen the hands and dim the outside polish. When the body is wearied with much toil the desire to cultivate the mind, or the cultivation it has already received, is gradually wiped out. Thus it was with my parents. They had dropped from swelldom to peasantism. They were among and of the peasantry. None of their former acquaintances came within their circle now, for the iron ungodly hand of class distinction has settled surely down upon Australian society—Australia's democracy is only a tradition of the past.

I say naught against the lower life. The peasantry are the bulwarks of every nation. The life of a peasant is, to a peasant who is a peasant with a peasant's soul, when times are good and when seasons smile, a grand life. It is honest, clean, and wholesome. But the life of a peasant to me is purgatory. Those around me worked from morning till night and then enjoyed their well-earned sleep. They had but two states of existence—work and sleep.

There was a third part in me which cried out to be fed. I longed for the arts. Music was a passion with me. I borrowed every book in the neighbourhood and stole hours from rest to read them. This told upon me and made my physical burdens harder for me than for other children of my years around me. That third was the strongest part of me. In it I lived a dream-life with writers, artists, and musicians. Hope, sweet, cruel, delusive Hope, whispered in my ear that life was long with much by and by, and in that by and by my dream-life would be real. So on I went with that gleaming lake in the distance beckoning me to come and sail on its silver waters, and Inexperience, conceited, blind Inexperience, failing to show the impassable pit between it and me.

To return to the dairying.

Old and young alike we earned our scant livelihood by the heavy sweat of our brows. Still, we *did* gain an honest living. We were not ashamed to look day in the face, and fought our way against all odds with the stubborn independence of our British ancestors. But when 1894 went out without rain, and '95, hot, dry, pitiless '95, succeeded it, there came a time when it was impossible to make a living.

The scorching furnace-breath winds shrivelled every blade of grass, dust and the moan of starving flock filled the air, vegetables became a thing of the past. The calves I had reared died one by one, and the cows followed in their footsteps.

I had left school then, and my mother and father and I spent the days in lifting our cows. When our strength proved inadequate, the help of neighbours had to be called in, and father would give his services in return. Only a few of our more well-to-do neighbours had been able to send their stock away, or had any better place to which to transfer them. The majority of them were in as tight a plight as ourselves. This cow-lifting became quite a trade, the whole day being spent in it and in discussing the bad prospect ahead if the drought continued.

Many an extra line of care furrowed the brows of the disheartened bushmen then. Not only was their living taken from them by the drought, but there is nothing more heartrending than to have poor beasts, especially dairy cows, so familiar, valued, and loved, pleading for food day after day in their piteous dumb way when one has it not to give.

We shore ourselves of all but the bare necessaries of life, but even they for a family of ten are considerable, and it was a mighty tussle to get both ends within cover of meeting. We felt the full force of the heavy hand of poverty—the most stinging kind of poverty too, that which still holds up its head and keeps an outside appearance. Far more grinding is this than the poverty inherited from generations which is not ashamed of itself, and has not as an accompaniment the wounded pride and humiliation which attacked us.

Some there are who argue that poverty does not mean unhappiness. Let those try what it is to be destitute of even one companionable friend, what it means to be forced to exist on an alien sphere of society, what it is like to be unable to afford a stamp to write to a friend; let them long as passionately as

I have longed for reading and music, and be unable to procure it because of poverty; let poverty force them into doing work against which every fibre of their being revolts, as it has forced me, and then see if their lives will be happy.

My school life had been dull and uneventful. The one incident of any note had been the day that the teacher, better known as old Harris, 'stood up' to the inspector. The latter was a precise, collar-and-cuffs sort of little man. He gave one the impression of having all his ideas on the subjects he thought worthy of attention carefully culled and packed in his brain-pan, and neatly labelled, so that he might without fluster pounce upon any of them at a moment's warning. He was gentlemanly and respectable, and discharged his duties punctiliously in a manner reflecting credit on himself and his position, but, comparing the mind of a philanthropist to the Murrumbidgee in breadth, his, in comparison, might be likened to the flow of a bucket of water in a dray-rut.

On the day in question—a precious hot one it was—he had finished examining us in most subjects, and was looking at our copy-books. He looked up from them, ahemed! and fastidiously straightened his waistcoat.

'Mr Harris!'

'Yes, sir.'

'Comparisons are odious, but, unfortunately, I am forced to draw one now.'

'Yes, sir.'

'This writing is much inferior to that of town scholars. It is very shaky and irregular. Also, I notice that the children seem stupid and dull. I don't like putting it so plainly, but, in fact, ah, they seem to be possessed with the proverbial stupidity of country people. How do you account for this?'

Poor old Harris! In spite of his drunken habits and inability to properly discharge his duties, he had a warm heart and much fellowshiply humanity in him. He understood and loved his pupils, and would not have aspersions cast upon them. Besides, the nip he had taken to brace himself to meet the inspector had been two or three, and they robbed him of the discretion which otherwise might have kept him silent.

'Si-r-r-r, I can and will account for it. Look you at every one of those children. Every one, right down to this little tot,' indicating a little girl of five, 'has to milk and work hard before and after school, besides walk on an average two miles to and from school in this infernal heat. Most of the elder boys and girls milk on an average fourteen cows morning and evening. You try that treatment for a week or two, my fine gentleman, and then see if your fist doesn't ache and shake so that you can't write at all. See if you won't look a trifly dozy. Stupidity of country people be hanged! If you had to work from morning till night in the heat and dust, and get precious little for it too, I bet you wouldn't have much time to scrape your finger-nails, read science notes, and look smart.' Here he took off his coat and shaped up to his superior.

The inspector drew back in consternation.

'Mr Harris, you forget yourself!'

At this juncture they went outside together. What happened there we never knew. That is all we heard of the matter except the numerous garbled accounts which were carried home that afternoon.

A DROUGHT IDYLL

'Sybylla, what are you doing? Where is your mother?'

'I'm ironing. Mother's down at the fowl-house seeing after some chickens. What do you want?'

It was my father who addressed me. Time, 2 o'clock p.m. Thermometer hung in the shade of the veranda registering 105½ degrees.

'I see Blackshaw coming across the flat. Call your mother. You bring the leg-ropes—I've got the dog-leg. Come at once; we'll give the cows another lift. Poor devils—might as well knock 'em on the head at once, but there might be rain next moon. This drought can't last for ever.'

I called mother, got the leg-ropes, and set off, pulling my sun-bonnet closely over my face to protect my eyes from the dust which was driving from the west in blinding clouds. The dog-leg to which father had referred was three poles about eight or ten feet long, strapped together so they could be stood up. It was an arrangement father had devised to facilitate our labour in lifting the cows. A fourth and longer pole was placed across the fork formed by the three, and to one end of this were tied a couple of leg-ropes, after being placed round the beast, one beneath the flank and one around the girth. On the other end of this pole we would put our weight while one man would lift with the tail and another with the horns. New-chum cows would sulk, and we would have great work with them; but those used to the performance would help themselves, and up they'd go as nice as a daisy. The only art needed was to draw the pole back quickly before the cows could move, or the leg-ropes would pull them over again.

On this afternoon we had six cows to lift. We struggled man-fully, and got five on their feet, and then proceeded to where the last one was lying, back downwards, on a shadeless stony spot on the side of a hill. The men slewed her round by the tail, while mother and I fixed the dog-leg and adjusted the ropes. We got the cow up, but the poor beast was so weak and knocked about that she immediately fell down again. We resolved to let her have a few minutes' spell before making another attempt at lifting. There was not a blade of grass to be seen, and the ground was too dusty to sit on. We were too overdone to make more than one-worded utterances, so waited silently in the blazing sun, closing our eyes against the dust.

Wearines! Weariness!

A few light wind-smitten clouds made wan streaks across the white sky, haggard with the fierce relentless glare of the after-noon sun. Weariness was written across my mother's delicate careworn features, and found expression in my father's knitted brows and dusty face. Blackshaw was weary, and said so, as he wiped the dust, made mud with perspiration, off his cheeks.

I was weary—my limbs ached with the heat and work. The poor beast stretched at our feet was weary. All nature was weary, and seemed to sing a dirge to that effect in the furnace-breath wind which roared among the trees on the low ranges at our back and smote the parched and thirsty ground. All were weary, all but the sun. He seemed to glory in his power, relentless and untiring, as he swung boldly in the sky, triumphantly leering down upon his helpless victims.

Weariness! Weariness!

This was life—my life—my career, my brilliant career! I was fifteen—fifteen! A few fleeting hours and I would be old as those around me. I looked at them as they stood there, weary, and turning down the other side of the hill of life. When young, no doubt they had hoped for, and dreamed of, better things—had even known them. But here they were. This had been their life; this was their career. It was, and in all probability would be, mine too. My life—my career—my brilliant career!

Weariness! Weariness!

The summer sun danced on. Summer is fiendish, and life is a curse, I said in my heart. What a great dull hard rock the world was! On it were a few barren narrow ledges, and on these, by exerting ourselves so that the force wears off our finger-nails, it allows us to hang for a year or two, and then hurls us off into outer darkness and oblivion, perhaps to endure worse torture than this.

The poor beast moaned. The lifting had strained her, and there were patches of hide worn off her the size of breakfast-plates, sore and most harrowing to look upon.

It takes great suffering to wring a moan from the patience of a cow. I turned my head away, and with the impatience and one-sided reasoning common to fifteen, asked God what He meant by this. It is well enough to heap suffering on human beings, seeing it is supposed to be merely a probation for a better world, but animals—poor, innocent animals—why are they tortured so?

'Come now, we'll lift her once more,' said my father. At it we went again; it is surprising what weight there is in the poorest cow. With great struggling we got her to her feet once more, and were careful this time to hold her till she got steady on her legs. Father and mother at the tail and Blackshaw and I at the horns, we marched her home and gave her a bran mash. Then we turned to our work in the house while the men sat and smoked and spat on the veranda, discussing the drought for an hour, at the end of which time they went to help someone else with their stock. I made up the fire and we continued our ironing, which had been interrupted some hours before. It was hot unpleasant work on such a day. We were forced to keep the doors and windows closed on account of the wind and dust. We were hot and tired, and our feet ached so that we could scarcely stand on them.

Weariness! Weariness!

Summer is fiendish and life is a curse, I said in my heart.

Day after day the drought continued. Now and again there would be a few days of the raging wind before mentioned, which carried the dry grass off the paddocks and piled it against the fences, darkened the air with dust, and seemed to promise rain, but ever it dispersed whence it came, taking with it the few clouds it had gathered up; and for weeks and weeks at a stretch, from horizon to horizon, was never a speck to mar the cruel dazzling brilliance of the metal sky.

Weariness! Weariness!

I said the one thing many times but, ah, it was a weary thing which took much repetition that familiarity might wear away a little of its bitterness!

CHAPTER 6

Revolt

In spite of our pottering and lifting, with the exception of five, all our cows eventually died; and even these and a couple of horses had as much as they could do to live on the whole of the thousand acres which, without reserve, were at their disposal. They had hardly any grass—it was merely the warmth and water which kept them alive. Needless to say, we were on our beam-ends financially. However, with a little help from more fortunate relatives, and with the money obtained from the sale of the cow-hides and mother's poultry, we managed to pay the interest on the money borrowed from the bishop, and keep bread in our mouths.

Unfortunately for us, at this time the bishop's agent proved a scoundrel and absconded. My father held receipts to show that to this agent he had regularly paid the interest of the money borrowed; but through some finicking point of law, because we had not money to contend with him, his lordship the bishop now refused to acknowledge his agent and one-time pillar of the cathedral, and, having law on his side, served a writ on us. In the face of our misfortunes this was too much: we begged for time, which plea he answered by putting in the bailiff and selling everything we possessed. Our five cows, two horses, our milk separator, plough, cart, dray, buggy, even our cooking utensils, books, pictures, furniture, father's watch—our very beds, pillows, and blankets. Not a thing besides what we stood up in was left us, and this was money for the payment of which my father held receipts.

But for the generosity of our relatives we would have been in a pretty plight. They sent us sufficient means to buy in every-thing, and our neighbours came to our rescue with enthusiasm and warm-hearted genuine sympathy. The bailiff—a gentleman to the core—seeing how matters stood, helped us to the utmost of his power.

Our goods were disposed of on the premises, and the neighbours arranged a mock sale, at which the bailiff winked. Our friends had sent the money, and the neighbours did the bidding—none bidding against each other—and thus our belongings went for a mere trifle. Every cloud has its silver lining, and the black cloud of poverty has a very bright silver lining.

In poverty you can get at the real heart of people as you can never do if rich. People are your friends from pure friendship and love, not from sponging self-interestedness. It is worth being poor once or twice in a lifetime just to experience the blessing and heartrestfulness of a little genuine reality in the way of love and friendship. Not that it is impossible for opulence to have genuine friends, but rich people, I fear, must ever have at their heart cankering suspicion to hint that the friendship and love lavished upon them is merely self-interestedness and sham, the implements of trade used by the fawning toadies who swarm around wealth.

In conjunction with the bishop's name, the approaching sale of our goods had been duly advertised in the local papers, and my father received several letters of sympathy from the clergy deploring the conduct of the bishop. These letters were from men unknown to father, who were unaware that Richard Melvyn was being sold off for a debt already paid.

By the generosity of relatives and the goodness of neighbours as kind as ever breathed, our furniture was our own again, but what were we to do for a living? Our crops were withering in the fields for want of rain, and we had but five cows—not an over-bright outlook. As I was getting to bed one night my mother came into my room and said seriously, 'Sybylla, I want to have a talk with you.'

'Talk away,' I responded rather sullenly, for I expected a long sing-song about my good-for-nothingness in general—a subject of which I was heartily tired.

'Sybylla, I've been studying the matter over a lot lately. It's not use, we cannot afford to keep you at home. You'll have to get something to do.'

I made no reply, and my mother continued, 'I'm afraid we will have to break up the home altogether. It's no use; your father has no idea of making a living. I regret the day I ever saw him. Since he has taken to drink he has no more idea of how to make a living than a cat. I will have to give the little ones to some of the relatives; the bigger ones will have to go out to service, and so will your father and I. That's all I can see ahead of us. Poor little Gertie is too young to go out in the world (she was not twelve months younger than I); she must go to your grandmother, I think.'

I still made no reply, so my mother inquired, 'Well, Sybylla, what do you think of the matter?'

'Do you think it absolutely necessary to break up the home?' I said.

'Well, you suggest something better if you are so clever,' said mother, crossly. 'That is always the way; if I suggest a thing it is immediately put down, yet there is never any one to think of things but me. What would you do? I suppose you think you could make a living on the place for us yourself.'

'Why can't we live at home? Blackshaw and Jansen have no bigger places than we, and families just as large, and yet they make a living. It would be terrible for the little ones to grow up separated; they would be no more to each other than strangers.'

'Yes; it is all very well for you to talk like that, but how is your father to start again with only five cows in the world? It's no use, you never talk sense. You'll find my way is always the best in the end.'

'Would it not be easier,' I replied, 'for our relations to each give a little towards setting us up again, than to be burdened with the whole responsibility of rearing a child? I'm sure they'd much prefer it.'

'Yes, perhaps it would be better, but I think *you* will have to get your own living. What would they say about having to support such a big girl as you are?'

'I will go and earn my own living, and when you get me weeded out of the family you will have a perfect paradise. Having no evil to copy, the children will grow up saints,' I said bitterly.

'Now, Sybylla, it is foolish to talk like that, for you know that you take no interest in your work. If you'd turn to and help me rear poultry and make dresses—and why don't you take to cooking?'

'Take to cooking!' I retorted with scorn. 'The fire that a fellow has to endure on that old oven would kill a horse, and the grit and dirt of clearing it up grinds on my very nerves. Besides, if I ever do want to do any extra fancy cooking, we either can't afford the butter or the currants, or else the eggs are too scarce! Cook be grannied!'

'Sybylla! Sybylla, you are getting very vulgar!'

'Yes, I once was foolish enough to try and be polite, but I've given it up. My style of talk is quite good enough for my company. What on earth does it matter whether I'm vulgar or not. I can feed calves and milk and grind out my days here just as well vulgar as unvulgar,' I answered savagely.

'There, you see you are always discontented about your home. It's no use; the only thing is for you to earn your own living.'

'I will earn my own living.'

'What will you do? Will you be examined for a pupil-teacher? That is a very nice occupation for girls.'

'What chance would I have in a competitive exam. against Goulburn girls? They all have good teachers and give up their time to study. I only have old Harris, and he is the most idiotic old animal alive; besides, I loathe the very thought of teaching. I'd as soon go on the wallaby.'

'You are not old enough to be a general servant or a cook; you have not experience enough to be a housemaid; you don't take to sewing, and there is no chance of being accepted as a hospital nurse: you must confess there is nothing you can do. You are really a very useless girl for your age.'

'There are heaps of things I could do.'

'Tell me a few of them.'

I was silent. The professions at which I felt I had the latent power to excel, were I but given a chance, were in a sphere far above us, and to mention my feelings and ambitions to my matter-of-fact practical mother would bring upon me worse ridicule than I was already forced to endure day by day.

'Mention a few of the things you could do.'

I might as well have named flying as the professions I was thinking of. Music was the least unmentionable of them, so I brought it forward.

'Music! But it would take years of training and great expense before you could earn anything at that! It is quite out of the question. The only thing for you to do is to settle down and take interest in your work, and help make a living at home, or else go out as a nurse-girl, and work your way up. If you have any ability in you it would soon show. If you think you could do such strokes, and the home work is not good enough for you, go out and show the world what a wonderful creature you are.'

'Mother, you are unjust and cruel!' I exclaimed. 'You do not understand me at all. I never thought I could do strokes. I cannot help being constituted so that grimy manual labour is hateful to me, for it *is* hateful to me, and I hate it more and more every day, and you can preach and preach till you go black in the face, and still I'll hate it more than ever. If I have to do it all my life, and if I'm cursed with a long life, I'll hate it just as much at the end as I do now. I'm sure it's not any wish of mine that I'm born with inclinations for better things. If I could be born again, and had the designing of myself, I'd be born the lowest and coarsest-minded person imaginable, so that I could find plenty of companionship, or I'd be born an idiot, which would be better still.'

'Sybylla!' said my mother in a shocked tone. 'It is a wonder God doesn't strike you dead; I never heard—'

'I don't believe there is a God,' I said fiercely, 'and if there is, He's not the merciful being He's always depicted, or He wouldn't be always torturing me for His own amusement.'

'Sybylla, Sybylla! That I should ever have nurtured a child to grow up like this! Do you know that—'

'I only know that I hate this life. I hate it, I hate it, I hate it,' I said vehemently.

'Talk about going out to earn your own living! Why, there's not a woman living would have you in her house above a day. You are a perfect she-devil. Oh God!' And my mother began to cry. 'What have I done to be cursed with such a child? There is not another woman in the district with such a burden put upon her. What have I done? I can only trust that my prayers to God for you will soften your evil heart.'

'If your prayers are answered, it's more than ever mine were,' I retorted.

'*Your* prayers!' said my mother, with scorn. 'The horror of a child not yet sixteen being so hardened. I don't know what to make of you, you never cry or ask forgiveness. There's dear little Gertie now, she is often naughty, but when I correct her she frets and worries and shows herself to be a human being and not a fiend.'

So saying my mother went out of the room.

'I've asked forgiveness once too often, to be sat upon for my pains,' I called out.

'I believe you're mad. That is the only feasible excuse I can make for your conduct,' she said as a parting shot.

'Why the deuce don't you two get to bed and not wrangle like a pair of cats in the middle of the night, disturbing a man's rest?' came in my father's voice from amid the bedclothes.

My mother is a good woman—a very good woman—and I am, I think, not quite all criminality, but we do not pull together. I am a piece of machinery which, not understanding, my mother winds up the wrong way, setting all the wheels of my composition going in creaking discord.

She wondered why I did not cry and beg forgiveness, and thereby give evidence of being human. I was too wrought up for tears. Ah, that tears might have come to relieve my overburdened heart! I took up the home-made tallow candle in its tin stick and looked at my pretty sleeping sister Gertie (she and I shared the one bed). It was as mother had said. If Gertie was scolded for any of her shortcomings, she immediately took refuge in tears, said she was sorry, obtained forgiveness, and straightaway forgot the whole matter. She came within the range of mother's understanding, I did not; she had feelings; mother thought, I had none. Did my mother understand me, she would know that I am capable of more depths of agony and more exquisite heights of joy in one day than Gertie will experience in her whole life.

Was I mad as mother had said? A fear took possession of me that I might be. I certainly was utterly different to any girl I had seen or known. What was the hot wild spirit which surged within me? Ah, that I might weep! I threw myself on my bed and moaned. Why was I not like other girls? Why was I not like Gertie? Why were not a new dress, everyday work, and an occasional picnic sufficient to fill my mind? My movements awakened Gertie.

'What is the matter, dear Sybylla? Come to bed. Mother has been scolding you. She is always scolding some one. That doesn't matter. You say you are sorry, and she won't scold any more. That's what I always do. Do get into bed. You'll be tired in the morning.'

'What does it matter if I will be. I wish I would be dead. What's the good of a hateful thing like I am being alive. No one wants or cares for me.'

'I love you, Sybylla, better than all the rest. I could not do without you,' and she put her pretty face to mine and kissed me.

What a balm to the tempest-tossed soul is a little love, though it may be fleeting and fickle! I was able to weep now, with wild hot tears, and with my sister's arms around me I fell asleep without undressing further.

CHAPTER 7

Was E'er a Rose Without Its Thorn?

I arose from bed next morning with three things in my head—
a pair of swollen eyes, a heavy pain, and a fixed determination
to write a book. Nothing less than a book. A few hours' work
in the keen air of a late autumn morning removed the swelling
from my eyes and the pain from my temples, but the idea of
relieving my feelings in writing had taken firm root in my brain.
It was not my first attempt in this direction. Two years previously
I had purloined paper and sneaked out of bed every night at
one or two o'clock to write a prodigious novel in point of length
and detail, in which a full-fledged hero and heroine performed
the duties of a hero and heroine in the orthodox manner. Knowing
our circumstances, my grandmother was accustomed, when
writing to me, to enclose a stamp to enable me to reply. These
I saved, and with them sent my book to the leading Sydney
publisher. After waiting many weeks I received a polite memo
to the effect that the story showed great ability, but the writer's
inexperience was too much in evidence for publication. The writer
was to study the best works of literature, and would one day,
no doubt, take a place among Australian novelists.

This was a very promising opinion of the work of a child of
thirteen, more encouraging than the great writers got at the start
of their literary career; but it seemed to even my childish intelligence that the memo was a stereotyped affair that the publisher
sent in answer to all the MSS. of fameless writers submitted to
him, and also sent in all probability without reading as much
as the name of the story. After that I wrote a few short stories
and essays; but now the spirit moved me to write another book—
not with any hope of success, as it was impossible for me to
study literature as advised. I seldom saw a book and could only
spare time in tiny scraps to read them when I did.

However, the few shillings I had obtained at odd times I spent on paper, and in secret robbed from much-needed rest a few hours weekly wherein to write. This made me very weary and slow in the daytime, and a sore trial to my mother. I was always forgetting things I should not have forgotten, because my thoughts were engaged in working out my story. The want of rest told upon me. I continually complained of weariness, and my work was a drag to me.

My mother knew not what to make of it. At first she thought I was lazy and bad, and punished me in various ways; but while my book occupied my mind I was not cross, gave her no impudence, and did not flare up. Then she began to fear I must be ill, and took me to a doctor, who said I was much too precocious for my years, and would be better when the weather got warmer. He gave me a tonic, which I threw out the window. I heard no more of going out as nurse-girl: father had joined a neighbour who had taken a road contract, and by this means the pot was kept, if not quite, at least pretty near, boiling.

Life jogged along tamely, and, as far as I could see, gave promise of going to the last slip-rails without a canter, until one day in July 1896 mother received a letter from her mother which made a pleasant change in my life, though, like all sweets, that letter had its bitter drop. It ran as follows:—

My dear daughter, Lucy,

Only a short letter this time, I am pressed for time, as four or five strangers have just come and asked to stay for the night, and as one of the girls is away, I have to get them beds. I am writing about Sybylla. I am truly grieved to hear she is such a source of grief and annoyance to you. The girl must surely be ill or she would never act as you describe. She is young yet, and may settle down better by and by. We can only entrust her to the good God who is ever near. Send her up to me as soon as you can. I will pay all expenses. The change will do her good, and if her conduct improves, I will keep her as long as you like. She is young to mention in regard to marriage, but in another year she will be as old as I was when

I married, and it might be the makings of her if she married early. At any rate she will be better away from Possum Gully, now that she is growing into womanhood, or she may be in danger of forming ties beneath her. She might do something good for herself up here: not that I would ever be a match-maker in the least degree, but Gertie will soon be coming on, and Sybylla, being so very plain, will need all the time she can get.

Your loving mother,
L. Bossier.

My mother gave me this letter to read, and, when I had finished perusing it, asked me would I go. I replied coldly:

'Yes. Paupers and beggars cannot be choosers, and grandmother might as well keep me at Caddagat as at Possum Gully'—for my grandmother contributed greatly to the support of our family.

As regards scenery, the one bit of beauty Possum Gully possessed was its wattles. Bowers of grown and scrubs of young ones adorned the hills and gullies in close proximity to the house, while groves of different species graced the flats. Being Sunday, on this afternoon I was at liberty for a few hours; and on receiving the intelligence contained in the letter, I walked out of the house over a low hill at the back into a gully, where I threw myself at the foot of a wattle in a favourite clump, and gave away to my thoughts.

So mother had been telling my grandmother of my faults—my grandmother whom I loved so dearly. Mother might have had enough honour and motherly protection to have kept the tale of my sins to herself. Though this intelligence angered, it did not surprise me, being accustomed to mother telling every neighbour what a great trial I was to her—how discontented I was, and what little interest I took in my work. It was the last part of the letter which finished up my feelings. Oh heavens! Surely if my mother understood the wild pain, the days and hours of agony pure and complete I have suffered on account of my appearance, she would never have shown me that letter.

I was to be given more time on account of being ugly—I was

not a valuable article in the marriage market, sweet thought! My grandmother is one of the good old school, who believed that a girl's only proper sphere in life was marriage; so, knowing her sentiments, her purpose to get me married neither surprised nor annoyed me. But I was plain. Ah, bosh! Oh! Ah! I cannot express what kind of a feeling that fact gave me. It sank into my heart and cut like a cruel jagged knife—not because it would be a drawback to me in the marriage line, for I had an antipathy to the very thought of marriage. Marriage to me appeared the most horribly tied-down and unfair-to-women existence going. It would be from fair to middling if there was love; but I laughed at the idea of love, and determined never, never, never to marry.

The other side of the letter—the part which gave me joy— was the prospect of going to Caddagat.

Caddagat, the place where I was born! Caddagat, whereat, enfolded in grandmotherly love and the petting which accrued therefrom, I spent some of my few sweet childish days. Caddagat, the place my heart fondly enshrines as home. Caddagat, draped by nature in a dream of beauty. Caddagat, Caddagat! Caddagat for me, Caddagat for ever! I say.

Too engrossed with my thoughts to feel the cold of the dull winter day, I remained in my position against the wattle-tree until Gertie came to inform me that tea was ready.

'You know, Sybylla, it was your turn to get the tea ready; but I set the table to save you from getting into a row. Mother was looking for you, and said she supposed you were in one of your tantrums again.'

Pretty little peacemaker! She often did things like that for me.

'Very well, Gertie, thank you. I will set it two evenings running to make up for it—if I'm here.'

'If you are here! What do you mean?'

'I am going away,' I replied, watching her narrowly to see if she cared, for I was very hungry for love.

'Going to run away because mother is always scolding you?'

'No, you little silly! I'm going up to Caddagat to live with grannie.'

'Always?'

'Yes.'

'Really?'

'Yes.'

'Honour bright?'

'Yes; really and truly and honour bright.'

'Won't you ever come back again?'

'I don't know about *never* coming back again; but I'm going up for always, as far as a person can lay out ahead of her. Do you care?'

Yes she cared. The childish mouth quivered, the pretty blue-eyed face fell, the ready tears flowed fast. I noticed every detail with savage comfort. It was more than I deserved, for, though I loved her passionately, I had ever been too much wrapped in self to have been very kind and lovable to her.

'Who will tell me stories now?'

It was a habit of mine to relate stories to her out of my own fertile imagination. In return for this she kept secret the fact that I sat up and wrote when I should have been in bed. I was obliged to take some means of inducing her to keep silence, as she—even Gertie, who firmly believed in me—on waking once or twice at unearthly hours and discovering me in pursuit of my nightly task, had been so alarmed for my sanity that I had the greatest work to prevent her from yelling to father and mother on the spot. But I bound her to secrecy, and took a strange delight in bringing to her face with my stories the laughter, the wide-eyed wonder, or the tears—just as my humour dictated.

'You'll easily get someone else to tell you stories.'

'Not like yours. And who will take my part when Horace bullies me?'

I pressed her to me.

'Gertie, Gertie, promise me you will love me a little always, and never, never forget me. Promise me.'

And with a weakly glint of winter sunshine turning her hair to gold, and with her head on my shoulder, Gertie promised—promised with the soluble promise of a butterfly-natured child.

SELF-ANALYSIS

N.B.—This is dull and egotistical. Better skip it. That's my advice.—S. P. M.

As a tiny child I was filled with dreams of the great things I was to do when grown up. My ambition was as boundless as the mighty bush in which I have always lived. As I grew it dawned upon me that I was a girl—the makings of a woman! Only a girl!—merely this and nothing more. It came home to me as a great blow that it was only men who could take the world by its ears and conquer their fate, while women, metaphorically speaking, were forced to sit with tied hands and patiently suffer as the waves of fate tossed them hither and thither, battering and bruising without mercy. Familiarity made me used to this yoke; I recovered from the disappointment of being a girl, and was reconciled to that part of my fate. In fact, I found that being a girl was quite pleasant until a hideous truth dawned upon me—I was ugly! That truth has embittered my whole existence. It gives me days and nights of agony. It is a sensitive sore that will never heal, a grim hobgoblin that nought can scare away. In conjunction with this brand of hell I developed a reputation of cleverness. Worse and worse! Girls! girls! Those of you who have hearts, and therefore a wish for happiness, homes, and husbands by and by, never develop a reputation of being clever. It will put you out of the matrimonial running as effectually as though it had been circulated that you had leprosy. So, if you feel that you are afflicted with more than ordinary intelligence, and especially if you are plain with it, hide your brains, cramp your mind, study to appear un-intellectual—it is your only chance. Provided a woman is beautiful allowance will be made for all her short-comings. She can be unchaste, vapid, untruthful, flippant, heartless, and even clever; so long as she is fair to see men will stand by her, and as men, in this world, are 'the dog on top', they are the power to truckle to. A plain woman will have nothing forgiven her. Her fate is such that the parents of uncomely female infants should be compelled to put them to death at their birth.

The next unpleasant discovery I made in regard to myself was that I was woefully out of my sphere. I studied the girls of my age around me, and compared myself with them. We had been reared side by side. They had had equal advantages; some, indeed, had had greater. We all moved in the one little, dull world, but they were not only in their world, they were of it; I was not. Their daily tasks and their little pleasures provided sufficient oil for the lamp of their existence—mine demanded more than Possum Gully could supply. They were totally ignorant of the outside world. Patti, Melba, Irving, Terry, Kipling, Caine, Corelli, and even the name of Gladstone, were only names to them. Whether they were islands or racehorses they knew not and cared not. With me it was different. Where I obtained my information, unless it was born in me, I do not know. We took none but the local paper regularly, I saw few books, had the pleasure of conversing with an educated person from the higher walks of life about once in a twelvemonth, yet I knew of every celebrity in literature, art, music, and drama; their world was my world, and in fancy I lived with them. My parents discouraged me in that species of foolishness. They had been fond of literature and the higher arts, but now, having no use for them, had lost interest therein.

I was discontented and restless, and longed unendurably to be out in the stream of life. 'Action! Action! Give me action!' was my cry. My mother did her best with me according to her lights. She energetically preached at me. All the old saws and homilies were brought into requisition, but without avail. It was like using common nostrums on a disease which could be treated by none but a special physician.

I was treated to a great deal of harping on that tiresome old string, 'Whatsoever your hand findeth to do, do it with all your might.' It was daily dinned into my ears that the little things of life were the noblest, and that all the great people I mooned about said the same. I usually retorted to the effect that I was well aware that it was noble, and that I could write as good an essay on it as any philosopher. It was all very well for great

41

people to point out the greatness of the little, empty, humdrum life. Why didn't they adopt it themselves?

> *The toad beneath the harrow knows*
> *Exactly where each tooth-point goes.*
> *The butterfly upon the road*
> *Preaches contentment to the toad.*

I wasn't anxious to patronize the dull kind of tame nobility of the toad; I longed for a few of the triumphs of the butterfly, decried though they are as hollow bubbles. I desired life while young enough to live, and quoted as my motto:

> *Though the pitcher that goes to the sparkling rill*
> *Too oft gets broken at last,*
> *There are scores of others its place to fill*
> *When its earth to the earth is cast.*
> *Keep that pitcher at home, let it never roam,*
> *But lie like a useless clod;*
> *Yet sooner or later the hour will come*
> *When its chips are thrown to the sod.*
>
> *Is it wise, then, say, in the waning day,*
> *When the vessel is crack'd and old,*
> *To cherish the battered potter's clay*
> *As though it were virgin gold?*
> *Take care of yourself, dull, boorish elf,*
> *Though prudent and sage you seem;*
> *Your pitcher will break on the musty shelf,*
> *And mine by the dazzling stream.*

I had sense sufficient to see the uselessness of attempting to be other than I was. In these days of fierce competition there was no chance for me—opportunity, not talent, was the main requisite. Fate had thought fit to deny me even one advantage or opportunity, thus I was helpless. I set to work to cut my coat according to my cloth. I manfully endeavoured to squeeze my spirit into 'that state of life into which it has pleased God to call me'. I crushed, compressed, and bruised, but as fast as I managed it on one side it burst out on another, and defied me to cram it into the narrow box of Possum Gully.

> *The restless throbbings and burnings*
> *That hope unsatisfied brings,*
> *The weary longings and yearnings*
> *For the mystical better things,*
> *Are the sands on which is reflected*
> *The pitiless moving lake,*
> *Where the wanderer falls dejected,*
> *By a thirst he never can slake.*

In a vain endeavour to slake that cruel thirst my soul groped in strange dark places. It went out in quest of a God, and finding one not, grew weary.

By the unknown way that the atmosphere of the higher life penetrated to me, so came a knowledge of the sin and sorrow abroad in the world—the cry of the millions oppressed, down-trodden, God-forsaken! The wheels of social mechanism needed readjusting—things were awry. Oh, that I might find a cure and give it to my fellows! I dizzied my brain with the problem; I was too much for myself. A man with these notions is a curse to himself, but a woman—pity help a woman of that description! She is not merely a creature out of her sphere, she is a creature without a sphere—a lonely being!

Recognizing this, I turned and cursed God for casting upon me a burden greater than I could bear—cursed Him bitterly, and from within came a whisper that there was nothing there to curse. There was no God. I was an unbeliever. It was not that I sought after or desired atheism. I longed to be a Christian, and fought against unbelief. I asked the Christians around me for help. Unsophisticated fool! I might as well have announced that I was a harlot. My respectability vanished in one slap. Some said it was impossible to disbelieve in the existence of a God: I was

43

only doing it for notoriety, and they washed their hands of me at once.

Not believe in God! I was mad!

If there really was a God, would they kindly tell me how to find Him?

Pray! pray!

I prayed, often and ardently, but ever came that heart-stilling whisper that there was nothing to pray to.

Ah, the bitter, hopeless heart-hunger of godlessness none but an atheist can understand! Nothing to live for in life—no hope beyond the grave. It plunged me into fits of profound melancholy.

Had my father occupied one of the fat positions of the land, no doubt as his daughter my life would have been so full of pleasant occupation and pleasure that I would not have developed the spirit which torments me now. Or had I a friend—one who knew, who had suffered and understood, one in whom I could lose myself, one on whom I could lean—I might have grown a nicer character. But in all the wide world there was not a soul to hold out a hand to me, and I said bitterly, 'There is no good in the world.' In softer moods I said, 'Ah, the tangle of it! Those who have the heart to help have not the power, and those who have the power have not the heart.'

Bad, like a too-strong opponent in a game of chess, is ever at the elbow of good to checkmate it like a weakly managed king.

I am sadly lacking in self-reliance. I needed some one to help me over the rough spots in life, and finding them not, at the age of sixteen I was as rank a cynic and infidel as could be found in three days' march.

CHAPTER 8

Possum Gully Left Behind. Hurrah! Hurrah!

If a Sydney man has friends residing in Goulburn, he says they are up the country. If a Goulburn man has friends at Yass, he says they are up the country. If a Yass man has friends at Young, he says they are up the country, and so on. Caddagat is 'up the country'.

Bound thither on the second Wednesday in August 1896, I bought a ticket at the Goulburn railway station, and at some time about 1 a.m. took my seat in a second class carriage of the mail-train on its way to Melbourne. I had three or four hours to travel in this train when I would have to change to a branch line for two hours longer. I was the only one from Goulburn in that carriage; all the other passengers had been in some time and were asleep. One or two opened their eyes strugglingly, stared glumly at the intruder, and then went to sleep again. The motion of the train was a joy to me, and sleep never entered my head. I stood up, and pressing my forehead to the cold window-pane, vainly attempted, through the inky blackness of the foggy night, to discern the objects which flew by.

I was too full of pleasant anticipation of what was ahead of me to think of those I had left behind. I did not regret leaving Possum Gully. Quite the reverse; I felt inclined to wave my arms and yell for joy at being freed from it. Home! God forbid that my experiences at Possum Gully should form the only food for my reminiscences of home. I had practically grown up there, but my heart refused absolutely to regard it as home. I hated it then, I hate it now, with its narrowing, stagnant monotony. It has and had not provided me with one solitary fond remembrance—only with dreary, wing-clipping, mind-starving recollections. No, no; I was not leaving home behind, I was flying homeward now. Home, home to Caddagat, home to ferny gullies, to the sweet sad rush of many mountain waters, to the majesty of rugged Borgongs; home to dear old grannie, and uncle and aunt, to books, to music; refinement, company, pleasure, and the dear old homestead I love so well.

All in good time I arrived at the end of my train journey, and was taken in charge by a big red-bearded man, who informed me he was the driver of the mail-coach, and had received a letter from Mrs Bossier instructing him to take care of me. He informed me also that he was glad to do what he termed 'that same', and I would be as safe under his care as I would be in God's pocket.

My twenty-six miles' coach drive was neither pleasant nor eventful. I was the only passenger, and so had my choice of seats. The weather being cold and wet, I preferred being inside the box, and curled myself up on the seat, to be interrupted every two or three miles by the good-natured driver inquiring if I was 'all serene'.

At the Halfway House, where a change of the team of five horses was affected, I had a meal and a warm, and so tuned myself up for the remainder of the way. It got colder as we went on, and at 2.30 p.m. I was not at all sorry to see the iron roofs of Gool-Gool township disclosing to my view. We first went to the post office, where the mail-bags were delivered, and then returned and pulled rein in front of the Woolpack Hotel. A tall young gentleman in a mackintosh and cap, who had been standing on the veranda, stepped out on the street as the coach stopped, and lifting his cap and thrusting his head into the coach, inquired, 'Which is Miss Melvyn?'

Seeing I was the only occupant, he laughed the pleasantest of laughs, disclosing two wide rows of perfect teeth, and turning to the driver, said, 'Is that your only passenger? I suppose it *is* Miss Melvyn?'

'As I wasn't present at her birth, I can't swear, but I believe her to be that same, as sure as eggs is eggs,' he replied.

My identity being thus established, the young gentleman with the greatest of courtesy assisted me to alight, ordered the hotel groom to stow my luggage in the Caddagat buggy, and harness the horses with all expedition. He then conducted me to the private parlour, where a friendly little barmaid had some refreshments on a tray awaiting me, and while warming my feet preparatory to eating I read the letter he had given me, which was addressed in my grandmother's handwriting. In it she told me that she and my aunt were only just recovering from bad colds, and on account of the inclemency of the weather thought it unwise to come to town to meet me; but Frank Hawden, the jackeroo, would take every care of me, settle the hotel bill, and tip the coach-driver. Caddagat was twenty-four miles distant from Gool-Gool, and the latter part of the road was very hilly. It was already past three o'clock, and, being rainy, the short winter afternoon would close in earlier; so I swallowed my tea and cake with all expedition, so as not to delay Mr Hawden, who was waiting to assist me into the buggy, where the groom was in charge of the horses in the yard. He struck up a conversation with me immediately.

'Seeing your name on yer bags, an' knowin' you was belonging to the Bossiers, I ask if yer might be a daughter of Dick Melvyn, of Bruggabrong, out by Timlinbilly.'

'Yes, I am.'

'Well, miss, please remember me most kindly to yer pa; he was a good boss was Dick Melvyn. I hope he's doin' well. I'm Billy Haizelip, brother to Mary and Jane. You remember Jane, I s'pose, miss?'

I hadn't time to say more than promise to send his remembrances to my father, for Mr Hawden, saying we would be in the dark, had whipped his horses and was bowling off at a great pace, in less than two minutes covering a rise which put Gool-Gool out of sight. It was raining a little, so I held over us the big umbrella, which grannie had sent, while we discussed the weather, to the effect that rain was badly needed and was a great novelty nowadays, and it was to be hoped it would continue. There had been but little, but the soil here away was of that rich loamy description which little water turns to mud. It clogged the wheels and loaded the break-blocks; and the near side horse

47

had a nasty way of throwing his front feet, so that he deposited soft red lumps of mud in our laps at every step. But, despite these trifling drawbacks, it was delightful to be drawn without effort by a pair of fat horses in splendid harness. It was a great contrast to our poor skinny old horse at home, crawling along in much-broken harness, clumsily and much mended with string and bits of hide.

Mr Hawden was not at all averse to talking. After emptying our tongues of the weather, there was silence for some time, which he broke with, 'So you are Mrs Bossier's grand-daughter, are you?'

'Not remembering my birth, I can't swear; but I believe myself to be that same, as sure as eggs is eggs,' I replied.

He laughed. 'Very good imitation of the coach-driver. But Mrs Bossier's grand-daughter! Well, I should smile!'

'What at?'

'Your being Mrs Bossier's grand-daughter.'

'I fear, Mr Hawden, there is a suspicion of something the reverse of complimentary in your remark.'

'Well, I should smile! Would you like to have my opinion of you?'

'Nothing would please me more. I would value your opinion above all things, and I'm sure—I feel certain—that you have formed a true estimate of me.'

At any other time his conceit would have brought upon himself a fine snubbing, but today I was in high feather, and accordingly very pleasant, and resolved to amuse myself by drawing him out.

'Well, you are not a bit like Mrs Bossier or Mrs Bell; they are both so good-looking,' he continued.

'Indeed!'

'I was disappointed when I saw you had no pretensions to prettiness, as there's not a girl up these parts worth wasting a man's affections on, and I was building great hopes on you. But I'm a great admirer of beauty,' he twaddled.

'I am very sorry for you, Mr Hawden. I'm sure it would take

48

quite a paragon to be worthy of such affection as I'm sure yours would be,' I replied sympathetically.

'Never mind. Don't worry about it. You're not a bad sort, and I think a fellow could have great fun with you.'

'I'm sure, Mr Hawden, you do me too much honour. It quite exhilarates me to think that I meet with your approval in the smallest degree,' I replied with the utmost deference. 'You are so gentlemanly and nice that I was alarmed at first lest you might despise me altogether.'

'No fear. You needn't be afraid of me; I'm not a bad sort of fellow,' he replied with the great encouragement.

By his accent and innocent style I detected he was not a colonial, so I got him to relate his history. He was an Englishman by birth, but had been to America, Spain, New Zealand, Tasmania, etc.; by his own make out had ever been a man of note, and had played Old Harry everywhere.

I allowed him to gabble away full tilt for an hour on this subject, unconscious that I had taken the measure of him, and was grinning broadly to myself. Then I diverted him by inquiring how long since the wire fence on our right had been put up. It bore evidence of recent erection, and had replaced an old cockatoo fence which I remembered in my childhood.

'Fine fence, is it not? Eight wires, a top rail, and very stout posts. Harry Beecham had that put up by contract this year. Twelve miles of it. It cost him a lot: couldn't get any very low tenders, the ground being so hard on account of the drought. Those trees are Five-Bob Downs—see, away over against the range. But I suppose you know the places better than I do.'

We were now within an hour of our destination. How familiar were many landmarks to me, although I had not seen them since I was eight years old.

A river ran on our right, occasionally a glimmer of its noisy waters visible through the shrubbery which profusely lined its banks. The short evening was drawing to a close. The white mists brought by the rain were crawling slowly down the hills, and settling in the hollows of the ranges on our left. A V-shaped rift in them, known as Pheasant Gap, came into view. Mr Hawden said it was well named, as it swarmed with lyrebirds. Night was falling. The skreel of a hundred curlews arose from the gullies—how I love their lonely wail!—and it was quite dark when we pulled up before the front gate of Caddagat.

A score of dogs rushed yelping to meet us, the front door was thrown open, lights and voices came streaming out.

I alighted from the buggy feeling rather nervous. I was a pauper with a bad character. How would my grandmother receive me? Dear old soul, I had nothing to fear. She folded me in a great warm-hearted hug, saying, 'Dear me, child, your face is cold. I'm glad you've come. It has been a terrible day, but we're glad to have the rain. You must be frozen. Get in to the fire, child, as fast as you can. Get in to the fire, get in to the fire. I hope you forgive me for not going to meet you.' And there was my mother's only sister, my tall graceful aunt, standing beside her, giving me a kiss and cordial hand-clasp, and saying, 'Welcome, Sybylla. We will be glad to have a young person to brighten up the old home once more. I am sorry I was too unwell to meet you. You must be frozen; come to the fire.'

My aunt always spoke very little and very quietly, but there was something in her high-bred style which went right home.

I could scarcely believe that they were addressing me. Surely they were making a mistake. This reception was meant for some grand relative honouring them with a visit, and not for the ugly, useless, bad little pauper come to live upon their bounty.

Their welcome did more than all the sermons I had ever heard put together towards thawing a little of the pitiless cynicism which encrusted my heart.

'Take the child inside, Helen, as fast as you can,' said grannie, 'while I see that the boy attends to the horses. The plaguey fellow can't be trusted any further than the length of his nose. I told him to tie up these dogs, and here they are yelp-yelping fit to deafen a person.'

I left my wet umbrella on the veranda, and aunt Helen led me into the dining-room, where a spruce maid was making a pleasant clatter in laying the table. Caddagat was a very old style of house, and all the front rooms opened onto the veranda without any such preliminary as a hall, therefore it was necessary to pass through the dining-room to my bedroom, which was a skillion at the back. While auntie paused for a moment to give some orders to the maid, I noticed the heavy silver serviette rings I remembered so well, and the old-fashioned dinner-plates, and the big fire roaring in the broad white fireplace; but more than all, the beautiful pictures on the walls and a table in a corner strewn with papers, magazines, and several very new-looking books. On the back of one of these I saw 'Corelli', and on another— great joy!—was *Trilby*. From the adjoining apartment, which was the drawing-room, came the sweet full tones of a beautiful piano. Here were three things for which I had been starving. An impulse to revel in them immediately seized me. I felt like clearing the table at a bound, seizing and beginning to read both books, and rushing in to the piano and beginning to play upon it there and then, and examine the pictures—all three things at once. Fortunately for the reputation of my sanity, however, aunt Helen had by this time conducted me to a pretty little bedroom, and saying it was to be mine, helped me to doff my cape and hat.

While warming my fingers at the fire my eyes were arrested by a beautiful portrait hanging above the mantelpiece. It represented a lovely girl in the prime of youth and beauty, and attired in floating white dinner draperies.

'Oh, aunt Helen! isn't she lovely? It's you, isn't it?'

'No. Do you not recognize it as your mother? It was taken just before her marriage. I must leave you now, but come out as soon as you arrange yourself—your grandmother will be anxious to see you.'

When aunt Helen left me I plastered my hair down in an instant without even a glance in the mirror. I took not a particle of interest in my attire, and would go about dressed anyhow. This was one symptom which inclined my mother to the belief of my possible insanity, as to most young girls dress is a great delight. I had tried once or twice to make myself look nice by dressing

51

prettily, but, by my own judgment, considering I looked as ugly as ever, I had given it up as a bad job.

The time which I should have spent in arranging my toilet passed in gazing at my mother's portrait. It was one of the loveliest faces imaginable. The features may not have been perfect according to rule of thumb, but the expression was simply angelic—sweet, winning, gentle, and happy. I turned from the contemplation of it to another photograph—one of my father—in a silver frame on the dressing-table. This, too, was a fine countenance, possessed of well-cut features and refined expression. This was the prince who had won Lucy Bossier from her home. I looked around my pretty bedroom—it had been my mother's in the days of her maidenhood. In an exclusive city boarding-school, and amid the pleasant surroundings of this home, her youth had been spent.

I thought of a man and his wife at Possum Gully. The man was blear-eyed, disreputable in appearance, and failed to fulfil his duties as a father and a citizen. The woman was work-roughened and temper-soured by endless care and an unavailing struggle against poverty. Could that pair possibly be identical with this?

This was life as proved by my parents! What right had I to expect any better yield from it? I shut my eyes and shuddered at the possibilities and probabilities of my future. It was for this that my mother had yielded up her youth, freedom, strength; for this she had sacrificed the greatest possession of woman.

Here I made my way to the dining-room, where grannie was waiting for me and gave me another hug.

'Come here, child, and sit beside me near the fire; but first let me have a look at you,' and she held me at arm's length.

'Dear, oh, dear, what a little thing you are, and not a bit like any of your relations! I am glad your skin is so nice and clear; all my children had beautiful complexions. Goodness me, I never saw such hair! A plait thicker than my arm and almost to your knees! It is that beautiful bright brown like your aunt's. Your mother's was flaxen. I must see your hair loose when you are going to bed. There is nothing I admire so much as a beautiful head of hair.'

The maid announced that dinner was ready, grannie vigorously rang a little bell, aunt Helen, a lady, and a gentleman appeared from the drawing-room, and Mr Hawden came in from the back. I discovered that the lady and gentleman were a neighbouring squatter and a new governess he was taking home. Grannie, seeing them pass that afternoon in the rain, had gone out and prevailed upon them to spend the night at Caddagat.

Mr Hawden took no notice of me now, but showed off to the others for my benefit. After dinner we had music and singing in the drawing-room. I was enjoying it immensely, but grannie thought I had better go to bed, as I had been travelling since about midnight last night. I was neither tired nor sleepy, but knew it useless to protest, so bade every one good night and marched off. Mr Hawden acknowledged my salute with great airs and stiffness, and aunt Helen whispered that she would come and see me by and by, if I was awake.

Grannie escorted me to my room, and examined my hair. I shook it out for her inspection. It met with her approval in every way. She pronounced it beautifully fine, silky, and wavy, and the most wonderful head of hair she had seen out of a picture.

A noise arose somewhere out in the back premises. Grannie went out to ascertain the cause of it and did not return to me, so I extinguished my lamp and sat thinking in the glow of the firelight.

For the first time my thoughts reverted to my leave-taking from home. My father had kissed me with no more warmth than if I had been leaving for a day only; my mother had kissed me very coldly, saying shortly, 'It is to be hoped, Sybylla, that your behaviour to your grandmother will be an improvement upon what it has ever been to me.' Gertie was the only one who had felt any sorrow at parting with me, and I knew that she was of such a disposition that I would be forgotten in a day or two. They would never miss me, for I had no place in their affections. True, I was an undutiful child, and deserved none. I possessed no qualities that would win either their pride or love, but my heart cried out in love for them.

Would Gertie miss me tonight, as I would have missed her had our positions been reversed? Not she. Would my absence from the noisy tea-table cause a blank? I feared not.

I thought of poor mother left toiling at home, and my heart grew heavy; I failed to remember my father's faults, but thought of his great patience with me in the years agone, and all my old-time love for him renewed itself. Why, oh, why, would they not love me a little in return! Certainly I had never striven to be lovable. But see the love some have lavished upon them without striving for it! Why was I ugly and nasty and miserable and useless—without a place in the world?

CHAPTER 9

Aunt Helen's Recipe

'Dear me, Sybylla, not in bed yet, and tears, great big tears! Tell me what is the cause of them.'

It was aunt Helen's voice; she had entered and lit the lamp.

There was something beautifully sincere and real about aunt Helen. She never fussed over any one or pretended to sympathize just to make out how nice she was. She was real, and you felt that no matter what wild or awful rubbish you talked to her it would never be retailed for any one's amusement—and, better than all, she never lectured.

She sat down beside me, and I impulsively threw my arms around her neck and sobbed forth my troubles in a string. How there was no good in the world, no use for me there, no one loved me or ever could on account of my hideousness.

She heard me to the end and then said quietly, 'When you are fit to listen I will talk to you.'

I controlled myself instantly and waited expectantly. What would she say? Surely not that tame old yarn anent this world being merely a place of probation, wherein we were allowed time to fit ourselves for a beautiful world to come. That old tune may be all very well for old codgers tottering on the brink of the grave, but to young persons with youth and romance and good health surging through their veins, it is most boresome. Would she preach that it was flying in the face of providence to moan about my appearance? it being one of the greatest blessings I had, as it would save me from countless temptations to which pretty girls are born. That was another piece of old croaking of the Job's comforter order, of which I was sick unto death, as I am sure there is not an ugly person in the world who thinks her lack of beauty a blessing to her. I need not have feared aunt Helen holding forth in that strain. She always said something brave and comforting which made me ashamed of myself and my selfish conceited egotism.

'I understand you, Sybylla,' she said slowly and distinctly, 'but you must not be a coward. There is any amount of love and good in the world, but you must search for it. Being misunderstood is one of the trials we all must bear. I think that even the most common-minded person in the land has inner thoughts and feelings which no one can share with him, and the higher one's organization the more one must suffer in that respect. I am acquainted with a great number of young girls, some of them good and true, but you have a character containing more than any three of them put together. With this power, if properly managed, you can gain the almost universal love of your fellows. But you are wild and wayward, you must curb and strain your spirit and bring it into subjection, else you will be worse than a person with the emptiest of characters. You will find that plain looks will not prevent you from gaining the *friendship* love of your fellows—the only real love there is. As for the hot fleeting passion of the man for the maid, which is wrongfully designated love, I will not tell you not to think of it, knowing that it is human nature to demand it when arriving at a certain age; but take this comfort: it as frequently passes by on the other side of those with well-chiselled features as those with faces of plainer mould.'

She turned her face away, sighed, and forgetful of my presence lapsed into silence. I knew she was thinking of herself.

Love, not *friendship* love, for anyone knowing her must give her love and respect, but the other sort of love had passed her by.

Twelve years before I went to Caddagat, when Helen Bossier had been eighteen and one of the most beautiful and lovable girls in Australia, there had come to Caddagat on a visit a dashing colonel of the name of Bell, in the enjoyment of a most extended furlough for the benefit of his health. He married aunt Helen and took her to some part of America where his regiment was stationed. I have heard them say she worshipped Colonel Bell, but in less than a twelvemonth he tired of his lovely bride, and becoming enamoured of another woman, he tried to obtain a divorce. On account of his wife's spotless character he was unable to do this; he therefore deserted her and openly lived with the other woman as his mistress. This forced aunt Helen to return to Caddagat, and her mother had induced her to sue for a judicial separation, which was easily obtained.

When a woman is separated from her husband it is the religion of the world at large to cast the whole blame on the wife. By reason of her youth and purity Mrs Bell had not as much to suffer in this way as some others. But, comparatively speaking, her life was wrecked. She had been humiliated and outraged in the cruellest way by the man whom she loved and trusted. He had turned her adrift, neither a wife, widow, nor maid, and here she was, one of the most estimably lovable and noble women I have ever met.

'Come, Sybylla,' she said, starting up brightly, 'I have a plan— will you agree to it? Come and take one good long look at yourself in the glass, then I will turn it to the wall, and you must promise me that for three or four weeks you will not look in a mirror. I will put as many as I can out of your way, and you must avoid the remainder. During this time I will take you in hand, and you must follow my directions implicitly. Will you agree? You will be surprised what a nice-looking little girl I will make of you.'

Of course I agreed. I took a long and critical survey of myself in the glass. There was reflected a pair of hands, red and coarsened with rough work, a round face, shiny and swollen with crying, and a small round figure enshrouded in masses of hair falling in thick waves to within an inch or two of the knees. A very ugly spectacle, I thought. Aunt Helen turned the face of the large mirror flat against the wall, while I remarked despond-ently, 'If you can make me only middling ugly, you must be a magician.'

'Come now, part of my recipe is that you must not think of yourself at all. I'll take you in hand in the morning. I hope you will like your room; I have arranged it on purpose to suit you. And now good night, and happy dreams.'

I awoke next morning in very fine spirits, and slithering out of my bed with alacrity, revelled—literally wallowed—in the appointments of my room. My poor old room at Possum Gully was lacking in barest necessaries. We could not afford even a wash-hand basin and jug; Gertie, the boys, and myself had to perform our morning ablutions in a leaky tin dish on a stool outside the kitchen door, which on cold frosty mornings was a pretty peppery performance: but this room contained everything dear to the heart of girlhood. A lovely bed, pretty slippers, dainty white China-matting and many soft skins on the floor, and in one corner a most artistic toilet set, and a wash-stand liberally supplied with a great variety of soap—some of it so exquisitely perfumed that I felt tempted to taste it. There were pretty pictures on the walls, and on a commodious dressing-table a big mirror and large hand-glasses, with their faces to the wall at present. Hairpins, fancy combs, ribbons galore, and a pretty work-basket greeted my sight, and with delight I swooped down upon the most excruciatingly lovely little writing-desk. It was stuffed full with all kinds of paper of good quality—fancy, all colours, sizes, and shapes, plain, foreign note, pens, ink, and a generous supply of stamps. I felt like writing a dozen letters there and then, and was on the point of giving way to my inclination, when my attention was arrested by what I considered the gem of the whole turn-out. I refer to a nice little bookcase containing copies of all our Australian poets, and two or three dozen novels which I had often longed to read. I read the first chapters of four of them, and then lost myself in Gordon, and sat on my dressing-table in my nightgown, regardless of cold, until brought to my senses by the breakfast-bell. I made great pace, scrambled into my clothes helter-skelter, and appeared at table when the others had been seated and unfolded their serviettes.

Aunt Helen's treatment for making me presentable was the wearing of gloves and a shady hat every time I went outside; and she insisted upon me spending a proper time over my toilet, and would not allow me to encroach upon it with the contents of my bookshelf.

'Rub off some of your gloomy pessimism and cultivate a little more healthy girlish vanity, and you will do very well,' she would say.

I observed these rites most religiously for three days. Then I contracted a slight attack of influenza, and in poking around the kitchen, doing one of the things I oughtn't at the time I shouldn't, a servant-girl tipped a pot of boiling pot-liquor over my right foot, scalding it rather severely. Aunt Helen and grannie put me to bed, where I yelled with pain for hours like a mad Red Indian, despite their applying every alleviative possible. The combined forces of the burn and influenza made me a trifle dicky, so a decree went forth that I was to stay in bed until recovered from both complaints. This effectually prevented me from running in the way of any looking-glasses.

I was not sufficiently ill to be miserable, and being a pampered invalid was therefore fine fun. Aunt Helen was a wonderful nurse. She dressed my foot splendidly every morning, and put it in a comfortable position many times throughout the day. Grannie brought me every dainty in the house, and sent special messengers to Gool-Gool for more. Had I been a professional glutton I would have been in paradise. Even Mr Hawden condescended so far as to express his regret concerning the accident, and favoured me with visits throughout each day; and one Sunday his gallantry carried him to a gully where he plucked a bouquet of maidenhair fern—the first of the season—and put them in a bowl beside my bed. My uncle Julius, the only other member of the family besides the servants, was away 'up the country' on some business or another, and was not expected home for a month or so.

The Bossiers and Beechams were leaders of swelldom among the squattocracy up the country, and firm and intimate friends. The Beechams resided at Five-Bob Downs, twelve miles from Caddagat, and were a family composed of two maiden ladies and their nephew, Harold. One of these ladies was aunt Helen's particular friend, and the other had stood in the same capacity to my mother in days gone by, but of late years, on account of her poverty, mother had been too proud to keep up communication with her. As for Harold Beecham, he was nearly as much at home at Caddagat as at Five-Bob Downs. He came and went with that pleasant familiarity practised between congenial spirits among squatterdom. The Bossiers and Beechams were congenial spirits in every way—they lived in the one sphere and held the one set of ideas, the only difference between them, and that an unnoticeable one, being that the Bossiers, though in comfortable circumstances, were not at all rich, while Harold Beecham was immensely wealthy. When my installation in the role of invalid took place, one Miss Beecham was away in Melbourne, and the other not well enough to come and see me, but Harold came regularly to inquire how I was progressing. He always brought me a number of beautiful apples. This kindness was because the Caddagat orchard had been too infested with codlin moth for grannie to save any last season.

Aunt Helen used to mischievously tease me about this attention.

'Here comes Harry Beecham with some more apples,' she would say. 'No doubt he is far more calculating and artful than I thought he was capable of being. He is taking time by the forelock and wooing you ere he sees you, and so will take the lead. Young ladies are in the minority up this way, and every one is snapped up as soon as she arrives.'

'You'd better tell him how ugly I am, auntie, so that he will carry apples twelve miles on his own responsibility, and when he sees me won't be vexed that all his work has been for nothing. Perhaps, though, it would be better not to describe me, or I will get no more apples,' I would reply.

Aunt Helen was a clever needlewoman. She made all grannie's dresses and her own. Now she was making some for me, which, however, I was not to see until I wore them. Aunt Helen had this as a pleasant surprise, and went to the trouble of blindfolding me while I was being fitted. While in bed, grannie and auntie being busy, I was often left hours alone, and during that time devoured the contents of my bookshelf.

The pleasure, so exquisite as to be almost pain, which I derived from the books, and especially the Australian poets, is beyond description. In the narrow peasant life of Possum Gully I had been deprived of companionship with people of refinement and education who would talk of the things I loved; but, at last! here was congeniality, here was companionship.

The weird witchery of mighty bush, the breath of wide sunlit plains, the sound of camp-bells and jingle of hobble chains, floating on the soft twilight breezes, had come to these men and had written a tale on their hearts as had been written on mine. The glory of the starlit heavens, the mighty wonder of the sea, and the majesty of thunder had come home to them, and the breathless fulness of the sunset hour had whispered of something more than the humour of tomorrow's weather. The wind and rain had a voice which spoke to Kendall, and he too had endured the misery of lack of companionship. Gordon, with his sad, sad humanism and bitter disappointment, held out his hand and took me with him. The regret of it all was I could never meet them—Byron, Thackeray, Dickens, Longfellow, Gordon, Kendall, the men I loved, all were dead; but, blissful thought! Caine, Paterson, and Lawson were still living, breathing human beings—two of them actually countrymen, fellow Australians!

I pored with renewed zeal over the terse realism and pathos of Lawson, and enjoyed Paterson's redolence of the rollicking side of the wholesome life beneath these sunny skies, which he depicted with grand touches of power flashing here and there. I learnt them by heart, and in that gloriously blue receptacle, by and by, where many pleasant youthful dreams are stowed, I put the hope that one day I would clasp hands with them, and feel and know the unspeakable comfort and heart-rest of congenial companionship.

CHAPTER 10

Everard Grey

Uncle Julius had taken a run down to Sydney before returning to Caddagat, and was to be home during the first week in September, bringing with him Everard Grey. This young gentleman always spent Christmas at Caddagat, but as he had just recovered from an illness he was coming up for a change now instead. Having heard much of him, I was curious to see him. He was grandmamma's adopted son, and was the orphan of very aristocratic English parents who had left him to the guardianship of distant relatives. They had proved criminally unscrupulous. By finding a flaw in deeds, or something which none but lawyers understand, they had deprived him of all his property and left him to sink or swim. Grannie had discovered, reared, and educated him. Among professions he had chosen the bar, and was now one of Sydney's most promising young barristers. His foster-mother was no end proud of him, and loved him as her own son.

In due time a telegram arrived from uncle Julius, containing instructions for the buggy to be sent to Gool-Gool to meet him and Everard Grey.

By this time I had quite recovered from influenza and my accident, and as they would not arrive till near nightfall, for their edification I was to be dressed in full-blown dinner costume, also I was to be favoured with a look at my reflection in a mirror for the first time since my arrival.

During the afternoon I was dispatched by grannie on a message some miles away, and meeting Mr Hawden some distance from the house, he took it upon himself to accompany me. Everywhere I went he followed after, much to my annoyance, because grannie gave me many and serious talkings-to about the crime of encouraging young men.

Frank Hawden had changed his tune, and told me now that it mattered not that I was not pretty, as pretty or not I was the greatest brick of a girl he had met. His idea for this opinion was that I was able to talk theatres with him, and was the only girl there, and because he had arrived at that overflowing age when young men have to be partial to some female whether she be ugly or pretty, fat or lean, old or young. That I should be the object of these puerile emotions in a fellow like Frank Hawden, filled me with loathing and disgust.

It was late in the afternoon when Hawden and I returned, and the buggy was to be seen a long way down the road, approaching at the going-for-the-doctor pace at which uncle Julius always drove.

Aunt Helen hustled me off to dress, but I was only half-rigged when they arrived, and so was unable to go out and meet them. Uncle Julius inquired for that youngster of Lucy's, and aunt Helen replied that she would be forthcoming when they were dressed for dinner. The two gentlemen took a nip, to put a little heart in them uncle Julius said, and auntie Helen came to finish my toilet while they were making theirs.

'There now, you have nothing to complain of in the way of looks,' she remarked at the completion of the ceremony. 'Come and have a good look at yourself.'

I was decked in my first evening dress, as it was a great occasion. It was only on the rarest occasion that we donned full war-paint at Caddagat. I think that evening dress is one of the prettiest and most idiotic customs extant. What can be more foolish than to endanger one's health by exposing at night the chest and arms— two of the most vital spots of the body—which have been covered all day? On the other hand, what can be more beautiful than a soft white bosom rising and falling amid a dainty nest of silk and lace? Every woman looks more soft and feminine in a *décolleté* gown. And is there any of the animal lines known pleasanter to the eye than the contour of shapely arms? Some there are who cry down evening dress as being immodest and indecent. These will be found among those whose chest and arms will not admit of being displayed, or among those who, not having been reared to the custom, dislike it with many other things from want of use.

Aunt Helen took me into the wide old drawing-room, now brilliantly lighted. A heavy lamp was on each of the four brackets in the corners, and another swung from the centre of the ceiling, and candelabra threw many lights from the piano. Never before had I seen this room in such a blaze of light. During the last week or two aunt Helen and I had occupied it every night, but we never lighted more than a single candle on the piano. This had been ample light for our purpose. Aunt Helen would sing in her sweet sad voice all the beautiful old songs I loved, while I curled myself on a mat at her side and read books—the music often compelling me to forget the reading, and the reading occasionally rendering me deaf to the music; but through both ever came the solemn rush of the stream outside in its weird melancholy, like a wind ceaselessly endeavouring to outstrip a wild vain regret which relentlessly pursued.

'Your uncle Julius always has the drawing-room lighted like this; he does not believe in shadowy half light—calls it sentimental bosh,' said aunt Helen in explanation.

'Is uncle like that?' I remarked, but my question remained unanswered. Leaving a hand-mirror with me, aunt Helen had slipped away.

One wall of the drawing-room was monopolized by a door, a big bookcase, and a heavy bevelled-edged old-fashioned mirror —the two last-mentioned articles reaching from floor to ceiling. Since my arrival the face of the mirror had been covered, but this evening the blue silken curtains were looped up, and it was before this that I stood.

I looked, and looked again in pleased surprise. I beheld a young girl with eyes and skin of the clearest and brightest, and lips of brilliant scarlet, and a chest and pair of arms which would pass muster with the best. If Nature had been in bad humour when moulding my face, she had used her tools craftily in forming my figure. Aunt Helen had proved a clever maid and dressmaker.

My pale blue cashmere dress fitted my fully developed yet girlish figure to perfection. Some of my hair fell in cunning little curls on my forehead; the remainder, tied simply with a piece of ribbon, hung in thick waves nearly to my knees. My toilet had altered me almost beyond recognition. It made me look my age—sixteen years and ten months—whereas before, when dressed carelessly and with my hair plastered in a tight coil, people not knowing me would not believe that I was under twenty. Joy and merriment lit up my face, which glowed with youth, health, and happiness, which rippled my lips in smiles, which displayed a splendid set of teeth, and I really believe that on that night I did not look out of the way ugly.

I was still admiring my reflection when aunt Helen returned to say that Everard and uncle Julius were smoking on the veranda and asking for me.

'What do you think of yourself, Sybylla?'

'Oh, aunt Helen, tell me that there is something about me not completely hideous!'

She took my face between her hands, saying:

'Silly child, there are some faces with faultless features, which would receive nothing more than an indifferent glance while beside other faces which might have few if any pretensions to beauty. Yours is one of the last mentioned.'

'But that does not say I am not ugly.'

'No one would dream of calling you plain, let alone ugly; brilliant is the word which best describes you.'

Uncle Julius had the upper part of his ponderous figure arrayed in a frock-coat. He did not take kindly to what he termed 'those skittish sparrow-tailed affairs'. Frock-coats suited him, but I am not partial to them on every one. They look well enough on a podgy, fat, or broad man, but on a skinny one they hang with such a forlorn, dying-duck expression, that they invariably make me laugh.

Julius John Bossier, better known as J. J. Bossier, and better still as Jay-Jay—big, fat, burly, broad, a jovial bachelor of forty, too fond of all the opposite sex ever to have settled his affections on one in particular—was well known, respected, and liked from Wagga Wagga to Albury, Forbes to Dandaloo, Bourke to Hay, from Tumut to Monaro, and back again to Peak Hill, as a generous man, a straight goer in business matters, and a jolly good fellow all round.

I was very proud to call him uncle.

'So this is yourself, is it!' he exclaimed, giving me a tremendous hug.

'Oh, uncle,' I expostulated, 'I'll wipe your old kisses off! Your breath smells horribly of whisky and tobacco.'

'Gammon, that's what makes my kisses so nice!' he answered; and, after holding me at arm's-length for inspection, 'By George, you're a wonderful-looking girl! You're surely not done growing yet, though! You are such a little nipper. I could put you in my pocket with ease. You aren't a scrap like your mother. I'll give the next shearer who passes a shilling to cut that hair off. It would kill a dog in the hot weather.'

'Everard, this is my niece, Sybylla' (aunt Helen was introducing us). 'You will have to arrange yourselves—what relation you are, and how to address each other.'

The admiration expressed in his clear sharp eyes gave me a sensation different to any I had ever experienced previously.

'I suppose I'm a kind of uncle and brother in one, and as either relationship entitles me to a kiss, I'm going to take one,' he said in a very gallant manner.

'You may take one if you can,' I said with mischievous defiance, springing off the veranda into the flower-garden. He accepted my challenge, and, being lithe as a cat, a tremendous scamper ensued. Round and round the flower-beds we ran. Uncle Jay-Jay's beard opened in a broad smile, which ended in a loud laugh. Everard Grey's coat-tails flew in the breeze he made, and his collar was too high for athletic purposes. I laughed too, and was lost, and we returned to the veranda—Everard in triumph, and I feeling very red and uncomfortable.

Grannie had arrived upon the scene, looking the essence of brisk respectability in a black silk gown and a white lace cap.

She cast on me a glance of severe disapproval, and denounced my conduct as shameful; but uncle Jay-Jay's eyes twinkled as he dexterously turned the subject.

'Gammon, mother! I bet you were often kissed when that youngster's age. I bet my boots now that you can't count the times you did the same thing yourself. Now, confess.'

Grannie's face melted in a smile as she commenced a little anecdote, with that pathetic beginning, 'When I was young.'

Aunt Helen sent me inside lest I should catch cold, and I stationed myself immediately inside the window so that I should not miss the conversation. 'I should think your niece is very excitable,' Mr Grey was saying to aunt Helen.

'Oh, very.'

'Yes; I have never seen any but very highly strung temperaments have that transparent brilliance of expression.'

'She is very variable—one moment all joy, and the next the reverse.'

'She has a very striking face. I don't know what it is that makes it so.'

'It may be her complexion,' said aunt Helen; 'her skin is whiter than the fairest blonde, and her eyebrows and lashes very dark. Be very careful you do not say anything that would let her know you think her not nice looking. She broods over her appearance in such a morbid manner. It is a weak point with her, so be careful not to sting her sensitiveness in that respect.'

'Plain-looking! Why, I think she has one of the most fascinating faces I've seen for some time, and her eyes are simply magnificent. What colour are they?'

'The grass is not bad about Sydney. I think I will send a truck of fat wethers away next week,' said uncle Jay-Jay to grannie.

'It is getting quite dark. Let's get in to dinner at once,' said grannie.

During the meal I took an opportunity of studying the appearance of Everard Grey. He had a typically aristocratic English face, even to the cold rather heartless expression, which is as established a point of an English blue blood as an arched neck is of a thoroughbred horse.

A ringer, whose wife had been unexpectedly confined, came for grannie when dinner was over, and the rest of us had a delightful musical evening. Uncle Jay-Jay bawled 'The Vicar of Bray' and 'Drink, Puppy, Drink' in a stentorian bass voice, holding me on his knee, pinching, tickling, pulling my hair, and shaking me up and down between whiles. Mr Hawden favoured us by rendering 'The Holy City'. Everard Grey sang several new songs, which was a great treat, as he had a well-trained and musical baritone voice. He was a veritable carpet knight, and though not a fop, was exquisitely dressed in full evening costume, and showed his long pedigreed blood in every line of his clean-shaven face and tall slight figure. He was quite a champion on the piano, and played aunt Helen's accompaniments while he made her sing song after song. When she was weary uncle Jay-Jay said to me, 'Now it's your turn, me fine lady. We've all done something to keep things rolling but you. Can you sing?'

'No.'

'Can this youngster sing, Helen?'

'She sings very nicely to herself sometimes, but I do not know how she would manage before company. Will you try something, Sybylla?'

Uncle Jay-Jay waited to hear no more, but carrying me to the music-stool, and depositing me thereon, warned me not to attempt to leave it before singing something.

To get away to myself, where I was sure no one could hear me, and sing and sing till I made the echoes ring, was one of the chief joys of my existence, but I had never made a success in singing to company. Besides losing all nerve, I had a very queer voice, which every one remarked. However, tonight I made an effort in my old favourite, 'Three Fishers Went Sailing'. The beauty of the full-toned Ronisch piano, and Everard's clever and sympathetic accompanying, caused me to forget my audience, and sing as though to myself alone, forgetting that my voice was odd.

When the song ceased Mr Grey wheeled abruptly on the stool and said, 'Do you know that you have one of the most wonderful natural voices I have heard. Why, there is a fortune in such a voice if it were trained! Such chest-notes, such feeling, such rarity of tone!'

'Don't be sarcastic, Mr Grey,' I said shortly.

'Upon my word as a man, I mean every word I say,' he returned enthusiastically.

Everard Grey's opinion on artistic matters was considered worth having. He dabbled in all the arts—writing, music, acting, and sketching, and went to every good concert and play in Sydney. Though he was clever at law, it was whispered by some that he would wind up on the stage, as he had a great leaning that way.

I walked away from the piano treading on air. Would I really make a singer? I with the voice which had often been ridiculed; I who had often blasphemously said that I would sell my soul to be able to sing just passably. Everard Grey's opinion gave me an intoxicated sensation of joy.

'Can you recite?' he inquired.

'Yes,' I answered firmly.

'Give us something,' said uncle Jay-Jay.

I recited Longfellow's 'The Slave's Dream'. Everard Grey was quite as enthusiastic over this as he had been about my singing.

'Such a voice! Such depth and width! Why, she could fill the Centennial Hall without an effort. All she requires is training.'

'By George, she's a regular dab! But I wish she would give us something not quite so glum,' said uncle Jay-Jay.

I let myself go. Carried away by I don't know what sort of a spirit, I exclaimed, 'Very well, I will, if you will wait till I make up, and will help me.'

I disappeared for a few minutes, and returned made up as a fat old Irish woman, with a smudge of dirt on my face. There was a general laugh.

Would Mr Hawden assist me? Of course he was only too delighted, and flattered that I had called upon him in preference to the others. What would he do?

I sat him on a footstool, so that I might with facility put my hand on his sandy hair, and turning to uncle, commenced:

'Shure, sir, seeing it was a good bhoy yez were afther to run errants, it's meself that has brought this youngsther for yer inspection. It's a jool ye'll have in him. Shure I rared him meself, and he says his prayers every morning. Kape sthill, honey! Faith, ye're not afraid of yer poor old mammy pullin' yer beautiful cur-r-rls?'

Uncle Jay-Jay was laughing like fun; even aunt Helen deigned to smile; and Everard was looking on with critical interest.

'Go on,' said uncle. But Mr Hawden got huffy at the ridicule which he suspected I was calling down upon him, and jumped up looking fit to eat me.

I acted several more impromptu scenes with the other occupants of the drawing-room. Mr Hawden emitted 'Humph!' from the corner where he grumpily sat, but Mr Grey was full of praise.

'Splendid! splendid!' he exclaimed. 'You say you have not had an hour's training, and never saw a play. Such versatility. Your fortune would be made on the stage. It is a sin to have such exceptional talent wasting in the bush. I must take her to Sydney and put her under a good master.'

'Indeed, you'll do no such thing,' said uncle. 'I'll keep her here to liven up the old barracks. You've got enough puppets on the stage without a niece of mine ever being there.'

I went to bed that night greatly elated. Flattery is sweet to youth. I felt pleased with myself, and imagined, as I peeped in the looking-glass, that I was not half bad-looking after all.

CHAPTER 11

Yah!

'Bah, you hideous animal! Ha ha! Your peerless conceit does you credit. So you actually imagined that by one or two out of every hundred you might be considered passable. You are the most uninteresting person in the world. You are small and nasty and bad, and every other thing that's abominable. That's what you are.'

This address I delivered to my reflection in the glass next morning. My elation of the previous night was as flat as a pancake. Dear, oh dear, what a fool I had been to softly swallow the flattery of Mr Grey without a single snub in return! To make up for my laxity, if he continued to amuse himself by plastering my vanity with the ointment of flattery, I determined to serve up my replies to him red-hot and well seasoned with pepper.

I finished my toilet, and in a very what's-the-good-o'-anything mood took a last glance in the glass to say, 'You're ugly, you're ugly and useless; so don't forget that and make a fool of yourself again.'

I was in the habit of doing this; it had long ago taken the place of a morning prayer. I said this, that by familiarity it might lose a little of its sting when I heard it from other lips, but somehow it failed in efficacy.

I was late for breakfast that morning. All the others were half through the meal when I sat down.

Grannie had not come home till after twelve, but was looking as brisk as usual.

'Come, Sybylla, I suppose this comes of sitting up too late, as I was not here to hunt you to bed. You are always very lively at night, but it's a different tune in the morning,' she said, when giving me the usual morning hug.

'When I was a nipper of your age, if I didn't turn out like

greased lightning every morning, I was assisted by a little strap oil,' remarked uncle Jay-Jay.

'Sybylla should be excused this morning,' interposed Mr Grey. 'She entertained us for hours last night. Little wonder if she feels languid this morning.'

'Entertained you! What did she do?' queried grannie.

'Many things. Do you know, gran, that you are robbing the world of an artist by keeping Sybylla hidden away in the bush? I must persuade you to let me take her to Sydney and have her put under the best masters in Sydney.'

'Under masters for what?'

'Elocution and singing.'

'I couldn't afford it.'

'But I'd bear the expense myself. It would only be returning a trifle of all you have done for me.'

'What nonsense! What would you have her do when she was taught?'

'Go on the stage, of course. With her talent and hair she would cause quite a sensation.'

Now grannie's notions re the stage were very tightly laced. All actors and actresses, from the lowest circus man up to the most glorious cantatrice, were people defiled in the sight of God, and utterly outside the pale of all respectability, when measured with her code of morals.

She turned energetically in her chair, and her keen eyes flashed with scorn and anger as she spoke.

'Go on the stage! A grand-daughter of mine! Lucy's eldest child! An actress—a vile, low, brazen hussy! Use the gifts God has given her with which to do good in showing off to a crowd of vile bad men! I would rather see her struck dead at my feet this instant! I would rather see her shear off her hair and enter a convent this very hour. Child, promise you will never be a bold bad actress.'

'I will never be a *bold bad* actress, grannie,' I said, putting great stress on the adjectives, and bringing out the actress very faintly.

'Yes,' she continued, calming down, 'I'm sure you have not enough bad in you. You may be boisterous, and not behave with sufficient propriety sometimes, but I don't think you are wicked enough to ever make an actress.'

Everard attempted to defend his case.

'Look here, gran, that's a very exploded old notion about the stage being a low profession. It might have been once, but it is quite the reverse nowadays. There are, of course, low people on the stage, as there are in all walks of life. I grant you that; but if people are good they can be good on the stage as well as anywhere else. On account of a little prejudice it would be a sin to rob Sybylla of the brilliant career she might have.'

'Career!' exclaimed his foster-mother, catching at the word. 'Career! That is all girls think of now, instead of being good wives and mothers and attending to their homes and doing what God intended. All they think of is gadding about and being fast, and ruining themselves body and soul. And the men are as bad to encourage them,' looking severely at Everard.

'There is a great deal of truth in what you say, gran, I admit. You can apply it to many of our girls, I am sorry to confess, but Sybylla could not be brought under that classification. You must look at her in a different way. If—'

'I look at her as the child of respectable people, and will not have the stage mentioned in connection with her.' Here grannie thumped her fist down on the table, and there was silence, complete, profound. Few dared argue with Mrs Bossier.

Dear old lady, she was never angry long, and in a minute or two she proceeded with her breakfast, saying quite pleasantly:

'Never mention such a subject to me again; but I'll tell you what you can do. Next autumn, some time in March or April, when the fruit-preserving and jam-making are done with, Helen can take the child to Sydney for a month or so, and you can show them round. It will be a great treat for Sybylla as she has never been in Sydney.'

'That's right, let's strike a bargain on that, gran,' said Everard.

'Yes; it's a bargain, if I hear no more about the stage. God intends His creatures for a better life than that.'

After breakfast I was left to entertain Everard for some while. We had a fine time. He was a perfect gentleman and a clever conversationalist.

I was always desirous of enjoying the company of society people who were well bred and lived according to etiquette, and possessed of leisure and culture sufficient to fill their minds with something more than the price of farm produce and a hard struggle for existence. Hitherto I had only read of such or seen them in pictures, but here was a real live one, and I seized my opportunity with vim. At my questioning and evident interest in his talk he told me of all the latest plays, actors, and actresses with whom he was acquainted, and described the fashionable balls, dinners, and garden-parties he attended. Having exhausted this subject, we fell to discussing books, and I recited snatches of poems dear to me. Everard placed his hands upon my shoulders and said:

'Sybylla, do you know you are a most wonderful girl? Your figure is perfect, your style refreshing, and you have a most interesting face. It is as ever-changing as a kaleidoscope—sometimes merry, then stern, often sympathetic, and always sad when at rest. One would think you had had some sorrow in your life.'

Lifting my skirt at either side, I bowed several times very low in what I called my stage bow, and called into requisition my stage smile, which displayed two rows of teeth as white and perfect as any twenty-guinea set turned out on a gold plate by a fashionable dentist.

'The handsome gentleman is very kind to amuse himself at the expense of a little country bumpkin, but he would do well to ascertain if his flattery would go down before administering it next time,' I said sarcastically, and I heard him calling to me as I abruptly went off to shut myself in my room.

'How dare anyone ridicule me by paying idle brainless compliments! I knew I was ugly, and did not want any one to perjure his soul pretending they thought differently. What right had I to be small? Why wasn't I possessed of a big aquiline nose and a tall commanding figure?' Thus I sat in burning discontent and ill-humour until soothed by the scent of roses and the gleam of soft spring sunshine which streamed in through my open window. Some of the flower-beds in the garden were completely carpeted with pansy blossoms, all colours, and violets—blue and white, single and double. The scent of mignonette, jonquils, and narcissi filled the air. I revelled in rich perfumes, and these tempted me forth. My ruffled feelings gave way before the delights of the old garden. I collected a number of vases, and, filling them with water, set them on a table in the veranda near one of the drawing-room windows. I gathered lapfuls of the lovely blossoms, and commenced arranging them in the vases.

Part of the old Caddagat house was built of slabs, and one of the wooden walls ran along the veranda side of the drawing-room, so the songs aunt Helen and Everard Grey were trying to the piano came as a sweet accompaniment to my congenial task.

Presently they left off singing and commenced talking. Under the same circumstances a heroine of a story would have slipped away; or, if that were impossible without discovery, she would have put her fingers in her ears, and would have been in a terrible state of agitation lest she should hear something not intended for her. I did not come there with a view to eaves-dropping. It is a degradation to which I never stoop. I thought they were aware of my presence on the veranda; but it appears they were not, as they began to discuss me (wonderfully interesting subject to myself), and I stayed there, without one word of disapproval from my conscience, to listen to their conversation.

'My word, didn't gran make a to-do this morning when I proposed to train Sybylla for the stage! Do you know that girl is simply reeking with talent; I must have her trained. I will keep bringing the idea before gran until she gets used to it. I'll work the we-should-use-the-gifts-God-has-given-us racket for all it is worth, and you might use your influence too, Helen.'

'No, Everard; there are very few who succeed on the stage. I would not use my influence, as it is a life of which I do not approve.'

'But Sybylla *would* succeed. I am a personal friend of the leading managers, and my influence would help her greatly.'

'Yes; but what would you do with her? A young gentleman couldn't take charge of a girl and bring her out without ruining her reputation. There would be no end of scandal, as the sister theory would only be nonsense.'

'There is another way; I could easily stop scandal.'

'Everard, what do you mean!'

'I mean marriage,' he replied deliberately.

'Surely, boy, you must be dreaming! You have only seen her for an hour or two. I don't believe in these sudden attachments.'

Perhaps she here thought of one (her own) as sudden, which had not ended happily.

'Everard, don't do anything rashly. You know you are very fickle and considered a lady-killer—be merciful to my poor little Sybylla, I pray. It is just one of your passing fancies. Don't wile her passionate young heart away and then leave her to pine and die.'

'I don't think she is that sort,' he replied laughingly.

'No, she would not die, but would grow into a cynic and sceptic, which is the worst of fates. Let her alone. Flirt as much as you will with society belles who understand the game, but leave my country maiden alone. I hope to mould her into a splendid character yet.'

'But, Helen, supposing I am in earnest at last, you don't think I'd make her a bad old hubby, do you?'

'She is not the girl for you. You are not the man who could ever control her. What I say may not be complimentary but it is true. Besides, she is not seventeen yet, and I do not approve of romantic young girls throwing themselves into matrimony. Let them develop their womanhood first.'

'Then I expect I had better hide my attractions under a bushel during the remainder of my stay at Caddagat?'

'Yes. Be as nice to the child as you like, but mind, none of those little ladies'-man attentions with which it is so easy to steal—'

I waited to hear no more, but, brimming over with a mixture of emotions, tore through the garden and into the old orchard. Bees were busy, and countless bright-coloured butterflies flitted hither and thither, sipping from hundreds of trees, white or pink with bloom—their beauty was lost upon me. I stood ankle-deep in violets, where they had run wild under a gnarled old apple-tree, and gave way to my wounded vanity.

'Little country maiden, indeed! There's no need for him to bag his attractions up. If he exerted himself to the utmost of his ability, he could not make me love him. I'm not a child. I saw through him in the first hour. There's not enough in him to win my love. I'll show him I think no more of him than of the caterpillars in the old tree there. I'm not a booby that will fall in love with every gussie I see. Bah, there's no fear of that! I hate and detest men!'

'I suppose you are rehearsing some more airs to show off with tonight,' sneered a voice behind me.

'No, I'm realisticing; and how *dare* you thrust your obnoxious presence before me when I wish to be alone! Haven't I often shown—'

'While a girl is disengaged, any man who is her equal has the right to pay his addresses to her if he is in earnest,' interrupted Mr Hawden. It was he who stood before me.

'I am well aware of that,' I replied. 'But it is a woman's privilege to repel those attentions if distasteful to her. You seem discinclined to accord me that privilege.'

Having delivered this retort, I returned to the house, leaving him standing there looking the fool he was.

I do not believe in spurning the love of a blackfellow if he behaves in a manly way; but Frank Hawden was such a drivel-ling mawkish style of sweetheart that I had no patience with him.

Aunt Helen and Everard had vacated the drawing-room, so I plumped down on the piano-stool and dashed into Kowalski's galop, from that into 'Gaîté de Coeur' until I made the piano dance and tremble like a thing possessed. My annoyance faded, and I slowly played that saddest of waltzes, 'Weber's Last'. I became aware of a presence in the room, and, facing about, confronted Everard Grey.

'How long have you been there?' I demanded sharply.

'Since you began to play. Where on earth did you learn to play? Your execution is splendid. Do sing "Three Fishers", please.'

'Excuse me; I haven't time now. Besides I am not competent to sing to you,' I said brusquely, and made my exit.

'Mr Hawden wants you, Sybylla,' called aunt Helen. 'See what he wants and let him get away to his work, or your grannie will be vexed to see him loitering about all the morning.'

'Miss Sybylla,' he began, when we were left alone, 'I want to apologize to you. I had no right to plague you, but it all comes of the way I love you. A fellow gets jealous at the least little thing, you know.'

'Bore me with no more such trash,' I said, turning away in disgust.

'But, Miss Sybylla, what am I to do with it?'

'Do with what?'

'My love.'

'Love!' I retorted scornfully. 'There is no such thing.'

'But there is, and I have found it.'

'Well, you stick to it—that's my advice to you. It will be a treasure. If you send it to my father he will get it bottled up and put it in the Goulburn museum. He has sent several things there already.'

'Don't make such a game of a poor devil. You know I can't do that.'

'Bag it up, then; put a big stone to make it sink, and pitch it in the river.'

'You'll rue this,' he said savagely.

'I may or may not,' I sang over my shoulder as I departed.

CHAPTER 12

One Grand Passion

I had not the opportunity of any more private interviews with Everard Grey till one morning near his departure, when we happened to be alone on the veranda.

'Well, Miss Sybylla,' he began, 'when I arrived I thought you and I would have been great friends; but we have not progressed at all. How do you account for that?'

As he spoke he laid his slender shapely hand kindly upon my head. He was very handsome and winning, and moved in literary, musical, and artistic society—a man from my world, a world away.

Oh, what pleasure I might have derived from companionship with him! I bit my lip to keep back the tears. Why did not social arrangements allow a man and a maid to be chums—chums as two men or two maids may be to each other, enjoying each other without thought beyond pure platonic friendship? But no; it could not be. I understood the conceit of men. Should I be very affable, I feared Everard Grey would imagine he had made a conquest of me. On the other hand, were I glum he would think the same, and that I was trying to hide my feelings behind a mask of brusquerie. I therefore steered in a bee-line between the two manners, and remarked with the greatest of indifference:

'I was not aware that you expected us to be such cronies— in fact, I have never given the matter a thought.'

He turned away in a piqued style. Such a beau of beaux, no doubt he was annoyed that an insignificant little country bumpkin should not be flattered by his patronage, or probably he thought me rude or ill-humoured.

Two mornings later uncle Jay-Jay took him to Gool-Gool *en route* for Sydney. When departing he bade me a kindly good-bye, made me promise to write to him, and announced his intention of obtaining the opinion of some good masters re my dramatic

79

talent and voice, when I came to Sydney as promised by my grandmother. I stood on the garden fence waving my handkerchief until the buggy passed out of sight among the messmate-trees about half a mile from the house.

'Well I hope, as that dandified ape has gone—and good riddance to him—that you will pay more heed to my attentions now,' said Mr Hawden's voice, as I was in the act of descending from the fence.

'What do you mean by your attentions?' I demanded.

'What do I mean! That is something like coming to business. I'll soon explain. You know what my intentions are very well. When I am twenty-four, I will come into my property in England. It is considerable, and at the end of that time I want to marry you and take you home. By Jove! I would just like to take you home. You'd surprise some English girls I know.'

'There would be more than one person surprised if I married you,' I thought to myself, and laughed till I ached with the motion.

'You infernal little vixen! What are you laughing at? You've got no more sense than a bat if such a solemn thing only provokes your mirth.'

'Solemn—why, it's a screaming farce!' I laughed more and more.

'What's a farce?' he demanded fiercely.

'The bare idea of you proposing to me.'

'Why? Have I not as much right to propose as any other man?'

'Man!' I laughed. 'That's where the absurdity arises. My child, if you were a man, certainly you could propose, but do you think I'd look at a boy, a child! If ever I perpetrate matrimony the participant in my degradation will be a fully developed man—not a hobbledehoy who falls in love, as he terms it, on an average about twice a week. Love! Ho!'

I moved in the direction of the house. He barred my path.

'You are not going to escape me like that, my fine lady. I will make you listen to me this time or you will hear more about it,' and he seized me angrily by the wrist.

I cannot bear the touch of any one—it is one of my idiosyncrasies. With my disengaged hand I struck him a vigorous blow on the nose, and wrenching myself free sprang away, saying, 'How dare you lay a finger on me! If you attempt such a thing again I'll make short work of you. Mark my words, or you'll get something more than a bleeding nose next time, I promise you.'

'You'll hear more of this! You'll hear more of this! You fierce, wild, touch-me-not thing,' he roared.

'Yes; my motto with men is touch-me-not, and it is your own fault if I'm fierce. If children attempt to act the role of a man with adult tools, they are sure to cut themselves. Hold hard a bit, honey, till your whiskers grow,' I retorted as I departed, taking flying leaps over the blossom-burdened flower-beds.

At tea that night, after gazing interestedly at Mr Hawden's nose for some time, uncle Julius inquired, 'In the name of all that's mysterious, what the devil have you been doing to your nose? You look as though you had been on the spree.'

I was quaking lest he would get me into a fine scrape, but he only muttered, 'By Jove!' with great energy, and glowered menacingly across the table at me.

After tea he requested an interview with grannie, which aroused my curiosity greatly. I was destined to hear all about it next morning. When breakfast was over grannie called me into her room and interviewed me about Mr Hawden's interview. She began without any preliminaries:

'Mr Hawden has complained of your conduct. It grieves me that any young man should have to speak to me of the behaviour of my own grand-daughter. He says you have been flirting with him. Sybylla, I scarcely thought you would be so immodest and unwomanly.'

On hearing this my thoughts of Frank Hawden were the reverse of flattering. He had persecuted me beyond measure, yet I had not deigned to complain of him to either uncle, grannie, or auntie, as I might reasonably have done, and have obtained immediate redress. He had been the one to blame in the case, yet for the rebuffs he had brought upon himself, went tattling to my grandmother.

'Is that all you have to say, grannie?'

'No. He wants to marry you, and has asked my consent. I told him it all rested with yourself and parents. What do you say?'

'Say,' I exclaimed, 'grannie, you are only joking, are you not?'

'No, my child, this is not a matter to joke about.'

'Marry that creature! A boy!' I uttered in consternation.

'He is no boy. He has attained his majority some months. He is as old as your grandfather was when we married. In three years you will be almost twenty, and by that time he will be in possession of his property which is very good—in fact, he will be quite rich. If you care for him there is nothing against him as I can see. He is healthy, has a good character, and comes of a high family. Being a bit wild won't matter. Very often, after they sow their wild oats, some of those scampy young fellows settle down and marry a nice young girl and turn out very good husbands.'

'It is disgusting, and you ought to be downright ashamed of yourself, grannie! A man can live a life of bestiality and then be considered a fit husband for the youngest and purest girl! It is shameful! Frank Hawden is not wild, he hasn't got enough in him to be so. I hate him. No, he hasn't enough in him to hate. I loathe and despise him. I would not marry him or any one like him though he were King of England. The idea of marriage even with the best man in the world seems to me a lowering thing,' I raged; 'but with him it would be pollution—the lowest degradation that could be heaped upon me! I will never come down to marry any one—' here I fell a victim to a flood of excited tears.

I felt there was no good in the world, especially in men—the hateful creatures!—and never would be while it was not expected of them, even by rigidly pure, true Christians such as my grandmother. Grannie, dear old grannie, thought I should marry any man who, from a financial point of view, was a good match for me. That is where the sting came in. No, I would never marry. I would procure some occupation in which I could tread my life out, independent of the degradation of marriage.

'Dear me, child,' said grannie, concernedly, 'there is no need to distress yourself so. I remember you were always fearfully passionate. When I had you with me as a tiny toddler, you would fret a whole day about a thing an ordinary child would forget inside an hour. I will tell Hawden to go about his business. I would not want you to consider marriage for an instant with anyone distasteful to you. But tell me truly, have you ever flirted with him? I will take you word, for I thank God you have never yet told me a falsehood!'

'Grannie,' I exclaimed emphatically, 'I have discouraged him all I could. I would scorn to flirt with any man.'

'Well, well, that is all I want to hear about it. Wash your eyes, and we will get our horses and go over to see Mrs Hickey and her baby, and take her something good to eat.'

I did not encounter Frank Hawden again till the afternoon, when he leered at me in a very triumphant manner. I stiffened myself and drew out of his way as though he had been some vile animal. At this treatment he whined, so I agreed to talk the matter over with him and have done with it once and for all.

He was on his way to water some dogs, so I accompanied him out to the stables near the kennels, to be out of hearing of the household.

I opened fire without any beating about the bush.

'I ask you, Mr Hawden, if you have any sense of manliness, from this hour to cease persecuting me with your idiotic professions of love. I have two sentiments regarding it, and in either you disgust me. Sometimes I don't believe there is such a thing as love at all—that is, love between men and women. While in this frame of mind I would not listen to professions of love from an angel. Other times I believe in love, and look upon it as a sacred and solemn thing. When in that humour, it seems to me a desecration to hear you twaddling about the holy theme, for you are only a boy, and don't know how to feel. I would not have spoken thus harshly to you, but by your unmanly conduct you have brought it upon yourself. I have told you straight all that I will ever deign to tell you on the subject, and take much pleasure in wishing you good afternoon.'

I walked away quickly, heedless of his expostulations.

My appeal to his manliness had no effect. Did I go for a ride, or a walk in the afternoon to enjoy the glory of the sunset, or a stroll to drink in the pleasures of the old garden, there would I find Frank Hawden by my side, yah, yah, yahing about the way I treated him, until I wished him at the bottom of the Red Sea.

However, in those glorious spring days the sense of life was too pleasant to be much clouded by the trifling annoyance Frank Hawden occasioned me. The graceful wild clematis festooned the shrubbery along the creeks with great wreaths of magnificent white bloom, which loaded every breeze with perfume; the pretty bright green senna shrubs along the river-banks were decked in blossoms which rivalled the deep blue of the sky in brilliance; the magpies built their nests in the tall gum-trees, and savagely attacked unwary travellers who ventured too near their domain; the horses were rolling fat, and invited one to get on their satin backs and have a gallop; the cry of the leather-heads was heard in the orchard as the cherry season approached. Oh, it was good to be alive!

At Caddagat I was as much out of the full flood of life for which I craved as at Possum Gully, but here there were sufficient pleasant little ripples on the stream of existence to act as a stop-gap for the present.

CHAPTER 13

He

Here goes for a full account of my first, my last, my only *real* sweetheart, for I considered the professions of that pestiferous jackeroo as merely a grotesque caricature on the genuine article.

On making my first appearance before my lover, I looked quite the reverse of a heroine. My lovely hair was not conveniently escaping from the comb at the right moment to catch him hard in the eye, neither was my thrillingly low sweet voice floating out on the scented air in a manner which went straight to his heart, like the girls I had read of. On the contrary, I much resembled a female clown. It was on a day towards the end of September, and I had been up the creek making a collection of ferns. I had on a pair of men's boots with which to walk in the water, and was garbed in a most dilapidated old dress, which I had borrowed from one of the servants for the purpose. A pair of gloves made of basil, and a big hat, much torn in struggling through the undergrowth, completed my make-up. My hair was most unbecomingly screwed up, the short ends sticking out like a hurrah's nest.

It was late in the day when, returning from my ramble, I was met on the doorstep by aunt Helen.

'While you are in that trim, I wish you would pluck some lemons for me. I'm sure there is no danger of you ruining your turn-out. A sketch of you would make a good item for the *Bulletin*,' she said.

I went readily to do her bidding, and fetching a ladder with rungs about two feet six apart, placed it against a lemon-tree at the back of the house, and climbed up.

Holding a number of lemons in my skirt, I was making a most ungraceful descent, when I heard an unknown footstep approaching towards my back.

People came to Caddagat at all hours of the day, so I was not in the least disconcerted. Only a tramp, an agent, or a hawker, I bet, I thought, as I reached my big boot down for another rung of the ladder without turning my head to see whom it might be.

A pair of strong brown hands encircled my waist, I was tossed up a foot or so and then deposited lightly on the ground, a masculine voice saying, 'You're a mighty well-shaped young filly—"a waist rather small, but a quarter superb".'

'How dare anyone speak to me like that,' I thought, as I faced about to see who was parodying Gordon. There stood a man I had never before set eyes on, smiling mischievously at me. He was a young man—a very young man, a bushman—tremendously tall and big and sunburnt, with an open pleasant face and chestnut moustache—not at all an awe-inspiring fellow, in spite of his unusual, though well-proportioned and carried, height. I knew it must be Harold Beecham, of Five-Bob Downs, as I had heard he stood six feet three and a half in his socks.

I hurriedly let down my dress, the lemons rolling in a dozen directions, and turned to flee, but that well-formed figure bounded before me with the agility of a cat and barred my way.

'Now, not a step do you go, my fine young blood, until you pick up every jolly lemon and put them away tidily, or I'll tell the missus on you as sure as eggs.'

It dawned on me that he had mistaken me for one of the servant-girls. That wasn't bad fun. I determined not to undeceive but to have a lark with him. I summed him up as conceited, but not with the disgusting conceit with which some are afflicted, or perhaps blessed. It was rather an air of I-have-always-got-what-I-desire-and-believe, -if-people-fail-it-is-all-their-own-fault, which surrounded him.

'If you please, sir,' I said humbly, 'I've gathered them all up, will you let me go now.'

'Yes, when you've given me a kiss.'

'Oh, sir, I couldn't do that!'

'Go on, I won't poison you. Come now, I'll make you.'

'Oh, the missus might catch me.'

'No jolly fear; I'll take all the blame if she does.'

'Oh don't, sir; let me go, please,' I said in such unfeigned distress, for I feared he was going to execute his threat, that he laughed and said:

'Don't be frightened, sissy, I never kiss girls, and I'm not going to start at this time of day, and against their will to boot. You haven't been long here, have you? I haven't seen you before. Stand out there till I see if you've got any grit in you, and then I am done with you.'

I stood in the middle of the yard, the spot he indicated, while he uncurled his long heavy stock-whip with its big lash and scented myall handle. He cracked it round and round my head and arms, but I did not feel the least afraid, as I saw at a glance that he was exceedingly dexterous in the bushman's art of handling a stock-whip, and knew, if I kept perfectly still, I was quite safe. It was thanks to uncle Jay-Jay that I was able to bear the operation with unruffled equanimity, as he was in the habit of testing my nerves in this way.

'Well, I never! Not so much as blinked an eyelash! Thorough-bred!' He said after a minute or so, 'Where's the boss?'

'In Gool-Gool. He won't be home till late.'

'Is Mrs Bossier in?'

'No, she's not, but Mrs Bell is somewhere around in front.'

'Thanks.'

I watched him as he walked away with an easy swinging stride, which spoke of many long, long days in the saddle. I felt certain as I watched him that he had quite forgotten the incident of the little girl with the lemons.

'Sybylla, hurry up and get dressed. Put on your best bib and tucker, and I will leave Harry Beecham in your charge, as I want to superintend the making of some of the dishes myself this evening.'

'It's too early to put on my evening dress, isn't it, auntie?'

'It is rather early; but you can't spare time to change twice.

Dress yourself completely; you don't know what minute your uncle and his worship will arrive.'

I had taken a dip in the creek, so had not to bathe, and it took me but a short time to don full war-paint—blue evening dress, satin slippers, and all. I wore my hair flowing, simply tied with a ribbon. I slipped out into the passage and called aunt Helen. She came.

'I'm ready, auntie. Where is he?'

'In the dining-room.'

'Come into the drawing-room and call him. I will take charge of him till you are at leisure. But, auntie, it will be a long time till dinner—how on earth will I manage him?'

'Manage him!' she laughed; 'he is not at all an obstreperous character.'

We had reached the drawing-room by this, and I looked at myself in the looking-glass while aunt Helen went to summon Harold Augustus Beecham, bachelor, owner of Five-Bob Downs, Wyambeet, Wallerawang West, Quat-Quatta, and a couple more stations in New South Wales, besides an extensive one in Queensland.

I noticed as he entered the door that since I had seen him he had washed, combed his stiff black hair, and divested himself of his hat, spurs, and whip—his leggings had perforce to remain, as his nether garment was a pair of closely fitting grey cloth riding-breeches, which clearly defined the shapely contour of his lower limbs.

'Harry, this is Sybylla. I'm sure you need no further introduction. Excuse me, I have something on the fire which is likely to burn.' And aunt Helen hurried off leaving us facing each other.

He stared down at me with undisguised surprise. I looked up at him and laughed merrily. The fun was all on my side. He was a great big man—rich and important. I was a chit—an insignificant nonentity—yet, despite his sex, size, and importance, I was complete master of that situation, and knew it: thus I laughed.

I saw that he recognized me again by the dusky red he flushed beneath his sun-darkened skin. No doubt he regretted having

called me a filly above all things. He bowed stiffly, but I held
out my hand, saying:

'Do shake hands. When introduced I always shake hands with
anyone I think I'll like. Besides, I seem to know you well. Just
think of all the apples you brought me!'

He acceded to my request, holding my hand a deal longer
than necessary, and looking at me helplessly. It amused me greatly,
for I saw that it was he who did not know how to manage me,
and not I that couldn't manage him.

' 'Pon my honour, Miss Melvyn, I had no idea it was you,
when I said—' Here he boggled completely, which had the effect
of reviving my laughter.

'You had no right to be dressed like that—deceiving a fellow.
It wasn't fair.'

'That's the best of it. It shows what a larrikin Don Juan sort
of character you are. You can't deceive me now if you pretend
to be a virtuous well-behaved member of society.'

'That is the first time I've ever meddled with any of the kitchen
fry, and, by Jove, it will be the last!' he said energetically. 'I've
got myself into a pretty mess.'

'What nonsense you talk,' I replied. 'If you say another word
about it, I'll write a full account of it and paste it in my scrap-
book. But if you don't worry about it, neither will I. You said
nothing very uncomplimentary; in fact, I was quite flattered.'

I was perched on the high end of a couch, and he was leaning
with big careless ease on the piano. Had grannie seen me, I would
have been lectured about unladylike behaviour.

'What is your uncle at today?' he inquired.

'He's not at anything. He went to Gool-Gool yesterday on
the jury. Court finishes up today, and he is going to bring the
judge home tonight. That's why I am dressed so carefully,' I
answered.

'Good gracious! I never thought of court this time as I wasn't
called on the jury, and for a wonder hadn't so much as a case
against a Chinaman. I was going to stay tonight, but can't if
his worship is going to dine here.'

'Why? You're surely not afraid of Judge Fossilt? He's a very simple old customer.'

'Imagine dining with a judge in this toggery!' and he glanced down his great figure at his riding gear.

'That doesn't matter; he's near-sighted. I'll get you put at the far end of the table under my wing. Men don't notice dress. If you weren't so big uncle or Frank Hawden could oblige you.'

'Do you think I could pass muster?'

'Yes; after I brush you down you'll look as spruce as a brass penny.'

'I did brush myself,' he answered.

'You brush yourself!' I retorted. 'There's a big splash of mud on your shoulder. You couldn't expect to do anything decently, for you're only a man, and men are the uselessest, good-for-nothingest, clumsiest animals in the world. All they're good for is to smoke and swear.'

I fetched a clothes brush.

'You'll have to stand on the table to reach me,' he said, looking down with amused indulgence.

'As you are so impertinent you can go dusty,' and I tossed the brush away.

The evening was balmy, so I invited him into the garden. He threw his handkerchief over my chest, saying I might catch cold, but I scouted the idea.

We wandered into an arbour covered with wistaria, banksia, and Maréchal Niel roses, and I made him a buttonhole.

A traveller pulled rein in the roadway, and, dismounting, threw his bridle over a paling of the garden fence while he went inside to try and buy a loaf of bread.

I jumped up, frightening the horse so that it broke away, pulling off the paling in the bridle-rein. I ran to bring a hammer to repair the damage. Mr Beecham caught the horse while I attempted to drive the nail into the fence. It was a futile attempt. I bruised my fingers. He took the hammer from me, and fixing the paling in its place with a couple of well-aimed blows, said laughingly:

'You drive a nail! You couldn't expect to do anything. You're only a girl. Girls are the helplessest, uselessest, troublesomest little creatures in the world. All they're good for is to torment and pester a fellow.'

I had to laugh.

At this juncture we heard uncle Jay-Jay's voice, so Mr Beecham went towards the back, whence it proceeded, after he left me at the front door.

'Oh, auntie, we got on splendidly! He's not a bit of trouble. We're as chummy as though we had been reared together,' I exclaimed.

'Did you get him to talk?'

'Oh yes.'

'Did you really?' in surprise.

When I came to review the matter I was forced to confess that I had done all the talking, and young Beecham the listening; moreover I described him as the quietest man I had ever seen or heard of.

The judge did not come home with uncle Jay-Jay as expected so it was not necessary for me to shelter Harold Beecham under my wing. Grannie greeted him cordially as 'Harold, my boy'— he was a great favourite with her. She and uncle Julius monopolized him for the evening. There was great talk of trucking sheep, the bad outlook as regarded the season, the state of the grass in the triangle, the Leigh Spring, the Bimbalong, and several other paddocks, and of the condition of the London wool market. It did not interest me, so I dived into a book, only occasionally emerging therefrom to smile at Mr Beecham.

He had come to Caddagat for a pair of bullocks which had been fattening in grannie's home paddock. Uncle gave him a start with them next morning. When they came out on the road I was standing in a bed of violets in a tangled corner of the garden, where roses climbed to kiss the lilacs, and spiraea stooped to rest upon the wallflowers, and where two tall kurrajongs stood like sentries over all. Harold Beecham dismounted, and, leaning over the fence, lingered with me, leaving the bullocks to uncle Jay-Jay. Uncle raved vigorously. Women, he asserted, were the bane of society and the ruination of all men; but he had always considered Harold as too sensible to neglect his business to stand grinning at a pesky youngster in short skirts and a pigtail. Which was the greatest idiot of the two he didn't know.

His grumbling did not affect Harold in the least.

'Complimentary to both of us,' he remarked as he leisurely threw himself across his great horse, and smiled his pleasant quiet smile, disclosing two rows of magnificent teeth, untainted by contamination with beer or tobacco. Raising his panama hat with the green fly-veil around it, he cantered off. I wondered as I watched him if anything ever disturbed his serenity, and desired to try. He looked too big and quiet to be ruffled by such emotions as rage, worry, jealousy, or even love. Returning to the house, I put aunt Helen through an exhaustive catechism concerning him.

Question. Auntie, what age is Harold Beecham?

Answer. Twenty-five last December.

Q. Did he ever have any brothers or sisters?

A. No. His birth caused his mother's death.

Q. How long has his father been dead?

A. Since Harold could crawl.

Q. Who reared him?

A. His aunts.

Q. Does he ever talk any more than that?

A. Often a great deal less.

Q. Is he really very rich?

A. If he manages to pull through these seasons he will be second to none but Tyson in point of wealth.

Q. Is Five-Bob a very pretty place?

A. Yes; one of the show places of the district.

Q. Does he often come to Caddagat?

A. Yes, he often drops in.

Q. What makes his hair so black and his moustache that light colour?

A. You'll have to study science to find that out. I'm sure I can't tell you.

Q. Does he—?

'Now, Sybylla,' said auntie, laughing, 'you are taking a suspicious interest in my sunburnt young giant. Did I not tell you he was taking time by the forelock when he brought the apples?'

'Oh, auntie, I am only asking questions because—'

'Yes, because, because, I understand perfectly. Because you are a girl, and all the girls fall a victim to Harry's charms at once. If you don't want to succumb meekly to your fate, "Heed the spark or you may dread the fire." That is the only advice I can tender you.'

This was a Thursday, and on the following Sunday Harold Beecham reappeared at Caddagat and remained from three in the afternoon until nine at night. Uncle Julius and Frank Hawden were absent. The weather had taken a sudden backward lurch into winter again, so we had a fire. Harold sat beside it all the time, and interposed yes and no at the proper intervals in grannie's brisk business conversation, but he never addressed one word to me beyond 'Good afternoon, Miss Melvyn,' on his arrival, and 'Good night, Miss Melvyn,' when leaving.

I studied him attentively all the while. What were his ideas and sentiments it were hard to tell: he never expressed any. He was fearfully and wonderfully quiet. Yet his was an intelligent silence, not of that wooden brainless description which casts a damper on company, neither was it of the morose or dreaming order.

CHAPTER 14

Principally Letters

Caddagat, 29th *Sept.*, 1896

My dearest Gertie,

I have started to write no less than seven letters to you, but
something always interrupted me and I did not finish them.
However, I'll finish this one in the teeth of Father Peter
himself. I will parenthesize all the interruptions. (A traveller
just asked me for a rose. I had to get up and give him one.)
Living here is lovely. (Another man inquired the way to
Somingley Gap, and I've just finished directing him.) Grannie
is terribly nice. You could not believe. She is always giving
me something, and takes me wherever she goes. Auntie is an
angel. I wish you could hear the piano. It is a beauty. There
are dozens of papers and books to read. Uncle is a dear old
fellow. You should hear him rave and swear sometimes when
he gets in a rage. It is great fun. He brings me lollies, gloves,
ribbons, or something every time he comes from town. (Two
Indian hawkers have arrived, and I am going out to see their
goods. There were nineteen hawkers here last week. I am
sitting on a squatter's chair and writing on a table in the
veranda, and the road goes right by the flower-garden. That is
how I see everyone.) Have you had rain down there this
week? They have great squawking about the drought up here.
I wish they could see Goulburn, and then they'd know what
drought means. I don't know what sort of a bobberie they
would kick up. It's pretty dry out on the run, but everyone
calls the paddocks about the house an oasis. You see there are
such splendid facilities for irrigation here. Uncle has put on a
lot of men. They have cut races between the two creeks
between which the house is situated. Every now and again
they let the water from these over the orchard gardens and

about a hundred acres of paddock land around the house. The grass therein is up to the horses' fetlocks. There is any amount of rhubarb and early vegetables in the garden. Grannie says there is a splendid promise of fruit in the orchard, and the flower-garden is a perfect dream. This is the dearest old place in the world. Dozens of people plague grannie to be let put their horses in the grass—especially shearers, there are droves of them going home now—but she won't let them; wants all the grass for her own stock. Uncle has had to put another man on to mind it, or at night all the wires are cut and the horses put in. (An agent, I think by the cut of him, is asking for grannie. I'll have to run and find her.) It is very lively here. Never a night but we have the house full of agents or travellers of one sort or another, and there are often a dozen swaggies in the one day.

Harold Beecham is my favourite of all the men hereaway. He is delightfully big and quiet. He isn't good-looking, but I like his face. (Been attending to the demands of a couple of impudent swaggies. Being off the road at Possum Gully, you escape them.) For the love of life, next time you write, fire into the news at once and don't half-fill your letter telling me about the pen and your bad writing. I am scribbling at the rate of 365 miles an hour, and don't care a jot whether it is good writing or not.

Auntie, uncle, Frank Hawden and I, are going to ride to Yabtree church next Sunday. It is four miles beyond Five-Bob Downs, so that is sixteen miles. It is the nearest church. I expect it will be rare fun. There will be such a crowd coming home, and that always makes the horses delightfully frisky. (A man wants to put his horses in the paddock for the night, so I will have to find uncle.) I never saw such a place for men. It is all men, men, men. You cannot go anywhere outside the house but you see men coming and going in all directions. It wouldn't do to undress without bothering to drop the window-blind like we used at Possum Gully. Grannie and uncle say it is a curse to be living beside the road, as it costs them a tremendous lot a year. There are seven lemon-trees here, loaded (another hawker). I hope you think of me sometimes. I am just as ugly as ever. (A traveller wants to buy a loaf of bread.)

With stacks of love to all at home, and a whole dray-load for yourself, from your loving sister,

Sybylla.

Remember me to Goulburn, drowsing lazily in its dreamy graceful hollow in the blue distance.

Caddagat, 29th *Sept.,* 1896

Dear Everard,

Thank you very much for the magazines and 'An Australian Bush Track'. I suppose you have quite forgotten us and Caddagat by this time. The sun has sunk behind the gum-trees, and the blue evening mists are hanging lazily in the hollows of the hills. I expect you are donning your 'swallow-tail' preparatory to leading some be-satined 'faire ladye' in to a gorgeous dinner, thence to the play, then to a dance probably. No doubt all around you is bustle, glare of lights, noise, and fun. It is such a different scene here. From down the road comes the tinkle of camp-bells and jingle of hobble-chains. From down in that sheltered angle where the creek meets the river comes the gleam of camp-fires through the gathering twilight, and I can see several tents rigged for the night, looking like white specks in the distance.

I long for the time to come when I shall get to Sydney. I'm going to lead you and aunt Helen a pretty dance. You'll have to keep going night and day. It will be great. I must get up and dance a jig on the veranda when I think of it. You'll have to show me everything—slums and all. I want to find out the truth of heaps of things for myself.

Save for the weird rush of the stream and the kookaburras' goodnight, all is still, with a mighty far-reaching stillness which can be felt. Now the curlews are beginning their wild

moaning cry. From the rifts in the dark lone ranges, far down
the river, it comes like a hunted spirit until it makes me feel—

At this point I said, 'Bah! I'm mad to write to Everard Grey
like this. He would laugh and call me a poor little fool.' I tore
the half-finished letter to shreds, and consigned it to the kitchen
fire. I substituted a prim formal note, merely thanking him for
the books and magazine he had sent me. To this I never received
an answer. I heard through his letters to grannie that he was
much occupied. Had been to Brisbane and Melbourne on important
cases, so very likely had not time to be bothered with me; or,
he might have been like the majority of his fellows who make
a great parade of friendship while with one, then go away and
forget one's existence in an hour.

While at Caddagat there were a few duties allotted to me.
One of these was to attend to the drawing-room; another was
to find uncle Jay-Jay's hat when he mislaid it—often ten times
per day. I assisted my grandmother to make up her accounts
and write business letters, and I attended to tramps. A man was
never refused a bit to eat at Caddagat. This necessitated the
purchase of an extra ton of flour per year, also nearly a ton
of sugar, to say nothing of tea, potatoes, beef, and all broken
meats which went thus. This was not reckoning the consumption
of victuals by the other class of travellers with which the house
was generally full year in and year out. Had there been any charge
for their board and lodging, the Bossiers would surely have made
a fortune. I interviewed on an average fifty tramps a week, and
seldom saw the same man twice. What a great army they were!
Hopeless, homeless, aimless, shameless souls, tramping on from
north to south, and east to west, never relinquishing their heart-
sickening, futile quest for work—some of them so long on the
tramp that the ambitions of manhood had been ground out of
them, and they wished for nothing more than this.

There were all shapes, sizes, ages, kinds, and conditions of
men—the shamefaced boy in the bud of his youth, showing by
the way he begged that the humiliation of the situation had not

yet worn off, and poor old creatures tottering on the brink of the grave, with nothing left in life but the enjoyment of beer and tobacco. There were strong men in their prime who really desired work when they asked for it, and skulking cowards who hoped they would not get it. There were the diseased, the educated, the ignorant, the deformed, the blind, the evil, the honest, the mad, and the sane. Some in real professional beggars' style called down blessings on me; others were morose and glum, while some were impudent and thankless, and said to supply them with food was just what I should do, for the swagmen kept the squatters— as, had the squatters not monopolized the land, the swagmen would have had plenty. A moiety of the last-mentioned—dirty, besotted, ragged creatures—had a glare in their eyes which made one shudder to look at them, and, while spasmodically twirling their billies or clenching their fists, talked wildly of making one to 'bust up the damn banks', or to drive all the present squatters out of the country and put the people on the land—clearly showing that, because they had failed for one reason or another, it had maddened them to see others succeed.

In a wide young country of boundless resources, why is this thing? This question worried me. Our legislators are unable or unwilling to cope with it. They trouble not to be patriots and statesmen. Australia can bring forth writers, orators, financiers, singers, musicians, actors, and athletes which are second to none of any nation under the sun. Why can she not bear sons, men! of soul, mind, truth, godliness, and patriotism sufficient to rise and cast off the grim shackles which widen round us day by day?

I was the only one at Caddagat who held these silly ideas. Harold Beecham, uncle Julius, grannie, and Frank Hawden did not worry about the cause of tramps. They simply termed them a lazy lot of sneaking creatures, fed them, and thought no more of the matter.

I broached the subject to uncle Jay-Jay once, simply to discover his ideas thereon.

I was sitting on a chair in the veranda sewing; he, with his

98

head on a cushion, was comfortably stretched on a rug on the floor.

'Uncle Boss, why can't something be done for tramps?'

'How done for 'em?'

'Couldn't some means of employing them be arrived at?'

'Work!' he ejaculated. 'That's the very thing the crawling divils are terrified they might get.'

'Yes; but couldn't some law be made to help them?'

'A law to make me cut up Caddagat and give ten of 'em each a piece, and go on the wallaby myself, I suppose?'

'No, uncle; but there was a poor young fellow here this morning who, I feel sure, was in earnest when he asked for work.'

'Helen!' bawled uncle Jay-Jay.

'Well, what is it?' she inquired, appearing in the doorway.

'Next time Sybylla is giving a tramp some tucker, you keep a sharp eye on her or she will be sloping one of these days. There was a young fellow here today with a scarlet moustache and green eyes, and she's clean gone on him, and has been bullying me to give him half Caddagat.'

'What a disgusting thing to say! Uncle, you ought to be ashamed of yourself,' I exclaimed.

'Very well, I'll be careful,' said aunt Helen, departing.

'What with the damned flies, and the tramps, and a pesky thing called Sybylla, a man's life ain't worth a penny to him,' said uncle.

We fell into silence, which was broken presently by a dirty red-bearded face appearing over the garden gate, and a man's voice:

'Good day, boss! Give us a chew of tobaccer?'

'I'm not the boss,' said uncle with assumed fierceness.

'Then who is?' inquired the man.

Uncle pointed his thumb at me, and, rolling out on the floor again as though very sleepy, began to snore. The tramp grinned, and made his request of me. I took him round to the back, served him with flour, beef, and an inch or two of rank tobacco out of a keg which had been bought for the purpose. Refusing a drink of milk which I offered, he resumed his endless tramp with a 'So long, little missy. God bless your pleasant face.'

I watched him out of sight. One of my brothers—one of God's children under the Southern Cross. Did these old fellows really believe in the God whose name they mentioned so glibly? I wondered. But I am thankful that while at Caddagat it was only rarely that my old top-heavy thoughts troubled me. Life was so pleasant that I was content merely to be young—a chit in the first flush of teens, health, hope, happiness, youth—a heedless creature recking not for the morrow.

CHAPTER 15

When the Heart is Young

About a week or so after I first met Harold Beecham, aunt Helen allowed me to read a letter she had received from the elder of the two Misses Beecham. It ran as follows:

My dearest Helen,

This is a begging letter, and I am writing another to your mother at the same time. I am asking her to allow her grand-daughter to spend a few weeks with me, and I want you to use your influence in the matter. Sarah has not been well lately, and is going to Melbourne for a change, and as I will be lonely while she is away Harold insists upon me having someone to keep me company—you know how considerate the dear boy is. I hardly like to ask you to spare your little girl to me. It must be a great comfort to have her. I could have got Miss Benson to stay with me, but Harold will not hear of her. He says she is too slow, and would give us both the mopes. But he says your little niece will keep us all alive. Julius was telling me the other day that he could not part with her, as she makes 'the old barracks', as he always calls Caddagat, echo with fun and noise. I am so looking forward to seeing her, as she is dear Lucy's child. Give her my love, &c., &c.

and as a postscript the letter had—'Harold will go up for Sybylla on Wednesday afternoon. I do hope you will be able to spare her to me for a while.'

'Oh, auntie, how lovely!' I exclaimed. 'What are you laughing at?'

'For whom do you think Harry wants the companion? It is nice to have an old auntie, as a blind, is it not? Well, all is fair in love and war. You have permission to use me in any way you like.'

I pretended to miss her meaning.

Grannie consented to Miss Beecham's proposal, and ere the day arrived I had a trunk packed with some lovely new dresses, and was looking forward with great glee to my visit to Five-Bob Downs.

One o'clock on Wednesday afternoon arrived; two o'clock struck, and I was beginning to fear no one was coming for me, when, turning to look out the window for the eighteenth time, I saw the straight blunt nose of Harold Beecham passing. Grannie was serving afternoon tea on the veranda. I did not want any, so got ready while my escort was having his.

It was rather late when we bowled away at a tremendous pace in a red sulky, my portmanteau strapped on at the back, and a thoroughbred American trotter, which had taken prizes at Sydney shows, harnessed to the front. We just whizzed! It was splendid! The stones and dust rose in a thick cloud from the whirling wheels and flying hoofs, and the posts of the wire fence on our left passed like magic as we went. Mr Beecham allowed me to drive after a time while he sat ready to take the reins should an emergency arise.

It was sunset—most majestic hour of the twenty-four—when we drove up to the great white gates which opened into the avenue leading to the main homestead of Five-Bob Downs station—beautiful far-reaching Five-Bob Downs! Dreamy blue hills rose behind, and wide rich flats stretched before, through which the Yarrangung river, glazed with sunset, could be seen like a silver snake winding between shrubberied banks. The odour from the six-acred flower-garden was overpowering and delightful. A breeze gently swayed the crowd of trees amid the houses, and swept over the great orchard which sloped down from the south side of the houses. In the fading sunlight thirty iron roofs gleamed and glared, and seemed like a little town; and the yelp of many dogs went up at the sound of our wheels. Ah! beautiful, beautiful Five-Bob Downs!

It seemed as though a hundred dogs leapt forth to greet us when that gate flew open, but I subsequently discovered there were but twenty-three.

Two female figures came out to meet us—one nearly six feet high, the other, a tiny creature, seemed about eighteen inches, though, of course, was more than that.

'I've brought her, aunt Gussie,' said Harold, jumping out of the sulky, though not relinquishing the reins, while he kissed the taller figure, and the small one attached itself to his leg saying, 'Dimme wide.'

'Hullo! Possum, why wasn't old Spanker let go? I see he's not among the dogs,' and my host picked the tiny individual up in his arms and got into the sulky to give her the desired ride, while after being embraced by Miss Beecham and lifted to the ground by her nephew, I went with the former over an asphalted tennis-court, through the wide garden, then across a broad veranda into the great, spreading, one-storeyed house from which gleamed many lights.

'I am so glad you have come, my dear. I must have a good look at you when we get into the light. I hope you are like your mother.'

This prospect discomfited me. I knew she would find a very ugly girl with not the least resemblance to her pretty mother, and I cursed my appearance under my breath.

'Your name is Sybylla,' Miss Beecham continued, 'Sybylla Penelope. Your mother used to be very dear to me, but I don't know why she doesn't write to me now. I have never seen her since her marriage. It seems strange to think of her as the mother of eight—five boys and three girls, is it not?'

Miss Beecham had piloted me through a wide hall and along an extended passage out of which a row of bedrooms opened, into one of which we went.

'I hope you will be comfortable here, child. You need not dress for dinner while you are here; we never do, only on very special occasions.'

'Neither do we at Caddagat,' I replied.

'Now, child, let me have a good look at you without your hat.'

'Oh, please don't!' I exclaimed, covering my face with my hands.

'I am so dreadfully ugly that I cannot bear to have anyone look at me.'

'What a silly little girl! You are not like your mother, but you are not at all plain-looking. Harold says you are the best style of girl he has seen yet, and sing beautifully. He got a tuner up from Sydney last week, so we will expect you to entertain us every night.'

I learnt that what Harold pronounced good no one dared gainsay at Five-Bob Downs.

We proceeded direct to the dining-room, and had not been there long when Mr Beecham entered with the little girl on his shoulder. Miss Beecham had told me she was Minnie Benson, daughter of Harold's married overseer on Wyambeet, his adjoining station. Miss Beecham considered it would have been more seemly for her nephew to have selected a little boy as a play-thing, but his sentiments regarding boys were that they were machines invented for the torment of adults.

'Well, O'Doolan, what sort of a day has it been?' Harold inquired, setting his human toy upon the floor.

'Fine wezzer for yim duts,' she promptly replied.

'Harold, it is shameful to teach a little innocent child such abominable slang; and you might give her a decent nickname,' said Miss Beecham.

'O'Doolan, this is Miss Melvyn, and you have to do the same to her as you do to me.'

The little thing held out her arms to me. I took her up, and she hugged and kissed me, saying:

'I luz oo, I luz oo,' and turning to Mr Beecham, 'zat anuff?'

'Yes, that will do,' he said; and she struggled to be put down.

Three jackeroos, an overseer, and two other young men came in, were introduced to me, and then we began dinner.

O'Doolan sat on a high chair beside Mr Beecham, and he attended to all her wants. She did everything he did, even taking mustard, and was very brave at quelling the tears that rose to the doll-like blue eyes. When Mr Beecham wiped his moustache, it was amusing to see her also wipe an imaginary one.

After dinner the jackeroos and the three other men repaired

to a sitting-room in the backyard, which was specially set apart for them, and where they amused themselves as they liked. My host and hostess, myself, and the child, spent the evening in a tiny sitting-room adjoining the dining-room. Miss Beecham entertained me with conversation and the family albums, and Harold amused himself entirely with the child.

Once when they were absent for a few minutes, Miss Beecham told me it was ridiculous the way he fussed with the child, and that he had her with him more than half his time. She also asked me what I thought of her nephew. I evaded the question by querying if he was always so quiet and good-tempered.

'Oh dear, no. He is considered a particularly bad-tempered man. Not one of the snarling nasty tempers, but—'

Here the re-entry of the owner of the temper put a stop to this conversation.

Harold gave O'Doolan rides on his back, going on all fours. She shouted in childish glee, and wound up by curling her small proportions on his broad chest, and going to sleep there.

Mrs Benson had sent for little O'Doolan, and Harold took her home next day. He invited me to accompany him, so we set out in the sulky with O'Doolan on my lap. It was a pleasant drive of twelve miles to and from Wyambeet. O'Doolan was much distressed at parting from Mr Beecham, but he promised to come for her again shortly.

'One little girl at a time is enough for me to care for properly,' he said to me in the winning manner with which, and his wealth, unintentionally and unconsciously made slaughter among the hearts of the fair sex.

CHAPTER 16

When Fortune Smiles

'Now, Harold, you have compelled Sybylla to come here, you must not let the time drag with her,' said Miss Beecham.

It was the second day after my arrival at Five-Bob. Lunch was over, and we had adjourned to the veranda. Miss Beecham was busy at her work-table; I was ensconced on a mat on the floor reading a book; Harold was stretched in a squatter's chair some distance away. His big brown hands were clasped behind his head, his chin rested on his broad chest, his eyes were closed, he occasionally thrust his lower lip forward and sent a puff of breath upwards to scatter the flies from his face; he looked a big monument of comfort, and answered his aunt's remarks lazily:

'Yes, aunt, I'll do my best;' and to me, 'Miss Melvyn, while here, please bear in mind that it will be no end of pleasure to me to do anything for your enjoyment. Don't fail to command me in any way.'

'Thank you, Mr Beecham. I will not fail to avail myself of your offer.'

'The absurdity of you two children addressing each other so formally,' said Miss Beecham. 'Why, you are a sort of cousins almost, by right of old friendship between the families. You must call me aunt.'

After this Mr Beecham and I called each other nothing when in Miss Beecham's hearing, but adhered to formality on other occasions.

Harold looked so comfortable and lazy that I longed to test how far he meant the offer he had made me.

'I'm just dying for a row on the river. Would you oblige me?' I said.

'Just look at the thermometer!' exclaimed Miss Augusta. 'Wait till it gets cooler, child.'

'Oh, I love the heat!' I replied. 'And I am sure it won't hurt his lordship. He's used to the sun, to judge from all appearances.'

'Yes, I don't think it can destroy my complexion,' he said good-humouredly, rubbing his finger and thumb along his stubble-covered chin. The bushmen up-country shaved regularly every Sunday morning, but never during the week for anything less than a ball. They did this to obviate the blue—what they termed 'scraped pig'—appearance of the faces of city men in the habit of using the razor daily, and to which they preferred the stubble of a seven-days' beard. 'I'll take you to the river in half an hour,' he said, rising from his seat. 'First I must stick on one of Warrigal's shoes that he's flung. I want him tomorrow, and must do it at once, as he always goes lame if ridden immediately after shoeing.'

'Shall I blow the bellows?' I volunteered.

'Oh no, thanks. I can manage myself. It would be better though if I had some one. But I can get one of the girls.'

'Can't you get one of the boys?' said his aunt.

'There's not one in. I sent every one off to the Triangle paddock today to do some drafting. They all took their quart pots and a snack in their saddle-bags, and won't be home till dark.'

'Let me go,' I persisted; 'I often blow the bellows for uncle Jay-Jay, and think it great fun.'

The offer of my services being accepted, we set out.

Harold took his favourite horse, Warrigal, from the stable, and led him to the blacksmith's forge under an open, stringybark-roofed shed, nearly covered with creepers. He lit a fire and put a shoe in it. Doffing his coat and hat, rolling up his shirt-sleeves, and donning a leather apron, he began preparing the horse's hoof.

When an emergency arose that necessitated uncle Jay-Jay shoeing his horses himself, I always manipulated the bellows, and did so with great decorum, as he was very exacting and I feared his displeasure. In this case it was different. I worked the pole with such energy that it almost blew the whole fire out of the pan, and sent the ashes and sparks in a whirlwind around Harold. The horse—a touchy beast—snorted and dragged his foot from his master's grasp.

'That the way to blow?' I inquired demurely.

'Take things a little easier,' he replied.

I took them so very easily that the fire was on the last gasp and the shoe nearly cold when it was required.

'This won't do,' said Beecham.

I recommenced blowing with such force that he had to retreat.

'Steady! steady!' he shouted.

'Sure O'i can't plaze yez anyhows,' I replied.

'If you don't try to plaze me directly I'll punish you in a way you won't relish,' he said laughingly. But I knew he was thinking of a punishment which I would have secretly enjoyed.

'If you don't let me finish this work I'll make one of the men do it tonight by candle-light when they come home tired. I know you wouldn't like them to do that,' he continued.

' 'Arrah, go on, ye're only tazin'!' I retorted. 'Don't you remember telling me that Warrigal was such a nasty-tempered brute that he allowed no one but yourself to touch him?'

'Oh well, then, I'm floored, and will have to put up with the consequences,' he good-humouredly made answer.

Seeing that my efforts to annoy him failed, I gave in, and we were soon done, and then started for the river—Mr Beecham clad in a khaki suit and I in a dainty white wrapper and fly-away sort of hat. In one hand my host held a big white umbrella, with which he shaded me from the hot rays of the October sun, and in the other was a small basket containing cake and lollies for our delectation.

Having traversed the half-mile between the house and river, we pushed off from the bank in a tiny boat just big enough for two. In the teeth of Harold's remonstrance I persisted in dangling over the boat-side to dabble in the clear, deep, running water. In a few minutes we were in it. Being unable to swim, but for my companion it would have been all up with me. When I rose to the surface he promptly seized me, and without much effort, clothes and all, swam with me to the bank, where we landed— a pair of sorry figures. Harold had mud all over his nose, and in general looked very ludicrous. As soon as I could stand I laughed.

'Oh, for a snapshot of you!' I said.

'We might have both been drowned,' he said sternly.

'Mights don't fly,' I returned. 'And it was worth the dip to see you looking such a comical article.' We were both minus our hats.

His expression relaxed.

'I believe you would laugh at your own funeral. If I look queer, you look forty times worse. Run for your life and get a hot bath and a drop of spirits or you'll catch your death of cold. Aunt Augusta will take a fit and tie you up for the rest of the time in case something more will happen to you.'

'Catch a death of cold!' I ejaculated. 'It is only good, pretty little girls, who are a blessing to everyone, who die for such trifles; girls like I am always live till nearly ninety, to plague themselves and everybody else. I'll sneak home so that your aunt won't see me, and no one need be a bit the wiser.'

'You'll be sun-struck!' he said in dismay.

'Take care you don't get daughter-struck,' I said perkily, turning to flee, for it had suddenly dawned upon me that my thin wet clothing was outlining my figure rather too clearly for propriety.

By a circuitous way I managed to reach my bedroom unseen. It did not take me long to change my clothes, hang them to dry, and appear on the main veranda where Miss Augusta was still sewing. I picked up the book I had left on the mat, and, taking up a position in a hammock near her, I commenced to read.

'You did not stay long at the river,' she remarked. 'Have you been washing your head? I never saw the like of it. Such a mass of it. It will take all day to dry.'

Half an hour later Harold appeared dressed in a warm suit of tweed. He was looking pale and languid, as though he had caught a chill, and shivered as he threw himself on a lounge. I was feeling none the worse for my immersion.

'Why did you change your clothes, Harold? You surely weren't cold on a day like this. Sybylla has changed hers too, when I come to notice it, and her hair is wet. Have you had an accident?' said Miss Augusta, rising from her chair in a startled manner.

'Rubbish!' ejaculated Harold in a tone which forbade further questioning, and the matter dropped.

She presently left the veranda, and I took the opportunity to say, 'It is yourself that requires the hot bath and a drop of spirits, Mr Beecham.'

'Yes; I think I'll take a good stiff nobbler. I feel a trifle squeamish. It gave me a bit of a turn when I rose to the top and could not see you. I was afraid the boat might have stunned you in capsizing, and you would be drowned before I could find you.'

'Yes; I would have been such a loss to the world in general if I had been drowned,' I said satirically.

Several jackeroos, a neighbouring squatter, and a couple of bicycle tourists turned up at Five-Bob that evening, and we had a jovial night. The great, richly furnished drawing-room was brilliantly lighted, and the magnificent Erard grand piano sang and rang again with music, now martial and loud, now soft and solemn, now gay and sparkling. I made the very pleasant discovery that Harold Beecham was an excellent pianist, a gifted player on the violin, and sang with a strong, clear, well-trained tenor, which penetrated far into the night. How many, many times I have lived those nights over again! The great room with its rich appointments, the superb piano, the lights, the merriment, the breeze from the east, rich with the heavy intoxicating perfume of countless flowers; the tall perfect figure, holding the violin with a master hand, making it speak the same language as I read in the dark eyes of the musician, while above and around was the soft warmth of an Australian summer night.

Ah, health and wealth, happiness and youth, joy and light, life and *love*! What a warm-hearted place is the world, how full of pleasure, good, and beauty, when fortune smiles! *When fortune smiles!*

Fortune did smile, and broadly, in those days. We played tricks on one another, and had a deal of innocent fun and frolic. I was a little startled one night on retiring to find a huge goanna near the head of my bed. I called Harold to dislodge the creature, when it came to light that it was roped to the bedpost. Great was the laughter at my expense. Who tethered the goanna I never discovered, but I suspected Harold. In return for this joke, I collected all the portable clocks in the house—about twenty—and arrayed them on his bedroom table. The majority of them were Waterburys for common use, so I set each alarm for a different hour. Inscribing a placard 'Hospital for Insane', I erected it above his door. Next morning I was awakened at three o'clock by fifteen alarms in concert outside my door. When an hour or two later I emerged I found a notice on my door, 'This way to the Zoo'.

It was a very busy time for the men at Five-Bob. Waggons were arriving with shearing supplies, for it was drawing nigh unto the great event of the year. In another week's time the bleat of thousands of sheep, and the incense of much tar and wool, would be ascending to the heavens from the vicinity of Five-Bob Downs. I was looking forward to the shearing. There never was any at Caddagat. Uncle did not keep many sheep, and always sold them long-woolled and rebought after shearing.

I had not much opportunity of persecuting Harold during the daytime. He and all his subordinates were away all day, busy drafting, sorting, and otherwise pottering with sheep. But I always, and Miss Augusta sometimes, went to meet them coming home in the evening. It was great fun. The dogs yelped and jumped about. The men were dirty with much dust, and smelt powerfully of sheep, and had worked hard all day in the blazing sun, but they were never too tired for fun, or at night to dance, after they had bathed and dressed. We all had splendid horses. They reared and pranced; we galloped and jumped every log which came in our path. Jokes, repartee, and nonsense rattled off our tongues. We did not worry about thousands of our fellows— starving and reeking with disease in city slums. We were selfish. We were heedless. We were happy. We were young.

Harold Beecham was a splendid host. Anyone possessed of the least talent for enjoyment had a pleasant time as his guest. He was hospitable in a quiet unostentatious manner. His overseer, jackeroos, and other employees were all allowed the freedom of home, and could invite whom they pleased to Five-Bob Downs. It is all very well to talk of good hosts. Bah, I could be a good hostess myself if I had Harold Beecham's superior implements of the art! With an immense station, plenty of house-room, tennis courts, musical instruments; a river wherein to fish, swim, and boat; any number of horses, vehicles, orchards, gardens, guns, and ammunition no object, it is easy to be a good host.

I had been just a week at Five-Bob when uncle Julius came to take me home, so I missed the shearing. Caddagat had been a dull hole without me, he averred, and I must return with him that very day. Mr and Miss Beecham remonstrated. Could I not be spared at least a fortnight longer? It would be lonely without me. Thereupon uncle Jay-Jay volunteered to procure Miss Benson from Wyambeet as a substitute. Harold declined the offer with thanks.

'The schemes of youngsters are very transparent,' said uncle Jay-Jay and Miss Augusta, smiling significantly at us. I feigned to be dense, but Harold smiled as though the insinuation was not only known, but also agreeable to him.

Uncle was inexorable, so home I had to go. It was sweet to me to hear from the lips of my grandmother and aunt that my absence had been felt.

As a confidante aunt Helen was the pink of perfection—tactful and sympathetic. My feather-brained chatter must often have bored her, but she apparently was ever interested in it.

I told her long yarns of how I had spent my time at the Beechams; of the deafening duets Harold and I had played on the piano; and how he would persist in dancing with me, and he being so tall and broad, and I so small, it was like being stretched on a hay-rack, and very fatiguing. I gave a graphic account of the arguments—tough ones they were too—that Miss Augusta had with the overseer on religion, and many other subjects; of one jackeroo who gabbed never-endingly about his great relations at home; another who incessantly clattered about spurs, whips, horses, and sport; and the third one—Joe Archer—who talked literature and trash with me.

'What was Harry doing all this time?' asked auntie. 'What did he say?'

Harold had been present all the while, yet I could not call to mind one thing he had said. I cannot remember him ever holding forth on a subject or cause, as most people do at one time or another.

CHAPTER 17

Idylls of Youth

In pursuance of his duty a government mail-contractor passed Caddagat every Monday, dropping the Bossier mail as he went. On Thursday we also got the post, but had to depend partly on our own exertions.

A selector at Dogtrap, on the Wyambeet run, at a point of the compass ten miles down the road from Caddagat, kept a hooded van. Every Thursday he ran this to and from Gool-Gool for the purpose of taking to market vegetables and other farm produce. He also took parcels and passengers, both ways, if called upon to do so. Caddagat and Five-Bob gave him a great deal of carrying, and he brought the mail for these and two or three other places. It was one of my duties, or rather privileges, to ride thither on Thursday afternoon for the post, a leather bag slung round my shoulders for the purpose. I always had a splendid mount, and the weather being beautifully hot, it was a jaunt which I never failed to enjoy. Frank Hawden went with me once or twice—not because grannie or I thought his escort necessary. The idea was his own; but I gave him such a time that he was forced to relinquish accompanying me as a bad job.

Harold Beecham kept a snivelling little Queensland black boy as a sort of black-your-boots, odd-jobs slavey or factotum, and he came to Dogtrap for the mail, but after I started to ride for it Harold came regularly for his mail himself. Our homeward way lay together for two miles, but he always came with me till nearly in sight of home. Some days we raced till our horses were white with lather; and once or twice mine was in such a state that we dismounted, and Harold unsaddled him and wiped the sweat off with his towel saddle-cloth, to remove the evidence of hard riding, so that I would not get into a scrape with uncle Jay-Jay. Other times we dawdled, so that when we parted the

114

last rays of sunset would be laughing at us between the white trunks of the tall gum-trees, the kookaburras would be making the echoes ring with their mocking good-night, and scores of wild duck would be flying quickly roostward. As I passed through the angle formed by the creek and the river, about half a mile from home, there came to my ears the cheery clink-clink of hobble-chains, the jangle of horse-bells, and the gleam of a dozen camp-fires. The shearing was done out in Riverina now, and the men were all going home. Day after day dozens of them passed along the long white road, bound for Monaro and the cool country beyond the blue peaks to the south-east, where the shearing was about to begin. When I had come to Caddagat the last of them had gone 'down' with horses poor; now they were travelling 'up' with their horses—some of them thoroughbreds—rolling fat, and a cheque for their weeks of back-bending labour in their pockets. But whether coming or going they always made to Caddagat to camp. That camping-ground was renowned as the best from Monaro to Riverina. It was a well-watered and sheltered nook, and the ground was so rich that there was always a mouthful of grass to be had there. It was a rare thing to see it without a fire; and the empty jam-tins, bottles, bits of bag, paper, tent-pegs, and fish-tins to be found there would have loaded a dozen waggons.

Thursday evening was always spent in going to Dogtrap, and all the other days had their pleasant tasks and were full of wholesome enjoyment. The blue senna flowers along the river gave place to the white bloom of the tea-tree. Grannie, uncle, and aunt Helen filled the house with girl visitors for my pleasure. In the late afternoon, as the weather got hot, we went for bogeys in a part of the river two miles distant. Some of the girls from neighbouring runs brought their saddles, others from town had to be provided therewith, which produced a dearth in side-saddles, and it was necessary for me to take a man's. With a rollicking gallop and a bogey ahead, that did not trouble me. Aunt Helen always accompanied us on our bathing expeditions to keep us in check. She was the only one who bothered with a bathing-dress. The rest of us reefed off our clothing, in our hurry sending buttons in all directions, and plunged into the pleasant water. Then—such water-fights, frolic, laughter, shouting and roaring fun as a dozen strong healthy girls can make when enjoying themselves. Aunt Helen generally called time before we were half inclined to leave. We would linger too long, then there would be a great scramble for clothes, next for horses, and with wet hair streaming on our towels, we would go home full belt, twelve sets of galloping hoofs making a royal clatter on the hard dusty road. Grannie made a rule that when we arrived late we had to unsaddle our horses ourselves, and not disturb the working men from their meal for our pleasure. We mostly were late, and so there would be a tight race to see who would arrive at table first. A dozen heated horses were turned out unceremoniously, a dozen saddles and bridles dumped down anywhere anyhow, and their occupants, with wet dishevelled hair and clothing in glorious disarray, would appear at table averring that they were starving.

The Caddagat folk were enthusiastic anglers. Fishing was a favourite and often enjoyed amusement of the household. In the afternoon a tinful of worms would be dug out of one of the water-races, tackle collected, horses saddled, and grannie, uncle, aunt, Frank Hawden, myself, and any one else who had happened to drop in, would repair to the fish-holes three miles distant. I hate fishing. Ugh! The hideous barbarity of shoving a hook through a living worm, and the cruelty of taking the fish off the hook! Uncle allowed no idlers at the river—all had to manipulate a rod and line. Indulging in pleasant air-castles, I generally forgot my cork till the rod would be jerked in my hand, when I would pull—too late! the fish would be gone. Uncle would lecture me for being a jackdaw, so next time I would glare at the cork unwinkingly, and pull at the first signs of it bobbing—too soon! the fish would escape again, and I would again be in disgrace. After a little experience I found it was a good plan to be civil to Frank Hawden when the prospect of fishing hung around, and then he would attend to my line as well as his own, while I read a book which I smuggled with me. The fish-hole was such a shrub-hidden nook that, though the main road passed within two hundred yards, neither we nor the horses could be seen by the travellers thereon. I lay on the soft moss and leaves and drank deeply of the beauties of nature. The soft rush of the river, the scent of the shrubs, the golden sunset, occasionally the musical clatter of hoofs on the road, the gentle noises of the fishers fishing, the plop, plop of a platypus disporting itself mid stream, came to me as sweetest elixir in my ideal, dream-of-a-poet nook among the pink-based, grey-topped, moss-carpeted rocks.

I was a creature of joy in those days. Life is made up of little things. It was a small thing to have a little pocket-money to spend on anything that took my fancy—a very small thing, and yet how much pleasure it gave me. Though eating is not one of the great aims of my life, yet it was nice to have enough of any delicacy one fancied. Not that we ever went hungry at home, but when one has nothing to eat in the hot weather but bread and beef it gives them tendency to dream of fruit and cool dainties. When one thinks of the countless army of one's fellows who are daily selling their very souls for the barest necessaries of life, I suppose we—irresponsible beings—should be thankful to God for allowing us, by scratching and scraping all our lives, to keep a crust in our mouth and a rag on our back. I am not thankful, I have been guilty of what Pat would term a 'digresshion'—I started about going for the mail at Dogtrap. Harold Beecham never once missed taking me home on Thursdays, even when his shearing was in full swing and he must have been very busy. He never once uttered a word of love to me—not so much as one of the soft nothings in which young people of opposite sexes often deal without any particular significance. Whether he went to all the bother and waste of time accruing from escorting me home out of gentlemanliness alone, was a mystery to me. I desired to find out, and resolved to drive instead of ride to Dogtrap one day to see what he would say.

Grannie assented to the project. Of course I could drive for

117

once if I didn't feel able to ride, but the horses had been spelling for a long time and were very frisky. I must take Frank with me or I might get my neck broken.

I flatly opposed the idea of Frank Hawden going with me. He would make a mull of the whole thing. It was no use arguing with grannie and impressing upon her the fact that I was not the least nervous concerning the horses. I could take Frank with me in the buggy, ride, or stay at home. I preferred driving. Accordingly the fat horses were harnessed to the buggy, and with many injunctions to be careful and not forget the parcels, we set out. Frank Hawden's presence spoilt it all, but I determined to soon make short work of him.

There was one gate to go through, about four miles from the house. Frank Hawden got out to open it. I drove through, and while he was pushing it to, laid the whip on the horses and went off full tilt. He ran after me shouting all manner of things that I could not hear on account of the rattle of the buggy. One horse began kicking up, so, to give him no time for further pranks, I drove at a good round gallop, which quickly left the lovable jackeroo a speck in the distance. The dust rose in thick clouds, the stones rattled from the whirling wheels, the chirr! chirr! of a myriad cicadas filled the air, and the white road glistened in the dazzling sunlight. I was enjoying myself tip-top, and chuckled to think of the way I had euchred Frank Hawden. It was such a good joke that I considered it worth two of the blowings-up I was sure of getting from grannie for my conduct.

It was not long before I fetched up at Dogtrap homestead, where, tethered to the 'six-foot' paling fence which surrounded the flower-garden, was Harold Beecham's favourite, great, black, saddle-horse Warrigal. The vicious brute turned his beautiful head, displaying a white star on the forehead, and snorted as I approached. His master appeared on the veranda raising his soft panama hat, and remarking, 'Well I never! You're not by yourself, are you?'

'I am. Would you please tell Mrs Butler to bring out grannie's parcels and post at once. I'm afraid to dawdle, it's getting late.'

He disappeared to execute my request and reappeared in less than a minute.

'Mr Beecham, please would you examine Barney's harness. Something must be hurting him. He has been kicking up all the way.'

Examining the harness and noticing the sweat that was dripping from the animals, panting from their run, he said:

'It looks as though you've been making the pace a cracker. There is nothing that is irritating Barney in the least. If he's putting on any airs it is because he is frisky and not safe for you to drive. How did Julius happen to let you away by yourself?'

'I'm not frightened,' I replied.

'I see you're not. You'd be game to tackle a pair of wild elephants, I know, but you must remember you're not much bigger than a sparrow sitting up there, and I won't let you go back by yourself.'

'You cannot stop me.'

'I can.'

'You can't.'

'I can.'

'You can't.'

'I can.'

'How?'

'I'm going with you,' he said.

'You're not.'

'I am.'

'You're not.'

'I am.'

'You ar-r-re not.'

'I am.'

'You are, a-r-re not.'

'We'll see whether I will or not in a minute or two,' he said with amusement.

'But, Mr Beecham, I object to your company. I am quite capable of taking care of myself; besides, if you come home with me I will not be allowed out alone again—it will be altogether unpleasant for me.'

119

Mrs Butler now appeared with the mail and some parcels, and Harold stowed them in the buggy.

'You'd better come in an' 'ave a drop of tay-warter, miss, the kittle's bilin'; and I have the table laid out for both of yez.'

'No, thank you, Mrs Butler. I can't possibly stay today, it's getting late. I must hurry off. Good-bye! Good afternoon, Mr Beecham.'

I turned my buggy and pair smartly round and was swooping off. Without a word Harold was at their heads and seized the reins. He seized his horse's bridle, where it was over the paling, and in a moment had him tied on the off-side of Barney, then stepping quietly into the buggy he put me away from the driver's seat as though I were a baby, quietly took the reins and whip, raised his hat to Mrs Butler, who was smiling knowingly, and drove off.

I was highly delighted with his action, as I would have despised him as a booby had he given in to me, but I did not let my satisfaction appear. I sat as far away from him as possible, and pretended to be in a great huff. For a while he was too fully occupied in making Barney 'sit up' to notice me, but after a few minutes he looked round, smiling a most annoying and pleasant smile.

'I'd advise you to straighten out your chin. It is too round and soft to look well screwed up that way,' he said provokingly.

I tried to extinguish him with a look, but it had not the desired effect.

'Now you had better be civil, for I have got the big end of the whip,' he said.

'I reserve to myself the right of behaving as I think fit in my own uncle's buggy. You are an intruder; it is yourself that should be civil.'

I erected my parasol and held it so as to tease Harold. I put it down so that he could not see the horses. He quietly seized my wrist and held it out of his way for a time, and then loosing me said, 'Now, behave.'

I flouted it now, so that his ears and eyes were endangered, and he was forced to hold his hat on.

'I'll give you three minutes to behave, or I'll put you out,' he said with mock severity.

'Shure it's me wot's behavin' beautiful,' I replied, continuing my nonsense.

He pulled rein, seized me in one arm, and lifted me lightly to the ground.

'Now, you can walk till you promise to conduct yourself like a Christian!' he said, driving at a walk.

'If you wait till I promise anything, you'll wait till the end of the century. I'm quite capable of walking home.'

'You'll soon get tired of walking in this heat, and your feet will be blistered in a mile with those bits of paper.'

The bits of paper to which he alluded were a pair of thin-soled white canvas slippers—not at all fitted for walking the eight miles on the hard hot road ahead of me. I walked resolutely on, without deigning a glance at Harold, who had slowed down to a crawling walk.

'Aren't you ready to get up now?' he inquired presently.

I did not reply. At the end of a quarter of a mile he jumped out of the buggy, seized upon me, lifted me in, and laughed, saying, 'You're a very slashing little concern, but you are not big enough to do much damage.'

We were about half-way home when Barney gave a tremendous lurch, breaking a trace and some other straps. Mr Beecham was at the head of the plunging horse in a twinkling. The harness seemed to be scattered everywhere.

'I expect I had better walk on now,' I remarked.

'Walk, be grannied! With two fat lazy horses to draw you?' returned Mr Beecham.

Men are clumsy, stupid creatures regarding little things, but in their right place they are wonderful animals. If a buggy was smashed to smithereens, from one of their many mysterious pockets they would produce a knife and some string, and put the wreck into working order in no time.

Harold was as clever in this way as any other man with as much bushman ability as he had, so it was not long ere we were bowling along as merrily as ever.

Just before we came in sight of Caddagat he came to a standstill, jumped to the ground, untied Warrigal, and put the reins in my hand, saying—

'I think you can get home safely from here. Don't be in such a huff—I was afraid something might happen you if alone. You needn't mention that I came with you unless you like. Goodbye.'

'Good-bye, Mr Beecham. Thank you for being so officious,' I said by way of a parting shot.

'Old Nick will run away with you for being so ungrateful,' he returned.

'Old Nick will have me anyhow,' I thought to myself as I drove home amid the shadows. The hum of the cicadas was still, and dozens of rabbits, tempted out by the cool of the twilight, scuttled across my path and hid in the ferns.

I wished the harness had not broken, as I feared it would put a clincher on my being allowed out driving alone in future.

Joe Slocombe, the man who acted as groom and rouseabout, was waiting for me at the entrance gate.

'I'm glad you come at last, Miss Sybyller. The missus has been in a dreadful stoo for fear something had happened yuz. She's been runnin' in an' out like a gurrl on the look-out fer her lover, and was torkin' of sendin' me after yuz, but she went to her tea soon as she see the buggy come in sight. I'll put all the parcels on the back veranda, and yuz can go in at woncest or yuz'll be late fer yer tea.'

'Joe, the harness broke and had to be tied up. That is what kept me so late,' I explained.

'The harness broke!' he exclaimed. 'How the doose is that! Broke here in the trace, and that strap! Well, I'll be hanged! I thought them straps couldn't break only onder a tremenjous strain. The boss is so dashed partickler too. I believe he'll sool me off the place; and I looked at that harness only yesterday.

I can't make out how it come to break so simple. The boss will rise the devil of a shine, and say you might have been killed.'

This put a different complexion on things. I knew Joe Slocombe could mend the harness with little trouble, as it was because he was what uncle Jay-Jay termed a 'handy divil' at saddlery that he was retained at Caddagat. I said carelessly:

'If you mend the harness at once, Joe, uncle Julius need not be bothered about it. As it happened, there is no harm done, and I won't mention the matter.'

'Thank you, miss,' he said eagerly. 'I'll mend it at once.'

Now that I had that piece of business so luckily disposed of, I did not feel the least nervous about meeting grannie. I took the mail in my arms and entered the dining-room, chirping pleasantly:

'Grannie, I'm such a good mail-boy. I have heaps of letters, and did not forget one of your commissions.'

'I don't want to hear that now,' she said, drawing her dear old mouth into a straight line, which told me I was not going to palm things off as easily as I thought. 'I want a reason for your conduct this afternoon.'

'Explain what, grannie?' I inquired.

'None of that pretence! Not only have you been most outrageously insulting to Mr Hawden when I sent him with you, but you also deliberately and wilfully disobeyed me.'

Uncle Julius listened attentively, and Hawden looked at me with such a leer of triumph that my fingers tingled to smack his ears. Turning to my grandmother, I said distinctly and cuttingly:

'Grannie, I did not intentionally disobey you. Disobedience never entered my head. I hate that thing. His presence was detestable to me. When he got out at the gate I could not resist the impulse to drive off and leave him there. He looked such a complete jackdaw that you would have laughed yourself to see him.'

'Dear, oh dear! You wicked hussy, what will become of you!' And grannie shook her head, trying to look stern, and hiding a smile in her serviette.

'Your manners are not improving, Sybylla. I fear you must be incorrigible,' said aunt Helen.

When uncle Jay-Jay heard the whole particulars of the affair, he lay back in his chair and laughed fit to kill himself.

'You ought to be ashamed to always encourage her in her tomboyish ways, Julius. It grieves me to see she makes no effort to acquire a ladylike demeanour,' said grannie.

Mr Hawden had come off second-best, so he arose from his half-finished meal and stamped out, banging the door after him, and muttering something about 'a disgustingly spoilt and petted tomboy', 'a hideous barbarian', and so forth.

Uncle Jay-Jay related that story to everyone, dwelling with great delight upon the fact that Frank Hawden was forced to walk four miles in the heat and dust.

CHAPTER 18

As Short as I Wish Had Been the Majority of Sermons to Which I Have Been Forced to Give Ear

When alone I confessed to aunt Helen that Harold had accompanied me to within a short distance of home. She did not smile as usual, but looked very grave, and, drawing me in front of her, said:

'Sybylla, do you know what you are doing? Do you love Harry Beecham? Do you mean to marry him?'

'Aunt Helen, what a question to ask! I never dreamt of such a thing. He has never spoken a word of love to me. Marriage! I am sure he does not for an instant think of me in that light. I'm not seventeen.'

'Yes, you are young, but some people's age cannot be reckoned by years. I am glad to see you have developed a certain amount of half-real and half-assumed youthfulness lately, but when the novelty of your present life wears away, your old mature nature will be there, so it is of no use feigning childishness. Harold Beecham is not given to speech—action with him is the same thing. Can you look at me straight, Sybylla, and say that Harold has not extended you something more than common politeness?'

Had aunt Helen put that question to me a day before, I would have blushed and felt guilty. But today not so. The words of the jackeroo the night before had struck home. 'A hideous barbarian,' he had called me, and it seemed to me he had spoken the truth. My life had been so pleasant lately that I had overlooked this fact, but now it returned to sting with redoubled bitterness. I had no lovable qualities to win for me the love of my fellows, which I so much desired.

I returned aunt Helen a gaze as steady as her own, and said bitterly:

'Aunt Helen, I can truly say he has never, and will never extend

125

to me more than common politeness. Neither will any other man. Surely you know enough of masculine human nature to see there is no danger of a man losing his heart to a plain woman like me. Love in fancy and song is a pretty myth, embracing unity of souls, congeniality of tastes, and such like commodities. In workaday reality it is the lowest of passions, which is set alight by the most artistic nose and mouth, and it matters not if its object is vile, low, or brainless to idiocy, so long as it has these attributes.'

'Sybylla, Sybylla,' said auntie sadly, as if to herself. 'In the first flush of girlhood, and so bitter. Why is this?'

'Because I have been cursed with the power of seeing, thinking, and, worse than all, feeling, and branded with the stinging affliction of ugliness,' I replied.

'Now, Sybylla, you are going to think of yourself again. Something has put you out. Be sensible for once in a way. What you have said of men's love may be true in a sense, but it is not always so, and Harry is not that kind of man. I have known him all his life, and understand him, and feel sure he loves you truly. Tell me plainly, do you intend to accept him?'

'Intend to accept him!' I echoed. 'I haven't once thought of such a possibility. I never mean to marry anyone.'

'Don't you care for Harold? Just a little? Think.'

'How could I care for him?'

'For many, many reasons. He is young, and very kind and gentle. He is one of the biggest and finest-looking men you could find. He is a man whom no one could despise, for he has nothing despicable about him. But, best of all, he is true, and that, I think, is the bedrock of all virtues.'

'But he is so conceited,' I remarked.

'That does not make him any the less lovable. I know another young person very conceited, and it does not prevent me from loving her dearly,' here aunt Helen smiled affectionately at me. 'What you complain of in Harold will wear off presently—life has been very easy for him so far, you see.'

'But, auntie, I'm sure he thinks he could have any girl for the asking.'

126

'Well, he has a great number to choose from, for they all like him.'

'Yes, just for his money,' I said scornfully. 'But I'll surprise him if he thinks he can get me for the asking.'

'Sybylla, never flirt. To play with a man's heart, I think, is one of the most horribly unwomanly actions our sex can be guilty of.'

'I would scorn to flirt with any man,' I returned with vigour. 'Play with a man's heart! You'd really think they had such a thing, aunt Helen, to hear you talk. Hurt their vanity for a few days is the most a woman could do with any of them. I am sick of this preach, preach about playing with men's hearts. It is an old fable which should have been abolished long ago. It does not matter how a woman is played with.'

'Sybylla, you talk at random. The shortcomings of men are no excuse for you to be unwomanly,' said aunt Helen.

CHAPTER 19

The 9th of November 1896

The Prince of Wales's birthday up the country was celebrated as usual thereaway by the annual horse-races on the Wyambeet course, about fourteen miles from Caddagat.

The holding of these races was an elderly institution, and was followed at night by a servants' ball given by one of the squatters. Last year it had been Beecham's ball, the year before Bossier's, and this year it was to take place in the woolshed of James Grant of Yabtree. Our two girls, the gardener, and Joe Slocombe the groom, were to be present, as also were all the other employees about. Nearly every one in the district—masters and men—attended the races. We were going, Frank Hawden volunteering to stay and mind the house.

We started at nine o'clock. Grannie and uncle Boss sat in the front seat of the buggy, and aunt Helen and I occupied the back. Uncle always drove at a good round gallop. His idea was to have good horses, not donkeys, and not to spare them, as there were plenty more to be had any day. On this morning he went off at his usual pace. Grannie urged as remonstrance that the dust was fearful when going at that rate. I clapped my hands and exclaimed, 'Go it, Mr Bossier! Well done, uncle Jay-Jay! Hurrah for Clancy!'

Uncle first said he was glad to see I had the spirit of an Australian, and then threatened to put my nose above my chin if I failed to behave properly. Grannie remarked that I might have the spirit of an Australian, but I had by no means the manners of a lady; while aunt Helen ventured a wish that I might expend all my superfluous spirits on the way, so that I would be enabled to deport myself with a little decorum when arrived at the racecourse.

We went at a great pace; lizards and goannas scampered out

of the way in dozens, and, clambering trees, eyed us unblinkingly as we passed. Did we see a person or vehicle a tiny speck ahead of us—in a short time were as far away in the background.

'Please, uncle, let me drive,' I requested.

'Couldn't now. Your grannie can't sit in the back-seat—neither could I—and look like a tame cockatoo while you sat in front. You ask Harry to let you drive him. I bet he'll consent; he's sure to be in a sulky with a spare seat on spec. We're sure to overtake him in a few minutes.'

There was a vehicle in the distance which proved to be from Five-Bob Downs, but as we overhauled it, it was the drag, and not a sulky. Harold occupied the driver's seat, and the other occupants were all ladies. I noticed the one beside him was wearing a very big hat, all ruffles, flowers, and plumes.

'Shall I pull up and get you a seat?' inquired uncle Jay-Jay. 'No, no, no.'

The boss of Five-Bob drew to his side of the road, and when we had passed uncle began to tease:

'Got faint-hearted, did you? The flower-garden on that woman's hat corked your chances altogether. Never mind, don't you funk; I'll see that you have a fair show. I'll get you a regular cart-wheel next time I go to town, and we'll trim it up with some of old Barney's tail. If that won't fetch him, I'm sure nothing will.'

Before we got to the racecourse Barney went lame through getting a stone in his hoof; this caused a delay which enabled the Five-Bob trap to catch us, and we pulled rein a little distance apart at the same time, to alight.

Mr Beecham's groom went to his horses' heads while Harold himself assisted his carriageful of ladies to set foot on the ground. Aunt Helen and grannie went to talk to them, but I stayed with uncle Jay-Jay while he took the horses out. Somehow I was feeling very disappointed. I had expected Harold Beecham to be alone. He had attended on me so absolutely everywhere I had met him lately, that I had unconsciously grown to look upon him as mine exclusively; and now, seeing he would belong to his own party of ladies for the day, things promised to be somewhat flat without him.

'I told that devil of a Joe to be sure and turn up as soon as I arrived. I wanted him to water the horses, but I can't see him anywhere—the infernal, crawling, doosed idiot!' ejaculated uncle Julius.

'Never mind, uncle, let him have his holiday. I suppose he'd like to have time to spoon with his girl. I can easily water the horses.'

'That would suit Joe, I have no doubt; but I don't pay him to let you water the horses. I'll water 'em myself.'

He led one animal, I took the other, and we went in the direction of water a few hundred yards away.

'You run along to your grannie and the rest of them, and I'll go by myself,' said uncle, but I kept on with the horse.

'You mustn't let a five-guinea hat destroy your hopes altogether,' he continued, with a mischievous twinkle in his eyes. 'If you stick to your guns you have a better show than anyone to bag the boss of Five-Bob.'

'I am at a loss to interpret your innuendo, Mr Bossier,' I said stiffly.

'Now, little woman, you think you are very smart, but you can't deceive me. I've seen the game you and Harry have been up to this last month. If it had been any other man, I would have restricted your capers long ago.'

'Uncle—' I began.

'Now, Sybylla, none of your crammers. There is no harm in being a bit gone on Harry. It's only natural, and just what I'd expect. I've known him since he was born, and he's a good all-round fellow. His head is screwed on the right way, his heart is in the right place, and his principles are tip-top. He could give you fal-de-rals and rubbish to no end, and wouldn't be stingy either. You'll never get a better man. Don't you be put out of the running so cheaply: hold your own and win, that's my advice to you. There is nothing against him, only temper—old Nick himself isn't a patch on him for temper.'

'Temper!' I exclaimed. 'He is always so quiet and pleasant.'

'Yes, he controls it well. He's a fellow with a will like iron, and that is what you want, as I find you have none of your own. But be careful of Harry Beecham in a temper. He is like a raging lion, and when his temper dies away is a sulking brute, which is the vilest of all tempers. But he is not vindictive, and is easy managed, if you don't mind giving in and coaxing a little.'

'Now, uncle, you have had your say, I will have mine. You seem to think I have more than a friendly regard for Mr Beecham, but I have not. I would not marry him even if I could. I am so sick of every one thinking I would marry any man for his possessions. I would not stoop to marry a king if I did not love him. As for trying to win a man, I would scorn any action that way; I never intend to marry. Instead of wasting so much money on me in presents and other ways, I wish you would get me something to do, a profession that will last me all my life, so that I may be independent.'

'No mistake, you're a rum youngster. You can be my companion till further orders. That's a profession that will last you a goodish while.'

With this I had to be contented, as I saw he considered what I had said as a joke.

I left uncle and went in quest of grannie, who, by this, was beyond the other side of the course, fully a quarter of a mile away. Going in her direction I met Joe Archer, one of the Five-Bob jackeroos, and a great chum of mine. He had a taste for literature, and we got on together like one o'clock. We sat on a log under a stringybark-tree and discussed the books we had read since last we met, and enjoyed ourselves so much that we quite forgot about the races or the flight of time until recalled from book-land by Harold Beecham's voice.

'Excuse me, Miss Melvyn, but your grannie has commissioned me to find you as we want to have lunch, and it appears you are the only one who knows the run of some of the tucker bags.'

'How do you do, Mr Beecham? Where are they going to have lunch?'

'Over in that clump of box-trees,' he replied, pointing in the direction of a little rise at a good distance.

'How are you enjoying yourself?' he asked, looking straight at me.

'Treminjous intoirely, sor,' I replied.

'I suppose you know the winner of every race,' he remarked, quizzically watching Joe Archer, who was blushing and as uneasy as a schoolgirl when nabbed in the enjoyment of an illicit love-letter.

'Really, Mr Beecham, Mr Archer and I have been so interested in ourselves that we quite forgot there was such a thing as a race at all,' I returned.

'You'd better see where old Boxer is. He might kick some of the other horses if you don't keep a sharp look-out,' he said, turning to his jackeroo.

'Ladies before gentlemen,' I interposed. 'I want Mr Archer to take me to grannie, then he can go and look after old Boxer.'

'I'll escort you,' said Beecham.

'Thank you, but I have requested Mr Archer to do so.'

'In that case, I beg your pardon, and will attend to Boxer while Joe does as you request.'

Raising his hat he walked swiftly away with a curious expression on his usually pleasant face.

'By Jove, I'm in for it!' ejaculated my escort. 'The boss doesn't get that expression on his face for nothing. You take my tip for it, he felt inclined to seize me by the scruff of the neck and kick me from here to Yabtree.'

'Go on!'

'It's a fact. He did not believe in me not going to do his bidding immediately. He has a roaring derry on disobedience. Everyone has to obey him like winkie or they can take their beds up and trot off quick and lively.'

'Mr Beecham has sufficient sense to see I was the cause of your disobedience,' I replied.

'That's where it is. He would not have cared had it been some other lady, but he gets mad if any one dares to monopolize you.

I don't know how you are going to manage him. He is a pretty hot member sometimes.'

'Mr Archer, you presume! But throwing such empty banter aside, is Mr Beecham really bad-tempered?'

'Bad-tempered is a tame name for it. You should have seen the dust he raised the other day with old Benson. He just did perform.'

I was always hearing of Harold Beecham's temper, and wished I could see a little of it. He was always so imperturbably calm, and unfailingly good-tempered under the most trying circumstances, that I feared he had no emotions in him, and longed to stir him up.

Grannie greeted me with, 'Sybylla, you are such a tiresome girl. I don't know how you have packed these hampers, and we want to have lunch. Where on earth have you been?'

Miss Augusta Beecham saluted me warmly with a kiss, and presented me to her sister Sarah, who also embraced me. I went through an introduction to several ladies and gentlemen, greeted my acquaintances, and then set to work in dead earnest to get our provisions laid out—the Five-Bob Downs party had theirs in readiness. Needless to say, we were combining forces. I had my work completed when Mr Beecham appeared upon the scene with two young ladies. One was a bright-faced little brunette, and the other a tall light blonde, whom, on account of her much trimmed hat, I recognized as the lady who had been sitting on the box-seat of the Beecham drag that morning.

Joe Archer informed me in a whisper that she was Miss Blanche Derrick from Melbourne, and was considered one of the greatest beauties of that city.

This made me anxious to examine her carefully, but I did not get an opportunity of doing so. In the hurry to attend on the party, I missed the honour of an introduction, and when I was at leisure she was sitting at some distance on a log, Harold Beecham shading her in a most religious manner with a dainty parasol. In the afternoon she strolled away with him, and after I had attended to the remains of the feast, I took Joe Archer in tow. He informed me that Miss Derrick had arrived at Five-Bob three days before, and was setting her cap determinedly at his boss.

'Was she really very handsome?' I inquired.

'By Jove, yes!' he replied. 'But one of your disdainful haughty beauties, who wouldn't deign to say good-day to a chap with less than six or seven thousand a year.'

I don't know why I took no interest in the races. I knew nearly all the horses running. Some of them were uncle's; though he never raced horses himself, he kept some swift stock which he lent to his men for the occasion.

Of more interest to me than the races was the pair strolling at a distance. They were fit for an artist's models. The tall, broad, independent figure of the bushman with his easy gentlemanliness, his jockey costume enhancing his size. The equally tall majestic form of the city belle, whose self-confident fashionable style spoke of nothing appertaining to girlhood, but of the full-blown rose—indeed, a splendid pair physically!

Then I thought of my lack of beauty, my miserable five-feet-one-inch stature, and I looked at the man beside me, small and round-shouldered, and we were both dependent children of indigence. The contrast we presented to the other pair struck me hard, and I laughed a short bitter laugh.

I excused myself to my companion, and acceded to the request of several children to go on a flower- and gum-hunting expedition. We were a long time absent, and returning, the little ones scampered ahead and left me alone. Harold Beecham came to meet me, looking as pleasant as ever.

'Am I keeping grannie and uncle waiting?' I inquired.

'No. They have gone over an hour,' he replied.

'Gone! How am I to get home? She must have been very angry to go and leave me. What did she say?'

'On the contrary, she was in great fiddle. She said to tell you not to kill yourself with fun, and as you are not going home, she left me to say good night. I suppose she kisses you when performing that ceremony,' he said mischievously.

'Where am I going tonight?'

'To Five-Bob Downs, the camp of yours truly,' he replied.

'I haven't got a dinner dress, and am not prepared. I will go home.'

'We have plenty dinner dresses at Five-Bob without any more. It is Miss Melvyn we want,' he said.

'Oh, bother you!' I retorted. 'Men are such stupid creatures, and never understand about dress or anything. They think you could go to a ball in a wrapper.'

'At all events, they are cute enough to know when they want a young lady at their place, no matter how she's dressed,' he said good-humouredly.

On reaching the racecourse I was surprised to see aunt Helen there. From her I learnt that grannie and uncle Jay-Jay had really gone home, but Mr Beecham had persuaded them to allow aunt Helen and me to spend the night at Five-Bob Downs, our host promising to send or take us home on the morrow. Now that I was to have aunt Helen with me I was delighted at the prospect, otherwise I would have felt a little out of it. With aunt Helen, however, I was content anywhere, and built a castle in the air, wherein one day she and I were always to live together—for ever! Till death!

Going home aunt Helen occupied a front seat with Harold and Miss Derrick, and I was crammed in at the back beside Miss Augusta, who patted my hand and said she was delighted to see me.

A great concourse of young men and women in vehicles and on horseback, and in expectation of great fun, were wending their way to Yabtree—nearly every trap containing a fiddle, concertina, flute, or accordion in readiness for the fray.

CHAPTER 20

Same Yarn—continued

Every station hand from Five-Bob, male and female, had gone to the ball at Yabtree. Harold and his overseer had to attend to the horses, while the jackeroos started a fire in the kitchen, opened windows and doors which had been locked all day, and saw to the comfort of the gentleman guests.

Aunt Helen and I shared the one bedroom. As we had not fresh dresses to put on we had to make the best of our present toilet.

I unplaited my hair (shook the dust out of it) and wore it flowing. We washed and dusted ourselves, and wore as adornments— roses. Crimson and cream roses paid the penalty of peeping in the window. Aunt Helen plucked some of them, which she put in my hair and belt, and pinned carefully at my throat, and then we were ready. Miss Beecham assured us there was nothing to be done, as the maids had set the table and prepared the viands for a cold meal before leaving in the morning, so we proceeded to the drawing-room to await the arrival of the other visitors. They soon made their appearance. First, two stout old squatters with big laughs and bigger corporations, then Miss Augusta Beecham, next Joe Archer the overseer, and the two other jackeroos. After these appeared a couple of governesses, Mr, Mrs, and Miss Benson, a clergyman, an auctioneer, a young friend of Harold's from Cootamundra, a horse-buyer, a wool-classer, Miss Sarah Beecham, and then Miss Derrick brought herself and her dress in with great style and airs. She was garbed in a sea-green silk, and had jewellery on her neck, arms, and hair. Her self-confident mien was suggestive of the conquest of many masculine hearts. She was a big handsome woman. Beside her, I in my crushed white muslin dress was as overshadowed as a little white handkerchief would be in comparison to a gorgeous shawl heavily wrought in silks and velvet. She was given the best seat as though she were a princess. She sat down with great indifference, twirled a bracelet round her wrist, languidly opened her fan, and closed her eyes as she wafted it slowly to and fro.

'By Jove, isn't she a splendid creature!' enthusiastically whispered a gentleman sitting beside me.

I looked at her critically. She was very big, and in a bony stiff way was much developed in figure. She had a nice big nose, and a long well-shaped face, a thin straight mouth, and empty light eyes. If my attention had not been called to her I would not have noticed her one way or the other, but being pointed to as a beauty, I weighed her according to my idea of facial charm, and pronounced her one of the most insipid-looking people I had set eyes upon.

She was the kind of woman with whom men become much infatuated. She would never make a fool of herself by letting her emotions run away with her, because she had no emotions, but lived in a sea of unruffled self-consciousness and self-confidence. Any man would be proud to introduce her as his wife to his friends whom he had brought home to dinner. She would adorn the head of his table. She would never worry him with silly ideas. She would never act with impropriety. She would never become a companion to her husband. Bah, a man does not want his wife to be a companion! There were myths and fables in the old day; so there are now. The story that men like a companion as well as a wife is an up-to-date one.

This train of thought was interrupted by our host, who appeared in the doorway, clad from sole to neck in white. We steered for the dining-room—twenty-two all told—thirteen men and nine representatives of the other sex.

Aunt Helen got one seat of honour near the head of the table and Miss Derrick another. I drifted to the foot among the unimportant younger fry, where we had no end of fun and idle chatter. We had to wait on ourselves, and as all formality was dispensed with, it was something like a picnic.

The heat was excessive. Every window and door were open,

137

and the balmy, almost imperceptible, zephyrs which faintly rustled the curtains and kissed our perspiration-beaded brows were rich with many scents from the wide old flower-garden, which, despite the drought, brought forth a wealth of blossom.

When done eating we had to wash the dishes. Such a scamper ensued back and forwards to the kitchen, which rang with noise and merriment. Everyone was helping, hindering, laughing, joking, teasing, and brimming over with fun and enjoyment. When we had completed this task, dancing was proposed. Some of the elderly and more sensible people said it was too hot, but all the young folks did not care a rap for the temperature. Harold had no objections, Miss Derrick was agreeable, Miss Benson announced herself ready and willing, and Joe Archer said he was 'leppin'' to begin, so we adjourned to the dancing-room and commenced operations.

I played the piano for the first quadrille, and aunt Helen for the second dance. It was most enjoyable. There was a table at one end of the room on which was any amount of cherries, lollies, cake, dainties, beers, syrups, and glasses, where all could regale themselves without ceremony or bother every time the inclination seized them. Several doors and windows of the long room opened into the garden, and, provided one had no fear of snakes, it was delightful to walk amid the flowers and cool oneself between dances.

A little exertion on such a night made us very hot. After the third dance the two old squatters, the horse-buyer, the clergyman, and Mr Benson disappeared. Judging from the hilarity of their demeanour and the killing odour of their breaths when they returned an hour or so later, during their absence they must have conscientiously sampled the contents of every whisky decanter on the dining-room sideboard.

I could not dance, but had no lack of partners, as, ladies being in the minority, the gentlemen had to occasionally put up with their own sex in a dance.

'Let's take a breeze now and have a song or two, but no more dancing for a while,' said some of them; but Harold Beecham said, 'One more turn, and then we will have a long spell and a change of programme.'

He ordered Joe Archer to play a waltz, and the floor soon held several whirling couples. Harold 'requested the pleasure' of me—the first time that night. I demurred. He would not take a refusal.

'Believe me, if I felt competent, Mr Beecham, I would not refuse. I cannot dance. It will be no pleasure to you.'

'Allow me to be the best judge of what is a pleasure to me,' he said, quietly placing me in position.

He swung me once round the room, and then through an open window into the garden.

'I am sorry that I haven't had more time to look after you today. Come round into my room. I want to strike a bargain with you,' were his words.

I followed him in the direction of a detached building in the garden. This was Harold's particular domain. It contained three rooms—one a library and office, another an arsenal and deed-room, and the third, into which he led me, was a sort of sitting-room, containing a piano, facilities for washing, a table, easy-chairs, and other things. As we entered I noticed the lamp, burning brightly on the table, gleamed on the face of a clock on the wall, which pointed to half past ten.

We stood beside the table, some distance apart, and, facing me, he said:

'It is no use of me making a long yarn about nothing. I'm sure you know what I want to say better than I do myself. You always are wonderfully smart at seeing through a fellow. Tell me, will it be yes or no?'

This was an experience in love. He did not turn red or white, or yellow or green, nor did he tremble or stammer, or cry or laugh, or become fierce or passionate, or tender or anything but just himself, as I had always known him. He displayed no more emotion than had he been inviting me to a picnic. This was not as I had pictured a man would tell his love, or as I had read of it, heard of it, or wished it should be. A curious feeling—

disappointment, perhaps—stole over me. His matter-of-fact coolness flabbergasted me.

'Is this not rather sudden? You have given me no intimation of your intentions,' I stammered.

'I didn't think it wise to dawdle any longer,' he replied. 'Surely you have known what I've been driving at ever since I first clapped eyes on you. There's plenty of time. I don't want to hurry you, only I want you to be engaged to me for safety.'

He spoke as usual in his slow twangy drawl, which would have proclaimed his Colonial nationality anywhere. No word of love was uttered to me and none requested from me.

I put it down to his conceit. I thought that he fancied he could win any woman, and me without the least palaver or trouble. I felt annoyed. I said aloud, 'I will become engaged to you;' to myself I added, 'Just for a little while, the more to surprise and take the conceit out of you when the time comes.'

Now that I understand his character I know that it was not conceit, but just his quiet unpretending way. He had meant all his actions towards me, and had taken mine in return.

'Thank you, Sybylla, that is all I want. We will talk about the matter more some other time. I will go up to Caddagat next Sunday. You have surprised me nearly out of my wits,' here he laughed. 'I never dreamt you would say yes so easily, just like any other girl. I thought I would have a lot of trouble with you.'

He approached me and was stooping to kiss me. I cannot account for my action or condemn it sufficiently. It was hysterical—the outcome of an overstrung, highly excitable, and nervous temperament. Perhaps my vanity was wounded, and my tendency to strike when touched was up in arms. The calm air of ownership with which Harold drew near annoyed me, or, as Sunday-school teachers would explain it, Satan got hold of me. He certainly placed a long strong riding-whip on the table beneath my hand. As Harold stooped with the intention of pressing his lips to mine, I quickly raised the whip and brought it with all my strength right across his face. The instant the whip had descended I would have smashed my arm on the door-post to recall that blow. But that was impossible. It had left a great weal on the healthy sun-tanned skin. His moustache had saved his lips, but it had caught his nose, the left cheek, had blinded the left eye, and had left a cut on the temple from which drops of blood were rolling down his cheek and staining his white coat. A momentary gleam of anger shot into his eyes and he gave a gasp, whether of surprise, pain, or annoyance, I know not. He made a gesture towards me. I half expected and fervently wished he would strike. The enormity of what I had done paralysed me. The whip fell from my fingers and I dropped on to a low lounge behind me, and placing my elbows on my knees crouchingly buried my face in my hands; my hair tumbled softly over my shoulders and reached the floor, as though to sympathetically curtain my humiliation. Oh, that Harold would thrash me severely! It would have infinitely relieved me. I had done a mean unwomanly thing in thus striking a man, who by his great strength and sex was debarred retaliation. I had committed a violation of self-respect and common decency; I had given a man an ignominious blow in the face with a riding-whip. And that man was Harold Beecham, who with all his strength and great stature was so wondrously gentle—who had always treated my whims and nonsense with something like the amused tolerance held by a great Newfoundland for the pranks of a kitten.

The clock struck eleven.

'A less stinging rebuke would have served your purpose. I had no idea that a simple caress from the man whose proposal of marriage you had just accepted would be considered such an unpardonable familiarity.'

Harold's voice fell clearly, calmly, cuttingly on the silence. He moved away to the other end of the room and I heard the sound of water.

A desire filled me to tell him that I did not think he had attempted a familiarity, but that I had been mad. I wished to say I could not account for my action, but I was dumb. My tongue refused to work, and I felt as though I would choke. The splash of the water came from the other end of the room. I knew he must be suffering acute pain in his eye. A far lighter blow had kept me sleepless a whole night. A fear possessed me that I might have permanently injured his sight. The splash of water ceased. His footfall stopped beside me. I could feel he was within touching distance, but I did not move.

Oh, the horrible stillness! Why did he not speak? He placed his hand lightly on my head.

'It doesn't matter, Syb. I know you didn't mean to hurt me. I suppose you thought you couldn't affect my dark, old, saddle-flap-looking phiz. That is one of the disadvantages of being a big lumbering concern like I am. Jump up. That's the girl.'

I arose. I was giddy, and would have fallen but for Harold steadying me by the shoulder. I looked up at him nervously and tried to ask his forgiveness, but I failed.

'Good heavens, child, you are as white as a sheet! I was a beast to speak harshly to you.' He held a glass of water to my lips and I drank.

'Great Jupiter, there's nothing to worry about! I know you hadn't the slightest intention of hurting me. It's nothing—I'll be right in a few moments. I've often been amused at and have admired your touch-me-not style. You only forgot you had something in your hand.'

He had taken it quite as a matter of fact, and was excusing me in the kindest possible terms.

'Good gracious, you mustn't screw over such a trifling accident! It's nothing. Just tie this handkerchief on for me, please, and then we'll go back to the others or there will be a search-party after us.'

He could have tied the handkerchief just as well himself— it was only out of kindly tact he requested my services. I accepted his kindness gratefully. He sank on his knee so that I could reach him, and I tied a large white handkerchief across the injured part. He could not open his eye, and hot water poured from it, but he made light of the idea of it paining. I was feeling better now, so we returned to the ballroom. The clock struck the half-hour after eleven as we left the room. Harold entered by one door and I by another, and I slipped into a seat as though I had been there some time.

There were only a few people in the room. The majority were absent—some love-making, others playing cards. Miss Beecham was one who was not thus engaged. She exclaimed at once:

'Good gracious, boy, what have you done to yourself?'

'Looks as if he had been interviewing a belligerent tramp,' said aunt Helen, smilingly.

'He's run into the clothes-line, that's what he's done,' said Miss Augusta confidently, after she had peeped beneath the bandage.

'You ought to get a bun for guessing, aunt Gus,' said Harold laughing.

'I told them to put the clothes-line up when they had done with them. I knew there would be an accident.'

'Perhaps they were put up high enough for ordinary purposes,' remarked her nephew.

'Let me do something for you, dear.'

'No, thank you, aunt Gus. It is nothing,' he said carelessly, and the matter dropped.

Harold Beecham was not a man to invite inquiry concerning himself.

Seeing I was unobserved by the company, I slipped away to indulge in my foolish habit of asking the why and the wherefore of things. Why had Harold Beecham (who was a sort of young sultan who could throw the handkerchief where he liked) chosen me of all women? I had no charms to recommend me—none of the virtues which men demand of the woman they wish to make their wife. To begin with, I was small, I was erratic and unorthodox, I was nothing but a tomboy—and, cardinal disqualification, I was ugly. Why, then, had he proposed matrimony to me? Was it merely a whim? Was he really in earnest?

The night was soft and dark; after being out in it for a time I could discern the shrubs dimly silhouetted against the light. The music struck up inside again. A step approached me on the gravelled walk among the flowers, and Harold called me softly by name. I answered him.

143

'Come,' he said, 'we are going to dance; will you be my partner?'

We danced, and then followed songs and parlour games, and it was in the small hours when the merry goodnights were all said and we had retired to rest. Aunt Helen dropped to sleep in a short time; but I lay awake listening to the soft distant call of the mopokes in the scrub beyond the stables.

CHAPTER 21

My Unladylike Behaviour Again

Joe Archer was appointed to take us home on the morrow. When our host was seeing us off—still with his eye covered—he took opportunity of whispering to me his intention of coming to Caddagat on the following Sunday.

Early in the afternoon of that day I took a book, and, going down the road some distance, climbed up a broad-branched willow-tree to wait for him.

It was not long before he appeared at a smart canter. He did not see me in the tree, but his horse did, and propping, snorted wildly, and gave a backward run. Harold spurred him, he bucked spiritedly. Harold now saw me and sang out:

'I say, don't frighten him any more or he'll fling me, saddle and all. I haven't got a crupper or a breastplate.'

'Why haven't you, then? Hang on to him. I do like the look of you while the horse is going on like that.'

He had dismounted, and had thrown the bridle rein over a post of the fence.

'I came with nothing but a girth, and that loose, as it was so hot; and I was as near as twopence to being off, saddle and all. You might have been the death of me,' he said good-humouredly.

'Had I been, my fortune would have been made,' I replied.

'How do you make that out? You're as complimentary as ever.'

'Everyone would be wanting to engage me as the great noxious weed-killer and poisonous insect exterminator if I made away with you,' I answered. I gave him an invitation to take a seat with me, and accepting, he swung up with easy grace. There was any amount of accommodation for the two of us on the good-natured branches of the old willow-tree.

When he had settled himself, my companion said, 'Now, Syb,

I'm ready for you. Fire away. But wait a minute, I've got some-ting here for you which I hope you'll like.'

As he searched in his pockets, I noticed that his eye had quite recovered, though there was still a slight mark on his cheek. He handed me a tiny morocco case, which on being opened disclosed a costly ring. I have about as much idea of the prices of things as a turkey would have. Perhaps that ring cost thirty pounds or possibly fifty guineas, for all I know. It was very heavy, and had a big diamond supported on either side by a large sapphire, and had many small gems surrounding it.

'Let me see if it fits,' he said, taking my hand; but I drew it away.

'No; don't you put it on. That would make us irrevocably engaged.'

'Isn't that what we intend to be?' he said in a tone of surprise.

'Not just yet; that is what I want to say to you. We will have three months' probation to see how we get on. At the end of that time, if we manage to sail along smoothly, we'll have the real thing; until then we will not be any more than we have been to each other.'

'But what am I to do in the meantime?' he asked, with amuse-ment curving the corners of his mouth.

'Do! Do the usual thing, of course; but don't pay me any special attentions, or I'll be done with you at once.'

'What's your idea for this?'

'It is no use making fools of ourselves; we might change our minds.'

'Very well; so be it,' he said laughing. 'I might have known you would have things arranged different from any other girl. But you'll take the ring and wear it, won't you? Let me put it on.'

'No; I won't let you put a finger on me till the three months are up. Then, if we definitely make up our minds, you can put it on; but till then, don't for the life of you hint by word or sign that we have any sort of an arrangement between us. Give me the ring and I'll wear it sometimes.'

He handed it to me again, and I tried it on. It was a little large. Harold took it, and tried to put it on one of his fingers. It would fit on none but the very top of his little finger. We laughed heartily at the disparity in the size of our hands.

' 'I'll agree to your bargain,' he said. 'But you'll be really engaged to me all the same.'

'Yes; under those conditions. Then it will not matter if we have a tiff. We can part, and no one will be the wiser.'

On my suggesting that it was now time to go to the house, he swung himself down by a branch and turned to assist me. Descending from that tree was a feat which presented no difficulties to me when no one was by, but now it seemed an awkward performance.

'Just lead your horse underneath, so that I can get on to his back, thence to the ground quite easily,' I said.

'No fear! Warrigal wouldn't stand that kind of dodge. Won't I do? I don't think your weight will quite squash me,' he returned, placing himself in leap-frog position, and I stepped on to his back and slid from there to the ground quite easily.

That afternoon, when leaving the house, I had been followed by one of the dogs, which, when I went up the willow-tree, amused himself chasing water lizards along the bank of the creek. He treed one, and kept up a furious barking at the base of its refuge. The yelping had disturbed grannie where she was reading on the veranda, and coming down the road under a big umbrella to see what the noise was about, as luck would have it she was in the nick of time to catch me standing on Harold Beecham's back. Grannie frequently showed marked displeasure regarding what she termed my larrikinism, but never before had I seen her so thoroughly angry. Shutting her umbrella, she thrust at me with it, saying, 'shame! shame! You'll come to some harm yet, you immodest, bold, bad hussy! I will write to your mother about you. Go home at once, miss, and confine yourself in your room for the remainder of the day, and don't dare eat anything until tomorrow. Spend the time in fasting, and pray to God to make you better. I don't know what makes you so forward with men.

147

Your mother and aunt never gave me the slightest trouble in that way.'

She pushed me from her in anger, and I turned and strode housewards without a word or glancing behind. I could hear grannie deprecating my conduct as I departed, and Harold quietly and decidedly differing from her.

From the time of my infancy punishment of any description never had a beneficial effect upon me. But dear old grannie was acting according to her principles in putting me through a term of penance, so I shut myself in my room as directed, with good-will towards her at my heart. I was burning with shame. Was I bold and immodest with men, as accused of being? It was the last indiscretion I would intentionally have been guilty of. In associating with men I never realize that the trifling difference of sex is sufficient to be a great wall between us. The fact of sex never for an instant enters my head, and I find it as easy to be chummy with men as with girls: men in return have always been very good, and have treated me in the same way.

On returning from her walk grannie came to my room, brought me some preachy books to read, and held out to me the privilege of saying I was sorry, and being restored to my usual place in the society of the household.

'Grannie, I cannot say I am sorry and promise to reform, for my conscience does not reproach me in the least. I had no evil—not even a violation of manners—in my intentions; but I am sorry that I vexed you,' I said.

'Vexing me is not the sinful part of it. It is your unrepentant heart that fills me with fears for your future. I will leave you here to think by yourself. The only redeeming point about you is, you do not pretend to be sorry when you are not.'

The dear old lady shook her head sorrowfully as she departed.

The afternoon soon ran away, as I turned to my bookcase for entertainment and had that beautiful ring to admire.

I heard them come in to tea, and I thought Harold had gone till I heard uncle Jay-Jay address him:

'Joe Archer told me you ran into a clothes-line on race-night, and ever since then mother has kept up a daddy of a fuss about ours. We've got props about a hundred feet long, and if you weren't in the know you'd think we had a telegraph wire to old St Peter up above.'

I wondered what Harold thought of the woman he had selected as his future wife being shut up for being a 'naughty girl'. The situation amused me exceedingly.

About nine o'clock he knocked at my window and said:

'Never mind, Syb. I tried to get you off, but it was no go. Old people often have troublesome straitlaced ideas. It will blow over by tomorrow.'

I did not answer; so he passed on with firm regular footfall, and presently I heard his horse's hoof-beats dying away in the darkness, and the closing and locking of doors around me as the household retired for the night.

During the following fortnight I saw Harold a good many times at cricket-matches, hare-drives, and so forth, but he did not take any particular notice of me. I flirted and frolicked with my other young men friends, but he did not care. I did not find him an ardent or a jealous lover. He was so irritatingly cool and matter-of-fact that I wished for the three months to pass so that I might be done with him, as I had come to the conclusion that he was barren of emotion or passion of any kind.

CHAPTER 22

Sweet Seventeen

Monday arrived—last day of November and seventeenth anniversary of my birth—and I celebrated it in a manner which I capitally enjoyed.

It was the time of the annual muster at Cummabella—a cattle-station seventeen miles eastward from Caddagat—and all our men were there assisting. Word had been sent that a considerable number of beasts among those yarded bore the impress of the Bossier brand on their hides; so on Sunday afternoon uncle Jay-Jay had also proceeded thither to be in readiness for the final drafting early on Monday morning. This left us manless, as Frank Hawden, being incapacitated with a dislocated wrist, was spending a few weeks in Gool-Gool until he should be fit for work again.

Uncle had not been gone an hour when a drover appeared to report that twenty thousand sheep would pass through on the morrow. Grass was precious. It would not do to let the sheep spread and dawdle at their drovers' pleasure. There was not a man on the place; grannie was in a great stew; so I volunteered my services. At first she would not hear of such a thing, but eventually consented. With many injunctions to conduct myself with proper stiffness, I started early on Monday morning. I was clad in a cool blouse, a holland riding-skirt, and a big straw hat; was seated on a big bay horse, was accompanied by a wonderful sheep-dog, and carried a long heavy stock-whip. I sang and cracked my stock-whip as I cantered along, quite forgetting to be reserved and proper. Presently I came upon the sheep just setting out for their day's tramp, with a black boy ahead of them, of whom I inquired which was the boss. He pointed towards a man at the rear wearing a donkey-supper hat. I made my way through the sheep in his direction, and asked if he were in charge of them. On being answered in the affirmative, I informed him that I was Mr Bossier's niece, and, as the men were otherwise engaged, I would see the sheep through.

'That's all right, miss. I will look out that you don't have much trouble,' he replied, politely raising his hat, while a look of amusement played on his face.

He rode away, and shouted to his men to keep the flock strictly within bounds and make good travelling.

'Right you are, boss,' they answered; and returning to my side he told me his name was George Ledwood, and made some remarks about the great drought and so on, while we rode in the best places to keep out of the dust and in the shade. I asked questions such as whence came the sheep? whither were they bound? and how long had they been on the road? And having exhausted these orthodox remarks, we fell a-talking in dead earnest without the least restraint. I listened with interest to stories of weeks and weeks spent beneath the sun and stars while crossing widths of saltbush country, mulga and myall scrubs, of encounters with blacks in Queensland, and was favoured with a graphic description of a big strike among the shearers when the narrator had been boss-of-the-board out beyond Bourke. He spoke as though well educated, and a gentleman—as drovers often are. Why, then, was he on the road? I put him down as a scapegrace, for he had all the winning pleasant manner of a ne'er-do-well.

At noon—a nice, blazing, dusty noon—we halted within a mile of Caddagat for lunch. I could have easily ridden home for mine, but preferred to have it with the drovers for fun. The men boiled the billy and made the tea, which we drank out of tin pots, with tinned fish and damper off tin plates as the completion of the *menu*, Mr Ledwood and I at a little distance from the men. Tea boiled in a billy at a bush fire has a deliciously aromatic flavour, and I enjoyed my birthday lunch immensely. Leaving the cook to collect the things and put them in the spring-cart, we continued on our way, lazily lolling on our horses and chewing gum-leaves as we went.

When the last of the sheep got off the Caddagat run it was nearing two o'clock.

Mr Ledwood and I shook hands at parting, each expressing a wish that we might meet again some day.

I turned and rode homewards. I looked back and saw the drover gazing after me. I waved my hand; he raised his hat and smiled, displaying his teeth, a gleam of white in his sunbrowned face. I kissed my hand to him; he bowed low; I whistled to my dog; he resumed his way behind the crawling sheep; I cantered home quickly and dismounted at the front gate at 2.30 p.m., a dusty, heated, tired girl.

Grannie came out to question me regarding the sex, age, condition, and species of the sheep, what was their destination, whether they were in search of grass or were for sale, had they spread or eaten much grass, and had the men been civil?

When I had satisfactorily informed her on all these points, she bade me have something to eat, to bathe and dress, and gave me a holiday for the remainder of the day.

My hair was grey with dust, so I washed all over, arrayed myself in a cool white dress, and throwing myself in a squatter's chair in the veranda, spread my hair over the back of it to dry. Copies of Gordon, Kendall, and Lawson were on my lap, but I was too physically content and comfortable to indulge in even these, my sworn friends and companions. I surrendered myself to the mere joy of being alive. How the sunlight blazed and danced in the roadway—the leaves of the gum-trees gleaming in it like a myriad gems! A cloud of white, which I knew to be cockatoos, circled over the distant hilltop. Nearer they wheeled until I could hear their discordant screech. The thermometer on the wall rested at 104 degrees despite the dense shade thrown on the broad old veranda by the foliage of creepers, shrubs, and trees. The gurgling rush of the creek, the scent of the flower-laden garden, and the stamp, stamp of a horse in the orchard as he attempted to rid himself of tormenting flies, filled my senses. The warmth was delightful. Summer is heavenly, I said—life is a joy.

Aunt Helen's slender fingers looked artistic among some pretty fancy-work upon which she was engaged. Bright butterflies flitted round the garden, and thousands of bees droned lazily among the flowers. I closed my eyes—my being filled with the beauty of it all.

I could hear grannie's pen fly over the paper as she made out a list of Christmas supplies on a table near me.

'Helen, I suppose a hundredweight of currants will be sufficient?'

'Yes; I should think so.'

'Seven dozen yards of unbleached calico be enough?'

'Yes; plenty.'

'Which tea-service did you order?'

'Number two.'

'Do you or Sybylla want anything extra?'

'Yes; parasols, gloves, and some books.'

'Books! Can I get them at Hordern's?'

'Yes.'

Grannie's voice faded on my ears, my thoughts ran on uncle Jay-Jay. He had promised to be home in time for my birthday spread, and I was sure he had a present for me. What would it be?—something nice. He would be nearly sure to bring someone home with him from Cummabella, and we would have games and fun to no end. I was just seventeen, only seventeen, and had a long, long life before me wherein to enjoy myself. Oh, it was good to be alive! What a delightful place the world was!— so accommodating, I felt complete mistress to it. It was like an orange—I merely had to squeeze it and it gave forth sweets plenteously. The stream sounded far away, the sunlight blazed and danced, grannie's voice was a pleasant murmur in my ear, the cockatoos screamed over the house and passed away to the west. Summer is heavenly and life is a joy, I reiterated. Joy! Joy! There was joy in the quit! quit! of the green-and-crimson parrots, which swung for a moment in the rose-bush over the gate, and then whizzed on into the summer day. There was joy in the gleam of the sun and in the hum of the bees, and it throbbed in my heart. Joy! Joy! A jackass laughed his joy as he perched on the telegraph wire out in the road. Joy! Joy! Summer is a dream of delight and life is a joy, I said in my heart. I was repeating the one thing over and over—but ah! it was a measure of happiness which allowed of much repetition. The cool murmur of the creek grew far away, I felt my poetry books slip off my knees and fall to the floor, but I was too content to bother about them—too happy to need their consolation, which I had previously so often and so hungrily sought. Youth! Joy! Warmth!

The clack of the garden gate, as it swung to, awoke me from a pleasant sleep. Grannie had left the veranda, and on the table where she had been writing aunt Helen was filling many vases with maidenhair fern and La France roses. A pleasant clatter from the dining-room announced that my birthday tea was in active preparation. The position of the yellow sunbeams at the far end of the wide veranda told that the dense shadows were lengthening, and that the last of the afternoon was wheeling westward. Taking this in, in an instant I straightened the piece of mosquito-netting, which, to protect me from the flies, some-one—auntie probably—had spread across my face, and feigned to be yet asleep. By the footsteps which sounded on the stoned garden walk, I knew that Harold Beecham was one of the individuals approaching.

'How do you do, Mrs Bell? Allow me to introduce my friend, Archie Goodchum. Mrs Bell, Mr Goodchum. Hasn't it been a roaster today? Considerably over 100 degrees in the shade. Terribly hot!'

Aunt Helen acknowledged the introduction, and seated her guests, saying:

'Harry, have you got an artistic eye? If so, you can assist me with these flowers. So might Mr Goodchum, if he feels disposed.'

Harold accepted the proposal, and remarked:

'What is the matter with your niece? It is the first time I ever saw her quiet.'

'Yes; she is a noisy little article—a perfect whirlwind in the house—but she is a little tired this afternoon; she has been seeing those sheep through today.'

'Don't you think it would be a good lark if I get something and tickle her?' said Goodchum.

'Yes, do,' said Harold; 'but look out for squalls. She is a great little fizzer.'

'Then she might be insulted.'

'Not she,' interposed auntie. 'No one will enjoy the fun more than herself.'

I had my eyes half open beneath the net, so saw him cautiously approach with a rose-stem between his fingers. Being extremely sensitive to tickling, so soon as touched under the ear I took a flying leap from the chair, somewhat disconcerting my tormentor.

He was a pleasant-looking young fellow somewhere about twenty, whose face was quite familiar to me.

He smiled so good-humouredly at me that I widely did the same in return, and he came forward with extended hand, exclaiming, 'At last!'

The others looked on in surprise, Harold remarking suspiciously, 'You said you were unacquainted with Miss Melvyn, but an introduction does not seem necessary.'

'Oh, yes it is,' chirped Mr Goodchum. 'I haven't the slightest idea of the young lady's name.'

'Don't know each other!' ejaculated Harold; and grannie, who had appeared upon the scene, inquired stiffly what we meant by such capers if unacquainted.

Mr Goodchum hastened to explain.

'I have seen the young lady on several occasions in the bank where I am employed, and I had the good fortune to be of a little service to her one day when I was out biking. Her harness, or at least the harness on the horse she was driving, broke, and I came to the rescue with my pocket-knife and some string, thereby proving, if not ornamental, I was useful. After that I tried hard to find out who she was, but my inquiries always came to nothing. I little dreamt who Miss Melvyn was when Harry, telling me she was a Goulburn girl, asked if I knew her.'

'Quite romantic,' said aunt Helen, smiling; and a great thankfulness overcame me that Mr Goodchum had been unable to discover my identity until now. It was right enough to be un-earthed as Miss Melvyn, grand-daughter of Mrs Bossier of Caddagat, and great friend and intimate of the swell Beechams of Five-Bob Downs station. At Goulburn I was only the daughter of old Dick Melvyn, broken-down farmer-cockatoo, well known by reason of his sprees about the commonest pubs in town.

Mr Goodchum told us it was his first experience of the country, and therefore he was enjoying himself immensely. He also mentioned that he was anxious to see some of the gullies around Caddagat, which, he had heard, were renowned for the beauty of their ferns. Aunt Helen, accordingly, proposed a walk in the direction of one of them, and hurried off to attend to a little matter before starting. While waiting for her, Harold happened to say it was my birthday, and Mr Goodchum tendered me the orthodox wishes, remarking, 'It is surely pardonable at your time of life to ask what age you have attained today?'

'Seventeen.'

'Oh! oh! "sweet seventeen, and never been kissed"; but I suppose you cannot truthfully say that, Miss Melvyn?'

'Oh yes, I can.'

'Well, you won't be able to say it much longer,' he said, making a suggestive move in my direction. I ran, and he followed, grannie reappearing from the dining-room just in time to see me bang the garden gate with great force on my pursuer.

'What on earth is the girl doing now?' I heard her inquire.

However, Mr Goodchum did not execute his threat; instead we walked along decorously in the direction of the nearest ferns, while Harold and aunt Helen followed, the latter carrying a sun-bonnet for me.

After we had climbed some distance up a gully aunt Helen called out that she and Harold would rest while I did the honours of the fern grots to my companion.

We went on and on, soon getting out of sight of the others.

'What do you say to my carving our names on a gum-tree, the bark is so nice and soft?' said the bank clerk; and I seconded the proposal.

'I will make it allegorical,' he remarked, setting to work.

He was very deft with his penknife, and in a few minutes had carved S. P. M. and A. S. G., encircling the initials by a ring and two hearts interlaced.

'That'll do nicely,' he remarked, and turning round, 'Why, you'll get a sunstroke; do take my hat.'

I demurred, he pressed the matter, and I agreed on condition he allowed me to tie his handkerchief over his head. I was wearing his hat and tying the ends of a big silk handkerchief beneath his chin when the cracking of a twig caused me to look up and see Harold Beecham with an expression on his face that startled me.

'Your aunt sent me on with your hood,' he said jerkily.

'You can wear it—I've been promoted,' I said flippantly, raising my head-gear to him and bowing. He did not laugh as he usually did at my tricks, but frowned darkly instead.

'We've been carving our names, at least, I have,' remarked Goodchum.

Harold tossed my sun-bonnet on the ground, and said shortly, 'Come on, Goodchum, we must be going.'

'Oh, don't go, Mr Beecham. I thought you came on purpose for my birthday tea. Auntie has made me a tremendous cake. You must stay. We never dreamt of you doing anything else.'

'I've changed my mind,' he replied, striding on at such a pace that we had difficulty in keeping near him. As we resumed our own head-wear, Goodchum whispered, 'A bulldog ant must have stung the boss. Let's ask him.'

On reaching the house we found other company had arrived in the persons of young Mr Goodjay from Cummabella, his sister, her governess, and a couple of jackeroos. They were seated on the veranda, and uncle Jay-Jay, attired in his shirt-sleeves, was appearing through the dining-room door with half a dozen bottles of home-made ginger ale in his arms. Dumping them down on the floor, he produced a couple of tots from his shirt-pockets, saying, 'Who votes for a draw of beer? Everyone must feel inclined for a swig. Harry, you want some; you don't look as though the heat was good for your temper. Hullo, Archie! Got up this far. Take a draw out of one of these bottles. If there had been a dozen pubs on the road, I'd have drunk every one of 'em dry today. I never felt such a daddy of a thirst on me before.'

'Good gracious, Julius!' exclaimed grannie, as he offered the governess a pot full of beer, 'Miss Craddock can't drink out of that pint.'

'Those who don't approve of my pints, let 'em bring their own,' said that mischievous uncle Jay-Jay, who was a great hand at acting the clown when he felt that way inclined.

I was dispatched for glasses, and after emptying the bottles uncle proposed a game of tennis first, while the light lasted, and tea afterwards. This proposition being carried with acclamation, we proceeded to the tennis court. Harold came too—he had apparently altered his intention of going home immediately.

There were strawberries to be had in the orchard, also some late cherries, so uncle ordered me to go and get some. I procured a basket, and willingly agreed to obey him. Mr Goodchum offered to accompany me, but Harold stepped forward saying he would go, in such a resolute tragic manner that Goodchum winked audaciously, saying waggishly, 'Behold, the hero descends into the burning mine!'

CHAPTER 23

Ah, For One Hour of Burning Love, 'Tis Worth an Age of Cold Respect!

We walked in perfect silence, Harold not offering to carry my little basket. I did not dare lift my eyes, as something told me the face of the big man would not be pleasant to look upon just then. I twirled the ring he had given me round and round my finger. I occasionally put it on, wearing the stones on the palm-side of my finger, so that it would not be taken for other than one of two or three aunt Helen had lent me, saying I was at liberty to use them while at Caddagat, if it gave me any pleasure.

The Caddagat orchard contained six acres, and being a narrow enclosure, and the cherries growing at the extreme end from the house, it took us some time to reach them. I led the way to our destination—a secluded nook where grape-vines clambered up fig-trees, and where the top of gooseberry bushes met the lower limbs of cherry-trees. Blue and yellow lupins stood knee-high, and strawberries grew wild among them. We had not uttered a sound, and I had not glanced at my companion. I stopped; he wheeled abruptly and grasped my wrist in a manner which sent the basket whirling from my hand. I looked up at his face, which was blazing with passion, and dark with a darker tinge than Nature and the sun had given it, from the shapely swelling neck, in its soft well-turned-down collar, to where the stiff black hair, wet with perspiration, hung on the wide forehead.

'Unhand me, sir!' I said shortly, attempting to wrench myself free, but I might as well have tried to pull away from a lion.

'Unhand me!' I repeated.

For answer he took a firmer hold, in one hand seizing my arm above the elbow, and gripping my shoulder with the other so tightly that, through my flimsy covering, his strong fingers bruised me so severely that in a calmer moment I would have squirmed and cried out with pain.

'How dare you touch me!' He drew me so closely to him that, through his thin shirt—the only garment on the upper part of his figure—I could feel the heat of his body, and his big heart beating wildly.

At last! at last! I had waked this calm silent giant into life. After many an ineffectual struggle I had got at a little real love or passion, or call it by any name—something wild and warm and splendidly alive that one could feel, the most thrilling, electric, and exquisite sensation known.

I thoroughly enjoyed the situation, but did not let this appear. A minute or two passed and he did not speak.

'Mr Beecham, I'll trouble you to explain yourself. How dare you lay your hands upon me?'

'Explain!' he breathed rather than spoke, in a tone of concentrated fury. 'I'll make *you* explain, and I'll do what I like with you. I'll touch you as much as I think fit. I'll throw you over the fence if *you* don't explain to *my* satisfaction.'

'What is there that I can explain?'

'Explain your conduct with other men. How dare you receive their attentions and be so friendly with them!'

'How dare you speak to me like that! I reserve the right of behaving as I please without your permission.'

'I won't have a girl with my engagement ring on her finger going on as you do. I think I have a right to complain, for I could get any amount of splendid women in every way to wear it for me, and behave themselves properly too,' he said fiercely.

I tossed my head defiantly, saying, 'Loose your hold of me, and I'll quickly explain matters to my own satisfaction and yours, Harold Beecham.'

He let me go, and I stepped a pace or two away from him, drew the costly ring from my finger, and, with indifference and contempt, tossed it to his feet, where the juice of crushed strawberries was staining the ground, and facing him, said mockingly:

'Now, speak to the girl who wears your engagement ring,

for I'll degrade myself by wearing it no more. If you think I think you as great a catch as you think yourself, just because you have a little money, you are a trifle mistaken, Mr Beecham, that is all. Ha ha ha! So you thought you had a right to lecture me as your future slave! Just fancy! I never had the slightest intention of marrying you. You were so disgustingly conceited that I have been attempting to rub a little of it out of you. Marry you! Ha ha! Because the social laws are so arranged that a woman's only sphere is marriage, and because they endeavour to secure a man who can give them a little more ease, you must not run away with the idea that it is yourself they are angling for, when you are only the bothersome appendage with which they would have to put up, for the sake of your property. And you must not think that because some women will marry for a home they all will. I trust I have explained to your satisfaction, Mr Beecham. Ha ha ha!'

The jealous rage had died out of his face and was succeeded by trembling and a pallor so ghastly, that I began to have a little faith in descriptions of love which I had hitherto ridiculed.

'Are you in earnest?' he asked in a deadly calm voice.

'Most emphatically I am.'

'Then all I can say is that I haven't much respect for you, Miss Melvyn. I always considered that there were three classes of women—one, that would marry a blackfellow if he had money; another, that were shameless flirts, and who amuse themselves by flirting and disgracing the name of woman; and a third class that were pure and true, on whom a man could stake his life and whom he could worship. I thought you belonged to this class, but I have been mistaken. I know you always try to appear heartless and worthless, but I fancied it was only your youth and mischief, and imagined you were good underneath; but I have been mistaken,' he repeated with quiet contempt.

His face had regained its natural colour, and the well-cut pleasant mouth, clearly seen beneath the soft drooping moustache, had hardened into a sullen line which told me he would never be first to seek reconciliation—not even to save his life.

'Bah!' I exclaimed sarcastically. 'It appears that we all labour under delusions. Go and get a beautiful woman to wear your ring and your name. One that will be able to say yes and no at the right time; one who will know how to dress properly; one who wouldn't for the world do anything that other women did not also; one who will know where to buy the best groceries and who will readily sell herself to you for your wealth. That's the sort of woman that suits men, and there are plenty of them; procure one, and don't bother with me. I am too small and silly, and have nothing to recommend me. I fear it speaks little for your sense or taste that you ever thought of me. Ta-ta, Mr Beecham,' I said over my shoulder with a mocking smile, and walked away.

When about half-way down the orchard reflection pulled me up shortly under an apple-tree.

I had said what I had said because, feeling bitter for the want of love, and because full of pain myself, I rejoiced with a sort of revenge to see the same feeling flash across another's face. But now I was cool, and, forgetting myself, thought of Harold.

I had led him on because his perpetually calm demeanour had excited in me a desire to test if it were possible to disturb him. I had thought him incapable of emotion, but he had proved himself a man of strong and deep emotion; might he not also be capable of feeling—of love? He had not been mean or nasty in his rage, and his anger had been righteous. By accepting his proposal of marriage, I had given him the right of expressing his objection to any of my actions of which he disapproved. I on my part had the liberty of trying to please him or of dissolving our engagement. Perhaps in some cases there was actually something more than wounded vanity when a man's alleged love was rejected or spurned. Harold had seemed to suffer, to really experience keen disappointment. I was clearly in the wrong, and had been unwomanly beyond a doubt, as, granting that Harold Beecham was conceited, what right had I to constitute myself his judge or to take into my own hands the responsibility of correcting him? I felt ashamed of my conduct; I was sorry to have hurt any one's feelings. Moreover, I cannot bear to be at ill-will with my fellows, and am ever the first to give in after having quarrelled. It is easier than sulking, and it always makes the other party so self-complacent that it is amusing as well as convenient, and—and—and—I found I was very, very fond of Harold Beecham.

I crept noiselessly up the orchard. He had his back to me, and had moved to where a post of the fence was peeping out among the greenery. He had his elbow placed thereon, and his forehead resting on his hand. His attitude expressed dejection. Maybe he was suffering the torture of a broken ideal.

His right hand hung limply by his side. I do not think he heard me approach.

My heart beat quickly, and a fear that he would snub me caused me to pause. Then I nerved myself with the thought that it would be only fair if he did. I had been rude to him, and he had a right to play tit-for-tat if he felt so disposed. I expected my action to be spurned or ignored, so very timidly slipped my fingers into his palm. I need not have been nervous, for the strong brown hand, which had never been known to strike a cowardly blow, completely enfolded mine in a gentle caressing clasp.

'Mr Beecham, Harold, I am so sorry I was so unwomanly, and said such horrible things. Will you forgive me, and let us start afresh?' I murmured. All flippancy, bitterness, and amusement had died out of me; I was serious and in earnest. This must have expressed itself in my eyes, for Harold, after gazing searchingly right there for a time, seemed satisfied, and his mouth relaxed to its habitually lovable expression as he said:

'Are you in earnest? Well, that is something more like the little woman.'

'Yes, I'm in earnest. Can you forgive me?'

'There is nothing to forgive, as I'm sure you didn't mean and don't remember the blood curdling sentiments you aired.'

'But I did mean them in one sort of a way, and didn't in another. Let us start afresh.'

'How do you mean to start afresh?'

'I mean for us to be chums again.'

'Oh, chums!' he said impatiently; 'I want to be something more.'

'Well, I will be something more if you will try to make me,' I replied.

'How? What do you mean?'

'I mean you never try to make me fond of you. You have never uttered one word of love to me.'

'Why, bless me!' he ejaculated in surprise.

'It's a fact. I have only flirted to try and see if you cared, but you didn't care a pin.'

'Why, bless me, didn't you say I was not to show any affection yet awhile? And talk about not caring—why, I have felt fit to kill you and myself many a time the last fortnight, you have tormented me so; but I have managed to keep myself within bounds till now. Will you wear my ring again?'

'Oh no; and you must not say I am flirting if I cannot manage to love you enough to marry you, but I will try my best.'

'Don't you love me, Syb? I have thought of nothing else but you night and day since I saw you first. Can it be possible that you don't care a straw for me?' and a pained expression came upon his face.

'Oh, Harold, I'm afraid I very nearly love you, but don't hurry me too much! You can think me sort of secretly engaged to you if you like, but I won't take your ring. Keep it till we see how we get on.' I looked for it, and finding it a few steps away, gave it to him.

'Can you really trust me again after seeing me get in such a vile beast of a rage? I often do that, you know,' he said.

'Believe me, Hal, I liked it so much I wish you would get in a rage again. I can't bear people who never let themselves go, or rather, who have nothing in them to carry them away—they cramp and bore me.'

'But I have a frightful temper. Satan only knows what I will do in it yet. Would you not be frightened of me?'

'No fear,' I laughed; 'I would defy you.'

'A tomtit might as well defy me,' he said with amusement.

164

'Well, big as you are, a tomtit having such superior facilities for getting about could easily defy you,' I replied.

'Yes, unless it was caged,' he said.

'But supposing you never got it caged,' I returned.

'Syb, what do you mean?'

'What could I mean?'

'I don't know. There are always about four or five meanings in what you say.'

'Oh, thanks, Mr Beecham! You must be very astute. I am always thankful when I am able to dish one meaning of my idle gabble.'

The glorious summer day had fallen asleep on the bosom of the horizon, and twilight had merged into dusk, as, picking up the basket, Harold and I returned cherry- and strawberry-less to the tennis court. The players had just ceased action, and the gentlemen were putting on their coats. Harold procured his, and thrust his arms into it, while we were attacked on all sides by a flood of banter.

My birthday tea was a great success, and after it was done we enjoyed ourselves in the drawing-room. Uncle Jay-Jay handed me a large box, saying it contained a present. Everyone looked on with interest while I hurriedly opened it, when they were much amused to see—nothing but a doll and materials to make it clothes! I was much disappointed, but uncle said it would be more in my line to play with that than to worry about tramps and politics.

I took care to behave properly during the evening, and when the good-byes were in full swing had an opportunity of a last word with Harold, he stooping to hear me whisper:

'Now that I know you care, I will not annoy you any more by flirting.'

'Don't talk like that. I was only mad for a moment. Enjoy yourself as much as you like. I don't want you to be like a nun. I'm not quite so selfish as that. When I look at you and see how tiny you are, and how young, I feel it is brutal to worry you at all, and you don't detest me altogether for getting in such an infernal rage?'

'No. That is the very thing I liked. Good night!'

'Good night,' he replied, taking both my hands in his. 'You are the best little woman in the world, and I hope we will spend all your other birthdays together.'

'It's to be hoped you've said something to make Harry a trifle sweeter than he was this afternoon,' said Goodchum. Then it was:

'Good night, Mrs Bossier! Good night, Harry! Good night, Archie! Good night, Mr Goodchum! Good-bye, Miss Craddock! Ta-ta, Miss Melvyn! So long, Jay-Jay! Good-bye, Mrs Bell! Good-bye, Miss Goodjay! Good night, Miss Melvyn! Good night, Mr Goodjay! Good night, Mrs Bossier! Good-bye, Miss Melvyn! Good night all!'

I sat long by my writing-table that night—thinking long, long thoughts, foolish thoughts, sad ones, merry ones, old-headed thoughts, and the sweet, sweet thoughts of youth and love. It seemed to me that men were not so invincible and invulnerable as I had imagined them—it appeared they had feeling and affections after all.

I laughed a joyous little laugh, saying, 'Hal, we are quits,' when, on disrobing for the night, I discovered on my soft white shoulders and arms—so susceptible to bruises—many marks, and black.

It had been a very happy day for me.

CHAPTER 24

Thou Knowest Not What a Day May Bring Forth

The next time I saw Harold Beecham was on Sunday the 13th of December. There was a hammock swinging under a couple of trees in an enclosure, half shrubbery, partly orchard and vegetable garden, skirting the road. In this I was gently swinging to and fro, and very much enjoying an interesting book and some delicious gooseberries, and seeing Harold approaching pretended to be asleep, to see if he would kiss me. But no, he was not that style of man. After tethering his horse to the fence and vaulting himself over it, he shook me and informed me I was as sound asleep as a log, and had required no end of waking.

My hair tumbled down. I accused him of disarranging it, and ordered him to repair the damage. He couldn't make out what was the matter with it, only that 'It looks a bit dotty.'

'Men are queer creatures,' I returned. 'They have the most wonderful brains in some ways, but in little things they are as stupid as owls. It is no trouble to them to master geology, mineralogy, anatomy, and other things, the very name of which gives me a headache. They can see through politics, mature mighty water reservoir schemes, and manage five stations at once, but they couldn't sew on a button or fix one's hair to save their life.'

I cannot imagine how the news had escaped me, for the story with which Harold Beecham surprised and startled me on that long hot afternoon had been common talk for some time.

He had come to Caddagat purposely to explain his affairs to me, and stated as his reason for not having done so earlier that he had waited until the last moment thinking he might pull himself up.

Business to me is a great mystery, into which I haven't the slightest desire to penetrate. I have no brains in that direction, so will not attempt to correctly reproduce all that Harold Beecham told me on that afternoon while leaning against a tree at my feet and looking down at me as I reclined in the hammock.

There was great mention of bogus bonds, bad investments, liabilities and assets and personal estates, and of a thing called an official assignee—whatever that is—voluntary sequestration, and a jargon of such terms that were enough to mither a Barcoo lawyer.

The gist of the matter, as I gathered it, was that Harold Beecham, looked upon as such a 'lucky beggar', and envied as a pet of fortune, had been visited by an unprecedented run of crushing misfortunes. He had not been as rich and sound in position as the public had imagined him to be. The failure of a certain bank two or three years previously had given him a great shaking. The tick plague had ruined him as regarded his Queensland property, and the drought had made matters nearly as bad for him in New South Wales. The burning of his wool last year, and the failure of the agents in whose hands he had placed it, this had pushed him farther into the mire, and now the recent 'going bung' of a building society—his sole remaining prop— had run him entirely ashore.

He had sequestrated his estate, and as soon as practicable was going through the courts as an insolvent. The personal estate allowed him from the debris of his wealth he intended to settle on his aunts, and he hoped it might be sufficient to support them. Himself, he had the same prospects as the boundary-riders on Five-Bob Downs.

I had nothing to say. Not that Harold was a much-to-be-pitied man when one contrasted his lot with that of millions of his fellows as deserving as he; but, on the other hand, considering he had been reared in wealth and as the master of it since his birth, to be suddenly rendered equal with a labourer was pretty hard lines.

'Oh, Harold, I am so sorry for you!' I managed to stammer at last.

'Don't worry about me. There's many a poor devil, crippled and ill, though rolling in millions, who would give all his wealth to stand in my boots today,' he said, drawing his splendid figure to its full height, while a look of stern pride settled on the strong features. Harold Beecham was not a whimpering cur. He would never tell anyone his feelings on the subject; but such a sudden reverse of fortune, tearing from him even his home, must have been a great blow to him.

'Syb, I have been expecting this for some years; now that it is done with, it is a sort of grim relief. The worst of all is that I've had to give up all hope of winning you. That is the worst of all. If you didn't care for me when I was thought to be in a position to give you all that girls like, you could never look at me now that I'm a pauper. I only hope you will get some fellow who will make you as happy as I would have tried to had you let me.'

I sat and wondered at the marvellous self-containment of the man before me. With this crash impending, just imagine the worry he must have gone through! But never had the least suspicion that he was troubled found betrayal on his brow.

'Good-bye, Syb,' he said; 'though I'm a nobody now, if I could ever be of use to you, don't be afraid to ask me.'

I remember him wringing the limp hand I mechanically stretched out to him and then slowly revaulting the fence. The look of him riding slowly along with his broad shoulders drooping despondently waked me to my senses. I had been fully engrossed with the intelligence of Harold's misfortune—that I was of sufficient importance to concern him in any way had not entered my head; but it suddenly dawned on me that Harold had said that I was, and he was not in the habit of uttering idle nothings.

While fortune smiled on him I had played with his manly love, but now that she frowned had let him go without even a word of friendship. I had been poor myself, and knew what awaited him in the world. He would find that they who fawned on him most would be first to turn their backs on him now. He would be rudely disillusioned regarding the fables of love and friendship, and would become cynical, bitter, and sceptical of there being any disinterested good in human nature. Suffering the cold heart-weariness of this state myself, I felt anxious at any price to save Harold Beecham from a like fate. It would be a pity to let one so young be embittered in that way.

There was a short cut across the paddocks to a point of the road where he would pass; and with these thought flashing through my mind, hatless and with flying hair, I ran as fast as I could, scrambling up on the fence in a breathless state just as he had passed.

'Hal, Hal!' I called. 'Come back, come back! I want you.'

He turned his horse slowly.

'Well, Syb, what is it?'

'Oh, Hal, dear Hal! I was thinking too much to say anything; but you surely don't think I'd be so mean as to care a pin whether you are rich or poor—only for your own sake? If you really want me, I will marry you when I am twenty-one if you are as poor as a crow.'

'It is too good to be true. I thought you didn't care for me. Sybylla, what do you mean?'

'Just what I say,' I replied, and without further explanation, jumping off the fence I ran back as fast as I had come.

When half-way home I stopped, turned, looked, and saw Harold cantering smartly homewards, and heard him whistling a merry tune as he went.

After all, men are very weak and simple in some ways.

I laughed long and sardonically, apostrophizing myself thus:

'Sybylla Penelope Melvyn, your conceit is marvellous and unparalleled! So you actually imagined that you were of sufficient importance to assist a man through life—a strong, healthy young man too, standing six feet three and a half in his socks, a level-headed business man, a man of high connections, spotless character, and influential friends, an experienced bushman, a man of sense, and, above all, a man—a man! The world was made for men.

'Ha ha! You, Sybylla, thought this! You, a hit in your teens, an ugly, poor, useless, unimportant, little handful of human flesh, and, above, or rather below, all, a woman—only a woman! It would indeed be a depraved and forsaken man who would need your services as a stay and support! Ha ha! The conceit of you!'

CHAPTER 25

Because?

The Beechams were vacating Five-Bob almost immediately—
before Christmas. Grannie, aunt Helen, and uncle Jay-Jay went
down to say good-bye to the ladies, who were very heartbroken
about being uprooted from Five-Bob, but they approved of their
nephew settling things at once and starting on a clean sheet.
They intended taking up their residence—hiding themselves, they
termed it—in Melbourne. Harold would be detained in Sydney
some time during the settling of his affairs, after which he intended
to take anything that turned up. He had been offered the management of Five-Bob by those in authority, but could not bring
himself to accept managership where he had been master. His
great desire, now that Five-Bob was no longer his, was to get
as far away from old associations as possible.

He had seen his aunts off, superintended the muster of all stock
on the place, dismissed all the female and most of the male
employees, and surrendered the reins of government, and as
Harold Augustus Beecham, boss of Five-Bob, on Monday, the
21st of December 1896, was leaving the district for ever. On
Sunday, the 20th of December, he came to bid us good-bye and
to arrive at an understanding with me concerning what I had
said to him the Sunday before. Grannie, strange to say, never
suspected that there was likely to be anything between us. Harold
was so undemonstrative, and had always come and gone as he
liked at Caddagat: she overlooked the possibility of his being
a lover, and in our intercourse allowed us almost the freedom
of sister and brother or cousins.

On this particular afternoon, after we had talked to grannie
for a little while, knowing that he wished to interview me, I
suggested that he should come up the orchard with me and get
some gooseberries. Without demur from anybody we set off, and

were scarcely out of hearing before Harold asked me had I really meant what I said.

'Certainly,' I replied. 'That is, if you really care for me, and think it wise to choose me of all my sex.'

Ere he put it in words I read his answer in the clear brown eyes bent upon me.

'Syb, you know what I feel and would like, but I think it would be mean of me to allow you to make such a sacrifice.'

I knew I was not dealing with a booby, but with a sensible clear-sighted man, and so studied to express myself in a way which would not for an instant give him the impression that I was promising to marry him because—what I don't know and it doesn't matter much, but I said:

'Hal, don't you think it is a little selfish of you to want to throw me over just because you have lost your money? You are young, healthy, have good character and influential connections, and plenty of good practical ability and sense, so, surely, you will know no such thing as failure if you meet the world bravely. Go and be the man you are; and if you fail, when I am twenty-one I will marry you, and we will help each other. I am young and strong, and am used to hard work, so poverty will not alarm me in the least. If you want me, I want you.'

'Syb, you are such a perfect little brick that I couldn't be such a beggarly cur as to let you do that. I knew you were as true as steel under your funny little whims and contrariness; and could you really love me now that I am poor?'

I replied with vigour:

'Do you think I am that sort, that cares for a person only because he has a little money? Why! that is the very thing I am always preaching against. If a man was a lord or a millionaire I would not have him if I loved him not, but I would marry a poor cripple if I loved him. It wasn't because you owned Five-Bob Downs that I liked you, but because you have a big heart in which one would have room to get warm, and because you are true, and because you are kind and big and—' Here I could feel my voice getting shaky, and being afraid I would make a fool of myself by crying, I left off.

'Syb, I will try and fix matters up a bit, and will claim you in that time if I have a home.'

'Claim me, home or not, if you are so disposed, but I will make this condition. Do not tell anyone we are engaged, and remember you are perfectly free. If you see a woman you like more than me, promise me on your sacred word that you will have none of those idiotic unjust ideas of keeping true to me. Promise.'

'Yes, I will promise,' he said easily, thinking then, no doubt, as many a one before him has thought, that he would never be called upon to fulfil his word.

'I will promise in return that I will not look at another man in a matrimonial way until the four years are up, so you need not be jealous and worry yourself; for, Hal, you can trust me, can you not?'

Taking my hand in his and looking at me with a world of love in his eyes, which moved me in spite of myself, he said:

'I could trust you in every way to the end of the world.'

'Thank you, Harold. What we have said is agreed upon—that is, of course, as things appear now: if anything turns up to disturb this arrangement it is not irrevocable in the least degree, and we can lay out more suitable plans. Four years will not be long, and I will be more sensible at the end of that time—that is, of course, if I ever have any sense. We will not write or have any communication, so you will be perfectly free if you see anyone you like better than me to go in and win. Do you agree?'

'Certainly; any little thing like that you can settle according to your fancy. I'm set up as long as I get you one way or another—that's all I want. It was a bit tough being cleared out from all the old ways, but if I have you to stand by me it will be a great start. Say what you said last Sunday, again. Syb, say you will be my wife.'

I had expected him to put it in that way, and believing in doing all or nothing, had laid out that I would put my hand in his and promise what he asked. But now the word wife finished me up. I was very fond of Harold—fond to such an extent that had I a fortune I would gladly have given it all to him: I felt capable of giving him a life of servitude, but I loved him—big, manly, lovable, wholesome Harold—from the crown of his head to the sole of his foot he was good in my sight, but lacking in that power over me which would make me desirous of being the mother of his children.

As for explaining my feelings to him—ha! He would laughingly call them one of my funny little whims. With his orthodox, practical, plain, commonsense views of these things, he would not understand me. What was there to understand? Only that I was queer and different from other women. But he was waiting for me to speak. I had put my hand to the plough and could not turn back. I could not use the word wife, but I put my hand in his, looked at him steadily, and said—

'Harold, I meant what I said last Sunday. If you want me— if I am of any use to you—I will marry you when I attain my majority.'

He was satisfied.

He bade us good-bye early that afternoon, as he intended departing from Five-Bob when the morrow was young, and had two or three little matters to attend to previous to his departure.

I accompanied him a little way, he walking and leading his horse. We parted beneath the old willow-tree.

'Good-bye, Harold. I mean all I have said.'

I turned my face upwards; he stooped and kissed me once— only once—one light, gentle, diffident kiss. He looked at me long and intently without saying a word, then mounted his horse, raised his hat, and rode away.

I watched him depart along the white dusty road, looking like a long snake in the glare of the summer sun, until it and he who travelled thereon disappeared among the messmate- and hickory-trees forming the horizon.

I stood gazing at the hills in the distance on which the blue dreaming mists of evening were gathering, until tears stole down my cheeks.

I was not given to weeping. What brought them? I hardly knew. It was not because Harold was leaving, though I would miss him much. Was it because I was disappointed in love? I persuaded myself that I loved Harold as much as I could ever love any one, and I could not forsake him now that he needed me. But, but, but, I did not want to marry, and I wished that Harold had asked anything of me but that, because—because, I don't know what, and presently felt ashamed for being such a selfish coward that I grudged to make a little sacrifice of my own inclinations to help a brother through life.

'I used to feel sure that Harry meant to come up to the scratch, but I suppose he's had plenty to keep him going lately without bothering his head about a youngster in short frocks and a pig-tail,' remarked uncle Jay-Jay that night.

'Well, Sybylla, poor Harry has gone: we will all—even you included—miss him very much, I am sure. I used to think that he cared for you. It may be that he has not spoken to us on account of his financial failure, and it may be that I made a mistake,' said aunt Helen when she was bidding me good night.

I held my peace.

CHAPTER 26

Boast Not Thyself of Tomorrow

We felt the loss of the Beechams very, very much. It was sad
to think of Five-Bob—pleasant, hospitable Five-Bob—as shut up,
with no one but a solitary caretaker there pending the settling
of the Beecham insolvency; with flowers running to seed un-
heeded in the wide old garden, grass yellowing on the lawns,
fruit wasting in wain-loads in the great orchard, kennels, stables,
fowl-houses, and cow-yards empty and deserted. But more than
all, we missed the quiet, sunburnt, gentlemanly, young giant whose
pleasant countenance and strapping figure were always welcome
at Caddagat.

Fortunately, Christmas preparations gave us no rest for the
soles of our feet, and thus we had little time to moon about
such things: in addition, uncle Jay-Jay was preparing for a trip,
and fussed so that the whole place was kept in a state of ferment.

We had fun, feasting, and company to no end on Christmas
Day. There were bank clerks and young fellows out of offices
from Gool-Gool, jackeroos and governesses in great force from
neighbouring holdings, and we had a merry time.

On Boxing Day uncle Jay-Jay set out on a tour to New Zealand,
intending to combine business with pleasure, as he meant to bring
back some stud stock if he could make a satisfactory bargain.
Boxing Day had fallen on a Saturday that year, and the last of
our guests departed on Sunday morning. It was the first time
we had had any quietude for many weeks, so in the afternoon
I went out to swing in my hammock and meditate upon things
in general. Taking with me a bountiful supply of figs, apricots,
and mulberries, I laid myself out for a deal of enjoyment in the
cool dense shade under the leafy kurrajong- and cedar-trees.

To begin with, Harold Beecham was gone, and I missed him
at every turn. I need not worry about being engaged to be married,

as four years was a long, long time. Before that Harold might take a face to someone else, and leave me free; or he might die, or I might die, or we both might die, or fly, or cry, or sigh, or do one thing or another, and in the meantime that was not the only thing to occupy my mind: I had much to contemplate with joyful anticipation.

Towards the end of February a great shooting and camping party, organized by grannie, was to take place. Aunt Helen, grannie, Frank Hawden, myself, and a number of other ladies and gentlemen, were going to have ten days or a fortnight in tents among the blue hills in the distance, which held many treasures in the shape of lyrebirds, musk, ferns, and such scenery as would make the thing perfection. After this auntie and I were to have our three months' holiday in Sydney, where, with Everard Grey in the capacity of showman, we were to see everything from Manly to Parramatta, the Cyclorama to the Zoo, the theatres to the churches, the restaurants to the jails, and from Anthony Hordern's to Paddy's Market. Who knows what might happen then? Everard had promised to have my talents tested by good judges. Might it not be possible for me to attain one of my ambitions—enter the musical profession? Joyful dream! Might I not be able to yet assist Harold in another way than matrimony?

Yes, life was a pleasant thing to me now. I forgot all my wild unattainable ambitions in the little pleasures of everyday life. Such a thing as writing never entered my head. I occasionally dreamt out a little yarn which, had it appeared on paper, would have brimmed over with pleasure and love—in fact, have been redolent of life as I found it. It was nice to live in comfort, and among ladies and gentlemen—people who knew how to conduct themselves properly, and who paid one every attention without a bit of fear of being twitted with 'laying the jam on'.

I ate another fig and apricot, a mulberry or two, and was interrupted in the perusal of my book by the clatter of galloping hoofs approaching along the road. I climbed on to the fence to see who it could be who was coming at such a breakneck pace. He pulled the rein opposite me, and I recognized a man from

Dogtrap. He was in his shirt-sleeves; his horse was all in a lather, and its scarlet nostrils were wide open, and its side heaving rapidly.

'I say, miss, hunt up the men quickly, will you?' he said hurriedly. 'There's a tremenjous fire on Wyambeet, and we're short-handed. I'm goin' on to knock them up at Bimbalong.'

'Hold hard,' I replied. 'We haven't a man on the place, only Joe Slocombe, and I heard him say he would ride down the river and see what the smoke was about; so he will be there. Mr Hawden and the others have gone out for the day. You go back to the fire at once; I'll rouse them up at Bimbalong.'

'Right you are, miss. Here's a couple of letters. My old moke flung a shoe and went dead lame at Dogtrap; an' wile I was saddlun another, Mrs Butler stuffed 'em in me pocket.'

He tossed them over the fence, and, wheeling his mount, galloped the way he had come. The letters fell, address upwards, on the ground—one to myself and one to grannie, both in my mother's handwriting. I left them where they lay. The main substance of mother's letters to me was a hope that I was a better girl to my grannie than I had been to her—a sentiment which did not interest me.

'Where are you off to?' inquired grannie, as I rushed through the house.

I explained.

'What horse are you going to take?'

'Old Tadpole. He's the only one available.'

'Well, you be careful and don't push him too quickly up that pinch by Flea Creek, or he might drop dead with you. He's so fat and old.'

'All right,' I replied, snatching a bridle and running up the orchard, where old Tadpole had been left in case of emergency. I clapped a side-saddle on his back, a hat on my head, jumped on just as I was, and galloped for my life in the direction of Bimbalong, seven miles distant. I eased my horse a little going up Flea Creek pinch, but with this delay reached my destination in half an hour, and sent the men galloping in the direction of the fire. I lingered for afternoon tea, and returned at my leisure.

It was sundown when I got in sight of Caddagat. Knowing the men would not be home for some time, I rode across the paddock to yard the cows. I drove them home and penned the calves, unsaddled my horse and returned him to the orchard, then stood upon the hillside and enjoyed the scene. It had been a fearfully hot day, with a blasting, drought-breathed wind; but the wind had dropped to sleep with the sunlight, and now the air had cooled. Blue smoke wreathed hill and hollow like a beauteous veil. I had traversed drought-baked land that after-noon, but in the immediate vicinity of Caddagat house there was no evidence of an unkind season. Irrigation had draped the place with beauty, and I stood ankle-deep in clover. Oh, how I loved the old irregularly built house, with here and there a patch of its low iron roof peeping out of a mass of greenery, flowers, and fruit—the place where I was born—home! Save for the murmur of the creek, the evening was wrapped in silence—sweet-breathed, balmy-browed, summer quietude. I stretched out my hand and stained my fingers, next my lips and teeth, with the sweet dark fruit of a mulberry-tree beside me. The shadows deepened; I picked up my sadde, and, carrying it housewards, put it in its place in the harness-room among the fig- and apricot-trees—laden to breaking point with ripe and ripening fruit. The two servant girls had departed on their Christmas holiday that morning, so grannie and auntie were the only members of the family at home. I could not see or hear them anywhere, so, presuming they were out walking, I washed my hands, lit a lamp, and sat down to my tea, where it had been left for me on the dining-table. I remembered—wonderful aberration from my usual thoughtlessness—that the book I had left in the hammock had a beautiful cover which the dew would spoil, so I left my tea to bring it in. Two little white squares struck my eye in the gathering dusk. I picked them up also, and, bringing them to the light, opened the one addressed to me, and read:

No doubt what I have to write will not be very palatable to you; but it is time you gave up pleasuring and began to meet the responsibilities of life. Your father is lazier if anything,

and drinks more than ever. He has got himself into great debt
and difficulties, and would have been sold off again but for
Peter M'Swat. You will remember Peter M'Swat? Well, he has
been good enough to lend your father £500 at 4 per cent,
which means £20 per year interest. Your father would have
no more idea of meeting this amount than a cat would have.
But now I am coming to the part of the matter which
concerns you. Out of friendship to your father, Mr M'Swat is
good enough to accept your services as governess to his
children, in lieu of interest on the money. I have told him you
will be in Yarnung on Friday the 8th of January 1897, where
he will meet you. Be careful to remember the date. I am sorry
I could not give you more notice; but he wants his children to
commence school as soon as possible, and he deserves every
consideration in the matter. Perhaps you will not find it as
pleasant as Caddagat; but he has been very good, and offers
you a fair number of holidays, and what he will give you is
equal to £20. That is a lot in these times, when he could easily
get so many better girls than you are in every way for half the
money, and make your father pay the interest, and thereby be
£10 in pocket. You will have to help Mrs M'Swat with the
work and sewing; but that will do you good, and I hope you
will try hard to give every satisfaction. I have also written to
your grandmother.

That letter wiped away every vestige of my appetite for the
dainties before me. M'Swat's! Send—me—to M'Swat's! I could
not believe it! It must be a nightmare! M'Swat's!

Certainly, I had never been there; but all those who had gave
graphic descriptions of the total ignorance of Mrs M'Swat.
Why, the place was quite tabooed on account of its squalor
and dirt!

The steel of my mother's letter entered my soul. Why had
she not expressed a little regret at the thing she was imposing
on me? Instead, there was a note of satisfaction running through
her letter that she was able to put an end to my pleasant life
at Caddagat. She always seemed to grudge me any pleasure.

I bitterly put it down as accruing from the curse of ugliness, as, when mentioning Gertie, it was ever, 'I have let Gertie go to such and such an entertainment. We could not very well afford it, but the poor little girl does not have many pleasures for her years.' I was smaller than Gertie, and only eleven months older; but to me it was 'You must think of something besides pleasure.'

The lot of ugly girls is not joyful, and they must be possessed of natures very absurdly sanguine indeed ever to hope for any enjoyment in life.

It was cruel, base, horrible of my mother to send me to M'Swat's. I would not go—not for £50 a day! I would not go! I would not! not for any consideration.

I stamped about in a fever of impatience until grannie appeared, when I handed both letters to her, and breathlessly awaited her verdict.

'Well, child, what do you say?'

'Say? I won't go! I can't! I won't! Oh, grannie, don't send me there—I would rather die.'

'My dear child, I would not be willing to part with you under any circumstances, but I cannot interfere between a mother and her child. I would not have allowed any one to do it with me, and believe in acting the same towards any other mother, even though she is my own daughter. However, there is time to get a reply before you would have to start, so I will write and see what can be done.'

The dear old lady, with her prompt businesslike propensities, sat down and wrote there and then. I wrote also—pleaded with my mother against her decree, begged her to leave me at Cadda-gat, and assured her I could never succeed at M'Swat's.

I did not sleep that night, so arose betimes to await the first traveller, whom I asked to post the letters.

We got an answer to them sooner than we expected—at least grannie did. Mother did not deign to write to me, but in her letter to grannie I was described as an abominably selfish creature, who would not consider her little brothers and sisters. I would never be any good; all I thought of was idleness and ease. Most decidedly I could not get out of going to M'Swat's, as mother had given her word.

'I am sorry for you,' said grannie, 'but it cannot be helped. You can stay there for two or three years, and then I can have you here again.'

I was inconsolable, and would not listen to reason. Ah! that uncle Jay-Jay had been at home to rescue me from this. Then aunt Helen brought her arguments to bear upon me, and persuaded me to think it was necessary for the benefit of my little brothers and sisters that I should take up this burden, which I knew would be too much for me.

It was a great wrench to be torn away from Caddagat—from refinement and comfort—from home! As the days till my departure melted away, how I wished that it were possible to set one's weight against the grim wheel of time and turn it back! Nights I did not sleep, but drenched my pillow with tears. Ah, it was hard to leave grannie and aunt Helen, whom I worshipped, and turn my back on Caddagat!

I suppose it is only a fancy born of the wild deep love I bear it, but to me the flowers seem to smell more sweetly there; and the shadows, how they creep and curl! oh, so softly and caressingly around the quaint old place, as the great sun sets amid the blue peaks; and the never-ceasing rush of the crystal fern-banked stream—I see and hear it now, and the sinking sun as it turns to a sheet of flame the mirror hanging in the backyard in the laundry veranda, before which the station hands were wont to comb and wash themselves. Oh, the memories that crowd upon me! Methinks I can smell the roses that clamber up the veranda posts and peep over the garden gate. As I write my eyes grow misty, so that I cannot see the paper.

The day for my departure arrived—hot, 110 degrees in the shade. It was a Wednesday afternoon. Frank Hawden was to take me as far as Gool-Gool that evening, and see me on to the coach next day. I would arrive in Yarnung about twelve or one o'clock on Thursday night, where, according to arrangement,

Mr M'Swat would be waiting to take me to a hotel, thence to his home next day.

My trunks and other belongings were stowed in the buggy, to which the fat horses were harnessed. They stood beneath the dense shade of a splendid kurrajong, and lazily flicked the flies off themselves while Frank Hawden held the reins and waited for me.

I rushed frantically round the house taking a last look at nooks and pictures dear to me, and then aunt Helen pressed my hand and kissed me, saying:

'The house will be lonely without you, but you must brighten up, and I'm sure you will not find things half as bad as you expect them.'

I looked back as I went out the front gate, and saw her throw herself into a chair on the veranda and cover her face with her hands. My beautiful noble aunt Helen! I hope she missed me just a little, felt just one pang of parting, for I have not got over that parting yet.

Grannie gave me a warm embrace and many kisses. I climbed on to the front seat of the buggy beside my escort, he whipped the horses—a cloud of dust, a whirr of wheels, and we were gone—gone from Caddagat!

We crossed the singing stream: on either bank great bushes of blackthorn—last native flower of the season—put forth their wealth of magnificent creamy bloom, its rich perfume floating far on the hot summer air. How the sunlight blazed and danced and flickered on the familiar and dearly loved landscape! Over a rise, and the house was lost to view, then good-bye to the crystal creek. The trees of Five-Bob Downs came within eye-range far away on our left. What merry nights I had spent there amid music, flowers, youth, light, love, and summer warmth, when the tide of life seemed full! Where now was Harold Beecham and the thirty or more station hands, who but one short month before had come and gone at his bidding, hailing him boss?

It was all over! My pleasant life at Caddagat was going into the past, fading as the hills which surrounded it were melting into a hazy line of blue.

CHAPTER 27

My Journey

The coach was a big vehicle, something after the style of a bus, the tilt and seats running parallel with the wheels. At the rear end, instead of a door, was a great tail-board, on the principle of a spring-cart. This was let down, and, after we scrambled over it into our seats, it was fixed half-mast, all the luggage piled thereon, and firmly roped into position. When this was completed, to any one on the ground only the heads of passengers were visible above the pile. Had the coach capsized we would have been in a nice fix, as the only means of exit was by crawling up through the back of the box-seat, which rose breast-high— an awkward feat.

Frank Hawden and I parted good friends. I leant out and waved my handkerchief, until a bend of the road hid him from sight.

It was noon, the thermometer registered 112 degrees in the shade, and the dust was simply awful. It rose in such thick grey clouds that often it was impossible to discern the team of five which pulled us, and there was danger of colliding with passing vehicles. We were very much crowded, there being sixteen passengers. When we settled down and got started, I discovered that I was the only representative of my sex, and that I was sandwiched between a perky youth in his teens and a Chinaman, while a black fellow and a man with a red beard sat opposite. A member of Parliament, farther up the seat, who had been patronizing New Year's Day races in a portion of his electorate, bawled loudly to his companion about 'the doin's of the 'Ouse'. In the perky youth I discovered a professional jockey; and when he found that I was a daughter of Dick Melvyn, the one-time great horse-breeder, he became very friendly. He gave me a couple of apples out of his tin box under the seat, from whence he also produced his whip for my inspection, and was good enough to say:

185

'If you can't stand the stink of that bloomin' chow, miss, just change seats with me. I've knocked about, so that I can easy stand some tough smells without much inconvenience.'

I cautioned him to talk lower for fear of hurting the China-man's feelings: this amused him immensely. He laughed very much, and, leaning over to the red-bearded man, repeated the joke:

'I say, this young lady is afraid I might hurt the chow's feelin's. Golly! Fancy a bloomin' chow havin' any!'

The other man also thought it a great joke. I changed seats with the jockey, which put me beside a young gentleman of a literary turn of mind, with whom I had some conversation about books when the dust, rumble of wheels, and turf talk of my other neighbour permitted. They were all very kind to me—gave me fruit, procured me drinks of water, and took turns in nursing a precious hat, for which, on account of the crush, no safe place could be found among the other luggage.

Before we had gone half our journey the horses knocked up. All the men were forced to walk up hills for miles and miles in the dust and heat, which did not conduce to their amiability, and many and caustic were the remarks and jokes made upon the driver. He wore out two whips upon his team, until the labour and excessive heat sent the perspiration rolling in rivulets down his face, leaving muddy tracks in the thick coating of dust there. The jockey assisted with his loaded instrument of trade, some of the passengers thrashed with sticks, and all swore under their breath, while a passing bullock-driver used his whip with such deadly effect, that the sweat which poured off the poor beasts was mingled with blood.

'Why the deuce don't you have proper horses?' demanded the red-bearded passenger.

The man explained that a ministerial party had chartered his best team to go on a tour of inspection to a mine; a brother coachman had been 'stuck up' for horses, and borrowed a couple from him, whereupon he was forced to do with animals which had been turned out for a spell, and the heat and overloading accounted for a good part of the contretemps. However, we managed to catch our train, but had to rush for it without waiting for refreshments. Nice articles we looked—our hair grey with dust, and our faces grimy. The men took charge of me as carefully as though I had been specially consigned to their care. One procured my ticket, another secured me a seat, while a third took charge of my luggage; and they were just as thoughtful when we had to change trains. Off we went. Grannie had packed me quite a large box full of dainties. I produced it, the men provided drinks, and we had quite a pleasant picnic, with all the windows down to catch a little air.

I love the rush and roar of the train, and wished on this occasion that it might go on and on for ever, never giving me time to think or stop. But, alas, at 1.20 we pulled up at Yarnung, where a man came inquiring for a young lady named Melvyn. My fellow passengers collected my belongings, and I got out.

'Good-bye, gentlemen; thank you very much for your kindness.'

'Good-bye, miss; you're welcome. Some of us might meet again yet. Ta-ta!'

A shriek, a jerk, and the great train rushed on into the night, leaving me there on the insignificant little platform, feeling how lonely and unhappy, no one knew or cared.

Mr M'Swat shouldered most of my luggage, I took the remainder, and we trudged off in the dark without a word on either side. The publican had given M'Swat the key, so that we might enter without disturbing the household, and he escorted me to a bedroom, where I tumbled into bed with expedition.

CHAPTER 28

To Life

It is indelibly imprinted on my memory in a manner which royal joy, fame, pleasure, and excitement beyond the dream of poets could never efface, not though I should be cursed with a life of five-score years. I will paint it truthfully—letter for letter as it was.

It was twenty-six miles from Yarnung to Barney's Gap, as M'Swat's place was named. He had brought a light waggonette and pair to convey me thither.

As we drove along, I quite liked my master. Of course, we were of calibre too totally unlike ever to be congenial companions, but I appreciated his sound common sense in the little matters within his range, and his bluntly straightforward, fairly good-natured, manner. He was an utterly ignorant man, with small ideas according to the sphere which he fitted, and which fitted him; but he was 'a man for a' that, an' a' that'.

He and my father had been boys together. Years and years ago M'Swat's father had been blacksmith on my father's station, and the little boys had played together, and, in spite of their then difference in station, had formed a friendship which lived and bore fruit at this hour. I wished that their youthful relations had been inimical, not friendly.

We left the pub in Yarnung at nine, and arrived at our destination somewhere about two o'clock in the afternoon.

I had waxed quite cheerful, and began to look upon the situation in a sensible light. It was necessary that I should stand up to the guns of life at one time or another, and why not now? M'Swat's might not be so bad after all. Even if they were dirty, they would surely be willing to improve if I exercised tact in introducing a few measures. I was not afraid of work, and would do many things. But all these ideas were knocked on the head, like a dairyman's surplus calves, when on entering Barney's Gap we descended a rough road to the house, which was built in a narrow gully between two steep stony hills, which, destitute of grass, rose like grim walls of rock, imparting a desolate and prison-like aspect.

Six dogs, two pet lambs, two or three pigs, about twenty fowls, eight children which seemed a dozen, and Mrs M'Swat bundled out through the back door at our approach. Those children, not through poverty—M'Swat made a boast of his substantial banking account—but on account of ignorance and slatternliness, were the dirtiest urchins I have ever seen, and were so ragged that those parts of them which should have been covered were exposed to view. The majority of them had red hair and wide hanging-open mouths. Mrs M'Swat was a great, fat, ignorant, pleasant-looking woman, shockingly dirty and untidy. Her tremendous, flabby, stockingless ankles bulged over her unlaced hobnailed boots; her dress was torn and unbuttoned at the throat, displaying one of the dirtiest necks I have seen. It did not seem to worry her that the infant she held under her arm like a roll of cloth howled killingly, while the other little ones clung to her skirts, attempting to hide their heads in its folds like so many emus. She greeted me with a smacking kiss, consigned the baby to the charge of the eldest child, a big girl of fourteen, and seizing upon my trunks as though they were feather-weight, with heavy clodhopping step disappeared into the house with them. Returning, she invited me to enter, and following in her wake, I was followed by the children through the dirtiest passage into the dirtiest room, to sit upon the dirtiest chair, to gaze upon the other dirtiest furniture of which I have ever heard. One wild horrified glance at the dirt, squalor, and total benightedness that met me on every side, and I trembled in every limb with suppressed emotion and the frantic longing to get back to Caddagat which possessed me. One instant showed me that I could never, never live here.

'Have ye had yer dinner?' my future mistress inquired in a rough uncultivated voice. I replied in the negative.

'Sure, ye'll by dyin' of hunger; but I'll have it in a twinklin'.'

She threw a crumpled and disgustingly filthy cloth three-cornered ways on to the dusty table and clapped thereon a couple of dirty knives and forks, a pair of cracked plates, two poley cups and chipped saucers. Next came a plate of salt meat, red with saltpetre, and another of dark, dry, sodden bread. She then disappeared to the kitchen to make the tea, and during her absence two of the little boys commenced to fight. One clutched the tablecloth, and over went the whole display with a bang—meat-dish broken, and meat on the dusty floor; while the cats and fowls, ever on the alert for such occurrences, made the most of their opportunities. Mrs M'Swat returned carrying the tea, which was spilling by the way. She gave those boys each a clout on the head which dispersed them roaring like the proverbial town bull, and alarmed me for the safety of their ear-drums. I wondered if their mother was aware of their having ear-drums. She grabbed the meat, and wiping it on her greasy apron, carried it around in her hand until she found a plate for it, and by that time the children had collected the other things. A cup was broken, and another, also a poley, was put in its stead.

Mr M'Swat now appeared, and after taking a nip out of a rum bottle which he produced from a cupboard in the corner, he invited me to sit up to dinner.

There was no milk. M'Swat went in entirely for sheep, keeping only a few cows for domestic purposes: these, on account of the drought, had been dry for some months. Mrs M'Swat apologized for the lack of sugar, stating she was quite out of it and had forgotten to send for a fresh supply.

'You damned fool, to miss such a chance wen I was goin' to town with the waggonette! I mightn't be goin' in again for munce [months]. But sugar don't count much. Them as can't do without a useless luxury like that for a spell will never make much of a show at gettin' on in the wu-r-r-ld,' concluded Mr M'Swat, sententiously.

The children sat in a row and, with mouths open and interest in their big wondering eyes, gazed at me unwinkingly till I felt I must rush away somewhere and shriek to relieve the feeling of overstrained hysteria which was overcoming me. I contained myself sufficiently, however, to ask if this was all the family.

'All but Peter. Where's Peter, Mary Ann?'

'He went to the Red Hill to look after some sheep, and won't be back till dark.'

'Peter's growed up,' remarked one little boy, with evident pride in this member of the family

'Yes; Peter's twenty-one, and hes a mustatche and shaves,' said the eldest girl, in a manner indicating that she expected me to be struck dumb with surprise.

'She'll be surprised wen she sees Peter,' said a little girl in an audible whisper.

Mrs M'Swat vouchsafed the information that three had died between Peter and Lizer, and this was how the absent son came to be so much older than his brothers and sisters.

'So you have had twelve children?' I said.

'Yes,' she replied, laughing fatly, as though it were a joke.

'The boys found a bees' nest in a tree an' have been robbin' it the smornin',' continued Mrs M'Swat.

'Yes; we have ample exemplification of that,' I responded. It was honey here and honey there and honey everywhere. It was one of the many varieties of dirt on the horrible foul-smelling tablecloth. It was on the floor, the door, the chairs, the children's heads, and the cups. Mrs M'Swat remarked contentedly that it always took a couple of days to wear 'off of' things.

After 'dinner' I asked for a bottle of ink and some paper, and scrawled a few lines to grannie and my mother, merely reporting my safe arrival at my destination. I determined to take time to collect my thoughts before petitioning for release from Barney's Gap.

I requested my mistress to show me where I was to sleep, and she conducted me to a fairly respectable little bedroom, of which I was to be sole occupant, unless I felt lonely and would like Rose Jane to sleep with me. I looked at pretty, soft-eyed, dirty little Rose Jane, and assured her kind-hearted mother I would not be the least lonely, as the sickening despairing loneliness which filled my heart was not of a nature to be cured by having as a bedmate a frowzy wild child.

Upon being left alone I barred my door and threw myself on the bed to cry—weep wild hot tears that scalded my cheeks, and sobs that shook my whole frame and gave me a violent pain in the head.

Oh, how coarse and grating were the sounds to be heard around me! Lack, nay, not lack, but utter freedom from the first instincts of cultivation, was to be heard even in the great heavy footfalls and the rasping sharp voices which fell on my ears. So different had I been listening in a room at Caddagat to my grannie's brisk pleasant voice, or to my aunt Helen's low refined accents; and I am such a one to see and feel these differences.

However, I pulled together in a little while, and called myself a fool for crying. I would write to grannie and mother explaining matters, and I felt sure they would heed me, as they had no idea what the place was like. I would have only a little while to wait patiently, then I would be among all the pleasures of Caddagat again; and how I would revel in them, more than ever, after a taste of a place like this, for it was worse than I had imagined it could be, even in the nightmares which had haunted me concerning it before leaving Caddagat.

The house was of slabs, unlimed, and with very low iron roof, and having no sign of a tree near it, the heat was unendurable. It was reflected from the rocks on either side, and concentrated in this spot like an oven, being 122 degrees in the veranda now. I wondered why M'Swat had built in such a hole, but it appears it was the nearness of the point to water which recommended it to his judgment.

With the comforting idea that I would not have long to bear this, I bathed my eyes, and walked away from the house to try and find a cooler spot. The children saw me depart but not return, to judge from a discussion of myself which I heard in the dining-room, which adjoined my bed-chamber.

Peter came home, and the children clustered around to tell the news.

'Did she come?'

'Yes.'

'Wot's she like?'

'Oh, a rale little bit of a thing, not as big as Lizer!'

'And, Peter, she hes teeny little hands, as wite as snow, like that woman in the picter ma got off of the tea.'

'Yes, Peter,' chimed in another voice; 'and her feet are that little that she don't make no nise wen she walks.'

'It ain't only becos her feet are little, but cos she's got them beautiful shoes like wot's in picters,' said another.

'Her hair is tied with two great junks of ribbing, one up on her head an' another near the bottom; better than that bit er red ribbing wot Lizer keeps in the box agin the time she might go to town some day.'

'Yes,' said the voice of Mrs M'Swat, 'her hair is near to her knees, and a plait as thick as yer arm; and wen she writ a couple of letters in a minute, you could scarce see her hand move it was that wonderful quick; and she uses them big words wot you couldn't understand without bein' eddicated.'

'She has tree brooches, and a necktie better than your best one wots you keeps to go seeing Susie Duffy in,' and Lizer giggled slyly.

'You shut up about Susie Duffy, or I'll whack yuz up aside of the ear,' said Peter angrily.

'She ain't like ma. She's fat up here, and goes in like she'd break in the middle, Peter.'

'Great scissors! she must be a flyer,' said Peter. 'I'll bet she'll make you sit up, Jimmy.'

'I'll make _her_ sit up,' retorted Jimmy, who came next to Lizer. 'She thinks she's a toff, but she's only old Melvyn's darter, that pa has to give money to.'

'Peter,' said another, 'her face ain't got them freckles on like yours, and it ain't dark like Lizer's. It's reel wite, and pinky round here.'

'I bet she won't make me knuckle down to her, no matter wot colour she is,' returned Peter, in a surly tone.

No doubt it was this idea which later in the afternoon induced him to swagger forward to shake hands with me with a flash insolent leer on his face. I took pains to be especially nice to him, treating him with deference, and making remarks upon the extreme heat of the weather with such pleasantness that he was nonplussed, and looked relieved when able to escape. I smiled to myself, and apprehended no further trouble from Peter.

The table for tea was set exactly as it had been before, and was lighted by a couple of tallow candles made from bad fat, and their odour was such as my jockey travelling companion of the day before would have described as a tough smell.

'Give us a toon on the peeany,' said Mrs M'Swat after the meal, when the dishes had been cleared away by Lizer and Rose Jane. The tea and scraps, of which there was any amount, remained on the floor, to be picked up by the fowls in the morning.

The children lay on the old sofa and on the chairs, where they always slept at night until their parents retired, when there was an all-round bawl as they were wakened and bundled into bed, dirty as they were, and very often with their clothes on.

I acceded to Mrs M'Swat's request with alacrity, thinking that while forced to remain there I would have one comfort, and would spend all my spare time at the piano. I opened the instrument, brushed a little of the dust from the keys with my pocket-handkerchief, and struck the opening chords of Kowalski's 'Marche Hongroise'.

I have heard of pianos sounding like a tin dish, but this was not as pleasant as a tin dish by long chalks. Every note that I struck stayed down not to rise, and when I got them up the jarring, clanging, discordant clatter they produced beggars description. There was not the slightest possibility of distinguishing any tune on the thing. Worthless to begin with, it had stood in the dust, heat, and wind so long that every sign that it had once made music had deserted it.

I closed it with a feeling of such keen disappointment that I had difficulty in suppressing tears.

'Won't it play?' inquired Mr M'Swat.

'No; the keys stay down.'

'Then, Rose Jane, go ye an' pick 'em up while she tries again.'

I tried again, Rose Jane fishing up the keys as I went along. I perceived instantly that not one had the least ear for music or idea what it was; so I beat on the demented piano with both hands, and often with all fingers at once, and the bigger row I made the better they liked it.

CHAPTER 29

To Life—continued

Mr M'Swat very kindly told me I need not begin my duties until Monday morning, and could rest during Saturday and Sunday. Saturday, which was sickeningly hot and sultry, and which seemed like an eternity, I spent in arranging my belongings, brushing the dust from my travelling dress, and in mending a few articles. Next morning rain started to fall, which was a great God-send, being the first which had fallen for months, and the only rain I saw during my residence at Barney's Gap.

That was a hideous Sabbath. Without a word of remonstrance from their parents, the children entertained themselves by pushing each other into the rain, the smaller ones getting the worst of it, until their clothing was saturated with water. This made them very cold, so they sat upon the floor and yelled outrageously.

It was the custom of Peter to spend his Sundays in riding about, but today, being deterred by the rain, he slept some of the time, and made a muzzle for one of his dogs between whiles.

From breakfast to the midday meal I shut myself in my bedroom and wrote letters to my mother and grandmother. I did not rant, rave, or say anything which I ought not to have said to my elders. I wrote those letters very coolly and carefully, explaining things just as they were, and asked grannie to take me back to Caddagat, as I could never endure life at Barney's Gap. I told my mother I had written thus, and asked her if she would not let grannie take me again, would she get me some other situation?—what I did not care, so long as it brought emancipation from the M'Swat's. I stamped and addressed these missives, and put them by till a chance of posting should arise.

Mr M'Swat could read a little by spelling the long words and blundering over the shorter ones, and he spent the morning and all the afternoon in perusal of the local paper—the only literature with which Barney's Gap was acquainted. There was a long list of the prices of stock and farm produce in this edition, which perfectly fascinated its reader. The ecstasy of a man of fine, artistic, mental calibre, when dipping for the first time into the work of some congenial poet, would be completely wiped out in comparison to the utter soul-satisfaction of M'Swat when drinking in the items of that list.

'By damn, pigs was up last Toosday! Thames the things to make prawfit on,' he would excitedly exclaim; or—'Wheat's rose a shillun a bushel! By dad, I must double my crops this year.' When he had plodded to the end, he started at the beginning again.

His wife sat the whole afternoon in the one place, saying and doing nothing. I looked for something to read, but the only books in the house were a Bible, which was never opened, and a diary kept most religiously by M'Swat. I got permission to read this, and opening it, saw:

September

1*st*. Fine. Wint to boggie creak for a cow.

2*nd*. Fine. Got the chestnut mair shod.

3*rd*. Fine. On the jury.

4*th*. Fine. Tail the lams 60 yeos 52 wethers.

5*th*. Cloudy. Wint to Duffys.

6*th*. Fine. Dave Duffy called.

7*th*. Fine. Roped the red filly.

8*th*. Showery. Sold the gray mair's fole.

9*th*. Fine. Wint to the Red hill after a horse.

10*th*. Fine. Found tree sheap ded in sqre padick.

I closed the book and put it up with a sigh. The little record was a perfect picture of the dull narrow life of its writer. Week after week that diary went on the same—drearily monotonous account of a drearily monotonous existence. I felt I would go mad if forced to live such a life for long.

'Pa has lots of diaries. Would I like to read them?'

They were brought and put before me. I inquired of Mr M'Swat which was the liveliest time of the year, and being told it was shearing and threshing, I opened one first in November:

November 1896

1*st*.   Fine. Started to muster sheap.

2*nd*.   Fine. Counten sheap very dusty 20 short.

3*rd*.   Fine. Stared shering. Joe Harris cut his hand bad and wint hoam.

4*th*.   Showery. Shering stoped on account of rane.

Then I skipped to December:

December 1896

1*st*.   Fine and hot. Stripped the weet 60 bages.

2*nd*.   Fine. Killed a snake very hot day.

3*rd*.   Fine. Very hot alle had a boagy in the river.

4*th*.   Fine. Got returns of woll 7½ fleece 5¼ bellies.

5*th*.   Fine. Awful hot got a serkeler from Tatersal by the poast.

6*th*.   Fine. Saw Joe Harris at Duffys.

There was no entertainment to be had from the diaries, so I attempted a conversation with Mrs M'Swat.

'A penny for your thoughts.'

'I wuz jist watchin' the rain and thinkin' it would put a couple a bob a head more on sheep if it keeps on.'

What was I to do to pass the day? I was ever very restless, even in the midst of full occupation. Uncle Jay-Jay used to accuse me of being in six places at once, and of being incapable of sitting still for five minutes consecutively; so it was simply endurance to live that long, long day—nothing to read, no piano on which to play hymns, too wet to walk, no one with whom to converse, no possibility of sleeping, as in an endeavour to kill a little of the time I had gone to bed early and got up late. There was nothing but to sit still, tormented by maddening regret. I pictured what would be transpiring at Caddagat now; what we had done this time last week, and so on, till the thing became an agony to me.

Among my duties before school I was to set the table, make all the beds, dust and sweep, and 'do' the girls' hair. After school I had to mend clothes, sew, set the table again, take a turn at nursing the baby, and on washing-day iron. This sounds a lot, but in reality was nothing, and did not half occupy my time. Setting the table was a mere sinecure, as there was nothing much to put on it; and the only ironing was a few articles outside my own, as Mr M'Swat and Peter did not wear white shirts, and patronised paper collars. Mrs M'Swat did the washing and a little scrubbing, also boiled the beef and baked the bread, which formed our unvaried menu week in and week out. Most peasant mothers with a family of nine have no time for idleness, but Mrs M'Swat managed things so that she spent most of the day rolling on her frowsy bed playing with her dirty infant, which was as fat and good-tempered as herself.

On Monday morning I marshalled my five scholars (Lizer, aged fourteen; Jimmy, twelve; Tommy, Sarah, and Rose Jane, younger) in a little back skillion, which was set apart as a school-room and store for flour and rock-salt. Like all the house, it was built of slabs, which, erected while green, and on account of the heat, had shrunk until many of the cracks were sufficiently wide to insert one's arm. On Monday—after the rain—the wind, which disturbed us through them, was piercingly cold, but as the week advanced summer and drought regained their pitiless sway, and we were often sunburnt by the rough gusts which filled the room with such clouds of dust and grit that we were forced to cover our heads until it passed.

A policeman came on Tuesday to take some returns, and to him I entrusted the posting of my letters, and then eagerly waited for the reply which was to give me glorious release.

The nearest post-office was eight miles distant, and thither Jimmy was dispatched on horseback twice a week. With trembling expectancy every mail-day I watched for the boy's return down the tortuous track to the house, but it was always, 'No letters for the school-missus.'

A week, a fortnight, dragged away. Oh, the slow horror of those never-ending days! At the end of three weeks Mr M'Swat went to the post unknown to me, and surprised me with a couple of letters. They bore the handwriting of my mother and grandmother—what I had been wildly waiting for—and now that they had come at last I had not the nerve to open them while any one was observing me. All day I carried them in my bosom till my work was done, when I shut myself in my room and tore the envelopes open to read first my grannie's letter, which contained two:

My dear child,

   I have been a long time answering your letter on account of
waiting to consult your mother. I was willing to take you
back, but your mother is not agreeable, so I cannot interfere
between you. I enclose your mother's letter, so you can see
how I stand in the matter. Try and do good where you are.
We cannot get what we would like in this world, and must
bow to God's will. He will always, &c.

MOTHER'S LETTER TO GRANNIE

My dear Mother,

   I am truly grieved that Sybylla should have written and
worried you. Take no notice of her; it is only while she is
unused to the place. She will soon settle down. She has always
been a trial to me, and it is no use of taking notice of her
complaints, which no doubt are greatly exaggerated, as she
was never contented at home. I don't know where her
rebellious spirit will eventually lead her. I hope M'Swat's will
tame her; it will do her good. It is absolutely necessary that
she should remain there, so do not say anything to give her
other ideas &c.

MOTHER'S LETTER TO ME

My dear Sybylla,

I wish you would not write and worry your poor old grandmother, who has been so good to you. You must try and put up with things; you cannot expect to find it like holidaying at Caddagat. Be careful not to give offence to any one, as it would be awkward for us. What is wrong with the place? Have you too much work to do? Do you not get sufficient to eat? Are they unkind to you, or what? Why don't you have sense and not talk of getting another place, as it is utterly impossible; and unless you remain there, how are we to pay the interest on that money? I've always been a good mother to you, and the least you might do in return is this, when you know how we are situated. Ask God &c.

Full of contempt and hatred for my mother, I tore her letters into tiny pieces and hurled them out the window. Oh, the hard want of sympathy they voiced! She had forced me to this place: it would have been different had I wanted to come of my own accord, and then sung out for a removal immediately; but no, against my earnest pleadings she had forced me here, and now would not heed my cry. And to whom in all the word can we turn when our mother spurns our prayer?

There never was any sympathy between my mother and myself. We are too unlike. She is intensely matter-of-fact and practical, possessed of no ambitions or aspirations not capable of being turned into cash value. She is very ladylike, and though containing no spice of either poet or musician, can take a part in conversation on such subjects, and play the piano correctly, because in her young days she was thus cultivated; but had she been born a peasant, she would have been a peasant, with no longings unattainable in that sphere. She no more understood me than I understand the works of a watch. She looked upon me as a discontented, rebellious, bad child, possessed of evil spirits, which wanted trouncing out of me; and she would have felt that she was sinning had she humoured me in any way, so after cooling I did not blame her for her letters. She was doing her duty according to her lights. Again, it was this way, grannie did not come to my rescue on this occasion on account of her attitude towards my father. The Bossiers were not at enmity with him, but they were so disgusted with his insobriety that they never visited Possum Gully, and did not assist us as much as they would have done had my father's failure been attributable to some cause more deserving of sympathy.

After reading my letters I wept till every atom of my body writhed with agonized emotion. I was aroused by Mrs M'Swat hammering at my door and inquiring:

'What ails ye, child? Did ye git bad noos from home?'

I recovered myself as by a miracle, and replied, no; that I was merely a little homesick, and would be out presently.

I wrote again to my mother, but as I could not truthfully say I was hungry or ill-treated, for, according to their ability, the M'Swats were very kind to me, she took no notice of my plaint, but told me that instead of complaining of monotony, it would suit me better if I cleared up the house a little.

Acting upon this advice, I asked Mr M'Swat to put a paling fence round the house, as it was useless trying to keep the house respectable while the fowls and pigs ran in every time the door was opened.

He was inclined to look with favour upon the proposition, but his wife sat upon it determinedly—said the fowls would lose the scraps. 'Would it not be possible to throw them over the fence to the fowls?' I asked; but this would cause too much waste, she considered.

Next I suggested that the piano should be tuned, but they were united in their disapproval of such a fearful extravagance. 'The peeany makes a good nise. What ails it?'

Then I suggested that the children should be kept tidier, for which I was insulted by their father. I wanted them to be dressed up like swells, and if he did that he would soon be a pauper like my father. This I found was the sentiment of the whole family regarding me. I was only the daughter of old hard-up Melvyn, consequently I had little weight with the children, which made things very hard for me as a teacher.

One day at lunch I asked my mistress if she would like the children to be instructed in table-manners. 'Certainly,' her husband replied, so I commenced.

'Jimmy, you must never put your knife in your mouth.'

'Pa does at any rate,' replied Jimmy.

'Yes,' said pa; 'and I'm a richer man today than them as didn't do it.'

'Liza, do not put a whole slice of bread to your mouth like that, and cram so. Cut it into small pieces.'

'Ma doesn't,' returned Liza.

'Ye'll have yer work cut out with 'em,' laughed Mrs M'Swat, who did not know how to correct her family herself, and was too ignorant to uphold my authority.

That was my only attempt at teaching manners there. In the face of such odds it was a bootless task, and as there were not enough knives and forks to go round, I could not inculcate the correct method of handling those implements.

Mrs M'Swat had but one boiler in which to do all her cooking, and one small tub for the washing, and there was seldom anything to eat but bread and beef; and this was not because they were poor, but because they did not know, or want to know, any better.

Their idea of religion, pleasure, manners, breeding, respectability, love, and everything of that ilk, was the possession of money, and their one idea of accumulating wealth was by hard sordid dragging and grinding.

A man who rises from indigence to opulence by business capabilities must have brains worthy of admiration, but the man who makes a fortune as M'Swat of Barney's Gap was making his must be dirt mean, grasping, narrow-minded, and soulless— to me the most uncongenial of my fellows.

I wrote once more to my mother, to receive the same reply. One hope remained. I would write to aunt Helen. She understood me somewhat, and would know how I felt.

Acting on this inspiration, I requested her to plead for me. Her answer came as a slap in the face, as I had always imagined her above the common cant of ordinary religionists. She stated that life was full of trials. I must try and bear this little cross patiently, and at the end of a year they might have me back at Caddagat. A year! A year at Barney's Gap! The possibility of such a thing made me frantic. I picked up my pen and bitterly reproached my aunt in a letter to which she did not deign to reply; and from that day to this she has rigidly ignored me— never so much as sending me the most commonplace message, or casually using my name in her letters to my mother.

Aunt Helen, is there such a thing as firm friendship when even yours—best of women—quibbled and went under at the hysterical wail from the overburdened heart of a child?

My predecessor, previous to her début at Barney's Gap, had spent some time in a lunatic asylum, and being a curious character, allowed the children to do as they pleased, consequently they knew not what it meant to be ruled, and were very bold. They attempted no insubordination while their father was about the house, but when he was absent they gave me a dog's life, their mother sometimes smiling on their pranks, often lazily heedless of them, but never administering any form of correction.

If I walked away from the house to get rid of them, they would follow and hoot at me; and when I reproved them they informed me they were not going 'to knuckle under to old Melvyn's darter, the damnedest fool in the world, who's lost all his prawperty, and has to borry money off of pa.'

Did I shut myself in my room, they shoved sticks in the cracks and made grimaces at me. I knew the fallacy of appealing to their father, as they and their mother would tell falsehoods, and my word would not be taken in contradiction of theirs. I had experience of this, as the postmistress had complained of Jimmy, to be insulted by his father, who could see no imperfection in his children.

M'Swat was much away from home at that time. The drought necessitated the removal of some of his sheep, for which he had rented a place eighty miles coastward. There he left them under the charge of a man, but he repaired thither frequently to inspect them. Sometimes he was away from home a fortnight at a stretch. Peter would be away at work all day, and the children took advantage of my defenceless position. Jimmy was the ringleader. I could easily have managed the others had he been removed. I would have thrashed him well at the start but for the letters I constantly received from home warning me against offence to the parents, and knew that to set my foot on the children's larrikinism would require measures that would gain their mother's ill-will at once. But when M'Swat left home for three weeks Jim got so bold that I resolved to take decisive steps towards subjugating him. I procured a switch—a very small one, as his mother had a great objection to corporal punishment— and when, as usual, he commenced to cheek me during lessons, I hit him on the coat-sleeve. The blow would not have brought tears from the eyes of a toddler, but this great calf emitted a wild yope, and opening his mouth let his saliva pour on to his slate. The others set up such blood-curdling yells in concert that I was a little disconcerted, but I determined not to give in. I delivered another tap, whereupon he squealed and roared so that he brought his mother to his rescue like a ton of bricks on stilts, a great fuss in her eyes which generally beamed with a cowful calm.

Seizing my arm she shook me like a rat, broke my harmless little stick in pieces, threw it in my face, and patting Jimmy on the shoulder, said:

'Poor man! She sharn't touch me Jimmy while I know. Sure you've got no sense. You'd had him dead if I hadn't come in.'

I walked straight to my room and shut myself in, and did not teach any more that afternoon. The children rattled on my door-handle and jeered:

'She thought she'd hit me, but ma settled her. Old poor Melvyn's darter won't try no more of her airs on us.'

I pretended not to hear. What was I to do? There was no one to whom I could turn for help. M'Swat would believe the

205

story of his family, and my mother would blame me. She would think I had been in fault because I hated the place.

Mrs M'Swat called me to tea, but I said I would not have any. I lay awake all night and got desperate. On the morrow I made up my mind to conquer or leave. I would stand no more. If, in all the wide world and the whole of life this was the only use for me, then I would die—take my own life if necessary.

Things progressed as usual next morning. I attended to my duties and marched my scholars into the schoolroom at the accustomed hour. There was no decided insubordination during the morning, but I felt Jimmy was waiting for an opportunity to defy me. It was a fearful day, possessed by a blasting wind laden with red dust from Riverina, which filled the air like a fog. The crockery ware became so hot in the kitchen that when taking it into the dining-room we had to handle it with cloths. During the dinner-hour I slipped away unnoticed to where some quince-trees were growing and procured a sharp rod, which I secreted among the flour-bags in the schoolroom. At half-past one I brought my scholars in and ordered them to their work with a confident air. Things went without a ripple until three o'clock, when the writing lesson began. Jimmy struck his pen on the bottom of the bottle every time he replenished it with ink.

'Jimmy,' I gently remonstrated, 'don't jab your pen like that—it will spoil it. There is no necessity to shove it right to the bottom.'

Jab, jab, went Jimmy's pen.

'Jimmy, did you hear me speak to you?'

Jab went the pen.

'James, I am speaking to you!'

Jab went the pen again.

'James,' I said sternly, 'I give you one more chance.'

He deliberately defied me by stabbing into the ink-bottle with increased vigour. Liza giggled triumphantly, and the little ones strove to emulate her. I calmly produced my switch and brought it smartly over the shoulders of my refractory pupil in a way that sent the dust in a cloud from his dirty coat, knocked the pen from his fingers, and upset the ink.

He acted as before—yelled ear-drum-breakingly, letting the saliva from his distended mouth run on his copy-book. His brothers and sisters also started to roar, but bringing the rod down on the table, I threatened to thrash every one of them if they so much as whimpered; and they were so dumbfounded that they sat silent in terrified surprise.

Jimmy continued to bawl. I hit him again.

'Cease instantly, sir.'

Through the cracks Mrs M'Swat could be seen approaching. Seeing her, Jimmy hollered anew. I expected her to attack me. She stood five feet nine inches, and weighed about sixteen stones; I measured five feet one inch, and turned the scale at eight stones— scarcely a fair match; but my spirit was aroused, and instead of feeling afraid, I rejoiced at the encounter which was imminent, and had difficulty to refrain from shouting 'Come on! I'm ready, physically and mentally, for you and a dozen others such.'

My curious ideas regarding human equality gave me confidence. My theory is that the cripple is equal to the giant, and the idiot to the genius. As, if on account of his want of strength the cripple is subservient to the giant, the latter, on account of that strength, is compelled to give in to the cripple. So with the dolt and the man of brain, so with Mrs M'Swat and me.

The fact of not only my own but my family's dependence on M'Swat sank into oblivion. I merely recognized that she was one human being and I another. Should I have been deferential to her by reason of her age and maternity, then from the vantage which this gave her, she should have been lenient to me on account of my chit-ship and inexperience. Thus we were equal.

Jimmy hollered with renewed energy to attract his mother, and I continued to rain blows across his shoulders. Mrs M'Swat approached to within a foot of the door, and then, as though changing her mind, retraced her steps and entered the hot low-roofed kitchen. I knew I had won, and felt disappointed that the conquest had been so easy. Jimmy, seeing he was worsted, ceased his uproar, cleaned his copy-book on his sleeve, and sheepishly went on with his writing.

Whether Mrs M'Swat saw she had been in fault the day before I know not; certain it is that the children ever after that obeyed me, and I heard no more of the matter; neither, as far as I could ascertain, did the 'ruction' reach the ears of M'Swat.

'How long, how long!' was my cry, as I walked out ankle-deep in the dust to see the sun, like a ball of blood, sink behind the hills on that February evening.

CHAPTER 30

Where Ignorance is Bliss, 'Tis Folly to Be Wise

When by myself, I fretted so constantly that the traces it left upon me became evident even to the dull comprehension of Mrs M'Swat.

'I don't hold with too much pleasure and disherpation, but you ain't had overmuch of it lately. You've stuck at home pretty constant, and ye and Lizer can have a little fly round. It'll do yous good,' she said.

The dissipation, pleasure, and flying round allotted to 'Lizer' and me were to visit some of the neighbours. Those, like the M'Swats, were sheep-farming selectors. They were very friendly and kind to me, and I found them superior to my employers, in that their houses were beautifully clean; but they lived the same slow life, and their soul's existence fed on the same small ideas. I was keenly disappointed that none of them had a piano, as my hunger for music could be understood only by one with a passion for that art.

I borrowed something to read, but all that I could get in the way of books were a few *Young Ladies' Journals*, which I devoured ravenously, so to speak.

When Lizer's back would be turned, the girls would ask me how I managed to live at Barney's Gap, and expressed themselves of the opinion that it was the most horrible hole in the world, and Mrs M'Swat the dirtiest creature living, and that they would not go there for £50 a week. I made a point of never saying anything against Mrs M'Swat; but I fumed inwardly that this life was forced upon me, when girls with no longings or aspirations beyond being the wife of a Peter M'Swat recoiled from the thought of it.

My mother insisted upon my writing to her regularly, so once a week I headed a letter 'Black's Camp', and condemned the place, while mother as unfailingly replied that these bad times I should be thankful to God that I was fed and clothed. I knew this as well as any one, and was aware there were plenty of girls willing to jump at my place; but they were of different temperament to me, and when one is seventeen, that kind of reasoning does not weigh very heavily.

My eldest brother, Horace, twin brother of my sister Gertie, took it upon himself to honour me with the following letter:

Why the deuce don't you give up writing those letters to mother? We get tongue-pie on account of them, and it's not as if they did you any good. It only makes mother more determined to leave you where you are. She says you are that conceited you think you ought to have something better, and you're not fit for the place you have, and she's glad it is such a place, and it will do you the world of good and take the nonsense out of you—that it's time you got a bit of sense. Sullivan's Ginger. After she gets your letters she does jaw, and wishes she never had a child, and what a good mother she is, and what bad devils we are to her. You are a fool not to stay where you are. I wish I could get away to M'Swat or Mack Pot, and I would jump at the chance like a good un. The boss still sprees and loafs about town till some one has to go and haul him home. I'm about full of him, and I'm going to leave home before next Christmas, or my name ain't what it is. Mother says the kiddies would starve if I leave; but Stanley is coming on like a haystack, I tell him, and he does kick up, and he ought to be able to plough next time. I ploughed when I was younger than him. I put in fourteen acres of wheat and oats this year, and I don't think I'll cut a wheelbarrow-load of it. I'm full of the place. I never have a single penny to my name, and it ain't father's drinking that's all to blame; if he didn't booze it wouldn't be much better. It's the slowest hole in the world, and I'll chuck it and go shearing or droving. I hate this dairying, it's too slow for a funeral: there would be more life in trapping 'possums out on Timlinbilly. Mother always says to have patience, and when the drought breaks and good seasons come round again things will be better, but it's no good of trying to stuff me like that. I remember when the seasons were wet. It was no good growing anything, because every one grew so much that there was no market, and the sheep died of foot-rot and you couldn't give your butter away, and it is not much worse to have nothing to sell than not be able to sell a thing when you have it. And the long and short of it is that I hate dairying like blue murder. It's as tame as a clucking hen. Fancy a cove sitting down every morning and evening pulling at a cow's tits fit to bust himself, and then turning an old separator, and washing it up in a dish of water like a blooming girl's work. And if you go to a picnic, just when the fun commences you have to nick off home and milk, and when you tog yourself on Sunday evening you have to undress again and lay into the milking, and then you have to change everything on you and have a bath, or your best girl would scent the cow-yard on you, and not have you within cooee of her. We won't know what rain is when we see it; but I suppose it will come in floods and finish the little left by the drought. The grasshoppers have eaten all the fruit and even the bark off the trees, and the caterpillars made a croker of the few tomatoes we kept alive with the suds. All the cockeys round here and dad are applying to the Government to have their rents suspended for a time. We have not heard yet whether it will be granted, but if Gov. doesn't like it, they'll have to lump it, for none of us have a penny to bless ourselves with, let alone dub up for taxes. I've written you a long letter, and if you growl about the spelling and grammar I won't write to you any more, so there, and you take my tip and don't write to mother on that flute any more, for she won't take a bit of notice.

Yr loving brother,

Horace.

So! Mother had no pity for me, and the more I pleaded with her the more determined she grew upon leaving me to suffer on, so I wrote to her no more. However, I continued to correspond with grannie, and in one of her letters she told me that Harry Beecham (that was in February) was still in Sydney settling his affairs; but when that was concluded he was going to Queensland. He had put his case in the hands of squatters he had known in his palmy days, and the first thing that turned up in managing or overseeing he was to have; but for the present he had been offered the charge of 1600 head of bullocks from a station up near the Gulf of Carpentaria overland to Victoria. Uncle Jay-Jay was not home yet: he had extended his tour to Hong Kong, and grannie was afraid he was spending too much money, as in the face of the drought she had difficulty in making both ends meet, and feared she would be compelled to go on the banks. She grieved that I was not becoming more reconciled to my place. It was dull, no doubt, but it would do my reputation no harm, whereas, were I in a lively situation, there might be numerous temptations hard to resist. Why did I not try to look at it in that way?

She sent a copy of the *Australasian*, which was a great treat to me, also to the children, as they were quite ignorant of the commonest things in life, and the advent of this illustrated paper was an event to be recorded in the diary in capital letters. They clustered round me eagerly to see the pictures. In this edition there chanced to be a page devoted to the portraits of eleven Australian singers, and our eyes fell on Madame Melba, who was in the middle. As what character she was dressed I do not remember, but she looked magnificent. There was a crown upon her beautiful head, the plentiful hair was worn flowing, and the shapely bosom and arms exposed.

'Who's that?' they inquired.

'Madame Melba; did you ever hear her name?'

'Who's Madame Melba? What's she do? Is she a queen?'

'Yes, a queen, and a great queen of song;' and being inspired with great admiration for our own Australian cantatrice, who was great among the greatest prima-donnas of the world, I began to tell them a little of her fame, and that she had been recently offered £40,000 to sing for three months in America.

They were incredulous. Forty thousand pounds! Ten times as much as 'pa' had given for a paid-up selection he had lately bought. They told me it was no use of me trying to tell them fibs. No one would give a woman anything to sing, not even one pound. Why, Susie Duffy was the best singer on the Murrumbidgee, and she would sing for any one who asked her, and free of charge.

At this juncture Jimmy, who had been absent, came to see the show. After gazing for a few seconds he remarked what the others had failed to observe, 'Why, the woman's naked!'

I attempted to explain that among rich people in high society it was customary to dress like that in the evening, and that it looked very pretty.

Mrs M'Swat admonished me for showing the children low pictures.

'She must be a very bold woman,' said Jimmy; and Lizer pronounced her mad because, as she put it, 'It's a wonder she'd be half-undressed in her photo; you'd think she oughter dress herself up complete then.'

Lizer certainly acted upon this principle, as a photo of her, which had been taken by a travelling artist, bore evidence that for the occasion she had arrayed herself in two pairs of ill-fitting cuffs, Peter's watch and chain, strings, jackets, flowers, and other gewgaws galore.

'There ain't no such person as Madame Melber; it's only a fairy-tale,' said Mrs M'Swat.

'Did you ever hear of Gladstone?' I inquired.

'No; where is that place?'

'Did you ever hear of Jesus Christ?'

'Sure, yes; he's got something to do with God, ain't he?'

After that I never attempted to enlighten them regarding our celebrities.

Oh, how I envied them their ignorant contentment! They were as ducks on a duck-pond; but I was as a duck forced for ever to live in a desert, ever wildly longing for water, but never reaching it outside of dreams.

CHAPTER 31

Mr M'Swat and I Have a Bust-up

Men only, and they merely on business, came to Barney's Gap—
women tabooed the place. Some of them told me they would
come to see me, but not Mrs M'Swat, as she always allowed
the children to be as rude to them as they pleased. With the
few individuals who chanced to come M'Swat would sit down,
light his pipe, and vulgarly and profusely expectorate on the
floor, while they yarned and yarned for hours and hours about
the price of wool, the probable breeding capacity of the male
stock they kept, and of the want of grass—never a word about
their country's politics or the events of the day; even the news
of the 'Mountain Murders' by Butler had not penetrated here.
I wondered if they were acquainted with the names of their
Governor and Prime Minister.

It was not the poor food and the filthy way of preparing it
that worried me, or that Mr M'Swat used 'damn' on an average
twice in five minutes when conversing, or that the children for
ever nagged about my father's poverty and tormented me in a
thousand other ways—it was the dead monotony that was killing
me.

I longed feveredly for something to happen. Agony is a tame
word wherewith to express what that life meant to me. Solitary
confinement to a gipsy would be something on a par.

Every night unfailingly when at home M'Swat sat in the bosom
of his family and speculated as to how much richer he was than
his neighbours, what old Reece lived on, and who had the best
breed of sheep and who was the smartest at counting these
animals, until the sordidness of it turned me dizzy, and I would
steal out under the stars to try and cool my heated spirit. This
became a practice with me, and every night I would slip away
out of hearing of the household to sing the songs I had heard

at Caddagat, and in imagination to relive every day and hour there, till the thing became too much for me, and I was scarcely responsible for my actions. Often I knelt on the parched ground beneath the balmy summer sky to pray—wild passionate prayers that were never answered.

I was under the impression that my nightly ramble was not specially noticed by any one, but I was mistaken. Mr M'Swat, it appears, suspected me of having a lover, but was never able to catch me red-handed.

The possibility of a girl going out at night to gaze at the stars and dream was as improbable a thought for him as flying is to me, and having no soul above mud, had I attempted an explanation he would have considered me mad, and dangerous to have about the place.

Peter, junior, had a sweetheart, one Susie Duffy, who lived some miles on the other side of the Murrumbidgee. He was in the habit of courting her every Sunday and two or three nights during the week, and I often heard the clang of his stirrup-irons and the clink of hobble-chain when he returned late; but on one occasion I stayed out later than usual, and he passed me going home. I stood still and he did not see me, but his horse shied violently. I thought he would imagine I was a ghost, so called out:

'It is I.'

'Well, I'll be hanged! What are ye doin' at this time ev night. Ain't yuz afraid of ghosts?'

'Oh dear no. I had a bad headache and couldn't sleep, so came out to try if a walk would cure it,' I explained.

We were a quarter of a mile or so from the house, so Peter slackened his speed that I might keep pace with him. His knowledge of etiquette did not extend as far as dismounting. There is a great difference between rudeness and ignorance. Peter was not rude; he was merely ignorant. For the same reason he let his mother feed the pigs, clean his boots, and chop wood, while he sat down and smoked and spat. It was not that he was unmanly, as that this was the only manliness he had known.

I was alone in the schoolroom next afternoon when Mr M'Swat sidled in, and after stuttering and hawing a little, delivered himself of:

'I want to tell ye that I don't hold with a gu-r-r-r-l going out of nights for to meet young men: if ye want to do any coortin' yuz can do it inside, if it's a decent young man. I have no objections to yer hangin' yer cap up to our Peter, only that ye have no prawperty—in yerself I like ye well enough, but we have other views for Peter. He's almost as good as made it sure with Susie Duffy, an' as ole Duffy will have a bit ev prawperty I want him to git her, an' wouldn't like ye to spoil the fun.'

Peter was 'tall and freckled and sandy, face of a country lout', and, like Middleton's rouse-about, 'hadn't any opinions, hadn't any ideas', but possessed sufficient instinct and common bush-craft with which, by hard slogging, to amass money. He was developing a moustache, and had a 'gu-r-r-r-l'; he wore tight trousers and long spurs; he walked with a sidling swagger that was a cross between shyness and flashness, and took as much pride in his necktie as any man; he had a kind heart, honest principles, and would not hurt a fly; he worked away from morning till night, and contentedly did his duty like a bullock in the sphere in which God had placed him; he never had a bath while I knew him, and was a man according to his lights. He knew there was such a thing as the outside world, as I know there is such a thing as algebra; but it troubled him no more than algebra troubles me.

This was my estimation of Peter M'Swat, junior. I respected him right enough in his place, as I trust he respected me in mine, but though fate thought fit for the present to place us in the one groove, yet our lives were unmixable commodities as oil and water, which lay apart and would never meet until taken in hand by the omnipotent leveller—death.

Marriage with Peter M'Swat!

Consternation and disgust held me speechless, and yet I was half inclined to laugh at the preposterousness of the thing, when Peter's father continued:

'I'm sorry if you've got smitten on Peter, but I know you'll be sensible. Ye see I have a lot of childre, and when the place is divided among 'em it won't be much. I tell ye wot, old Duffy has a good bit of money and only two childre, Susie and Mick. I could get you to meet Mick—he mayn't be so personable as our Peter,' he reflected, with evident pride in his weedy firstborn, and he got no farther, for I had been as a yeast-bottle bubbling up, and now went off bang!

'Silence, you ignorant old creature! How dare you have the incomparable impertinence to mention my name in conjunction with that of your boor of a son. Though he were a millionaire I would think his touch contamination. You have fallen through for once if you imagine I go out at night to meet any one— I merely go away to be free for a few minutes from the suffocating atmosphere of your odious home. You must not think that because you have grasped and slaved and got a little money that it makes a gentleman of you; and never you *dare* to again mention my name in regard to matrimony with any one about here;' and with my head high and shoulders thrown back I marched to my room, where I wept till I was weak and ill.

This monotonous sordid life was unhinging me, and there was no legitimate way of escape from it. I formed wild plans of running away, to do what I did not care so long as it brought a little action, anything but this torturing maddening monotony; but my love for my little brothers and sisters held me back. I could not do anything that would put me for ever beyond the pale of their society.

I was so reduced in spirit that had Harold Beecham appeared then with a matrimonial scheme to be fulfilled at once, I would have quickly erased the fine lines I had drawn and accepted his proposal; but he did not come, and I was unacquainted with his whereabouts or welfare. As I remembered him, how lovable and superior he seemed in comparison with the men I met nowadays: not that he was any better than these men in their place and according to their lights, but his lights—at least not his lights, for Harold Beecham was nothing of a philosopher, but the furniture of the drawing-room which they illuminated—was more artistic.

What a prince of gentlemanliness and winning gallantries he was in his quiet way!

This information concerning him was in a letter I received from my grandmother at Easter:

Who should surprise us with a visit the other day but Harold Beecham. He was as thin as a whipping-post, and very sunburnt [I smiled, imagining it impossible for Harold to be any browner than of yore]. He has been near death's door with the measles—caught them in Queensland while droving, and got wet. He was so ill that he had to give up charge of that 1600 head of cattle he was bringing. He came to say good-bye to us, as he is off to Western Australia next week to see if he can mend his fortunes there. I was afraid he was going to be like young Charters, and swear he would never come back unless he made a pile, but he says he will back next Christmas three years for certain, if he is alive and kicking, as he says himself. Why he intends returning at that stipulated time I don't know, as he never was very communicative, and is more unsociable than ever now. He is a man who never shows his feelings, but he must feel the loss of his old position deeply. He seemed surprised not to find you here, and says it was a pity to set you teaching, as it will take all the life and fun out of you, and that is the first time I ever heard him express an opinion in any one's business but his own. Frank Hawden sends kind regard, &c.

Teaching certainly had the effect upon me anticipated by Harold Beecham, but it was not the teaching but the place in which I taught which was doing the mischief—good, my mother termed it.

I was often sleepless for more than forty-eight hours at a stretch, and cried through the nights until my eyes had black rings round them, which washing failed to remove. The neighbours described me as 'a sorrowful lookin' delicate creetur', that couldn't larf to save her life'—quite a different character to the girl who at Caddagat was continually chid for being a romp, a hoyden, a

218

boisterous tomboy, a whirlwind, and for excessive laughter at anything and everything. I got into such a state of nervousness that I would jump at the opening of a door or an unexpected footfall.

When cooling down, after having so vigorously delivered Mr M'Swat a piece of my mind, I felt that I owed him an apology. According to his lights (and that is the only fair way of judging our fellows) he had acted in a kind of fatherly way. I was a young girl under his charge, and he would have in a measure been responsible had I come to harm through going out in the night. He had been good-natured, too, in offering to help things along by providing an eligible, and allowing us to 'spoon' under his surveillance. That I was of temperament and aspirations that made his plans loathsome to me was no fault of his—only a heavy misfortune to myself. Yes; I had been in the wrong entirely.

With this idea in my head, sinking ankle-deep in the dust, and threading my way through the pigs and fowls which hung around the back door, I went in search of my master. Mrs M'Swat was teaching Jimmy how to kill a sheep and dress it for use; while Lizer, who was nurse to the baby and spectator of the peformance, was volubly and ungrammatically giving instructions in the art. Peter and some of the younger children were away felling stringybark-trees for the sustenance of the sheep. The fall of their axes and the murmur of the Murrumbidgee echoed faintly from the sunset. They would be home presently and at tea; I reflected it would be 'The old yeos looks terrible skinny, but the hoggets is fat yet. By crikey! They did go into the bushes. They chawed up stems and all—some as thick as a pencil.'

This information in that parlance had been given yesterday, the day before, would be given today, tomorrow, and the next day. It was the boss item on the conversational programme until further orders.

I had a pretty good idea where to find Mr M'Swat, as he had lately purchased a pair of stud rams, and was in the habit of admiring them for a couple of hours every evening. I went to

219

where they usually grazed, and there, as I expected, found Mr M'Swat, pipe in mouth, with glistening eyes, surveying his darlings.

'Mr M'Swat, I have come to beg your pardon.'

'That's all right, me gu-r-r-r-l. I didn't take no notice to anything ye might spit out in a rage.'

'But I was not in a rage. I meant every word I said, but I want to apologize for the rude way in which I said it, as I had no right to speak so to my elders. And I want to tell you that you need not fear me running away with Peter, even supposing he should honour me with his affections, as I am engaged to another man.'

'By dad, I'll be hanged!' he exclaimed, with nothing but curiosity on his wrinkled dried tobacco-leaf-looking face. He expressed no resentment on account of my behaviour to him.

'Are ye to be married soon? Has he got any prawperty? Who is he? I suppose he's respectable. Ye're very young.'

'Yes; he is renowned for respectability, but I am not going to marry him till I am twenty-one. He is poor, but has good prospects. You must promise me not to tell any one, as I wish it kept a secret, and only mention it to you so that you need not be disturbed about Peter.'

He assured me that he would keep the secret, and I knew I could rely on his word. He was greatly perturbed that my intended was poor.

'Never ye marry a man widout a bit er prawperty, me gu-r-r-r-l. Take my advice—the divil's in a poor match, no matter how good the man may be. Don't ye be in a hurry; ye're personable enough in yer way, and there's as good fish in the seas as ever come out of 'em. Yer very small; I admire a good lump of a woman meself—but don't ye lose heart. I've heerd some men say they like little girls, but, as I said, I like a good lump of a woman myself.'

'And you've got a good lump of a squaw,' I thought to myself.

Do not mistake me. I do not for an instant fancy myself above the M'Swats. Quite the reverse; they are much superior to me. Mr M'Swat was upright and clean in his morals, and in his little

220

sphere was as sensible and kind a man as one could wish for. Mrs M'Swat was faithful to him, contented and good-natured, and bore uncomplainingly, year after year, that most cruelly agonising of human duties—childbirth, and did more for her nation and her Maker than I will ever be noble enough to do.

But I could not help it that their life was warping my very soul. Nature fashions us all; we have no voice in the matter, and I could not change my organisation to one which would find sufficient sustenance in the mental atmosphere of Barney's Gap.

CHAPTER 32

Ta-ta to Barney's Gap

It chanced at last, as June gave place to July and July to August, that I could bear it no longer. I would go away even if I had to walk, and what I would do I did not know or care, my one idea being to leave Barney's Gap far and far behind. One evening I got a lot of letters from my little brothers and sisters at home. I fretted over them a good deal, and put them under my pillow; and as I had not slept for nights, and was feeling weak and queer, I laid my head upon them to rest a little before going out to get the tea ready. The next thing I knew was that Mrs M'Swat was shaking me vigorously with one hand, holding a flaring candle in the other, and saying:

'Lizer, shut the winder quick. She's been lyin' here in the draught till she's froze, and must have the nightmare, the way she's been singin' out that queer, an' I can't git her woke up. What ails ye, child? Are ye sick?'

I did not know what ailed me, but learnt subsequently that I laughed and cried very much, and pleaded hard with grannie and some Harold to save me, and kept reiterating, 'I cannot bear it, I cannot bear it,' and altogether behaved so strangely that Mr M'Swat became so alarmed that he sent seventeen miles for the nearest doctor. He came next morning, felt my pulse, asked a few questions, and stated that I was suffering from nervous prostration.

'Why, the child is completely run down, and in a fair way to contract brain fever!' he exclaimed. 'What has she been doing? It seems as though she had been under some great mental strain. She must have complete rest and change, plenty of diversion and nourishing food, or her mind will become impaired.'

He left me a bottle of tonic and Mr and Mrs M'Swat many fears. Poor kind-hearted souls, they got in a great state, and understood about as much of the cause of my breakdown as I do of the inside of the moon. They ascribed it to the paltry amount of teaching and work I had done.

Mrs M'Swat killed a fowl and stewed it for my delectation. There was part of the inside with many feathers to flavour the dish, and having no appetite, I did not enjoy it, but made a feint of so doing to please the good-natured cook.

They intended writing at once to give my parents notice when I would be put on the train. I was pronounced too ill to act as scribe; Lizer was suggested, and then Jimmy, but M'Swat settled the matter thus:

'Sure, damn it! I'm the proper one to write on an important business matther like this here.'

So pens, ink, and paper were laid on the dining-room table, and the great proclamation went forth among the youngsters, 'Pa is goin' to write a whole letter all by hisself.'

My door opened with the dining-room, and from bed I could see the proceeding. Mr M'Swat hitched his trousers well through the saddle-strap which he always wore as a belt, took off his coat and folded it on the back of a chair, rolled his shirt-sleeves up to his elbows, pulled his hat well over his eyes, and 'shaped up' to the writing material, none of which met with his approval. The ink was 'warter', the pens had not enough 'pint', and the paper was 'trash'; but on being assured it was the good stuff he had purchased especially for himself, he buckled to the fray, producing in three hours a half-sheet epistle, which in grammar, composition, and spelling quite eclipsed the entries of his diary. However, it served its purpose, and my parents wrote back that, did I reach Goulburn on a certain day, a neighbour who would be in town then would bring me home.

Now that it was settled that I had no more to teach the dirty children, out of dirty books, lessons for which they had great disinclination, and no more to direct Lizer's greasy fingers over the yellow keys of that demented piano in a vain endeavour to teach her 'choones', of which her mother expected her to learn on an average two daily, it seemed as though I had a mountain lifted off me, and I revived magically, got out of bed and packed my things.

I was delighted at the prospect of throwing off the leaden shackles of Barney's Gap, but there was a little regret mingled with my relief. The little boys had not been always bold. Did I express a wish for a parrot-wing or water-worn stone, or such like, after a time I would be certain, on issuing from my bedroom, to find that it had been surreptitiously laid there, and the little soft-eyed fellows would squabble for the privilege of bringing me my post, simply to give me pleasure. Poor little Lizer, and Rose Jane too, copied me in style of dress and manners in a way that was somewhat ludicrous but more pathetic.

They clustered round to say good-bye. I would be sure to write. Oh yes, of course, and they would write in return and tell me if the bay mare got well, and where they would find the yellow turkey-hen's nest. When I got well I must come back, and I wouldn't have as much work to do, but go for more rides to keep well, and so on. Mrs M'Swat very anxiously impressed it upon me that I was to explain to my mother that it was not her (Mrs M'S.'s) fault that I 'ailed' from overwork, as I had never complained and always seemed well.

With a kindly light on his homely sunburnt face, M'Swat said, as he put me on the train:

'Sure, tell yer father he needn't worry over the money. I'll never be hard on him, an' if ever I could help ye, I'd be glad.'

'Thank you; you are very good, and have done too much already.'

'Too much! Sure, damn it, wot's the good er bein' alive if we can't help each other sometimes. I don't mind how much I help a person if they have a little gratitood, but, damn it, I can't abear ingratitood.'

'Good-bye, Mr M'Swat, and thank you.'

'Good-bye, me gu-r-r-l, and never marry that bloke of yours if he don't git a bit er prawperty, for the divil's in a poor match.'

224

CHAPTER 33

Back at Possum Gully

They were expecting me on the frosty evening in September, and the children came bounding and shouting to meet me, when myself and luggage were deposited at Possum Gully, by a neighbour, as he passed in a great hurry to reach his own home ere it got too dark. They bustled me to a glowing fire in no time.

My father sat reading, and, greeting me in a very quiet fashion, continued the perusal of his paper. My mother shut her lips tightly, saying exultingly, 'It seems it was possible for you to find a worse place than home'; and that little speech was the thorn on the rose of my welcome home. But there was no sting in Gertie's greeting, and how beautiful she was growing, and so tall! It touched me to see she had made an especial dainty for my tea, and had put things on the table which were only used for visitors. The boys and little Aurora chattered and danced around me all the while. One brought for my inspection some soup-plates which had been procured during my absence; another came with a picture-book; and nothing would do them but that I must, despite the darkness, straightaway go out and admire a new fowl-house which 'Horace and Stanley built all by their-selves, and no one helped them one single bit.'

After Mrs M'Swat it was a rest, a relief, a treat, to hear my mother's cultivated voice, and observe her lady-like and refined figure as she moved about; and, what a palace the place seemed in comparison to Barney's Gap! simply because it was clean, orderly, and bore traces of refinement; for the stamp of indigent circumstances was legibly imprinted upon it, and many things which had been considered 'done for' when thirteen months be-fore I had left home, were still in use.

I carefully studied my brothers and sisters. They had grown

225

during my absence, and were all big for their age, and though some of them not exactly handsome, yet all pleasant to look upon—I was the only wanting in physical charms—also they were often discontented, and wished, as children will, for things they could not have; but they were natural, understandable children, not like myself, cursed with a fevered ambition for the utterly unattainable.

> *Oh, were I seated high as my ambition,*
> *I'd place this foot on naked necks of monarchs!*

At the time of my departure for Caddagat my father had been negotiating with beer regarding the sale of his manhood; on returning I found that he had completed the bargain, and held a stamped receipt in his miserable appearance and demeanour. In the broken-down man, regardless of manners, one would have failed to recognize Dick Melvyn, 'Smart Dick Melvyn', 'Jolly-good-fellow Melvyn', 'Thorough Gentleman', and 'Manly Melvyn' of the handsome face and ingratiating manners, one-time holder of Bruggabrong, Bin Bin East, and Bin Bin West. He never corrected his family nowadays, and his example was most deleterious to them.

Mother gave me a list of her worries in private after tea that night. She wished she had never married: not only was her husband a failure, but to all appearances her children would be the same. I wasn't worth my salt or I would have remained at Barney's Gap; and there was Horace—heaven only knew where he would end. God would surely punish him for his disrespect to his father. It was impossible to keep things together much longer, etc., etc.

When we went to bed that night Gertie poured all her troubles into my ear in a jumbled string. It was terrible to have such a father. She was ashamed of him. He was always going into town, and stayed there till mother had to go after him, or some of the neighbours were so good as to bring him home. It took all the money to pay the publican's bills, and Gertie was ashamed to be seen abroad in the nice clothes which grannie sent, as the neighbours said the Melvyns ought to pay up the old man's bills instead of dressing like swells; and she couldn't help it, and she was sick and tired of trying to keep up respectability in the teeth of such odds.

I comforted her with the assurance that the only thing was to feel right within ourselves, and let people say whatsoever entertained their poor little minds. And I fell asleep thinking that parents have a duty to children greater than children to parents, and they who do not fulfil their responsibility in this respect are as bad in their morals as a debauchee, corrupt the community as much as a thief, and are among the ablest underminers of their nation.

On the morrow, the first time we were alone, Horace seized the opportunity of holding forth on *his* woes. It was no use, he was choke full of Possum Gully: he would stick to it for another year, and then he would chuck it, even if he had to go on the wallaby. He wasn't going to be slaving for ever for the boss to swallow the proceeds, and there was nothing to be made out of dairying. When it wasn't drought it was floods and caterpillars and grasshoppers.

Among my brothers and sisters I quickly revived to a certain extent, and mother asserted her opinion that I had not been ill at all, but had made up my mind to torment her; had not taken sufficient exercise, and might have had a little derangement of the system but nothing more. It was proposed that I should return to Barney's Gap. I demurred, and was anathematized as ungrateful and altogether corrupt, that I would not go back to M'Swat, who was so good as to lend my father money out of pure friendship; but for once in my life I could not be made submit by either coercion or persuasion. Grannie offered to take one of us to Caddagat; mother preferred that Gertie should go. So we sent the pretty girl to dwell among her kindred in a land of comfort and pleasure.

I remained at Possum Gully to tread the same old life in its tame narrow path, with its never-ending dawn-till-daylight round of tasks; with, as its entertainments, an occasional picnic or funeral or a day in town, when, should it happen to be Sunday, I never fail to patronize one of the cathedrals. I love the organ music, and the hush which pervades the building; and there is much entertainment in various ways if one goes early and watches the well-dressed congregation filing in. The costumes and the women are pretty, and, in his own particular line, the ability of the verger is something at which to marvel. Regular attendants, of course, pay for and have reserved their seats, but it is in classing the visitors that the verger displays his talent. He can cull the commoners from the parvenu aristocrats, and put them in their respective places as skilfully as an expert horse-dealer can draft his stock at a sale. Then, when the audience is complete, in the middle and front of the edifice are to be found they of the white hands and fine jewels; and in the topmost seat of the synagogue, praying audibly, is one who has made all his wealth by devouring widows' houses; while pushed away to the corners and wings are they who earn their bread by the sweat of their brow; and those who cannot afford good linen are too proud to be seen here at all.

'The choir sings and the organ rings,' the uninteresting prayers are rattled off ('O come, let us worship, and fall down: and kneel before the Lord, our Maker'); a sermon, mostly of the debts of the concern, of the customs of the ancients, or of the rites and ceremonies of up-to-date churchism, is delivered, and the play is done, and as I leave the building a great hunger for a little Christianity fills my heart.

Oh that a preacher might arise and expound from the Book of books a religion with a God, a religion with a heart in it— a Christian religion, which would abolish the cold legend whose centre is respectability, and which rears great buildings in which the rich recline on silken hassocks while the poor perish in the shadow thereof.

Through the hot dry summer, then the heartless winter and the scorching summer again which have spent themselves since

Gertie's departure, I have struggled hard to do my duty in that state of life unto which it had pleased God to call me, and sometimes I have partially succeeded. I have had no books or papers, nothing but peasant surroundings and peasant tasks, and have encouraged peasant ignorance—ignorance being the mainspring of contentment, and contentment the bed-rock of happiness; but it is all to no purpose. A note from the other world will strike upon the chord of my being, and the spirit which has been dozing within me awakens and fiercely beats at its bars, demanding some nobler thought, some higher aspiration, some wider action, a more saturnalian pleasure, something more than the peasant life can ever yield. Then I hold my spirit tight till wild passionate longing sinks down, down to sickening dumb despair, and had I the privilege extended to Job of old—to curse God and die—I would leap at it eagerly.

CHAPTER 34

But Absent Friends are Soon Forgot

We received a great many letters from Gertie for a little while after she went up the country, but they grew shorter and farther between as time went on.

In one of grannie's letters there was concerning my sister: 'I find Gertie is a much younger girl for her age than Sybylla was, and not nearly so wild and hard to manage. She is a great comfort to me. Every one remarks upon her good looks.'

From one of Gertie's letters:

> Uncle Julius came home from Hong Kong and America last
> week, and brought such a lot of funny presents for every one.
> He had a lot for you, but he has given them to me instead as
> you are not here. He calls me his pretty little sunbeam, and
> says I must always live with him.

I sighed to myself as I read this. Uncle Jay-Jay had said much the same to me, and where was I now? My thoughts were ever turning to the people and old place I love so well, but Gertie's letters showed me that I was utterly forgotten and unmissed.

Gertie left us in October 1897, and it was somewhere about January 1898 that all the letters from Caddagat were full to overflowing with the wonderful news of Harold Beecham's reinstatement at Five-Bob Downs, under the same conditions as he had held sway there in my day.

From grannie's letters I learnt that some old sweetheart of Harold's father had bequeathed untold wealth to this her lost love's son. The wealth was in bonds and stocks principally, and though it would be some time ere Harold was actually in possession of it, yet he had no difficulty in getting advancements to any amount, and had immediately repurchased Five-Bob.

I had never dreamed of such a possibility. True, I had often

said were Harold a character in fiction instead of real life, some
relative would die opportunely and set him up in his former
position, but, here, this utterly unanticipated contingency had
arisen in a manner which would affect my own life, and what
were my feelings regarding the matter?

I think I was not fully aware of the extent of my lack of wifely
love for Harold Beecham, until experiencing the sense of relief
which stole over me on holding in my hand the announcement
of his return to the smile of fortune.

He was rich; he would not need me now; my obligation to
him ceased to exist; I was free. He would no longer wish to
be hampered with me. He could take his choice of beauty and
worth; he might even purchase a princess did his ambition point
that way.

One of Gertie's letters ran:

> That Mr Beecham you used to tell me so much about has
> come back to live at Five-Bob. He has brought his aunts back.
> Every one went to welcome them, and there was a great fuss.
> Aunt Helen says he (Mr B.) is very conservative; he has
> everything just as it used to be. I believe he is richer than ever.
> Every one is laughing about his luck. He was here twice last
> week, and has just left this evening. He is very quiet. I don't
> know how you thought him so wonderful. I think he is too
> slow, I have great work to talk to him, but he is very kind, and
> I like him. He seems to remember you well, and often says
> you were a game youngster, and could ride like old Nick
> himself.

I wrote to the owner of Five-Bob desiring to know if what
I heard concerning his good fortune was correct, and he replied
by return post:

> My dear little Syb,
>   Yes, thank goodness it is all true. The old lady left me
> nearly a million. It seems like a fairy yarn, and I will know
> how to value it more now. I would have written sooner, only
> you remember our bargain, and I was just waiting to get

things fixed up a little, when I'm off at great tracks to claim you in the flesh, as there is no need for us to wait above a month or two now if you are agreeable. I am just run to death. It takes a bit of jigging to get things straight again, but it's simply too good to believe to be back in the same old beat. I've seen Gertie a good many times, and find your descriptions of her were not at all overdrawn. I won't send any love in this, or there would be a 'bust-up' in the post-office, because I'd be sure to overdo the thing, and I'd have all the officials on to me for damages. Gather up your goods and chattels, because I'll be along in a week or two to take possession of you.

Yr devoted
Hal.

I screwed the letter in two and dropped it into the kitchen-fire.

I knew Harold meant what he had said. He was a strong-natured man of firm determinations, and having made up his mind to marry me would never for an instant think of anything else; but I could see what he could not see himself—that he had probably tired of me, and was becoming enamoured of Gertie's beauty.

The discordance of life smote hard upon me, and the letter I wrote was not pleasant. It ran:

To H. A. BEECHAM, Esq.,
  Five-Bob Downs Station,
    Gool-Gool, N.S.W.
Sir,

Your favour duly to hand. I heartily rejoice at your good fortune, and trust you may live long and have health to enjoy it. Do not for an instant consider yourself under any obligations to me, for you are perfectly free. Choose some one who will reflect more credit on your taste and sense.

With all good wishes,
Faithfully yrs,
S. Penelope Melvyn.

As I closed and directed this how far away Harold Beecham seemed! Less than two years ago I had been familiar with every curve and expression of his face, every outline of his great figure, every intonation of his strong cultivated voice; but now he seemed as the shadow of a former age.

He wrote in reply: What did I mean? Was it a joke—just a little of my old tormenting spirit? Would I explain immediately? He couldn't get down to see me for a fortnight at the least.

I explained, and very tersely, that I had meant what I said, and in return received a letter as short as my own:

Dear Miss Melvyn,

I regret your decision, but trust I have sufficient manhood to prevent me from thrusting myself upon any lady, much less you.

Your sincere friend,
Harold Augustus Beecham.

He did not demand a reason for my decision, but accepted it unquestionably. As I read his words he grew near to me, as in the days gone by.

I closed my eyes, and before my mental vision there arose an overgrown old orchard, skirting one of the great stock-routes from Riverina to Monaro. A glorious day was languidly smiling good night on abundance of ripe and ripening fruit and flowers. The scent of stock and the merry cry of the tennis-players filled the air. I could feel Harold's wild jolting heart-beats, his burning breath on my brow, and his voice husky with rage in my ear. As he wrote that letter I could fancy the well-cut mouth settling into a sullen line, as it had done on my birthday when, by caressing, I had won it back to its habitual pleasant expression; but on this occasion I would not be there. He would be angry just a little while—a man of his strength and importance could not long hold ill-will towards a woman, a girl, a child! as weak and insignificant as I. Then when I should meet him in the years to come, when he would be the faithful and loving husband of another woman, he would be a little embarrassed perhaps; but

233

I would set him at his ease, and we would laugh together re what he would term our foolish young days, and he would like me in a brotherly way. Yes, that was how it would be. The tiny note blackened in the flames.

So much for my romance of love! It had ended in a bottle of smoke, as all my other dreams of life bid fair to do.

I think I was not fully aware how near I had been to loving Harold Beecham until experiencing the sense of loss which stole over me on holding in my hand the acceptance of his dismissal. It was a something gone out of my life, which contained so few somethings, that I crushingly felt the loss of any one.

Our greatest heart-treasure is a knowledge that there is in creation an individual to whom our existence is necessary—some one who is part of our life as we are part of theirs, some one in whose life we feel assured our death would leave a gap for a day or two. And who can be this but a husband or wife? Our parents have other children and themselves, our brothers and sisters marry and have lives apart, so with our friends; but one's husband would be different. And I had thrown behind me this chance; but in the days that followed I knew that I had acted wisely.

Gertie's letters would contain: 'Harold Beecham, he makes me call him Harry, took me to Five-Bob last week, and it was lovely fun.'

Again it would be: 'Harry says I am the prettiest little girl ever was, Caddagat or anywhere else, and he gave me such a lovely bracelet. I wish you could see it.'

Or this:

We all went to church yesterday. Harry rode with me. There is to be a very swell ball at Wyambeet next month, and Harry says I am to keep nearly all my dances for him. Frank Hawden sailed for England last week. We have a new jackeroo. He is better-looking than Frank, but I don't like him as well.

234

Grannie's and aunt Helen's letter to my mother corroborated these admissions. Grannie wrote:

> Harry Beecham seems to be very much struck with Gertie. I think it would be a good thing, as he is immensely rich, and a very steady young fellow into the bargain. They say no woman could live with him on account of his temper; but he has always been a favourite of mine, and we cannot expect a man without some faults.

Aunt Helen remarked:

> Don't be surprised if you have young Beecham down there presently on an 'asking papa' excursion. He spends a great deal of time here, and has been inquiring the best route to Possum Gully. Do you remember him? I don't think he was here in your day. He is an estimable and likeable young fellow, and I think will make a good husband apart from his wealth. He and Gertie present a marked contrast.

Sometimes on reading this kind of thing I would wax rather bitter. Love, I said, was not a lasting thing; but knowledge told me that it was for those of beauty and winsome ways, and not for me. I was ever to be a lonely-hearted waif from end to end of the world of love—an alien among my own kin.

But there were other things to worry me. Horace had left the family roof. He averred he was 'full up of life under the old man's rule. It was too slow and messed up.' His uncle, George Melvyn, his father's eldest brother, who had so often and so kindly set us up with cows, had offered to take him, and his father had consented to let him go. George Melvyn had a large station outback, a large sheep-shearing machine, and other improvements. Thence, strong in the hope of sixteen years, Horace set out on horseback one springless spring morning ere the sun had risen, with all his earthly possessions strapped before him. Bravely the horse stepped out for its week's journey, and bravely its rider sat, leaving me and the shadeless, wooden sun-baked house on the side of the hill, with the regretlessness of teens—

235

especially masculine teens. I watched him depart until the clacking of his horse's hoofs grew faint on the stony hillside and his form disappeared amid the she-oak scrub which crowned the ridge to the westward. He was gone. Such is life. I sat down and buried my face in my apron, too miserable even for tears. Here was another article I ill could spare wrenched from my poorly and sparsely furnished existence.

True, our intercourse had not always been carpeted with rose-leaves. His pitiless scorn of my want of size and beauty had often given me a sleepless night; but I felt no bitterness against him for this, but merely cursed the Potter who had fashioned the clay that was thus described.

On the other hand, he was the only one who had ever stood up and said a word of extenuation for me in the teeth of a family squall. Father did not count; my mother thought me bad from end to end; Gertie, in addition to the gifts of beauty and lovable-ness, possessed that of holding with the hare and running with the hound; but Horace once had put in a word for me that I would never forget. I missed his presence in the house, his pounding of the old piano with four dumb notes in the middle, as he bawled thereto rollicking sea and comic songs; I missed his energetic dissertations on spurs, whips, and blood-horses, and his spirited rendering of snatches of Paterson and Gordon, as he came in and out, banging doors and gates, teasing the cats and dogs and tormenting the children.

236

CHAPTER 35

The 3rd of December 1898

It was a very hot day. So extreme was the heat that to save the lives of some young swallows my father had to put wet bags over the iron roof above their nest. A galvanized-iron awning connected our kitchen and house: in this some swallows had built, placing their nest so near the iron that the young ones were baking with the heat until rescued by the wet bagging. I had a heavy day's work before me, and, from my exertions of the day before, was tired at the beginning. Bush-fires had been raging in the vicinity during the week, and yesterday had come so close that I had been called out to carry buckets of water all the afternoon in the blazing sun. The fire had been allayed, after making a gap in one of our boundary fences. Father and the boys had been forced to leave the harvesting of the miserable pinched wheat while they went to mend it, as the small allowance of grass the drought gave us was precious, and had to be carefully preserved from neighbours' stock.

I had baked and cooked, scrubbed floors and whitewashed hearths, scoured tinware and cutlery, cleaned windows, swept yards, and discharged numerous miscellaneous jobs, and half-past two in the afternoon found me very dirty and very tired, and with very much more yet to do.

One of my half-starved poddy calves was very ill, and I went out to doctor it previous to bathing and tidying myself for my finishing household duties.

My mother was busy upon piles and piles of wearying mending, which was one of the most hopeless of the many slaveries of her life. This was hard work, and my father was slaving away in the sun, and mine was arduous labour, and it was a very hot day, and a drought-smitten and a long day, and poddy calves ever have a tendency to make me moralize and snarl. This was life, my life and my parents' life, and the life of those around us, and if I was a good girl and honoured my parents I would be rewarded with a long stretch of it. Yah!

These pagan meditations were interrupted by a footfall slowly approaching. I did not turn to ascertain who it might be, but trusted it was no one of importance, as the poddy and I presented rather a grotesque appearance. It was one of the most miserable and sickly of its miserable kind, and I was in the working uniform of the Australian peasantry. My tattered skirt and my odd and bursted boots, laced with twine, were spattered with white-wash, for coolness my soiled cotton blouse hung loose, and exceedingly dilapidated sun-bonnet surmounted my head, and a bottle of castor-oil was in my hand.

I supposed it was one of the neighbours or a tea-agent, and I would send them to mother.

The footsteps had come to a halt beside me.

'Could you tell me if—'

I glanced upwards. Horrors! There stood Harold Beecham, as tall and broad as of yore, even more sunburnt than ever, and looking very stylish in a suit of grey and a soft fashionable dinted-in hat; and it was the first time I have ever seen him in a white shirt and high collar.

I wished he would explode, or I might sink into the ground, or the calf would disappear, or that something might happen.

On recognizing me his silence grew profound, but an unmistakable expression of pity filled his eyes and stung me to the quick.

I have a faculty of self-pity, but my pride promptly refuses the slightest offer of sympathy from another.

I could feel my heart grow as bitterly cold as my demeanour was icily stiff, when I stood up and said curtly:

'This is a great surprise, Mr Beecham.'

'Not an unpleasant one, I hope,' he said pleasantly.

'We will not discuss the matter. Come inside out of the heat.'

'I'm in no hurry, Syb, and couldn't I help you with that poor little devil?'

'I'm only trying to give it another chance of life.'

'What will you do with it if it lives?'

'Sell it for a half a crown when it's a yearling.'

'It would pay better to shoot the poor little beggar now.'

'No doubt it would the owner of Five-Bob, but we have to be more careful,' I said tartly.

'I didn't mean to offend you.'

'I'm not offended,' I returned, leading the way to the house, imagining with a keen pain that Harold Beecham must be wondering how for an instant he could have been foolish enough to fancy such an object two years ago.

Thank goodness I have never felt any humiliation on account of my mother, and felt none then, as she rose to greet Harold upon my introduction. She was a lady, and looked it, in spite of the piles of coarse mending, and the pair of trousers, almost bullet-proof with patches, out of which she drew her hand, roughened and reddened with hard labour, in spite of her patched and faded cotton gown, and the commonest and most poverty-stricken of peasant surroundings, which failed to hide that she had not been always thus.

Leaving them together, I expeditiously proceeded to relieve the livery-stable horse, on which Harold had come, of the valise, saddle, and bridle with which it was encumbered, and then let it loose in one of the grassless paddocks near at hand.

Then I threw myself on a stool in the kitchen, and felt, to the bone, the sting of having ideas above one's position.

In a few minutes mother came hurrying out.

'Good gracious, what's the matter? I suppose you didn't like being caught in such a pickle, but don't get in the dumps about it. I'll get him some tea while you clean yourself, and then you'll be able to help me by and by.'

I found my little sister Aurora, and we climbed through the window into my bedroom to get tidy. I put a pair of white socks and shoes and a clean pinafore on the little girl, and combed her golden curls. She was all mine—slept with me, obeyed me, championed me; while I—well, I worshipped her.

239

There was a hole in the wall, and through it I could see without being seen.

Mother was dispensing afternoon tea and talking to Harold. It was pleasant to see that manly figure once again. My spirits rose considerably After all, if the place was poor, it was very clean, as I had scrubbed it all that morning, and when I came to consider the matter, I remembered that men weren't such terrible creatures, and never made one feel the sting of one's poverty half as much as women do.

'Aurora,' I said, 'I want you to go out and tell Mr Beecham something.'

The little girl assented. I carefully instructed her in what she was to say, and dispatched her. She placed herself in front of Harold—a wide-eyed mite of four, that scarcely reached above his knee—and clasping her chubby hands behind her, gazed at him fearlessly and unwinkingly.

'Aurora, you mustn't stand staring like that,' said mother.

'Yes, I must,' she replied confidently.

'Well, and what's your name?' said Harold laughingly.

'Aurora and Rory. I belong to Sybyller, and got to tell you somesing.'

'Have you? Let's hear it.'

'Sybyller says you's Mr Beecher; when you're done tea, you'd like me if I would 'scort you to farver and the boys, and 'duce you.'

Mother laughed. 'That's some of Sybylla's nonsense. She considers Rory her especial property, and delights to make the child attempt long words. Perhaps you would care to take a stroll to where they are at work, by and by.'

Harold said he would go at once, and accepting Rory's escort, and with a few directions from mother, they presently set out— she importantly trudging beneath a big white sun-bonnet, and he looking down at her in amusement. Presently he tossed her high above his head, and depositing her upon his shoulder, held one sturdy brown leg in his browner hand, while she held on by his hair.

'My first impressions are very much in his favour,' said mother,

240

when they had got out of hearing. 'But fancy Gertie the wife of that great man!'

'She is four inches taller than I am,' I snapped. 'And if he was as big as a gum-tree, he would be a man all the same, and just as soft on a pretty face as all the rest of them.'

I bathed, dressed, arranged my hair, got something ready for tea, and prepared a room for our visitor. For this I collected from all parts of the house—a mat from one room, a toilet-set from another, and so on—till I had quite an elaborately furnished chamber ready for my one-time lover.

They returned at dusk, Rory again seated on Harold's shoulder, and two of the little boys clinging around him.

As I conducted him to his room I was in a different humour from that of the sweep-like object who had met him during the afternoon. I laughed to myself, for, as on a former occasion during our acquaintance, I felt I was master of the situation.

'I say, Syb, don't treat a fellow as though he was altogether a stranger,' he said diffidently, leaning against the doorpost.

Our hands met in a cordial grasp as I said, 'I'm awfully glad to see you, Hal; but, but—'

'But what?'

'I didn't feel over delighted to be caught in such a stew this afternoon.'

'Nonsense! It only reminded me of the first time we met,' he said with a twinkle in his eye. 'That's always the way with you girls. You can't be civil to a man unless you're dressed up fit to stun him, as though you couldn't make fool enough of him without the aid of clothes at all.'

'You'd better shut up,' I said over my shoulder as I departed, 'or you will be saying something better left unsaid, like at our first meeting. Do you remember?'

'Do I not? Great Scot, it's just like old times to have you giving me impudence over your shoulder like that!' he replied merrily.

'Like, yet unlike,' I retorted with a sigh.

CHAPTER 36

Once Upon a Time, When the Days Were Long and Hot

Next day was Sunday—a blazing one it was too. I proposed that in the afternoon some of us should go to church. Father sat upon the idea as a mad one. Walk two miles in such heat for nothing! as walk we would be compelled to do, horse-flesh being too precious in such a drought to fritter it away in idle jaunts. Surprising to say, however, Harold, who never walked anywhere when he could get any sort of a horse, uttered a wish to go. Accordingly, when the midday dinner was over, he, Stanley, and I set out. Going to church was quite the event of the week to the residents around Possum Gully. It was a small Dissenting chapel, where a layman ungrammatically held forth at 3 p.m. every Sunday; but the congregation was composed of all denominations, who attended more for the sitting about on logs outside, and yarning about the price of butter, the continuance of the drought, and the latest gossip, before and after the service, than for the service itself.

I knew the appearance of Harold Beecham would make quite a miniature sensation, and form food for no end of conjecture and chatter. In any company he was a distinguished-looking man, and particularly so among these hard-worked farmer-selectors, on whose careworn features the cruel effects of the drought were leaving additional lines of worry. I felt proud of my quondam sweetheart. There was an unconscious air of physical lordliness about him, and he looked such a swell—not the black-clothed, clean-shaved, great display of white collar-and-cuffs swell appertaining to the office and city street, but of the easy sunburnt squatter type of swelldom, redolent of the sun, the saddle, the wide open country—a man who is a man, utterly free from the least suspicion of effeminacy, and capable of earning his bread by the sweat of his brow—with an arm ready and willing to save in an accident.

All eyes were turned on us as we approached, and I knew that the attentions he paid me out of simple courtesy—tying my shoe, carrying my book, holding my parasol—would be put down as those of a lover.

I introduced him to a group of men who were sitting on a log, under the shade of a stringybark, and leaving him to converse with them, made my way to where the women sat beneath a gum-tree. The children made a third group at some distance. We always divided ourselves thus. A young fellow had to be very far gone ere he was willing to run the gauntlet of all the chaff levelled at him had he the courage to single out a girl and talk to her.

I greeted all the girls and women, beginning at the great-grandmother of the community, who illustrated to perfection the grim sarcasm of the fifth commandment. She had worked hard from morning till night, until too old to do so longer, and now hung around with aching weariness waiting for her grave. She generally poured into my ears a wail about her 'rheumatisms', and 'How long it do be waiting for the Lord'; but today she was too curious about Harold to think of herself.

'Sure, Sybyller, who's that? Is he yer sweetheart? Sure he's as fine a man as iver I clapped me eyes on.'

I proceeded to give his pedigree, but was interrupted by the arrival of the preacher, and we all went into the weatherboard iron-roofed house of prayer.

After service, one of the girls came up to me and whispered, 'That is your sweetheart, isn't it, Sybyller? He was looking at you all the time in church.'

'Oh dear, no! I'll introduce him to you.'

I did so, and watched him as they made remarks about the heat and drought. There was nothing of the cad or snob about him, and his short season of adversity had rubbed all the little crudities off his character, leaving him a man that the majority of both sexes would admire: women for his bigness, his gentleness, his fine brown moustache—and for his wealth; men, because he was a manly fellow.

I know he had walked to church on purpose to get a chance of speaking to me about Gertie, before approaching her parents on the matter; but Stanley accompanied us, and, boy-like, never relaxed in vigilance for an instant, so there was no opportunity for anything but matter-of-fact remarks. The heat was intense. We wiped the perspiration and flies from our face frequently, and disturbed millions of grasshoppers as we walked. They had devoured all the fruit in the orchards about, and had even destroyed many of the trees by eating the bark, and now they were stripping the briers of foliage. In one orchard we passed, the apricot, plum, and peach-stones hung naked on their leafless trees as evidence of their ravages. It was too hot to indulge in any but the most desultory conversation. We dawdled along. A tiger-snake crossed our path. Harold procured a stick and killed it, and Stanley hung it on the top wire of a fence which was near at hand. After this we discussed snakes for a few yards.

A blue sea-breeze, redolent of the bush-fires which were raging at Tocumwal and Bombala, came rushing and roaring over the ranges from the east, and enshrouded the scene in its heavy fog-like folds. The sun was obscured, and the temperature suddenly took such a great drop that I felt chilled in my flimsy clothing, and I noticed Harold draw his coat together.

Stanley had to go after the cows, which were little better than walking hides, yet were yarded morning and evening to yield a dribble of milk. He left us among some sallie-trees, in a secluded nook, walled in by briers, and went across the paddock to round-up the cows. Harold and I came to a halt by tacit consent.

'Syb, I want to speak to you,' he said earnestly, and then came to a dead stop.

'Very well; "tear into it," as Horace would say; but if it is anything frightful, break it gently,' I said flippantly.

'Surely, Syb, you can guess what it is I have to say.'

Yes, I could guess, I *knew* what he was going to say, and the knowledge left a dull bitterness at my heart. I knew he was going to tell me that I had been right and he wrong—that he had found some one he loved better than me, and that some one being my sister, he felt I needed some explanation before he could go in and win; and though I had refused him for want of love, yet it gave me pain when the moment arrived that the only man who had ever pretended to love me was going to say he had been mistaken, and preferred my sister.

There was silence save for the whirr of the countless grasshoppers in the brier bushes. I knew he was expecting me to help him out, but I felt doggedly savage and wouldn't. I looked up at him. He was a tall grand man, and honest and true and rich. He loved my sister; she would marry him, and they would be happy. I thought bitterly that God was good to one and cruel to another—not that I wanted this man, but why was I so different from other girls?

But then I thought of Gertie, so pretty, so girlish, so understandable, so full of innocent winning coquetry. I softened. Could any one help preferring her to me, who was strange, weird, and perverse—too outspoken to be engaging, devoid of beauty and endearing little ways? It was my own misfortune and nobody's fault that my singular individuality excluded me from the ordinary run of youthful joyous-heartednesses, and why should I be nasty to these young people?

I was no heroine, only a common little bush-girl, so had to make the best of the situation without any fooling. I raised my eyes from the scanty baked wisps of grass at my feet, placed my hand on Hal's arms, and tiptoeing so as to bring my five-foot stature more on a level with his, said:

'Yes, Hal, I know what you want to say. Say it all. I won't be nasty.'

'Well, you see you are so jolly touchy, and have snubbed me so often, that I don't know how to begin; and if you know what I'm going to say, won't you give me an answer without hearing it?'

'Yes, Hal; but you'd better say it, as I don't know what conditions—'

'Conditions!'—catching me up eagerly at the word. 'If it is only conditions that are stopping you, you can make your own conditions if you will marry me.'

'Marry you, Harold! What do you mean? Do you know what you are saying?' I exclaimed.

'There!' he replied: 'I knew you would take it as an insult. I believe you are the proudest girl in the world. I know you are too clever for me; but I love you, and could give you everything you fancied.'

'Hal, dear, let me explain. I'm not insulted, only surprised. I thought you were going to tell me that you loved Gertie, and would ask me not to make things unpleasant by telling her of the foolish little bit of flirtation there had been between us.'

'Marry Gertie! Why, she's only a child! A mere baby, in fact. Marry Gertie! I never thought of her in that light; and did you think I was that sort of a fellow, Syb?' he asked reproachfully.

'No, Hal,' I promptly made answer. 'I did not think you were that sort of fellow; but I thought that was the only sort of fellow there was.'

'Good heavens, Syb! Did you really mean those queer little letters you wrote me last February? I never for an instant looked upon them as anything but a little bit of playful contrariness. And have you forgotten me? Did you not mean your promise of two years ago, that you speak of what passed between us as a paltry bit of flirtation? Is that all you thought of it?'

'No, I did not consider it flirtation; but that is what I thought you would term it when announcing your affection for Gertie.'

'Gertie! Pretty little Gertie! I never looked upon the child as anything but your sister, consequently mine also. She's a child.'

'Child! She is eighteen. More than a year older than I was when you first introduced the subject of matrimony to me, and she is very beautiful, and twenty times as good and lovable as I could ever be even in my best moments.'

'Yes, I know you are young in years, but there is nothing of the child in you. As for beauty, it is nothing. If beauty was all a man required, he could, if rich, have a harem full of it any day. I want some one to be true.'

> *'The world is filled with folly and sin,*
> *And love must cling where it can, I say;*
> *For beauty is easy enough to win,*
> *But one isn't loved every day,'*

I quoted from Owen Meredith.

'Yes,' he said, 'that is why I want you. Just think a moment; don't say no. You are not vexed with me—are you, Syb?'

'Vexed, Hal! I am scarcely inhuman enough to be angry on account of being loved.'

Ah, why did I not love him as I have it in me to love! Why did he look so exasperatingly humble? I was weak, oh, so pitifully weak! I wanted a man who would be masterful and strong, who would help me over the rough spots of life—one who had done hard grinding in the mill of fate—one who had suffered, who had understood. No; I could never marry Harold Beecham.

'Well, Syb, little chum, what do you say?'

'Say!'—and the words fell from me bitterly—'I say, leave me; go and marry the sort of woman you ought to marry. The sort that all men like. A good conventional woman, who will do the things she should at the proper time. Leave me alone.'

He was painfully agitated. A look of pain crossed his face.

'Don't say that, Syb, because I was a beastly cad once: I've had all that knocked out of me.'

'I am the cad,' I replied. 'What I said was nasty and unwomanly, and I wish I had left it unsaid. I am not good enough to be your wife, Hal, or that of any man. Oh, Hal, I have never deceived you! There are scores of good noble women in the world who would wed you for the asking—marry one of them.'

'But, Syb, I want you. You are the best and truest girl in the world.'

'Och! Sure, the blarney-stone is getting a good rub now,' I said playfully.

Annoyance and amusement struggled for mastery in his expression as he replied:

'You're the queerest girl in the world. One minute you snub

247

a person, the next you are the jolliest girl going, and then you get as grave and earnest as a fellow's mother would be.'

'Yes, I am queer. If you had any sense, you'd have nothing to do with me. I'm more queer, too. I am given to something which a man never pardons a woman. You will draw away as though I were a snake when you hear.'

'What is it?'

'I am given to writing stories, and literary people predict I will yet be an authoress.'

He laughed—his soft, rich laugh.

'That's just into my hand. I'd rather work all day than write the shortest letter; so if you will give me a hand occasionally, you can write as many yarns as you like. I'll give you a study, and send for a truck-load of writing-gear at once, if you like. Is that the only horror you had to tell me?'

I bowed my head.

'Well, I can have you now,' he said gently, folding me softly in his arms with such tender reverence that I cried out in pain, 'Oh, Hal, don't, don't!' and struggled free. I was ashamed, knowing I was not worthy of this.

He flushed a dusky red.

'Am I so hateful to you that you cannot bear my touch?' he asked half wistfully, half angrily.

'Oh no; it isn't that. I'm really very fond of you, if you'd only understand,' I said half to myself.

'Understand! If you care for me, that is all I want to understand. I love you, and have plenty of money. There is nothing to keep us apart. Now that I know you care for me, I *will* have you, in spite of the devil.'

'There will be a great tussle between you,' I said mischievously, laughing at him. 'Old Nick has a great hold on me, and I'm sure he will dispute your right.'

At any time Harold's sense of humour was not at all in accordance with his size, and he failed to see how my remark applied now.

He gripped my hands in a passion of pleading, as two years

previously he had seized me in jealous rage. He drew me to him. His eyes were dark and full of entreaty; his voice was husky.

'Syb, poor little Syb, I will be good to you! You can have what you like. You don't know what you mean when you say no.'

No; I would not yield. He offered me everything—but control. He was a man who meant all he said. His were no idle promises on the spur of the moment. But no, no, no, no, he was not for me. My love must know, must have suffered, must understand.

'Syb, you do not answer. May I call you mine? You must, you must, you must!'

His hot breath was upon my cheek. The pleasant, open, manly countenance was very near—perilously near. The intoxication of his love was overpowering me. I had no hesitation about trusting him. He was not distasteful to me in any way. What was the good of waiting for that other—the man who had suffered, who knew, who understood? I might never find him; and, if I did, ninety-nine chances to one he would not care for me.

'Syb, Syb, can't you love me just a little?'

There was a winning charm in his manner. Nature had endowed him liberally with virile fascination. My hard uncongenial life had rendered me weak. He was drawing me to him; he was irresistible. Yes; I would be his wife. I grew dizzy, and turned my head sharply backwards and took a long gasping breath, another and another, of that fresh cool air suggestive of the grand old sea and creak of cordage and bustle and strife of life. My old spirit revived, and my momentary weakness fled. There was another to think of than myself, and that was Harold. Under a master-hand I would be harmless; but to this man I would be as a two-edged sword in the hand of a novice—gashing his fingers at every turn, and eventually stabbing his honest heart.

It was impossible to make him see my refusal was for his good. He was as a favourite child pleading for a dangerous toy. I desired to gratify him, but the awful responsibility of the after-effects loomed up and deterred me.

'Hal, it can never be.'

He dropped my hands and drew himself up.

249

'I will not take your No till the morning. Why do you refuse me? Is it my temper? You need not be afraid of that. I don't think I'd hurt you; and I don't drink, or smoke, or swear very much; and I've never destroyed a woman's name. I would not stoop to press you against your will if you were like the ordinary run of women; but you are such a queer little party, that I'm afraid you might be boggling at some funny little point that could easily be wiped out.'

'Yes; it is only a little point. But if you wipe it out you will knock the end out of the whole thing—for the point is myself. I would not suit you. It would not be wise for you to marry me.'

'But I'm the only person concerned. If you are not afraid for yourself, I am quite satisfied.'

We faced about and walked homewards in unbroken silence— too perturbed to fall into our usual custom of chewing bush-leaves as we went.

I thought much that night when all the house was abed. It was tempting. Harold would be good to me, and would lift me from this life of poverty which I hated, to one of ease. Should I elect to remain where I was, till the grave there was nothing before me but the life I was leading now: my only chance of getting above it was by marriage, and Harold Beecham's offer was the one chance of a lifetime. Perhaps he could manage me well enough. Yes; I had better marry him.

And I believe in marriage—that is, I think it the most sensible and respectable arrangement for replenishing of a nation which has yet been suggested. But marriage is a solemn issue of life. I was as suited for matrimony as any of the sex, but only with an exceptional helpmeet—and Harold was not he. My latent womanliness arose and pointed this out so plainly that I seized my pen and wrote:

Dear Harold,

I will not get a chance of speaking to you in the morning, so write. Never mention marriage to me again. I have firmly made up my mind—it must be No. It will always be a comfort to me in the years to come to know that I was loved once, if only for a few hours. It is not that I do not care for you, as I like you better than any man I have ever seen; but I do not mean ever to marry. When you lost your fortune I was willing to accede to your request, as I thought you wanted me; but now that you are rich again you will not need me. I am not good enough to be your wife, for you are a good man; and better, because you do not know you are good. You may feel uncomfortable or lonely for a little while, because, when you make up your mind, you are not easily thwarted; but you will find that your fancy for me will soon pass. It is only a fancy, Hal. Take a look in the glass, and you will see reflected there the figure of a stalwart man who is purely virile, possessing not the slightest attribute of the weaker sex, therefore your love is merely a passing flame. I do not impute fickleness to you, but merely point out a masculine characteristic, and that you are a man, and only a man, pure and unadulterated. Look around, and from the numbers of good women to be found on every side choose one who will make you a fitter helpmeet, a more conventional comrade, than I could ever do. I thank you for the inestimable honour you have conferred upon me; but keep it till you find some one worthy of it, and by and by you will be glad that I have set you free.

Good-bye, Hal!

Your sincere and affec. friend,
Sybylla Penelope Melvyn.

Then I crept into bed beside my little sister, and though the air inside had not cooled, and the room was warm, I shivered so that I clasped the chubby, golden-haired little sleeper in my arms that I might feel something living and real and warm.

'Oh, Rory, Rory!' I whispered, raining upon her lonely-hearted tears. 'In all the world is there never a comrade strong and true to teach me the meaning of this hollow, grim little tragedy—life? Will it always be this ghastly aloneness? Why am I not good and pretty and simple like other girls? Oh, Rory, Rory, why was I ever born? I am of no use or pleasure to any one in all the world!'

251

CHAPTER 37

He That Despiseth Little Things, Shall Fall Little By Little

I

The morning came, breakfast, next Harold's departure. I shook my head and slipped the note into his hand as we parted. He rode slowly down the road. I sat on the step of the garden gate, buried my face in my hands, and reviewed the situation. I could see my life, stretching out ahead of me, barren and monotonous as the thirsty track along which Harold was disappearing. Today it was washing, ironing tomorrow, next day baking, after that scrubbing—thus on and on. We would occasionally see a neighbour or a tea-agent, a tramp or an Assyrian hawker. By hard slogging against flood, fire, drought, pests, stock diseases, and the sweating occasioned by importation, we could manage to keep bread in our mouths. By training and education I was fitted for nought but what I was, or a general slavey, which was many degrees worse. I could take my choice. Life was too much for me. What was the end of it, what its meaning, aim, hope, or use?

In comparison to millions I knew that I had received more than a fair share of the goods of life; but knowing another has leprosy makes our cancer none the easier to bear.

My mother's voice, sharp and cross, roused me. 'Sybylla, you lazy unprincipled girl, to sit scheming there while your poor old mother is at the wash-tub. You sit idling there, and then by and by you'll be groaning about this terrible life in which there's time for nothing but work.'

How she fussed and bothered over the clothes was a marvel to me. My frame of mind was such that it seemed it would not signify if all our clothes went to the dogs, and the clothes of our neighbours, and the clothes of the whole world, and the world itself for the matter of that.

'Sybylla, you are a dirty careless washer. You've put Stanley's trousers in the boil and the colour is coming out of them, and your father's best white handkerchief should have been with the first lot, and here it is now.'

Poor mother got crosser as she grew weary with the fierce heat and arduous toil, and as I in my abstraction continued to make mistakes, but the last straw was the breaking of an old cup which I accidently pushed off the table.

I got it hot. Had I committed an act of premeditated villainy I could not have received more lecturing. I deserved it—I was careless, cups were scarce with us, and we could not afford more; but what I rail against is the grindingly uneventful narrowness of the life in which the unintentional breaking of a common cup is good for a long scolding.

Ah, my mother! In my life of nineteen years I can look back and see a time when she was all gentleness and refinement, but the polish has been worn off it by years and years of scrubbing and scratching, and washing and patching, and poverty and husbandly neglect, and the bearing of burdens too heavy for delicate shoulders. Would that we were more companionable, it would make many an oasis in the desert of our lives. Oh that I could take an all-absorbing interest in patterns and recipes, bargains and orthodoxy! Oh that you could understand my desire to feel the rolling billows of the ocean beneath, to hear the pealing of a great organ through dimly lit arches, or the sob and wail of a violin in a brilliant crowded hall, to be swept on by the human stream.

Ah, thou cruel fiend—Ambition! Desire!

> *Soul of the leaping flame,*
> *Heart of the scarlet fire,*
> *Spirit that hath for name*
> *Only the name—Desire!*

To hot young hearts beating passionately in strong breasts, the sweetest thing is motion.

No, that part of me went beyond my mother's understanding.

253

On the other hand, there was a part of my mother—her brave cheerfulness, her trust in God, her heroic struggle to keep the home together—which went soaring on beyond my understanding, leaving me a coward weakling, grovelling in the dust.

Would that hot dreary day never close? What advantage when it did? The next and the next and many weeks of others just the same were following hard after.

If the souls of lives were voiced in music, there are some that none but a great organ could express, others the clash of a full orchestra, a few to which nought but the refined and exquisite sadness of a violin could do justice. Many might be likened unto common pianos, jangling and out of tune, and some to the feeble piping of a penny whistle, and mine could be told with a couple of nails in a rusty tin-pot.

Why do I write? For what does any one write? Shall I get a hearing? If so—what then?

I have voiced the things around me, the small-minded thoughts, the sodden round of grinding tasks—a monotonous, purposeless, needless existence. But patience, O heart, surely I can make a purpose! For the present, of my family I am the most suited to wait about common public-houses to look after my father when he is inebriated. It breaks my mother's heart to do it; it is dangerous for my brothers; imagine Gertie in such a position! But me it does not injure, I have the faculty for doing that sort of thing without coming to harm, and if it makes me more bitter and godless, well, what matter?

II

The next letter I received from Gertie contained:

I suppose you were glad to see Harry. He did not tell me he was going, or I would have sent some things by him. I thought he would be able to tell me lots about you that I was dying to hear, but he never said a word, only that you were all well. He went travelling some weeks ago. I missed him at first because he used to be so kind to me; but now I don't, because Mr Creyton, whom Harry left to manage Five-Bob, comes just as often as Harry used to, and is lots funnier. He brings me something nice every time. Uncle Jay-Jay teases me about him.

Happy butterfly-natured Gertie! I envied her. With Gertie's letter came also one from grannie, with further mention of Harold Beecham.

We don't know what to make of Harold Beecham. He was always such a steady fellow, and hated to go away from home even for a short time, but now he has taken an idea to rush away to America, and is not coming home till he has gone over the world. He is not going to see anything, because by cablegrams his aunts got he is one place today and hundreds of miles away tomorrow. It is some craze he has suddenly taken. I was asking Augusta if there was ever any lunacy in the family, and she says not that she knows of. It was a very unwise act to leave full management to Creyton and Benson in the face of such a drought. One warning and marvellous escape such as he has had ought to be enough for a man with any sense. I told him he'd be poor again if he didn't take care, but he said he didn't mind if all his property was blown into atoms, as it had done him more harm than good, whatever he means by talking that way. Insanity is the only reason I can see for his conduct. I thought he had his eye on Gertie, but I questioned her, and it appears he has never said anything to her. I wonder what was his motive for going to Possum Gully that time?

Travel was indeed an unexpected development on the part of Harold Beecham. He had such a marked aversion to anything of that sort, and never went even to Sydney or Melbourne for more than a few days at a stretch, and that on business or at a time of stock shows.

There were many conjectures re the motive of his visit to Possum Gully, but I held my peace.

CHAPTER 38

A Tale That is Told and a Day That is Done

> *There are others toiling and straining*
> *'Neath burdens graver than mine;*
> *They are weary, yet uncomplaining,—*
> *I know it, yet I repine:*
> *I know it, how time will ravage,*
> *How time will level, and yet*
> *I long with a longing savage,*
> *I regret with a fierce regret.*

A. L. GORDON.
Possum Gully, 25th *March*, 1899

Christmas, only distinguished from the fifty-two slow Sundays of the year by plum-pudding, roast turkey, and a few bottles of home-made beer, has been once more; New Year, ushered in with sweet-scented midsummer wattle and bloom of gum- and box-tree has gone; February has followed, March is doing likewise, and my life is still the same.

What the future holds I know not, and am tonight so weary that I do not care.

> *Time rules us all. And life, indeed, is not*
> *The thing we planned it out, ere hope was dead;*
> *And then, we women cannot choose our lot.*

Time is thorough in his work, and as that arch-cheat, Hope, gradually becomes a phantom of the past, the neck will grow inured to its yoke.

Tonight is one of the times when the littleness—the abject littleness—of all things in life comes home to me.

After all, what is there in vain ambition? King or slave, we all must die, and when death knocks at our door, will it matter whether our life has been great or small, fast or slow, so long as it has been true—true with the truth that will bring rest to the soul?

> *But the toughest lives are brittle,*
> *And the bravest and the best*
> *Lightly fall—it matters little;*
> *Now I only long for rest.*

To weary hearts throbbing slowly in hopeless breasts the sweetest thing is rest.

And my heart is weary. Oh, how it aches tonight—not with the ache of a young heart passionately crying out for battle, but with the slow dead ache of an old heart returning vanquished and defeated!

Enough of pessimistic snarling and grumbling! Enough! Enough! Now for a lilt of another theme:

I am proud that I am an Australian, a daughter of the Southern Cross, a child of the mighty bush. I am thankful I am a peasant, a part of the bone and muscle of my nation, and earn my bread by the sweat of my brow, as man was meant to do. I rejoice I was not born a parasite, one of the blood-suckers who loll on velvet and satin, crushed from the proceeds of human sweat and blood and souls.

Ah, my sunburnt brothers!—sons of toil and of Australia! I love and respect you well, for you are brave and good and true. I have seen not only those of you with youth and hope strong in your veins, but those with pathetic streaks of grey in your hair, large families to support, and with half a century sitting upon your work-laden shoulders. I have seen you struggle uncomplainingly against flood, fire, disease in stock, pests, drought, trade depression, and sickness, and yet have time to extend your hands and hearts in true sympathy to a brother in misfortune, and spirits to laugh and joke and be cheerful.

And for my sisters a great love and pity fills my heart. Daughters of toil, who scrub and wash and mend and cook, who are dressmakers, paperhangers, milkmaids, gardeners, and candlemakers all in one, and yet have time to be cheerful and tasty in your homes, and make the best of the few oases to be found along the narrow dusty track of your existence. Would that I were more worthy to be one of you—more a typical Australian peasant—cheerful, honest, brave!

I love you, I love you. Bravely you jog along with the rope of class distinction drawing closer, closer, tighter, tighter around you: a few more generations and you will be as enslaved as were ever the moujiks of Russia. I see it and know it, but I cannot help you. My ineffective life will be trod out in the same round of toil—I am only one of yourselves, I am only an unnecessary, little, bush commoner, I am only a—woman!

The great sun is sinking in the west, grinning and winking knowingly as he goes, upon the starving stock and drought-smitten wastes of land. Nearer he draws to the gum-tree scrubby horizon, turns the clouds to orange, scarlet, silver flame, gold! Down, down he goes. The gorgeous, garish splendour of sunset pageantry flames out; the long shadows eagerly cover all; the kookaburras laugh their merry mocking good-night; the clouds fade to turquoise, green, and grey; the stars peep shyly out; the soft call of the mopoke arises in the gullies! With much love and good wishes to all—Good night! Good-bye!

AMEN

MY CAREER
GOES BUNG

Precocious effort in art is naturally imitative, but in localities remote from literary activity there is no one for the embryo writer to copy. Thus I was twelve before I wrote anything to draw attention to myself. I must have been nearly thirteen when the idea of writing novels flowered into romances which adhered to the design of the trashy novelettes reprinted in the *Supplement to the Goulburn Evening Penny Post.* These stories, secretly devoured, presented a world enchanting to budding adolescence. They were prinked with castles with ivied towers and hooting owls, which were inhabited by the unaccommodating guardians, thrilling seducers and more thrilling rescuers of titled maidens, as pure as angels. I used to read my versions to two or three girls, who still gaily recall the entertainment we thus manufactured for ourselves.

An Englishman, to whom some of these lucubrations were shown, directed me to the Australian scene as the natural setting for my literary efforts. The idea sprouted. Huh! I'd show just how ridiculous the life around me would be as story material, and began in sardonically humorous mood on a full-fledged novel with the jibing title *My Brilliant (?) Career.* I remember declaring my need of a striking name for the rampageous heroine of my ambition. An elder friend—beloved by her young neighbours for her sympathy—thereupon gave me her two Christian names Penelope and Sybylla, which she said were wasting, as she was known by a diminutive—Penny. This was an inspiring gift.

But INEXPERIENCE cannot possibly achieve any intended

artistic effect. Removed as I as from anyone equipped to understand or direct my literary attempts it was inevitable that I, of all my audience, should be the most flabbergasted. The literalness with which *My Brilliant Career* was taken was a shock to one of any imagination.

My Career Goes Bung was planned as a corrective. I discussed with my father the absurdity of girls from all over the continent writing to tell me that I had expressed their innermost lives and emotions—confidences of fellowship in introversion, whereas I was a healthy extrovert. My father, equally with myself, lacked knowledge of practising authors, or association with people who had any conception of what authorship of fiction might entail. But he had wisdom.

'You mustn't spoil what you have done,' he said. 'You see, you have created an imaginary reality, and you must stick to it now. Something would be hurt in all those discontented little girls if they felt that your story lacked foundation. Besides, they are many, and I and you are only two.'

I felt that my father did not quite understand, and so did not show him the story. Now I know that he was a spiritual genius in a community where there was no realisation of his giftedness nor any more employment for it than for a Spanish comb in a bald head.

The pother raised by Sybylla Penelope in print so petrified me that I closed her book and have not yet reopened it. Could I bring myself to re-read it I could, perhaps, fabricate an essay to air the dubious guesses of psycho-analysis: but that would be a preface to my first printed volume while this is a foreword to its aftermath.

This was deposited in a portmanteau of MSS and finally left with someone in Chicago, U.S.A. while I went to the World War, which is now seen to have been merely practice manoeuvres for Global Armageddons. When I returned this caretaker said Mr X had needed a bag, and, as my old grip was quite out of fashion and contained nothing but useless papers, she had known I would be glad to oblige him. I was assured Mr X had put all the papers in the furnace: I need have no fear that they had

262

been left about. I made no complaint, being as sure as the caretaker that my MSS were of no consequence. Nevertheless I regret the loss of stories and plays, which glowed at the time, and which will not come again. I thought *My Career Goes Bung* had gone with this collection, and had forgotten the copy of it which survived in an old trunk valiantly preserved all the years by my mother.

I opened the packet with trepidation and to my relief found entertainment, but that, as Sybylla Penelope Melvyn would say, may be due solely to egotism. The MS had a dedication of gratitude to someone indicated by initials, but I cannot recall who this was nor why I should have been grateful to him or her. There was also a preface by Peter McSwat, 'Who kept a diary and paid his debts.' Time has cancelled this topical illusion, and it has been deleted with some matter which has been disposed of elsewhere. Otherwise I have kept faith with that girl who once was I. I have not meddled by corrections which would have resulted, probably, in no better than the substitution of one set of solecisms and clichés by another, for such abound in even the greatest English novels.

The novel returned to me out of the past with the impact of a discovery. Though a work of fiction, the people in it are oddly familiar: their story has with time shed any character but that of reality. It is now an irrefutable period piece, and, in the light of EXPERIENCE, it is to be discerned that while intentionally quite as little, unintentionally it was equally as autobiographical as my first printed romance; no more, no less.

This second portrait of Sybylla Penelope was classified as delicious by the only person to whom it was submitted at the time: that it was also regarded by him as 'too audacious for publication' seems quaint today, and indicates how smug behaviour must have been when it was written. It is to-day inveterately dedicated to all Australian writers who were as young, who are as young, and who each decade for ever will be forthcoming as young as I was when first I foolhardily tried to write.

MILES FRANKLIN
Australia

This tale's as true as true can be,
  For what is truth or lies?
So often much that's told by me
  When seen through other eyes,
Becomes thereby unlike so much
  These others tell to you,
And if things be the same as such,
  What is a scribe to do?

Why, tell his tale of course, my friend,
  Or hold his tongue for aye,
Or wait till fictive matters mend,
  Which may be by-and-bye,
So here's a tale of things a-near
  That you may read and lend
Without a fear—you'll need no tear—
  It hasn't any end.

CHAPTER 1

Explanatory

A wallaby would have done just as well as a human being to endure the nothingness of existence as it has been known to me. This, I suppose, is why I want to tell of the only two lively things that have happened in a dull, uninteresting life. You don't know me from a basket of gooseberries, or wouldn't if only I had kept myself to myself, but as I didn't, I shall endure the embarrassment of bringing myself to your attention again in any explanatory postscript. In company with ninety-nine per cent of my fellows, the subject of self is full of fascination to me. There are cogent reasons for this.

One of the interesting happenings is my entanglement with Henry Beauchamp. The other is my experience in writing a new style of autobiography. Such a departure grew out of my satiation with the orthodox style. I shall deal with the autobiography first. These notes are slightly and somewhat expurgatedly compiled from my diary.

I was at that stage of chrysalism when boys dream of becoming bushrangers, engine drivers, or champion pugilists. Nothing so garishly simple relieves a girl. I yearned to make the whole world into a beautiful place where there would be no sick and starving babies, where people of advancing years could be safe from penury, where all the animals could be fat and happy, and even our little sisters, the flowers, might not be bruised or plucked against their wish. The prospect of settling down to act tame hen in a tin pot circle, and to acknowledge men as superior merely owing to the accident of gender, revolted me.

Life among boys and girls at an institution such as the Stringybark Hill Public School, ere adolescence has arrived to mess things up, is a good example of democracy. There were no wealthy within competitive reach, money did not count to any extent, and beauty and birth did not count at all. We never heard of such things. Only the merit of brains and honesty weighed in the school room, and athletic prowess coupled with fair play on the playground.

Any sort of lessons except long addition sums were a joy and sinecure to me. On the playground, though small, I was fleet of foot and exceptionally agile, could vault as high as any boy of my own age till I was twelve, and was always chosen as captain whether the game happened to be cricket, rounders or prisoners' bar. A balance was preserved in my status by the fact that the dunces at lessons were always the best bats or runners outside, and that athletes when grown up had so much more glory than mere scholars.

I was impatient to be done with school so that I could take hold of life in the big world. I could not understand why people stayed in some lone hole with no more spunk in them than a milch cow, while the universe elsewhere teemed with adventure.

I expected to continue in enjoyment of the friendship and affection of my fellows, working for and winning a high place in all the activities that I essayed. I thought that there would be any number of activities to choose from. I was sure of winning love and acclamation because I never cheated in a game or put on airs over my ascendancy in them, and eagerly shared anything and everything within my power.

Thus came the last day under the rule of the gentle old teacher in the little slab school house among the tall trees on the stringybark range. Old Harris, as we called him behind his back, got drunk on occasion but was condoned by the kindly settlers because he knew and loved each child individually. He could bring what there was out of the thickest skulls and I rioted unrebuked and highly encouraged within his jurisdiction. He had been educated at one of the great colleges in England. I don't know which as he never mentioned it to the simple circle of Stringybark Hill. He was supposed to be related to big swells but that likewise he never mentioned unless he was a bit tipply and some flash intruder was putting on airs. He had the manners of an angel, a dear kind face, and wouldn't have harmed a grasshopper. These qualifications earned him the protection of the rudest and crudest. He taught a mere handful of children the rudiments of education for less than £3 a week and boarded with a family who were industrious, honest and kind, but could offer him no congeniality of mind or companionship of knowledge.

Ma condemned his fecklessness to be stuck there, but Pa would rub the top of his head—his own head—and remark, 'At Old Harris's age life boils down to a decent bed and a good feed, and those things are his.'

At the end of my last day with him he patted me on the shoulder—an unusual liberty for this diffident soul. He never seemed to have any egotism except when he was drunk. It must have been ingrowing like squeezed toenails. He made a little speech over me, the kind which youth accepts as drivel at the time, but which comes back vividly when youth has grown towards this drivelling knowledge itself. It returns to me now in the drivellage of my twentieth year, and here it is.

'Sybylla, you are a good girl—clean and true—and a gifted one to boot. You are as game as a young lion but I fear that the opposing forces will break your heart. You are a glad young thing now, but with your ability and temperament, alas, it will take more than ordinary conditions to keep you happy. You have a quicker brain than any scholar I ever had, but that will not help you unless you use it to hide the fact of its existence and to enhance your beauty; and of beauty you have ample to secure what would satisfy most of your sex, but which will never content you, so I might as well hold my tongue. At any rate, good fortune attend you. The old school house will be dull and lonely without you.'

I thought that he must have had a drop, but now when he is dead and six years have passed, I simply know that his experience of life was more than mine.

I was let out in advance and he stood looking after me as I swung down the path between the young trees which I had helped to plant on by-gone Arbor Days. Affection is a terribly binding thing. It always keeps me from breaking bonds, so I turned back every few steps to wave to the old man with a wistful regret that he was a finished chapter and that I could not take him with me into the glamorous young world towards which I was headed.

I had two miles to go by a short cut, which I followed for the joy of fallen logs to vault, and I sprang high every yard or two for the gum leaves that splashed their outline on the ground. The sky was a washing-bag blue with mountainous white clouds of thunderous splendour piled in the west. What a sunset it would be! I revelled in every scrap of beauty that came my way, and was excited to picture the beauty and adventure that I was going to broach beyond the ragged horizon to be seen from the tall fence post. The loveliest most thrilling thing in sight was the road that led from the front paddock to Goulburn, then on and on to Sydney—first port of call in my voyage of conquest. I climbed on to the garden post for a view before entering the house, my school days past.

'What are you doing there like a tom-boy?' inquired Ma. 'You must change your ways now. The happiest days you'll ever know are over—all play and no work and worry. You'll find life a different matter.'

LIFE a different matter—I should hope so!—like a blue ocean of adventure calling with a deafening invitation to embark.

CHAPTER 2

The Fettered Round

But how to get on to that ocean? I was on a small weedy waterhole that seldom swelled into a stream and there were many snags. Upon leaving school these multiplied like fury.

I entered into the life of struggling incompetent selectors. The chief burden of that, for the women, was unrestricted child-bearing, and I was now a woman, as Ma reminded me, a fact which made me rebellious. Ma said I was always a wilful and contradictory imp and that during the throes of rearing me, she was frequently put to such confusion that despite I was her first and last and only child there were times when she could have cheerfully wrung my neck. Ma said most girls felt the way I did at first, but soon settled down. All girls wished that they were men.

At that I flashed out like a tornado, insulted. Never in my life had I a wish to be a man. Such a suggestion fills me with revulsion. What I raged against were the artificial restrictions.

Girls! I do not address those feeble nauseating creepers who seem to fit into every one of the old ruts, the slimy hypocrites who are held up as womanly, but those who have some dash and spirit. You remember what we had to learn, girls, things that one cannot write in plain print or else truth would be abused as indecency; and there were other things too subtle to be expressed even to the elect, but which wielded the strongest subjecting influence. The dead dank gloom that settled on us upon learning that the eternal feminine was the infernal feminine! But Ma always said, 'You'll have to get used to it. There is no sense in acting like one possessed of a devil.'

A man can get used to having his legs cut off, and women have even greater endurance, or, seeing the conditions under which they live and work and dress and reproduce their species, they would have been extinct with the Great Auk, and what a pity they weren't!

Girls! Do you remember how we loathed the correct meek merely sexy specimens who had none of our foolhardy honesty, or any unsmutched ideals of life and love? We clamoured for the opportunity to be taken on our merits by LIFE: we wanted to play it as we played our games, where, if there was any doubt about us being bowled out, we did not want to hold on, we laid down our bats without whimpering.

The first foul blast from the tree of knowledge was that we weren't to be allowed any unadulterated HUMAN merits. Sexual attractions alias WOMANLINESS was to be our stock-in-trade. If we did not avail ourselves of it we were defenceless, and might even be execrated. How we abhorred the cunning girls who found no trouble with their role. In school they had been ranked by attainment, and their marks had seldom risen even to FAIR. Now in the hierarchy of mere gender their pandering intelligence was to score every time. We could come into line or find ourselves on an outside track alone.

Girls, how did you take it?

It seemed to develop into a storm between Ma and me. Ma at last said, 'Bother it, I have nothing to do with it. It is God's will.'

It was a relief to be indignant with God, but a trial not to be able to get at Him in any way. In my perturbation I collided with Great-aunt Jane, who said that the Lord loveth those whom He chasteneth. His way of saving the world did not appear to me as efficient for a being who was all-powerful. He so loved the world that He gave His only begotten Son to save it, and allowed Him to be nailed on a cross in ghastly agony—without saving anything considerable as far as history shows.

'Heaven knows what He would have permitted to be done to a daughter,' I remarked.

Aunt Jane stood this pretty well. 'Ah,' she laughed, 'you'll grow to sense. A husband and children of your own will put you in your place.'

The dire soul-crushings with which old wives threaten me consequent upon the glories of motherhood are enough to quell a quadruped. Aunt Jane repudiated the blame too, and said I should have to wait until the next world to have things righted.

'According to what I have heard, a woman who has had the hell of bearing twelve children to give some male object a heaven of begetting is just as likely to go to hell as the father: and the next world's joys are open equally to men, more so, in fact. That next-world-payment-of-debts is sloppy rubbish,' I snorted.

'You have a great deal to learn,' said Auntie. 'You are a rude ignorant girl. If you persist in thinking as you do, you'll come to harm.'

Pa rubbed his hair up on end and gently remarked, 'What is coming to harm in this debate, Aunt Jane, is your theology.'

Pa's words fell as healingly as rain on the dust. I was sorry I had been rude to Auntie. When I got Pa alone I questioned him further, and he said, as if talking to himself, 'As high as a people rises, so high will be its gods.'

'The trouble with the Church of England God,' Pa continued, 'is that he is made in the image of some darned old cackling prelate, so mean and cowardly that the Devil, for consistency and ability, is a gentleman beside him.' Pa had a twinkle in his eye as he added, 'But you know, it isn't gentlemanly to upset people of less mental powers than yourself; besides, it is dangerous. Think as much as you like, my girl, but let sleeping dogs lie unless you can do some real good by waking them up.'

Great-aunt spends a lot of time with us. She says Pa is the nicest man she has ever known in a house, that I should thank God on my knees every night for such a parent. This so differs from Ma's inculcations that I would attribute it to Auntie's love of contradiction, only that under cross-questioning she says that had she had such a father when a girl she would have thought herself in heaven. Her father was an unmerciful autocrat. His daughters had to live their lives under cover, so to speak, like mice. I wish I could be so dominating, but judging by Grandma and Ma and myself, this progenitor's progenitiveness is becoming diluted with the generations.

I concede that technically Ma is my primary parent and Pa merely secondary. The question of woman's emancipation and the justice which is her due make this fatally clear in theory, but when it comes to the practice of an affection which springs spontaneously from my human breast, Pa can have no second place; and when it comes to being understood, well—but—but—Ma says having children of my own will teach me. I wonder what.

I had lots of other stuffing in me too. Resiliently I renewed my attack on LIFE. Rebellion against artificial WOMANLINESS did not interfere with all that rushed out of my mind on the wings of imagination. There was one great recreation open to me, even at Possum Gully, which was a sop to energy. I could ride. I could ride tremendously. I loved horses and seemed to become part of them. In the district were any number of good horses, most of them owned by bachelors. As one of these bachelors said, 'A lovely high-spirited girl is just the thing to top-off a good horse.'

All kinds of horses, from racing stallions to hunting mares, were brought to me with the owners included as escorts and the source of chocolates in wonderful boxes. Some of the horses demanded skill and attention to handle, and that saved their owners from my dialectics and me from their love-making. There was no use in a man offering me a horse that was moke enough for love-dawdling, and that's how that worked out.

Pa forbade fences. Ma said that unless I meant to marry one of the men it was foolish and unladylike to be riding about with them; they would have no respect for me. If I really was against marriage I'd have to take up some trade or profession; she wished she had been trained to something so that she could be independent and not be dragged in the backwash of man's mismanagement.

This brought me to consider my prospects and to find that I hadn't any. I loved to learn things—anything, everything. To attend the University would have been heaven, but expense barred that. I could become a pupil-teacher, but I loathed the very name of this profession. I should have had to do the same work as a man for less pay, and, in country schools, to throw in free of remuneration, the specialty of teaching all kinds of needle-work. I could be a cook or a housemaid and slave all day under some nagging woman and be a social outcast. I could be a hospital nurse and do twice the work of a doctor for a fraction of his pay or social importance, or, seeing the tremendously advanced age, I could even be a doctor—a despised lady-doctor, doing the drudgery of the profession in the teeth of such prejudice that even the advanced, who fought for the entry of women into all professions, would in practice 'have more faith in a man doctor'. I could be a companion or governess to some woman appended to some man of property.

I rebelled against every one of these fates. I wanted to do something out of the ordinary groove. There *were* people who had done great things for the world, why not be one of such? Ma threw cold water on these haverings. Ma is the practical member of our ménage. She has to be, so that we have a ménage at all. Ma's thesis was that if all the millions who have gone have not improved the world, how was I going to do it in one slap? How would I start about it? Whereas, improvement seemed to me so simple that all that was needed was common sense and energy.

Pa was sympathetic. Ma says that I take after him, except when I am commendable. Pa has ever acknowledged the relationship with pride even during my most debbil-debbil stretches, which is very generous of Pa.

'There have been great women, haven't there, Pa?'

'Of course there have, and are, and will be again,' said he.

'But what on earth makes you think you might be one of them?' demanded Ma.

'Why shouldn't she be?' murmured Pa.

'You can't be anything without means these days.'

273

'The times are always the same. People make their opportunities.'

'She doesn't strike me as that kind.'

'Oh, I don't know,' maintained Pa. 'Greatness has sprung from unlikelier sources.'

CHAPTER 3

The Logic of Egotism

Poverty is a stultifying curse. We suffered from it. Ma blamed Pa. Pa never blamed anyone but himself. He had not always been poor. He was no business man. Bad seasons and foolish investments lost him his parental station. Ma considered his term in Parliament as Member for Gool-Gool his biggest financial mistake. Pa had been under heavy election expenses, and was robbed by a partner during his absence. Pa had had ambitions to improve the Colony through political action, and had failed. That was why Ma was alarmed by my symptoms. I was too young to remember Pa's Parliamentary term. Ma's abiding reference to it is that men are very fond of the sound of their own voices. Well, I like Pa's voice too, because it is never raised in blame.

Pa is tall and lean and lank and brown as is the ribbed sea sand, and he is fond of poetry. Byron is a favourite with him. He can quote Byron by the page.

> *This makes the madmen who have made men mad*
> *By their contagion; conquerors and kings,*
> *Founders of sects and systems, to whom add*
> *Sophists, bards, statesmen, all unquiet things.*

> * * *

> *He who surpasses or subdues mankind*
> *Must look down on the hate of those below.*

Such lines roll splendidly from him. Ma says a man betrays himself by what he extols. I asked if that also applies to women, but Ma says not nearly so accurately, as woman have to pretend to like so many things to humour men.

Ma extols Dr Watts. He is prosaic compared with Byron.

> *Not more than others I deserve,*
> *Yet God has given me more,*
> *For I have food while others starve,*
> *Or beg from door to door.*

Which suggests mean favouritism on the part of God, and a priggish self-satisfaction on the part of one who has petty deserts.

Satan finds some mischief still for idle hands to do, has often driven me exasperated and frustrated from meditation when a thought was filling out like a sail catching a breeze.

Dr Watts was the lighter side of Ma. She was also a whale on Shakespeare. I enjoyed him too, but Milton was too much of a good thing. Ma insisted that I should learn long slices of Milton as discipline and to elevate my thoughts.

> *Where joy for ever dwells; hail, horrors; hail,*
> *Infernal world; and thou, profoundest hell,*
> *Receive thy new possessor; one who brings*
> *A mind not to be changed by place or time.*
> *The mind is its own place, and in itself*
> *Can make a heaven of hell, a hell of heaven.*

'Bust' was the most ferocious expletive ever heard from women in Ma's family. It was considered the height of vulgarity and not allowed at all, really, but in the depths of some overpowering exasperation even Great-aunt Jane has been overheard expleting it. 'Bust Milton!' I said many times to myself. 'Paradise is lost surely enough while you have to be learning this stuff by heart.'

The most interesting line in the book was, 'Witness, William Yopp, Ann Yopp'. They were a funny note in the stiff gilt-edged volume. Why had they a name like that? They were attached to the information that Mrs Milton had got eight pounds for the twelve books of P.L. Poetry didn't seem to be a lucrative business, but of course that was over three hundred years ago, and to-day was different.

Ma said as I wasn't in a position to tackle professional training

I must help Pa on the place. He could not afford to hire men. This brought me back to my idea of a career at the top where there was plenty of room above the tame-fowl openings, which were all that lay before one so poor and isolated. Ma said I should take stock of my possibilities and banish all silly delusions. Ma assisted in this stock-taking. She dwelt upon my lack of special gifts and said we should not shrink from unpleasant facts about ourselves, we must face them and grow strong. We must accept God's will without whining. It must be dreadful to have a daughter as disappointing as I am to Ma, and it is just as hard for such a fiasco of a girl to have a superb mother. I did not know which of the two trials was the heavier, but Ma did. Hers was the trial and mine the failure to take advantage of my heredity in her. However, life went on.

At that date there was a parliamentary election. FREE-TRADE or PROTECTION became a war cry. Pa was called upon to support the Member for our electorate. Possum Gully livened up. We had meetings at our house and I accompanied Pa on the rounds. There were young men everywhere all eager to argue politics with me. How I chafed that women were classed with idiots and children! Of course I should have had to wait until I was twenty-one to vote, but I longed to stand for Parliament then just as I was with my hair in a plat and my skirts above my ankles. I hankered to tackle the job of Premier for a start. The young men all said they would vote for me when I put up. Our Member was one of those who advocated extending the franchise to women, so I adored him and we were great friends. He said I was one of his best canvassers.

Scorning tame-hen accomplishments and lacking special gifts of God, which lift a person from obscurity to fame through an art, a sport, or an invention, I returned to the thought of general greatness. Pa was very proud when old campaigners said I was a chip off the old block. He was strenuously in favour of woman suffrage. Ma expostulated with him for taking me about. She said we soon would not have even a poor roof to cover us. My Grandma got to hear of me and wrote letters blaming Ma. When

Great-aunt Jane next stayed with us she did her best to save me.

'You'll grow into one of those dreadful female agitators—eccentric women that men hate. You'll get the name of a man-hater if you don't take care.'

'This men-hating business seems to be as lop-sided as God's will for women. You condemn a woman if she doesn't worship men. She is the one in the wrong to hate the darling creatures, though they're pretty hatable by all accounts. Then if a girl is fond of men that also disgraces her. I do like logic and fair play.'

'So do I,' interposed Ma, 'but you'll have to resign yourself to it all being on the other side.'

'It's all silly nonsense. The men don't act as if they hated me. The old ones as well as the boys all are friendly wherever I go.'

'Men will always blather to a forward woman while she is young; but they won't respect her or marry her,' said Aunt Jane.

'She couldn't marry more than one at a time, however willing she is,' said Pa. 'She has plenty of time yet.'

When Pa and I were driving around the electorate together he talked about LIFE and said that my idea of being Premier was not fantastic. The political enfranchisement of women was inevitable, and women free could do what they liked with the world.

Votes for women was a magic talisman by which all evils and abuses were to be righted. Women no longer would have to pander to men through sexual attraction and pretend to be what they weren't. They would burgeon as themselves. Those were splendid days. Pa said I must educate myself in readiness as by the time I should be of age I could stand for Parliament and discover if I had ability as a statesman. As a beginning he suggested that I should study history and the lives of great people to learn how they conducted the business. To this end the poor dear once again postponed a new suit, which Ma truly said he needed to prevent his being mistaken for a scarecrow, and brought me home an armful of books, including some autobiographies.

That's how the trouble began.

The histories I left for later consumption, as the people in them are always so long dead and are nearly all kings and queens and military or political murderers who have no relation to the ordinary kind of people like those I know in Australia. The biographies of real people nearer our own day, and especially the autobiographies, where people told about themselves, filled me with excitement.

Judging by the way Ma always misunderstands my deeds and purposes and intentions, and by what she and Aunt Jane tell me that other people do think or will think of me, it seemed that an autobiography was a device for disseminating personal facts straight from the horse's mouth.

I read ardently, nay, furiously would better express the way that one tackles the things one wants to do. Grace Darling, Charlotte Brontë, Joan of Arc and Mrs Fry passed in review, evidently by dull old professors. These were a long time dead. Lives nearer to my own day had more appeal—until I read them. What I absorbed from autobiographies was not how to be great so much as the littleness of the great. Every one of those productions, whether the fiction that passes for reality or the decorated reality that is termed fiction was marred by the same thing—the false pose of the autobiographer.

Now, we are always warned against egotism as something more unforgivable, more unpopularising than vulgar sin. Yet everyone is a mass of egotism. They must be if they are to remain perpendicular. Henry Beauchamp later explained this to me. He says that little Jimmy Dripping is a much more important person to little Jimmy Dripping than the Prince of Wales is. If this were not so he says that the end of little Jimmy Dripping would soon be mud; that each fellow's self-importance is the only thing that keeps him going. Well then, why make such an unholy fuss about egotism?

Ma despised egotism because she had none herself and happened by an accident to be perfect. Pa and I seemed to have whips and whips, but of the wrong king. The best kind, the most profitable is like the hippo's epidermis. Another word for it is hide—HIDE. It works so that you think your own performance of sin or stupidity is quite all right, and only the other fellow's all quite wrong. Pa said that that kind of egotism was a magnificent battering ram for worldly success, but to have it you must be born without a sense of humour and without the ability to see yourself as others see you. I was beginning to suspect that a sense of humour was more profitable to the other fellow than to the owner.

The business of egotism needs to be regulated by give-and-take in real life or there would be general obstruction of all conversation and social intercourse, but that does not apply to an autobiography, at least not in conjunction with logic. The fact of an autobiography is in itself an egotism. People perpetrate autobiographies for the sole purpose of airing their own exploits. If they go off the track of displaying the writer they likewise cease to be autobiographies. Such documents are usually mawk-ishly egotistical instead of frankly so because they attempt the scientific impossibility of being unegotistical. Too, in autobi-ographies, the hero of the narrative tries to deprecate his goodness, while at the same time he often endeavours to depict himself as a saint worthy of wings. If he has a penny-dreadful parent he nevertheless paints himself as adoring him (or her) and by honouring one or both is a contestant for the doubtful prize of long life, which the bible promises people for enduring their immediate progenitors in any circumstances. (And I never could see in strict logic how that works.)

I have examined all available autobiographies since then but not one have I found by woman or man, scientist or simpleton, which did not assume the same pose. So little greatness did I find in the lives of the great as related by themselves that for a time I was diverted from the idea of becoming great myself by the notion of constructing a fictitious autobiography to make hay of the pious affectations of printed autobiographies as I know them.

Who has not read an autobiography beginning thus: 'At the risk of being egotistical I must admit,' etc. I determined to flout these pretences with an imitation autobiography that would wade in without apology or fear, biffing convention on the nose.

The days were goldenly long and warm, I was rabid for mental and physical action, and there was none in that state of discontent in which it had pleased God to place me. It makes me question His amiability in placing His victims. In addition to riding I swam in our weedy water-holes among leeches and turtles where there was also an occasional snake, but of mental pabulum there was no crumb to be found, except in books. I was a voracious reader, but after all, books pall on one when that one is throbbing to be doing something exciting. From Possum Gully to Spring Hill and round about to Wallaroo Plains there wasn't a real companion of my own age, nor any other age. The dissatisfaction of other girls stopped short at wondering why life should be so much less satisfactory to them than to their brothers, but they accepted it as the will of God. None of them was consumed with the idea of changing the world.

The idea of writing a book to make fun of the other books grew with cossetting. Ma said she had sufficient experience of my ideas to be chary of them. EXPERIENCE seems to stand by Ma like religion.

Pa rubbed the top of his head contemplatively and said, 'If you are man enough to write a book, I'll get you some paper.'

'How could an untried girl write a book?' demanded Ma. 'Why not start with a little story for the "Children's Corner"? You can't run before you learn to walk.'

CHAPTER 4

'Satan Finds Some Mischief Still.'

A ream of paper is a large quantity to one who has never written a book nor met anyone who has done so—480 sheets all to myself.

'That'll hold you for a bit,' said Pa.

'What a waste!' said Ma.

The pleasure of good penmanship on all that lovely white paper edged me on to begin upon my spontaneous career of slinging ink, of which this volume is to be the petite finale.

Ma admired classical features. Pa had them. Perhaps that is what misled her into a poor match, and why, no matter how often my looks are praised as lovely, she will not rank me as a beauty. She says such talk is to make a fool of me. So to be done with the uncertainty, I accept Ma's dictum that beauty lies in actions, and as my actions are all wrong, where could be my beauty? Nevertheless, bang went another convention. Men cared only for prettiness in girls, yet our house was a rendezvous for young men from all over the electorate and beyond it, who did not honestly come to talk politics with Pa, though they pretended that they did. I wasn't in danger of being embittered by a lack of admirers, nor of platonic men friends, as I was simple enough to think they were at the start. They teased me about dropping the Premiership and taking to writing.

Ma said there was no sight more nauseating than love-sick men all cackling and he-hawing and pretending they were angels who wouldn't let her pick up her thimble; while by-and-bye if I should marry one of them, most likely he would leave me to chop the wood and would turn her out of his house.

Pa said there was no use in quarrelling with NATURE or taking a jaundiced view.

Ma rejoined that EXPERIENCE had shown her that common sense was very rare.

It was a spring without a spring. The breezes had a strong dash of summer, but the cloudless skies looked down with an excess of that pitilessness which the Persian poet has advised us not to call upon. Not a speck the size of a man's hand came up for weeks to give even false hope, and the half-opened leaves withered on the rose bushes and orchard trees. The starving stock lacked strength to bring their young to birth, and the moan of dying creatures throughout that country side was a reproach to whatever power had placed them there. The earth was as dry as ashes. Isolated shrubs and plants, that had been the pride of settlers' drudging wives and daughters, died in spite of efforts to keep them alive with the slop water collected after household use. The wattle trees, however, because they were natives, were putting forth an unstinted meed of bloom with an optimism rivalling 'God's in His Heaven, all's right with the world'. Masses of lovely yellow fluff swayed to waves in the breeze and wafted perfume too chaste for the seventh heaven of oriental belief. This loveliness lacked competition in the grim landscape. I culled sprays to press between the leaves of some old book, and wondered would there ever come a day when I should be as homesick for a bower of wattle bloom set in a frame of gum-trees as I was now wild to escape to other lands of castles and chateaux and Gothic cathedrals.

The drought made work in the garden superfluous. I had leisure to utilise that ream of paper. The burlesque autobiography grew apace. My idea of ridicule speedily enlarged as a reticule into which anything could be packed. I could express my longing to escape to other lands and far great cities across the sheening ocean to strange ports above and below the Line, where big ships and little go for their cargoes. It was an opportunity to crystallise rebellion and to use up some of the words which pressed upon me like a flock of birds fluttering to be let out of their cages. There is artistic satisfaction in liberating words: and they entered into me and flew from me like fairies.

It was absorbing to allot parts to characters. Uncertainty when to interpolate 'Odds fish, ma'am,' or 'Gad Zooks,' put me off a historical track, though I had started in an ancient castle on an English moor. I was also in a quandary about style, but at that time dear old Mr Harris came to spend a few days with us prior to leaving the district. I let him into the secret. He was sympathetic in one way and discouraging in another. He said that the pursuit of literature was a precarious staff of life, but an engrossing hobby, if one had the leisure and the means. He asked me where the scene was set, a question I did not understand. He said if I would trust him to see the first chapter he could probably tell me.

We walked among the wattle blossom in the gully beyond the vegetable garden till we reached the top, where there were some rocks. We sat down, and he said, 'My dear Sybylla, I have read your beginning. Though immature it has promise.'

I nearly stifled in agonised expectation of his condemnation. My whole feeling had come to the surface as sensitive as the nerve of a tooth. I knew he would never be mean enough to tell Ma the full depth of my foolishness.

'Why do you write about a castle in England that you have never seen?' he asked gently.

Without waiting for my reply he continued, 'I'll tell you, my dear little girl. The castle in England is a castle in Spain, and "tho' 'twas never built," imagination makes it more enthralling than things near at hand. Why not try reality?'

I asked breathlessly what he meant.

'Well, instead of the roses on that castle wall, why not this fragrant bower of wattle? Instead of the wind moaning across the moor, why not the pitiless sun beating down on the cracked dusty earth?'

'But that couldn't be put in a book—not in a story!'

'Why not, child?'

'Everyone knows that, and it is so tame and ugly.'

'It would be most novel and informing to those who are as familiar with the castle or a slum street as you are with the wattles and the baked paddocks. Australia is crying out to be done: England is done to death.'

This was an expanding idea, like opening a window and letting me look into a place I had known before.

'You see, you know everyone in the Australian bush. You could picture them with a vigor and conviction that would be refreshing: and my dear, if you could project yourself upon the canvas it would be most successful.'

'Oh, I couldn't do that!' I shrank from this. 'Besides, I have never done anything like the heroines in novels. I am not sweetly good, and though Ma thinks I am possessed of a devil, I have never done anything really unrespectable. For example, I could never have been so unkind as to throw that dictionary back at the teacher like Becky Sharp did, though I *wish* I could do that kind of thing. It must be splendid.'

'If you could draw portraits of all the characters that furnish your life it would be a good beginning.'

'Oh, but I couldn't put in real people. They would not like to see themselves except as white-washed saints—like the yarns on the tombstones. I'd have to imagine people to make them interesting.'

'Um!' said he, and then with a chuckle, 'you go ahead. I shouldn't be surprised if they turn out to be more real that way. But there is one thing, my dear, be Australian. It is the highest form of culture and craftmanship in art to use local materials. That way you stand a chance of adding to culture. The other way you are in danger of merely imitating it, and though imitation is a form of flattery to the imitated, it is a form of weakness or snobbery in the perpetrator. You must find your own way and your own level. The material is in you: all that is required is industry in cultivation.'

I could hardly wait till the end of his visit to plaster the ideas he had put into my head upon the original burlesque. Ma said that Mr Harris was right to a certain extent, that to pretend to be what one was not was the height of vulgarity, but she couldn't see that an interesting book could be made of reality: it was dreary enough to live in the bush in drought time: no one could possibly find any pleasure in reading about such misfortune.

Ma always brings up EXPERIENCE. She has often routed Pa from the field of philosophy with the records of EXPERI-ENCE, and she now inquired what was the sense in wasting time and paper in this way? Why not do something practical? Pa though, is always willing to believe that the latest venture must be better than the preceding.

I set out to do the equivalent of taking two photographs on the one plate. I was to burlesque autobiography and create the girl of my admiration, and fill in with a lot of lifelike people as a protest against over-virtuous lay figures. One thing I have always envied in girls is the ability to fly into a towering rage. At school there were two bad-tempered dunces and they enjoyed my brain effort. I lived in terror of their temper and did their sums with alacrity. Poor Old Harris was careful not to stir them up, and they did pretty well what they liked. So my heroine was to be the antithesis of conventional heroines. All my people were to be created in the image of reality—none of them bad enough to be tarred and feathered, none good enough to be canonised. But people are never what they think themselves, and by the results which accrued it would seem that it is equally difficult to present a character as you intend.

Up to that date I do not remember being so fully interested in anything. I had a secret delight. I ceased to talk about it even to Pa. He and I had quite opposite tastes in stories. He liked adventure: Mayne Reed, Fenimore Cooper, Captain Marryat, Gil Blas, Rider Haggard, but I had one or two of George Gissing's books, Vanity Fair, Colonel Newcome and Esther Waters, and enjoyed that style. No, I could not write dashingly enough to interest Pa. Ma was reading an annotated edition of Shakespeare, and that took her above my sphere of effort.

Bewitchment shadowed the paper as I progressed. I could not do what I liked with the people. I often found them as troublesome as Ma found me, and I think in the end they made rather a pie of my theme, though I did not know it at the time. The book was a companion as well as an entertainment, a confidant and a twin soul. You know how a piece of lace that you have made yourself has a charm lacking in a much better piece made by someone else? So with that book. I used to climb on the hay in the shed behind the stables on Sunday afternoons and read it over—like doing all the parts in a play myself, though at the time I had not seen a play. I must have had a lot of ingrowing egotism, and it came out in this way as the pimples or boils that are common to boys.

I was sardonically amused to depict that reality suggested by Mr Harris.

Our home was of wood and of the usual pattern and situation in a particularly ugly portion of the bush. We were dished in a basin of low scrubby ranges which are familiar to the poorer settlers where the fertile patches are land-locked in a few big holdings by hard-headed fellows who got in early with capital and grants and convicts.

Instead of hedges we had dog-leg and brush fences, and stumps in the cultivation paddocks. There were fowl-houses covered with tin to render them safe against sharp-snouted spotted marsupial cats; the mess-mate roosting trees also had wide rings of tin around the trunks to save the turkeys by night. Cowsheds were roofed with stringybark. Fields of briars and rugged ranges were all around; a weedy water hole in the middle; the not-yet-bleached bones of beasts were a common decoration. No roofs but our own were within sight. It was a raw contrast to the English scenery on which I doted, with its thatched cottages, trailing roses, gabled farm houses, towered ancestral halls with Tudor chimneys amid oaks and elms and cawing rooks and moors and downs, wolds, woods, spinneys and brooks. Such reality as mine would look mighty queer in a book, something like a swaggie at a Government House party, but it was as easy to describe as falling off a log.

The people belonging to this scenery were so ordinary and respectable and decent that a yarn about them could not possibly attract the attention of a reader. The probability of readers must have popped up somewhere along the track. I had had no thought of them when I started. I'm sure nothing but genius could make the Possum Gully kind of reality interesting, and as I am only a jokist I had to bring out the paintpot of embellishment to heighten or lower the flat colourless effect.

There are times when our own case is so blinding that we are unable to feel or to see outside it. We are shut within ourselves. Sometimes these moods are merry and sometimes sad, but always self-sealed. If merry, so all-sufficient is our hilarity that grey skies or black nights have no power to damp our inward fire. But let us be sad, and the brilliance of the sun seems callous. We cannot reach outside ourselves. When young we demand so much that is beyond us that the first lessons in EXPERIENCE are the hoeing of the chastening row of disappointment.

I had a fever which fed upon itself like the green-eyed monster, and it was a great relief to be shedding it like a snake-skin. A desire to have someone to read the result came upon me towards the end. I don't know whether this was gregariousness or mere egotism, like my cat's when she brings home a kitten and dumps it for us to see. I was more selective than the cat. She doesn't pick her appreciators. She drops her kitten among us regardless of passing boots, and also regardless of who may be in the boots. I adore her and indulge her and so have been surprised that she did not bring me her kitten.

I was more demanding. I wanted someone who would understand. Who better than our greatest Australian author? I quite understood him since ever I was old enough to lisp a line of his ballads, what more sequential than his understanding of me? In the innocence of my heart, or it may have been the heartlessness of my innocence, I confidently sent him the manuscript. Having worshipped at his shrine with a whole-heartedness which we can enjoy but once in life, I felt sure of welcome within the gates of his interest.

In those days so entire was my unsophistication that I did not suspect that an author, even the AUSTRALIAN GREATEST, may not have earned thousands by his pen, and may be pestered by so many literary duds that he sees each fresh one draw near with weariness and terror.

To escape making a short story long, my idol welcomed my attempt with cheers for its ORIGINALITY, and asked would I trust him with the manuscript?

WOULD I ! ! ! ! !

I'd have given him any or all of my treasures, even my black-dappled-grey filly, a doll, a book of girls' stories or a little box covered with velvet and sea shells. When I come to think of it, these were my only treasures, and he could not take the filly with him to London whither he was going. I was excited by his acceptance of the manuscript. I once gave Ma a little story for her birthday. She thanked me, but did not look as if it were an enjoyable present, and never said whether she read it before burning it under the copper. I hoped the great Australian writer would read my offering before burning it, as I had taken pains to write it nicely—no blots or scratchings-out.

CHAPTER 5

Finishing School

This matter of the autobiography settled with satisfaction, I regained my chronic distaste for the kind of life into which it had pleased God to stuff me. The entertainment of fashioning my characters and acting their parts gave me the idea of being an actress. Acting appeared to be the only avocation open to a girl who was not a musical genius nor trained in anything but domesticity. Heaven knows why I had such a notion, for I loathed hypocrisy, and in my circle, acting was another name for this. I had never seen a play nor a mummer, nor even read one—a play I mean—except Shakespeare's. It must have been the delirium of day-dreaming. Fantasy.

My delirium escaped me one day and really startled poor Ma. We had a State child called Eustace to help about the place, or hinder, Ma said. He had once been an elephant's leg in a school play in Goulburn and considered it a great lark. I concocted a scene, in which I was to accidentally fight a duel with him. He refused to fight unless I wore trousers. I put on Pa's, but Eusty said Odds Fish, no dashing blade would fight with such a spectacle. So I tried a pair of Eusty's in which I showed a bit of knee like a fat boy. Eusty called me Greedy Guts. We staged the drama in the hay shed. Pa was concerned that we might have set alight to the straw. Ma said never, never let her hear of me again putting on trousers; showing my person, failing in self-respect before a State School boy!

My defence was that to act Shakespeare (whom everyone respects next to the bible), I should have to don doublet and hose. Me acting SHAKESPEARE! Ma was shocked to discover such foolishness in me. I must really be mad. This put me in a fantod so that Ma reported me to Pa and threatened to enlist the clergyman to exorcise the devil in me.

'Now,' said Pa, when left to rebuke me, 'you must be careful not to upset your mother. The game is not worth the candle.' The only thing wrong in the affair was that I had upset Ma: I must never upset Ma: she was a wonderful woman.

'She is not always right just because she is my mother,' I grumbled.

'The law is that the Queen can do no wrong,' said Pa.

'Yes, but a Queen is a being raised to false majesty.'

'Have you forgotten that a woman's kingdom is the home?'

Pa had a twinkle in his eyes, but I refused to melt. EXPERIENCE was certainly teaching me that a sense of humour is too often an advantage to the one who hasn't it. A lack of a sense of humour, like a lack of good-temper, can be used as a waddy.

Later Ma upbraided Pa because he had not severely trounced me. Pa said, 'I see nothing wrong with the child's intellect except that it is too bright for its uses.'

'If she comes to harm, you must take the consequences,' said Ma. 'I find her with a boy—swept up from the gutter or somewhere—in a pair of trousers exposing her flesh.'

'Eustace is a fine boy. He only needs a chance.'

'A chance to get into mischief and laziness. Dear me, where would a child of mine get notions of the stage—the lowest . . . '

Pa began to rub his hair gently on end and remarked, 'I suppose a sea bird reared in the middle of a desert would retain aquatic tendencies.'

'She does not take after my side of the house,' said Ma.

She was too perturbed about my aberration, as she called it, to leave me to Pa. She 'took me in hand'. I resented the evil she discerned in me, felt that she was unfair, but there was no appeal against Ma. She disabused my mind of any notion that I could go upon the stage. She ridiculed my every feature and every contour. Ma believes in finishing things. She says it is a sign of a weak mind to begin things and leave them half done. Ma has no weakness of mind. She always finishes the hardest task. She finished me to squashation like a sucked gooseberry.

291

I often longed for death or a nunnery as an escape from my depressing lack of desirable attributes.

But I was freed from notions. Never again would I have the conceit and delusions to think of the stage. Never would I have the effrontery to seek any but the humblest jobs. Should anyone flatter me I would know them for what they were at the first soft word. Ma had ensured me against making a fool of myself by attempting flights, but she had not helped me towards contentment. The native wombat role for me henceforth. Those who are low need fear no fall. I had always jeered at the Blackshaws, our neighbours, by saying they would never make fools of themselves and by adding that those who had not enough stuffing to make fools of themselves at times would never make anything else of themselves.

The finishing stroke in Ma's finishing school was the threat to report me to the nice little clergyman. I loved him dearly. Like Old Harris he was an outlet. I was so worked up that I warned Ma that I'd listen to what she told him. Ma said it was a grave pass to be dictated to in her own house by a creature she had brought into the world. She demanded an apology. I refused. If I expressed contrition to Pa all was washed out, but with Ma it was different. She said penitent gush was useless without reform in deeds. Ma was what she called consistent.

The clergyman came next day, and after dinner, when Pa was at the stables feeding his horses, I loitered in the passage to hear what Ma was saying. Sure enough, she was reporting me as an abnormal specimen. I was infuriated, but the clergyman's voice, in the tone of the Collects—perhaps it was the Twentieth Sunday after the Melbourne Cup—said, 'But my dear Mrs Melvyn, I cannot see anything wrong at all. That child has such glorious eyes that when they are fixed upon me I always find I can preach a better sermon.'

'She can be nice when she wants to.'

'Adolescence is a difficult time. You might let her come with me around the parish and to stay with my wife and daughters till I come next month. During our progress I could find time to talk to her on spiritual things: and I get so tired of driving, and she is such a clever whip.'

That was one in the eye of Ma. I was as gay as a lark, and a willy-wagtail or two thrown in, when serving supper. I awaited breathlessly to hear the results of the clergyman's championship. Disillusion awaited me.

There was only a thin partition between my bed and Ma's, and I could always hear Ma's final injunctions to Pa. Tonight Pa opened the discourse. 'Mr David wants to take Sybylla with him.'

'So he said.' Ma's voice was a drought of common sense.

'Are you letting her go?'

'I am not.'

'Can't you spare her?'

'Not to Mr David.'

'Why?'

'Why should I let her run around with that silly old man?'

'He's not so silly.'

'All men are silly where there is a young girl.'

'I think you carry suspicion too far,' murmured Pa.

'His cloth doesn't protect a man from being blind to faults in a girl, though he would be dull to the problems of older women.'

Pa gave a loud grunt. In a little while Ma complained, 'I wish you wouldn't snore so.' Pa hadn't begun yet, so Ma was taking time by the forelock, as she often adjured me to do.

I lay awake pondering her words. Surely a clergyman, and such a nice lean helpless-looking little one as Mr David, would not be guilty of flattery or trying to make a fool of me; and he wasn't a bit like the pretentious Canon, who had once taken Mr David's place. Now, if it had been the Canon! I remember chortling when I read the table of consanguinity beginning, 'A man may not marry his grandmother,' but Pa had said that human nature was such that . . . well, such daunting things are attributed to human nature that one would prefer to be one of the higher animals and have decent instincts.

I had a good yarn with Mr David on his next visit. I had him alone because a neighbour who was ill sent for Ma, and Pa had driven her over. I confessed one thing that prejudiced me against God was that He had to be fed on everlasting praise. I had to grow strong on disapprobation, but God had to be praised unceasingly by measley creatures which He Himself had made. The Psalms were ridiculous with fulsome praise. Egotism in me had to be stemmed and denied, but God seemed to be a sticky mess of it. Another reason I could not respect God was that it seemed so despicable to continually spy upon distressed little girls for the purpose of condemnation.

Mr David chuckled and said, 'Poor God: He has need of young minds like yours to think their way to Him, not to rebel against Him. He needs your help to free Him from all the stupid misrepresentation. Sybylla, m'dear, God is aching for your loving help.'

The problem was thrown on me in a way that had never even been hinted in Possum Gully by anyone except Pa, and his theories were discredited by Little Jimmy Dripping's common sense.

This devastating idea haunted me day and night. The God made by disagreeable and selfish old men in their own image and erected as a bogey to control women and children retreated before it. Was there no God, only as He was made manifest by nobility and truth in ourselves? This idea, at first releasing, grew to be terrifying. It left one lost and alone. The European God with all His masculine bullying unfairness was at least something to be sure of, however unsatisfactory. No God except as we demonstrate Him! Whew! There was a burden too difficult and demanding to be borne. No wonder people evaded such a vast responsibility by hypocrisy, or sought less exacting conceptions of God in josses which could be placated by praise and candles and incense and other material bribes. It was a sobering revelation.

However, LIFE went on.

I loathed Possum Gully more and more. The horses were dog-poor. To ride them at the beginning of a bleak and droughty winter would have been wanton cruelty plus extravagance. March was crisp and cool, with a hint of frost which makes one feel as strong as a young colt, and I rebelled against the continual shining of pot lids, the unnecessary whitening of the hearth, just because Ma insisted upon being the top-notcher.

I took to the piano. Ma said that hard work and worry had driven piano-playing out of her. I said why not turn it the other way about, and drive out dullness with the piano, but Ma preferred to excel in spotless floors and windows. My thumping on the piano irritated her as a love of idleness, and I had to desist.

I hated every bit of the life but the sunsets and moonlight and the wild flowers. The watch-dog's bark was often the only incident of the day with its promise of a caller to break monotony. Sometimes this would be a tea agent or a stock inspector. The regular visitors were Mrs Oliver, Mrs Blackshaw, or Mrs Crispin come to spend the afternoon. I resented their inadequacy as society. It was not their fault. I loved them warmly, much more than they loved me, I am sure, and did more for them than they did for me, because I was something for them to criticise and cackle about. 'That Sybylla does this and that.' Someone was always reporting what the other said, and that annoyed Ma. Pa said rubbish, if criticism was sifted out of conversation people would be silent from Goulburn to Bourke and Broken Hill and beyond.

Poverty can make pioneering a sorry job. In any case it has always been heavier on women than on men. Possum Gully was a generation or two removed from frontier pioneering, though Australia never had a frontier. She had an outback which became back paddocks with familiarity. But all the trying part and none of the adventure of pioneering remained at Possum Gully. The inconvenient houses depending on the main strength of drudgery, the absence of comfort or beauty or any cultural possibilities or opportunities for self-development were still enough to induce Back Blocks lunacy in any one above a cow in ability.

Those good ladies all had large families, and their conversations were about recipes for cakes and puddings and little

Tommies' tummyaches, and then boasting bees as to who skinned her hands the most in washing her husband's trousers of moleskin. They and their daughters, following in their tracks, were held up to me as admirable. Horrors! Broken down drudges talking of uterine troubles and the weariness of child-bearing! I could not accept that as the fullness of life from any God worthy of worship or gratitude. These martyrs to stupidity were extolled in sententious tones as 'mothers of families'. They were populating Australia. I said that instead of Ned Crispin and others I should prefer Australia to remain populated by kangaroos and the dear little bears and kangaroo rats that were as thick about us as sheep. This was the sort of thing that made me entertaining to the Possum Gullyites, and troubled Ma.

Another winter wore away and a bit of a spring deluded the land. We had saved a few hundred sheep, and wool would be scarce because so many sheep had died. Just as shearing was coming on Pa had a call from an old colleague to help fight a by-election in Junee. This was a key electorate on Pa's side, and he said he could not let the country down. The shearing would take only a few days, and Mr Blackshaw offered to oversee it. He too saw the importance of Junee being saved for the right side.

This infuriated poor Ma. She said Pa might as well have been a drunkard who went on the booze at critical times. To leave our sole income to the superintendence of an outsider was not merely undignified, it was lunacy. Ma said I could now see why she tried to save me from my father's tendencies. She held that a man should first save his home and family, and the country could come second. Pa said if the country was not saved for the homes and liberty Australia might as well be under the Russian Czars.

At any rate Pa went, ran away in a crisis, Ma said, just because he loved to hear himself spouting on a platform. Ma said I would never understand what she had suffered, that life was a bitter thing with a useless husband. I ventured to say that Pa didn't have such a slashing life either. Ma maintained it was much harder for her, but that I could not understand that.

I was piqued by this accusation of lack in understanding. I said I could not understand it was easier for Pa because he was so proud of her and thought her so wonderful. He at least had the satisfaction of thinking what a stroke he had done to choose and win such a wife, while she must always be ashamed of herself for marrying so much beneath her; but that did not appease Ma. Quite the opposite! I gathered that Ma had the added affliction of me as a daughter, which couldn't matter so much to Pa because I took after him.

Then Mr Blackshaw's back was smitten and he could not rise from bed. All the men at one time or another had a bad back. It was Mr Blackshaw's turn. Ma was a deserted heroine.

'It is my turn to save the ship,' said I. 'You always say that I'll have to help Pa. I know how to pick up and roll a fleece, and Eusty can be tar boy and rouse-about.'

This did not dispose of the pressing. We had a hand-worked press of Pa's construction which Ma said showed what a helpless botcher Pa was, but all the neighbours used to borrow it, which further shows the standard of the neighbourhood, or that Pa wasn't so bad.

We turned the hayshed into a floor for two men with blades, who wanted to learn so that they could go down the Riverina next year. The skilled shearers had not yet returned to their little homes in the wallaby scrubs around us. These lads had to do their own work and come a distance each morning and they were very slow. All this prolonged the festival.

Ma vetoed the idea of my working in the shed. It would have been fun and a relief from the pot lids and d'oyleys. (It sometimes took half an hour to iron one of the prevalent d'oyleys.)

'You would be talked about,' said Ma, 'and the boys would be giggle-gaggling with you instead of attending to their work.'

She decided to attend to the shearing herself and let me do the cooking. This was a disappointment, as to press one's face into a nice fat sheep all white from the shears is a delight. The two shearers were selectors' sons in their teens. We knew each other minutely, but did not 'associate'. We were a grade higher socially, but had we shown it they would not have shorn for us, and would have slanged us throughout the neighbourhood. Ma and I managed to be too busy to sit down to meals with them, and thus was a gradation of the caste system preserved.

The shearing was saved but the country was lost in so far as Pa's man was rejected by the electors, and Pa did not have his election expenses paid.

CHAPTER 6

The Bread of the Mail Box Returns

The mail was left three times a week in a battered kerosene can nailed on the fence of the main road two miles away—that is if the mailman was not too drunk to sort it. He liked to keep any special letter a day or two till he read it and then gummed it up again. Other times he was content with tearing a corner off so that he could look in. He enlivened monotony by a lively interest in his neighbours' doings.

I was always hopeful of the mail. I don't know why, for the mail box only gives back the fruit of what is sown in it, and I had nothing to sow. It was at least a channel of possibility, a Tattersall's sweep that might throw up a prize, and I hungrily devoured the news of the great, reported in the newspapers.

There was no hope of any eruption in Possum Gully, it would need to be an irruption. There was no public road nearer than two miles. There was no stream to attract anglers, nor scenery for a painter, nor rocks for a geologist. My chiefest grudge against it has always been its ugliness. It is ragged rather than rugged, and lacks grandeur. We are too much in the ranges for them to be blue. They are merely sombre. The one glory that I dote and gloat on is the sunset. I love the sinking sun red as a fire between the trunks of the trees upon the hillside, and by running a quarter of a mile up the track can catch the afterglow of the grandeur of transfigured clouds on a more distant horizon.

Great was my astonishment one dull day to find a letter and a large parcel both addressed to me, and with English stamps. The letter had the corner torn off but not enough to divulge the contents. The parcel had been untied, but I was so surprised that I was not resentful of this. In all my life I had not received so much as a post card written by a hand in another country. I had no idea of the what and why of the parcel, but I trembled with excitement. I galloped part of the way home and in a little gully where the hop scrub was thickest got off to investigate.

The parcel was books. Oh, joy! Had old Harris gone back to England without letting us know? But they were all the same book. Each had the same picture on the cover. I had never seen so many of one book except school readers. And the title of the book was my spoof autobiography—and there was my name printed below it! ! ! ! It looked so different in print—so conspicuous somehow, that I was frightened.

The letter was from a man I did not know, a business letter, as his name was printed at the top of the stationery. This gentleman wrote that herewith under separate cover he had pleasure in sending me six presentation copies of my novel with the publishers' compliments. He would be glad to have my acknowledgment in due course.

There in the hop scrub I faced the biggest crisis I have known to date. What on earth was I to do about this? What would Ma say? It was a shock that this thing written as a lark could come back to me as a real book like one written by a grownup educated person. I never in the world thought of an author as resembling myself, not even the feminine ones.

There was a dreadful fascination in peeping between the leaves. There it all was, all my irreverence about God and parents, and the make-believe reality that I had piled on with a grin in a spirit of 'I'll show 'em reality as it is in Possum Gully.' I never had a book affect me like this one. It was as if the pages were on fire and the printing made of quicksilver. Was this because I knew what was in it, or was it just plain egotism, which no decent girl should have? I wished now that I had written a lady-like book that I could be pleased with. If only I had known it would be printed I should have done so. Those poor lost girls who have a baby without being married must feel like I did. There would be the baby but all the wild deep joy of it would be disgrace and trouble.

I thought of dropping the packet near home so that I could burn the books one by one secretly, but the mailman had opened them. He would ask Pa. No, I must face it. Ma and Pa were waiting for me, as I was late, and everyone looked forward to the mail, though the crop that Pa put in it mostly bore no fruit but bills.

Pa reached for the packet while Eusty took old Bandicoot's bridle.

'What's this?' asked Pa.

Ma came forward. She and Pa and Eusty each seized a book. Eusty and Pa regardless of evening jobs, there and then opened theirs.

'Golly!' screeched Eusty, inspecting the picture on the cover. 'Is that meant to be you on old Bandicoot? Bandicoot looks as if he is going to have a foal, and you look as if you are going to fall off and your clothes blow up!'

'I don't understand this,' said Ma dubiously. 'Some confidence trick man must have got hold of you. How did this book get to the printer?'

I explained that I had sent my ream of paper, when written upon to the GREATEST AUSTRALIAN AUTHOR, and he had asked me to let him keep it, and I thought it was only to read.

'Your father will be getting a big bill for this, and we'll be ruined. I wonder how much it has cost to print all this trash— it might be twenty pounds, or even fifty. You'll find EXPERI-ENCE a bitter and expensive teacher, but you must pay the price of your own wilfulness. What is hard and unjust is that I have continually to be paying it with you.'

'This is like a meteor falling in the paddock, let us investigate it,' said Pa.

Ma said, first things first; she must prepare the evening meal while I put the chooks to bed safe from the native cats: we couldn't all chase the shadow while the substance escaped us.

Eusty speedily arrived at his opinion. He had no impediment to arriving at his opinion on any subject. Old Harris said that Eusty was a perfect example of the cocksure Australian youth, possessed of the irreverence which resulted from lack of culture.

'I reckon this is a slashing lark,' he grinned. 'And crikey, if

301

it doesn't get people's nark up, I'm a goanna with two tails.'
Eusty further expressed himself as full up of it, as it was only
a blooming girl's book, and went about his jobs.

Pa wiped his pince-nez and looked thoughtfully into space
and murmured half to himself, 'Of course you are not to blame
for inexperience, but it's a very strange thing. I am tremendously
interested in what you have done, but you must not expect any
one else to be. It has just a local interest because you make
things seem so true, even things that have no relation to any
one we know, that it is like a looking glass. I really had no
idea that you had anything like this in your head. It would have
been wiser to consult me beforehand; I could have saved you
disappointment.'

With his kindness to any one in a scrape, he added, 'You must
try again and write something adventurous. Authors write many
books before they succeed, so you needn't worry that no one
will take any notice of you. I have sometimes thought of describing the old pioneer life that is fast disappearing, but when
I came to put pen on paper something always interrupted, or
the experiences seemed such small potatoes compared with the
Spanish Main or American pioneering, that they could not carry
interest beyond those who actually knew them.'

Ma made sure that the pigs and fowls had been fed, the calves
penned, the flowers watered, and kindling gathered ready for
the morning fire before she read her copy.

She said she was relieved that it was not as bad as she had
expected, for how could a girl without EXPERIENCE write a
book? She said it was lacking in discretion to have rung in such
peculiar characters. There would be unpleasantness with worthy
people who would think themselves ridiculed. She also said it
was unfilial to concoct an uncomplimentary exaggerated fabri-
cation in such a way that outsiders would think it represented
Pa and her. This was very mild and very handsome of Ma, but
she is superb in a real crisis, though often irritating in a trivial
rumpus. And what kind of a mad notion was it to rig up such
a headstrong unladylike girl to be mistaken for myself? Ma said

it was hard enough for a girl whose father could not provide for her, without handicapping herself with false reports. I was in danger of being put down as unwomanly, and men liked none but womanly girls. I shall never be a lady and poor Ma will never be anything else. So I plucked up to contend that it was womanized girls that men craved, and that it did not matter what men thought of me, as what I thought of them would even things up. 'What nonsense you talk,' said Ma. 'You will find that in this world men have it all their own way. We won't waste any more time on the silly book at present. I only hope it doesn't involve us in any expense. The publishers must have little to do, or a peculiar taste. Put the copies away where no one will see them. A nine days wonder soon fades.'

I sent a copy to Old Harris. He wrote that it was surprising to see such a novel issuing from the stately house of McMurwood—this alone assured my status. 'But my dear girl, I am troubled by the tenor of the book. Where is your radiance, your joyous sense of fun, your irrepressible high spirits? The pages seethe with discontents and pain. Have you been living alone in your spirit, suffering as we who had deepest affection for you did not dream? This distresses me. I cannot recognise you at all in these pages. Why not set our hearts at ease with a companion volume in which you give us your bright illuminating self?'

Pa said Old Harris was a wonderful man. Ma said how was a man wonderful who had wasted all his opportunities. Pa said that Mr Harris had understanding.

'Humph!' said Ma. 'All men, and the older they grow the sillier they are, *understand* a young woman, but a mature mother of a family or an old woman burdened to the earth with real griefs and troubles—thrust upon her by other people—could drop under their feet without attention.'

Pa said that it was useless to quarrel with NATURE.

And that was the end of the book. We got on with the drought. It was a hummer that year and took all our attention.

CHAPTER 7

'That Sybylla!'

It wasn't the end of the book after all. Because of the drought, and the horses being poor, visiting among the neighbours practically ceased, and it was some time before we knew what was going on. We were further like ostriches, because hard times had suspended our subscriptions to the papers.

Eusty went to Stony Flat—the neighbouring community centring in a school—with the Stringybark Hill boys who were meeting in a picnic and football match, and he came home with a briar bush of gossip.

'Golly, Sybylla, you've done it this time, I reckon,' announced he. 'Everybody is snake-headed about your blooming old book.'

'Where did they get it?' asked Ma. My heart missed a beat in dismay.

'Old Foxall can't keep enough on hand. They must have printed dozens more than those you had. Golly, I'm glad I'm not you. All the old blokes despise you and laugh at the idea of you trying to write a book.'

'That reminds me,' said Pa. 'The other day when I went over to Blackshaw, he got as red in the face as if he had been popping his brand on my sheep, and hid a book behind his back. I knew what it was, as he never read another book in his life, I'll swear. Poor old chap, he apologised and said he would put it on the fire, that he only got it to see if it was as wicked as people were saying. At any rate, my girl, you've made people read a book for the first time in their lives.'

'What did you say?' inquired Ma.

'I told him that a marvellous thing had happened in our midst, and they were too ignorant to know it. Then he got squiffy and thanked God that *his* daughters were different. It appears that the Wesleyan preacher last Sunday denounced you. He said that your attitude towards religion damns you.'

'People are magging more about your book than the drought or the price of wool,' chimed Eusty. 'Everybody is sorry for your Pa and Ma. They say you should have been kept under more.'

'Now you see what your policy of encouraging her has done,' said Ma.

'Agh! A lot of magpies chattering on the fence posts.'

I was in an agony of disgrace. I did not sleep that night. I lay awake shivering with ignominy and listening to the mopokes and plovers. I did not mind what people thought or were so silly as to mis-think about me, it was Ma. To have brought disgrace upon her and to be compelled to remain there and be tied to it in Possum Gully was a deadly tribulation.

A prophet denounced where he is known often has a great innings among strangers. Sometimes things are thus and sometimes otherwise. In my case it was both thus and otherwise. Otherwise came later: I must continue about thus.

Following his next sorties Eusty reported that Mrs Crispin had said to Mrs Oxley that she had not been to see poor Mrs Melvyn, as she did not know what to say about that Sybylla. 'Then they cackled,' said Eusty, 'and said something more about *that Sybylla* which I couldn't hear.'

'I'm sure that was no fault of your ears,' remarked Pa, and smiled to himself. I wondered why. I thought it callous of Pa.

Ma took the whole thing calmly. She was disapproving but that was business as usual.

At anyrate Eusty had great pleasure in the affair. His eyes popped and he danced a can-can after each report. 'You've done it, Sybylla,' he would giggle. 'All the girls reckon they ain't going to talk to any one so unwomanly. Elsie Blinder says her Ma says it is indelicate for a girl to write books at all.'

The trouble spread. It seemed to be more wide-spread than the drought, which that season was confined to the Southern Tableland. People arrived to condole with Pa about his hussy of a daughter, and had to scrunch on the brakes when they found

Pa so lost to all Possum Gully and Little Jimmy Dripping common sense as to be vain-glorious. He enjoyed being my father much more than I enjoyed being myself.

Every house in the district had the book, though hitherto the only reading had been the *'Penny Post'* and the bible or a circular from Tattersall's. It was the sensation of the age and at least relieved dullness. People in other Possum Gullies were equally excited, and not so annoyed. The mail bag grew fuller and fuller with the weeks. Girls from all over Australia wrote to say that I had expressed the innermost core of their hearts. Others attacked Pa for allowing his daughter to write such a book. As one man put it, 'Malicious lies without cause, for it is not a bit like us.' Another wrote, 'Of course she has altered little things here and there but everybody who reads the book will immediately know it is us because it is all so plain and true to life.'

Pa seemed to enjoy these outbursts. I could not see why. I was unnerved to have enraged people whom I had not thought of when writing, as well as others that I had not even heard of.

'You must answer these letters,' said Pa. 'It will give you a balanced sense of responsibility.'

I had to chew my pen for quite a time. I wrote humbly that I had not known the specific people but had meant simply to make fun of general reality. Pa said it was a generous letter, that it could not do any harm, neither would it do any good.

So I read the copies and then something came up in me and I jabbed down a postscript: 'I don't know you and am sorry that you are angry, but if the cap fits you and you make a noise and wear it, I can't help it.'

There was no reply to these letters.

Other letters to Ma put the cap on. The one from Grandma was a sizzler. To me she wrote that she had hoped her eyelids would be closed in death before such a disgrace had been brought upon her, but she did not blame me so much as my mother.

Ma got another letter, from an old neighbour when we had lived up the country, pitching into her and accusing her of aiding me in making fun of him because Ma had always been stuck up because she was a swell, and thought her family better than his.

It was dreadful that Ma, the one perfect member of our ménage, who was beautiful and good and clever, who had sacrificed her life for Pa and me, should have this to bear.

'I knew there was something wrong,' she remarked. 'There has been no one near the place to borrow so much as a bottle of yeast or half a hundred of flour for weeks.'

Ma is the most wonderful housekeeper in the district. The result is that the neighbours for miles around come to her when they want anything. They send to her when there is an accident, and more than once she has set an arm or leg in such a way that the doctor coming later has highly commended her skill and left it untouched. She can make dresses like a picture, and her pastry is so light and flaky that Pa says one needs a nosebag to keep it from flying away during consumption. Her bread is always taken for that of the best bakery, and so on, and so on. It is a sore trial for Ma to have such a poor husband, but added to that having her daughter, whom she had hoped would be a comfort, turning out to be a wolf in the barn, was indeed tragedy for Ma. It wasn't any pleasure to me, but I had brought it on myself. It was right that I should suffer, but Ma was suffering through no fault of her own. She was a genuine heroine.

I had to be utterly discredited. I stated that no one had known a thing about my writing a book. Pa was inculpated as far as supplying the paper, but had not suspected what I was to write. Ma was very generous and kind to everyone who complained. She wrote them nice letters explaining she entirely disapproved of me, that she had known nothing of my intentions, was grieved by my wicked wilfulness, which never came from her either by precept or example, and that she herself was the greatest victim to be mistaken for the mother in the foolish autobiography. 'But ma,' I said, 'I made up a woman with no resemblance to you on purpose, it is not my fault.'

But of course denial would not adjust matters. It showed the abnormal power of what was printed, and was my first inkling that what was printed could be wide of the facts. EXPERIENCE taught me that, but those who had never tried to write anything but a letter could not learn by experience.

'If the child had known enough to take a *nom-de-plume*, her relatives and friends would have been able to remain silent when she failed and to boast if she succeeded, without this pillaloo,' said Pa. Parliament had taught him about human nature.

I lay awake night after night wondering what I could do. I made up my mind to commit suicide so that Ma could be rid of me, but when I had worked myself up to it one day, Pa asked me to help him draft and brand a flock of sheep, and it was such a relief that instead of suiciding I decided to run away. Even that was not immediately practicable as I hadn't a railway fare, and if I left, Pa would not have had anyone to help with the place. I helped reap our bit of wheat that year, with a hook, and I milked the cows, so that Eusty could help Pa top the fences in the back paddock. I was awfully glad to keep to my own back yard. I did not want to give the girls the satisfaction of fumigating society by cutting me dead, as they all were threatening to do.

Then one day, who should come riding to the front gate but a strange gentleman in clerical attire. It was Father O'Toole who was in charge of the Roman Catholics of the parish. He told Ma that he would like to talk to that daughter of hers, if she did not object. Ma was hurt that a clergyman from another denomination should find it necessary to correct me, especially a Roman Catholic, as Catholics and Protestants have silly contentions concerning the copyright to heaven, but Ma is always a lady, so she invited Father O'Toole to come in.

Fortunately Pa had seen the arrival and came to my support. There was a great flow of geniality between them. Ma withdrew.

'Well, well, well,' said Father O'Toole, laughing so heartily that I smiled. 'Ye're a great girl and a right royal brave wan, but ye're all wrong on wan or two points that I'd like to indicate.'

Here was a learned man of religious authority taking me seriously. I felt seasick. I just sat.

'Now, whoi on earth did ye set up to interfere with the birthrate?' He laughed again. 'Arragh! Ye must have got ye'r ideas from that father of ye'rs.'

Pa rubbed his hands together as he does when really pleased, and said I formulated my ideas myself; but he added that if a young person had a mind made for ideas they came out of the air.

I did not know what Father O'Toole meant by interference with the birthrate, but he said my condemnation of large families for pioneer women. Why, bless him, the country is crying out for population. Pioneering and population, according to him, are two things that should go together like strawberries and cream.

It was inspiriting to have a real person to argue with. I put forward my pity for overburdened women dying worn-out before their time. I advanced cases where even the doctors said the women would die if they had any more babies. 'And what for?' I demanded. 'Just to delve away from week to week at a lot of dull tasks—some of them superfluous. No beauty but the sunset and the moonlight.'

His Reverence said that I was suffering from the divine discontent of genius, that it was a different matter with common people. If their noses weren't kept to the grindstone—Ha! Ha! Ha!—rearing families and working, they would get into all the devil's mischief in the world. Sure, we must fill up Australia and hold it from the Yellow Peril at our doors.

We must ourselves become a swarming menace to outswarm the Yellow Peril! What a reason for spoiling our part of the earth! What a fate, to be driven to a competition in emulation of guinea pigs!

I pointed out to the Reverend gentleman that he didn't add to the population himself, that he was safe from the burdens of both fathers and mothers, that if he were a woman he might think differently. No woman should be expected to have a big family in addition to drudging at a dozen different trades. I suggested that the unfortunate Yellow Peril women might be relieved to enter into an alliance with us to stem the swarming business.

'Ah, but ye're all wrong, ye're arguing against NATURE. Ye mustn't interfere with Nature.'

'As for that,' interposed Pa, 'All human civilization is a conquest of Nature.'

'Yes, but ye can't change human nature.' Father O'Toole laughed loudly.

'I don't think that to call an overdose of lust and verminous fecundity human nature is God's will,' I contended, 'and that I maintain, despite dads and the divils and all of divinity.'

'Whoi would ye set yourself up against all of theology?'

'And why not? if her thinking apparatus suggested it,' said Pa. 'I often think myself that we have to take out a licence to keep a dog but the most undesirable man is not restricted in thrusting upon his fellows and his unfortunate wife, as many as a dozen repetitions of himself.'

'Ah, 'tis only the old head talking through the young voice,' laughed Father O'Toole. 'It's to be hoped she won't be brought into too much trouble. Och, ye're a fine girl, and a beauty to boot. The pity of it that ye're not a boy! Then we could make a priest of ye, and the many theological arguments and disquisitions we could have would put a different complexion on these things entirely.'

Ma then brought in tea and the talk became ladylike and small. Our enlivening guest shook my hand kindly at parting as he said, 'Ye can count me wan of ye'r friends and admirers though I think ye're wrong, young woman, but ye must grow to years of discretion.'

Pa thanked him heartily for calling and invited him to come again which he promised to do, 'To see what fresh mischief this young lady will be at.'

'There's a man of the world,' observed Pa, as he went. 'I like him for coming openly as a friend, not a snake behind our backs.'

'Huh!' said Ma. 'He has the real old cackle like a political vote-catcher with his tongue in his cheek.'

The following day I got a horrifying letter. The signature was bold and plain, so were the contents. It was from old Mr Grayling who lived ten or fifteen miles away to the east. He was one of the most intimate of our friends. His wife had died about a year since. His daughters were Ma's great friends. He was seventy-two years of age—twenty-one years older than Pa.

I thought I was having a nightmare. It was a proposal of marriage. It sickened me to the core as something unclean.

Things were pretty bad for me, he said, when a blasted priest could think he had the right to denounce me, but that He (old Grayling) had faith in me. With his love and protection I could reinstate myself and be a very happy woman. He was a frantic Protestant and so set on his chart of the way to heaven that a cross drove him beserk as a symbol of popery rather than as the gallows on which Christ was crucified.

Old Grayling told me his age right out, but said he was younger at heart and otherwise than men half his age. Ugh! I cannot go on. UGH! UGH! UGH!

This was a desecration of all I had ever thought of love, of all the knights that were bold and heroes in lace and gold, and that sort of thing. Old Grayling was the most wrinkled man I know. He was stooped; he had only two or three barnacled fangs, and nothing gives a man such a mangy and impecunious appearance in the flesh as teeth like that. He had a BEARD. A straggly old-man one!

Petrified, sick, I hid behind the pig-sty for an hour or two. I had regarded him as a friendly grandfather. Why, he had three sons all with beards and bald heads and corporations! His granddaughters were older than I by years. It was as shocking as a case of indecent exposure against a bishop.

The pigs did not know what to think. They conversed to me and about me in the most friendly grunts. I love pigs. Observe how everyone cheers up at the mere mention or sight of pigs!

In the animal kingdom one cannot ask for more engaging companions. They were my only refuge in that landscape. I couldn't even tell Pa this. It was too disgusting a revelation about another man so old. I tried to comfort myself by thinking Old Grayling must be suffering from delirium tremens, and this the equivalent of seeing snakes; but there wasn't really any comfort in it as I had never heard of his being drunk.

I tore the letter into bits and strewed it in the pigsty but every word was in my head. When I reappeared Ma asked me to explain my peculiar behaviour. I said I had been looking for the nest of a kangaroo rat. Ma said that was childish of me, but I got away with it because she was absorbed in Anthony Hordern's catalogue that the mail had brought.

Another sleepless and tortured night. I was in a sorry pass if clergymen of divers denominations could preach against me and call to admonish me so that Old Grayling could think himself a rescuer. My former state when I had chafed against monotony and lack of opportunity to try my wings with birds of my own feather now seemed deliciously peaceful. I had written a yarn just for fun, and every sort of person took it seriously and it collected duds and freaks upon me. Here was something like one of those murders or fires or other disasters that happen to strangers. Disgrace had rained upon me as suddenly as a thunderstorm.

I was abashed with one side of me but with the other I wished that Father O'Toole had proposed to me too. That would have been a situation to turn one camp a yellow tinged with green and give the other that pea-green feeling trimmed with orange, which would have been jolly good for both.

CHAPTER 8

More Chickens of Inexperience

One day old Bismarck yelped and I looked out of the kitchen window to see Old Grayling approaching with a tall black blood which was being broken before my eyes on the bridle track between our place and one or two neighbours. A dry creek was almost impassable and mess-mate stumps were dotted thickly on either side of a narrow wriggling track. Along this came a man of 72 in a new single buggy—a show-ring affair—with a horse that leapt and sidled resentfully.

'Flash old fool!' remarked Pa. 'He is bursting out again now that the old woman is underground.'

'A wonder the family lets him run to such useless expense. He is mad to drive such a horse along that track,' said Ma.

The Graylings were mortgaged through the front door and out the back gate. I knew why that odious old man had that horse and a new vehicle. He had eschewed riding but had come in competition with the young men who headed in my direction on Sundays and holidays leading race horses and other prime specimens wearing a lady's bridle. He had been a reckless young man. The district yielded yarns of his escapades. It was a feat, if I had not been so apprehensive of him, to see him bring that buggy and rampageous horse among the stumps and into that creek and up again at a dangerous angle and around our wood heap and over the garden drain to the side gate.

He was warmly welcomed by Pa and Ma. I kept near Ma while tea was being served. When Old Grayling began to jockey me aside, I fled. He followed me to the garden, to the dairy, to the kitchen. I took the direction of a building to which no lady would be seen going. Desperation drove me to such a ruse. It was successful. The Graylings were renowned for gallantry.

I ran from there to the pigs again, risking the fleas for an unsuspected retreat. After a time Ma called. After some more time Pa hailed me with rousing coo-ees. The pigs talked to me but did not betray me. At length, peeping between the logs of the sty, I saw Mr Grayling departing at racing speed guiding his intractable horse safely along the difficult track. I slid up the back way and into the kitchen. Ma and Pa, who had lingered watching the driving skill, were talking about me.

'She must be mad,' it was Ma's voice. 'To disappear without rhyme or reason.'

'She shows no signs of madness,' said Pa. 'She might want to think.'

At this I appeared. Ma demanded an explanation of my antics. I gave none.

'You make yourself very agreeable to the young men, but flout poor old Mr Grayling. He waited till too late to drive home with that flighty horse just to say good-bye to you. Now is not the time to miss your manners if you want to live down the scandal and trouble you have caused.'

Pa came with me to feed the pigs. 'Your mother is right, you know, my girl. When we are kind to fine young men, it is not hospitality, it is self-indulgence. I always feel that any welcome I can give the Graylings is feeble compared with the welcome they give me.'

The cause of my action seemed too indecent to tell Pa. As for telling Ma I would rather have had her report me to the doctor and clergyman as raving mad. She would blame me for Old Grayling's sickening aberration, and constant misunderstanding hurt. 'Oh, Pa,' I said, 'I can't bear any more scandalmongering and fuss. I would as soon go and live with the pigs like the Prodigal Son.'

This surprised Pa. He sat upon the pig-sty fence talking to me for a long time. 'And you wanted to be famous,' he said banteringly. 'What you are undergoing is fame, the thing you wanted, in a very mild form.'

'I didn't want bad notoriety: it must have been fair renown that I dreamed about.'

'There is only one percent of that, mixed with exaggeration and scandal and envy. No one can make it otherwise, not even royalty, though it commands the press and the army. The smoking rooms are full of another story right around the world, always have been, even in days when one's head could be cut off for a disrespectful word about those in authority.' Pa here quoted Byron.

'Why, my girl, it is wonderful at your age to be denounced by a preacher and argued with by a priest, though I can't see what the stir is about, myself. I'm sorry that you did not write something much more rousing. Surely you are man enough to stand up to a little flutter like this. Use common sense. Think what you say about other people. You don't like them any the less, but if they heard your private criticism of their clothes and persons there wouldn't be a friend from Cape Otway to Cape Leeuwin. If you enter public life, you have to take all that as the chattering of magpies. As for people going to cut you dead, and that stuff that Eusty brings home; just walk out before them and smile, and they'll all be running to lick your boots and gain your favour.'

Pa then went on to tell me of his experiences as a member of the Legislature. 'Bless me, I was accused of being a traitor to the State when I tried to bring in measures to help the under dog. I was called the misappropriator of funds for trying to save a great public swindle, and the fellows who carried it through were knighted.'

Pa took me further into his confidence in a grown-up way.

'I was slandered—they even tried to defeat me by annoying your mother. They said she was a drunkard, which was madness, as you know.'

Poor Ma, herself perfect and circumspect, first to have suffered the backwash from Pa's opponents and now to undergo a repetition through me! It made me understand Ma's attitude.

'You are old enough to face these things now,' continued Pa and added in a whisper, 'they even accused me of carrying on with other women.'

This completely cheered me. I laughed until the pigs went whoof! whoof! whoof! all around the sty expecting a second helping. Pa and *other women*! was atrociously absurd, and Ma being accused of drunkenness was so abnormal that I was henceforward prepared for any stories about myself. Dear old Pa! Pa and OTHER WOMEN!

The prating about nothing new under the sun (Solomon) and the impossibility of upsetting antecedents, which met me when I wished to try something different, was gaining weight with me. Dismal. Now I could see why people have written those self-praising, white-washing autobiographies. People don't write autobiographies until they are old fogies. Otherwise they would have lacked time for EXPERIENCE, and EXPERIENCE had taught them before they started what it was teaching me now, that people can't endure their reality in print and so create an uncomfortable situation for the realistic autobiographer with his family and all concerned. Pa is always saying that when you get up in years you want peace, that it is only while you are very young or haven't any spiritual grist that you hanker for emotional tornadoes.

These lessons from Pa were a great help. Politics have seasoned him. He gives a whoof of contempt for gossip and scandal. He always turns what is said of him into a circus against the talebearer.

Things, all the same, are not simple. If I had stuck to my lords and ladies in England and a beautiful heroine who went through tophet to give the hero a chance to show-off as a deferred rescuer; if I had had the villain scrunching the gravel, and a jealous rival beauty biting her lips till the blood came and breaking the stem of a champagne glass between her jewelled fingers with rage (though I have not yet seen a champagne glass) I should have been acclaimed. My tale might have adorned the *Supplement to the Goulburn Evening Penny Post*. I love the tales in the *Penny Post*, full of mystery and glamour and castles and lords and gorgeous lovers. I don't know why on earth I became afflicted with this foolish notion of showing how comical the Possum Gully

316

sort of reality would look by comparison. Aunt Jane is right, no doubt, when she says I was born contrary.

It was Old Harris who got me into this trouble by adjuring me to be Australian and thus add to culture. CULTURE! Talk about culture!!! I wrote to him on the subject.

There were fresh inconsistencies teasing me. Ma said that if I wasn't womanly and all that sort of triffle-traffle, the men would not propose to me, and here I was beset with proposals from all over the place. Some of them were nearly as bad as Old Grayling's, though he was the dean of the faculty, but men cannot help nearly all being duds from the lover angle. I suppose their delirium of egotism keeps them perpendicular. I should never have the front to try to get a man to marry me, but you should see the objects that booby up to me and think they can have me for the asking.

There are others, always young and sometimes desirable who are so shy that I know them only in letters in which they confess they have followed me all day, recording my least action, or have sat on the same seat in Belmore Square and have heard the sound of my voice. There now!

One Sunday afternoon old Bismarck made an unusual commotion and called our attention to another exhibition of driving on the tortuous back track. A pair of spirited trotters swung around the stumps, down in to the creek at a dizzy angle and up over the mere footbridge of the garden drain to fetch-up at the side gate. The turn-out was too good for a tea agent: it must be a wool agent. All kinds of agents are rather regarded as parasites upon the squatters and selectors—middlemen who fatten on the profits of commodities which other men sweat to produce. He looked like someone who had got out of his way and had called for directions. I hoped he was not coming in. I used to long for any sort of caller, but that infernal book has resulted in my being a kind of puppet show, and I am heartily sick of it.

Pa went out shouting surprise and a boomer of a welcome. Ma followed corroborating him, and asking the man why they had not seen him all these years. Pa and he went to the stables, leading the lovely ponies with their saucy heads and wide red nostrils. Ma hastened to spread a hearthrug and a table cover, kept for high company, and said we'd have to prepare something for tea. We had tea on Sundays: other days Ma stuck to dinner at sundown instead of in the middle of the day. She was the only one in the neighbourhood who did—a relic of her early social status.

It was Henry Beauchamp from Moongudgeonby, one of the big stations up the country, where Ma and Pa came from. He had been at their wedding and, since those days had been in Queensland and down the Murray. I did up my hair to look grown-up in readiness to meet him. Ma seemed delighted that he had come. As I came out he was saying she was the loveliest bride he had ever seen.

'Married life soon altered that,' said Ma. 'You haven't a bride of your own yet?'

'Can't find one to come up to you,' said he. 'Is your daughter like yourself.'

'Oh, dear me, no,' said Ma expressively.

'Takes after you from what I hear,' said Mr Beauchamp, with a grin at Pa.

'They say so, but I think she is very much herself.' I loved Pa for that and took this moment to come in.

The typical Australian squatter, according to my idea, rose to meet me. He was a tall broad man, with a clipped black beard and two or three grey hairs around the temples. Quite old. I noticed at once. He was so tanned that his eyes, a sort of oyster grey, looked like white holes. He smiled, showing white teeth, without waiting to be introduced. It was trying to have to come out in contrast to Ma, but I did not think I was grown-up enough for him to notice me much. I hoped he would not miss my complexion, which is one of my unassailable points. Everyone raves about it. My admirers always wish they could eat it. Ma says I get it from her as Pa's side have muddy skins and that mine will soon go, that a complexion is a fleeting thing.

I think Henry Beauchamp noticed it and every other detail.

His glances were quick and penetrating as if they could see through one's clothes.

There was a great flow of geniality and high company talk. Ma and Pa asked questions and Mr Beauchamp replied in a soft cool voice. I liked looking at his teeth, but found his eyes on me wherever I went. This made me uneasy as I knew he was wondering how Ma, the perfect and unique, could have produced me. Pa and Ma had him in the evening while I did the work. I did not reappear until supper time at half past nine after which Ma showed Mr Beauchamp to the spare room.

It was a wild windy night with tins rattling and rafters creaking and Pa hoped for rain, but the morning sky was bright and cold. At breakfast Ma suggested that Mr Beauchamp should stay for the day. He accepted without quibble. He had had two big stages with his horses and a spell would do them good. They were a prize pair, had taken everything open to them at Bathurst, Junee, Cootamundra, Gool-Gool and half a dozen other shows. He was to judge the horses at the Goulburn Show and had come a day or two in advance to visit Pa.

It was washing day and Ma and I wondered how he would put in the time. Moongudgeonby is a show place, and our cockatoo farm has nothing to exhibit. However, our guest seemed content to go about talking to Pa. They leant upon all the places possible and talked, even on the pigsty, while the pigs whoofed and seemed as pleased as they were to see me. They leant upon the sheep yards, and Ma said she would be ashamed for anyone who came from real sheep yards to see such makeshifts, but Mr Beauchamp did not criticise. They leaned against the stable door, and on the cow-yard fence and over the garden gate and talked and talked, and talked and talked.

Ma and I had to pull foot to get the washing out and the lunch on and look like ladies who had nothing to do. Pa was so pleased with a chum from his original grade that he invited Mr Beauchamp to stay until the Show. He accepted without pressing. He did not seem to need exciting company. At lunch he said he would like one of the ladies to run into town with him next morning. Ma refused. He turned to me, but Pa said he would go, and it was a single-seated buggy. That settled that.

'Well then, I should like to take Miss Sybylla with me to the Show. A man by himself in a buggy looks forlorn, but Miss Sybylla would repair that.'

I had promised to meet Billy Olliver but decided to ask him to let me off. He could come any day. This would be a thrilling jaunt with an escort so old and important. Twenty-six was the oldest I had yet, except Old Grayling. I went about my tasks like quicksilver hoping that Ruby and Nellie Blackshaw and the Crispin girls would see me driving with Mr Beauchamp. They were going to look the other way when I came near. This would dish their airs.

The wind went out of my balloon while I was setting the table for dinner. Mr Beauchamp was beside the fire while Ma was darning. It had come up cold. As I entered Ma was saying, 'There seems to be no end to the annoyance caused by that silly book. I think it best to ignore all the scandal and it will die out. I assure you I knew nothing of it and have discouraged her all I can.'

As I put the tray down Ma continued pointedly. 'You asked if Sybylla resembled me. I should not like to think so. She has given me a lot of vexation. I have had two mothers here bullying me because I have not restrained her from driving their sons mad. Men are foolish to think they can make any impression on her.'

I felt myself reddening right through to my heels. Why will Ma hurt me so that I cannot sleep? She might have given me a chance with Mr Beauchamp. I was being most circumspect. An older man like that, what would he think? I could not go to the Show with him after this.

I made faces at Ma and tried to stop her, and I think Mr Beauchamp caught me, he was much amused, and led Ma on to say more.

'So Sybylla is a bit wild, is she? You must have spoilt her.'

'She has spoilt herself. Men can't see that they might as well try to catch the wind or that old hawk out there, but they giggle-gaggle around her and overlook the nice quiet girls who would make men happy.'

That was not fair of Ma. When I tried to escape Old Grayling, she said I was inhospitable. I treated everyone alike and they all admitted that I was friendly and full of fun.

I was so ashamed that I could not look Mr Beauchamp in the eyes. I placed the lamp at his end of the table with a vase of flowers between me and him but he peeped around it and said I was getting lost so far away.

I disappeared to the kitchen for the evening to finish the ironing and to set bread. Ma was in the dining-room writing letters to send by the men in the morning. Mr Blackshaw came over and he and Pa and Mr Beauchamp were in the drawing-room or 'front room' as the company room is called around Possum Gully.

Eusty had gone to bed and I had started on the ironing when Mr Beauchamp stood laughing at me from the doorway. I asked him if he wanted anything and he said, yes, a talk with me.

'I haven't time to talk,' I said, fearing that Ma would blame me if she came out and found him there.

'Aren't you going to ask me to sit down?'

'I beg your pardon,' I said, setting a stool before the fire. 'I thought Pa would be wanting to talk to you.'

I blithered away at the ironing. He placed the stool right before me.

'So you are a trouble to the lads of the district,' he said with a chuckle and a soft pedal in his voice. 'And your mother does not advertise you as a little dove.'

I thumped like everything so that I couldn't hear him, but he cupped his hands like coo-eeing. I was afraid that I'd laugh, so saying that I had forgotten the bread, I dashed away and collected the tub, the yeast, the flour and potatoes and began setting the sponge.

'You are the quickest human being I ever saw,' he remarked.

'You are carrying on like this just because you are upset by what your mother was telling me.'

'I'm not like what Ma says.'

'Oh, ho, what about that book?'

'It's not real.'

'I don't believe you are either. I have never seen anyone like you, and I've been about a bit in my time. I've had a bit too much time to be about in too,' he added, and laughed so infectiously that I nearly joined in.

'In that case,' said I, 'you had better not waste any more time here.'

'Oh, I don't grudge a little time to see if I can do anything to help my dear old friends with such a terrible daughter.'

I worked furiously at the bread-setting.

'Well now, tell me about the book.'

'I never talk about it. They all can think what they like. At least it has shown me how silly everyone is.'

'I thought it had shown how silly you are. That's what I gathered from your cousins as I came along. They said it was the silliest goat of a book they ever read, and just what they expected as you are the silliest goat of a girl they have ever known.'

I just stood and looked at him. I had not Pa's seasoning in meeting condemnation, especially from my cousins of whom I was so fond. At length I steadied enough to say, 'At anyrate the greatest writer in Australia says I could be great some day if I develop.'

'That poet fellow! Does his word count for anything? Writers are just skites, aren't they—half their time drunk and the rest of it cadging for a bit to eat?'

I was familiar with this point of view. All of my relations had it. None but Pa ever wrote so much as a letter to the newspapers, which put him among those sneered at as windbags trying to be important. I made the coffee and said, 'You will be wanting your supper,' and went to the dining-room.

Mr Beauchamp went around the house and came in from the front pretending that he had been to the stables to let his horses

322

out. Pa and Mr Blackshaw were still talking. I went to bed, leaving Ma to dispense supper. Another tortured night. I was so fond of my cousins. I always defended them if anyone dared to say they were not the prettiest liveliest girls up the country.

Mr Beauchamp and Pa left early in the morning and did not return until dinner time.

CHAPTER 9

It Was All Real, But How Much Was True?

Mr Beauchamp came straight to the kitchen after seeing about his horses.

'Last night you were quite put off your stride by what your mother and cousins think of you.'

'If you don't mind, the subject is closed.'

'Oh, no, it isn't,' he said with his provokingly contagious laugh. 'You were afraid it would affect my opinion of you.'

'Your opinion . . . '

'Now, now, don't try to break the bridle, or I'll tell your mother that you have been rude to me, and she won't permit that.'

I devoted myself to the washing-up.

'I'll wait. You are so quick that you soon will be ready.'

I turned my back on him.

'You have the prettiest neck and cheek from the back I ever saw,' he remarked casually. 'Don't be squiffy. I'll tell you something. Every word said against you weighs against those who say it. That sort of jealousy always works that way. All the girls from here to Timbuctoo are busy adoring you, and the one or two squeaks are pure jealousy.'

'I never was jealous of anyone in my life.'

'You have no one to be jealous of here. I wonder how you would shape among girls who could rival you.'

This was a new point of view to me—an idea. I began to examine it and was trapped into talking.

'There are only two kinds of parents,' he continued. 'Those who think their offspring can do nothing wrong, and those who think they can do nothing right. My old man was in the same class as your mother. Every word of disparagement by your mother made me more interested in you. I would never think of marrying anything but a jolly little flirt. That kind of girl knows

324

her way about, and you know when you have her. The booby might go off the rails at the least strain. Besides she has no fire or style.'

'Yes, but I intend to be as annoying as I can in accordance with the family critics.'

'Very clever of you: makes you provokingly attractive.' He chortled again, 'You are as full of mettle as a blood filly.'

'I'll tell Ma that you are vulgar.'

'She'd blame you. When she began to warn me against you, my interest was aroused. I know how to take the praise of fond mas with daughters on their hands. I'm not having any. There is no use in your playing up: the breed is there. Your father is the whitest man in Australia and any daughter reared by your mother is the real stuff, in a class by herself. There are a lot of old maids in your mother's family and that is another jolly good sign. Early marriage is often a sign of poor goods that have to be sold quickly.'

Here was another idea. An interesting man.

'I'm glad you approve of old maids because I have decided to be one.'

'But I shan't let you.'

'What have you got to do with it?'

'Haven't you noticed my influence with your mother? Do you suppose I'm here to talk about the pigs and old times to your father: nearly staked my pair coming up that track.'

'Aren't you married already?'

'No fear.'

'Didn't sell early—are you good material?'

'Better call me Henry,' he replied irrelevantly. 'It will make me seem quite ten years younger.'

'What for?'

'Well—you see—what age are you—eighteen?'

'Nearly.'

'Whew! Only seventeen! You'll make a delightful little wife when the nonsense is trained out of you. Any man would want to marry you because of your mother.'

325

'I don't know *your* mother, so I don't know if there is *any* reason at all why any one would want to marry *you*.'

He laughed consumedly, I too; it was so silly.

'It is a serious consideration for a man of thirty-six to think of a girl of eighteen. Twenty years on I'll be an old chap wanting to settle down and you'll be just in your prime.'

'Why consider such silly things without foundation?'

'Must I shave off my beard?'

'Why do you tolerate such a monstrosity?'

'It can go any minute you say.'

'You might collapse like Samson and then need a winch to hoist you about.'

'Do you like beards?'

'As if anyone could *like* a beard!'

'I must go to the barber tomorrow.'

'Don't shave it off just yet.'

'Why?'

'I shan't tell you.' I had the laugh to myself now. After only thirty-five hours he seemed to be buckling like the young men, and what a trophy he would be, with his beard, like a big bear on a chain. This matter of beard was a lively test. I had applied it with the result that all my young men friends who had had moustaches were now clean-shaven, while those who had been clean-shaven were assiduously growing moustaches. Some of the latter were of the cricket style—eleven hairs a side.

'Well now, when I marry you I don't think I'll approve of any more of this writing. I'd be jealous of it. You'd want to be wasting your spare time on that when I wanted to play with you.'

I flashed out at this. 'Supposing I said that you would have to give up breeding wool or horses and be hanging around ready to play with me.'

'That's a different matter. You're a woman, and Nature settled it long ago. I have nothing to do with it.'

'But I have, you conceited lord of creation!'

At this Ma came in the door looking trenchantly at me. 'Do

you know that your daughter has just called me a conceited lord of creation?'

'Men deserve what they get for being so foolish,' said Ma. 'You are not going to be as silly as the boys, are you?'

I left him to Ma.

The following morning he again invited me to go to the Show with him in his buggy, drawn by the dashing pair that seemed to run above the road instead of on it. Ma and Pa both said I could go, Ma adding the rider, 'If you behave yourself.'

'I'll see that she behaves,' said Mr Beauchamp in his good-humoured drawl.

'And I'll see that he behaves,' thinks I to myself, pricked to pay him out for his self-confidence. Billy Olliver was the instrument at hand. Billy's horse, Captain Phillip, was the best hunter of the year, and I had promised to take my habit and ride him in the lady's hack class. Well, my lord Henry could drive me to the door of the hotel, and when he came out I should be departing with Billy. There was time to send a letter and get the plot in train.

Then the Clerk of the Weather messed-up everything. We had suffered from a drought since Christmas, and it was now late in March. The sky was overcast. Henry received word to come in on the Wednesday for urgent business with the Show officials. He apologised, but said he would take charge of me the moment Pa and Ma arrived on Thursday morning, and would drive me to the Show Ground.

'Ha!' scoffed Ma. 'You'll find you won't have your own way with a hard-shelled old lady-killer.'

The drought took a notion to break on Wednesday. It poured all the afternoon so that I could hardly make old Bandicoot face it when I went to meet Great-aunt Jane, who was arriving from Gool-Gool; and the cattle went shivering campwards with humped backs and lowered heads. It was called a heavy thunderstorm, most opportune to lay the dust for the morrow, but rain fell again during the night. The morning was grey, but held up sufficiently for us to start. I shared the back seat with Aunt Jane.

The rain got heavier and heavier, obscuring the horizon, and Auburn Street was running creeks as we took refuge in the hotel yard. Mr Beauchamp and Billy were both at the front door awaiting us. They did not know each other, but had been talking.

The rain was so torrential that there was no hope of going to the Show Ground. Ring events were impossible until it lifted. When we came into the hotel parlour, Billy and Mr Beauchamp were both there. I introduced them. Billy immediately 'turned dawg' and looked most bilious.

Mr Beauchamp was in high spirits. Something seemed to so amuse him that he could not contain himself. I whispered to him that my plans, like his, had to be altered somewhat, that I was to be photographed on Mr Olliver's horse, but that Aunt Jane would companion him to the show. 'She's a dear,' I said. 'Ma is never done singing her praises, and says she wishes I was only a quarter as good.'

Mr Beauchamp's eyes danced. I withdrew to Billy. He muttered a curse on the drought having taken this day to break and said that young Masters had a wonderful gramophone at the Royal and had invited me to come and hear it if the rain continued.

We set off at once, Billy carrying the handbag with my habit, as I could dress at the Royal later. I had friends there in mine host and his wards. Mr Beauchamp came to the door and wished us well with unforced glee, but Billy looked angry and chapfallen.

'Is Beauchamp a married man?' he really hissed, as soon as we were safely in the street.

'No.'

'What's he doing here?'

'He's the Show judge, and Ma and Pa knew him up the country.'

'AAAAH! He told me he was staying at Possum Gully.'

I wondered what Mr Beauchamp could have said to Billy to make him so queer. He turned quite wooden. He had no reason to be glum, as I went off with him, keeping my word under Mr Beauchamp's nose. Billy bought me the regulation chocolates—a huge box—and we proceeded to the gramophone until the clouds should break. One of the Masters from out our way was the proud possessor. It played 'Arrah go on,' and some other songs. During the recital a messenger arrived with a note for me.

Mr Beauchamp wrote that my Great-aunt Jane showed the breed I came from. He had been going to tell my mother how I had deserted him, but he was so pleased with Auntie that he would let me off this time. It was signed *Harold Beecham*.

Billy growled, 'It's from that mug with the beard I suppose.'

Daddy Royal overheard him and chipped in, 'Miss Sybylla would get a hundred notes if the young men knew where to find her. If I put a notice on my door that she needed someone to drive her home this evening, the police would have to regulate the rush. If not, the young men of the district would be decaying; and they have eaten too much bull beef for that.'

Billy suggested we should go in a cab to see the pavilion exhibits. He was polite and thoughtful, helping me with my dress, and keeping the rain off me with a big new umbrella while we were getting in and out of the cab, but there was a sadness and quietness about him that I have not seen before. I hoped he was not catching a chill.

The rain kept on and on. There wasn't a hope of a ring event, so we came back to the Royal. The messenger was awaiting with another note. *Harold Beecham* reported that he and Auntie were getting on splendidly. He hoped that I and young Olliver were enjoying ourselves only half as much. If there was anything I would like him to do for me I had only to let him know. The postscript ran, 'Ask young Olliver if he will grow a beard for you.'

The messenger said he had to wait for a reply. I was delighted to oblige: 'Yes, there is something you can do, thank you very much. Propose to dear Aunt Jane. I should adore you for an uncle, and it is a pity to waste such an avuncular beard.'

I was pleased with the opportunity to use the word *avuncular*.

'Would you grow a beard for anyone you liked?' I asked Billy Olliver.

'I know what put that into your head,' he snorted, and fell into a deep gloom.

Daddy Royal invited me to lunch and put me on his right hand side and kept up a patter of teasing. Billy sat on the other side of me and had rather a bad time. He seemed unfledged in meeting it after Henry Beauchamp. Tame. The subject of beards came up among the girls of the house, and some wag asked Mine Host if he thought a man ought to grow a beard to please a lady.

'Of course he should. I'm a Methuselah and have a beard already, but if I had the honour, now, say, of escorting Miss Sybylla for a day, I'd grow my hair and train it in a peruke. Billy Olliver, give an account of yourself. Why have you the privilege of sitting where you sit today, when all the upstanding young men of the district would eat their hats to be where you are at this moment?'

Poor Billy looked worse and worse. I tried to comfort him, but was puzzled by his behaviour. Perhaps he was a philanthropist and liked me while convention was against me, but hadn't the know-how to act up to the situation which had suddenly overtaken us.

Another note arrived at the end of lunch.

'Your mischief is like a tonic. Never enjoyed myself more. Your father has invited me to spend a week with him after the Show, and then I'll get my innings. I bet young Olliver's cake is turning to dough already. Let me know your thoughts by the messenger.'

I wrote: 'My thought is that you are very silly. Don't blame me. I haven't said a word, but everyone in town will know that the messenger is from you.'

The messenger was back in twenty minutes: 'It's downright unkind of you not to mention me. What do you suppose I'm sending a man back and forth for but to keep myself to the front. If my only object was to employ a messenger I could give him five bob and let him rest his corns.'

Billy growled, 'You must be very spoony if you have to write to him every two minutes.'

Mr Beauchamp had me on tip-toe to play ball with him, but I could not make him angry. He laughed with imperturbable good humour.

330

The rain never let-up for a moment. Everyone settled down to a comfortable day indoors. We had a jolly time at the Royal with flirtation and chocolates, badinage and so on, mingled in equal parts. The prospects of grass for the winter cheered everyone.

'The rain'll do more good than the Show,' the publicans said, as they reaped an advance harvest.

As the afternoon deepened the messenger represented Pa, and I had to return to the Commercial. It was too wet to ride home with Billy, as we had intended, so I tucked in beside Aunt Jane.

Billy escorted me to the last and said good-bye with chocolates, the only backsheesh I was permitted to collect from admirers.

It was a long wet drive. In spite of macintoshes, umbrellas and rugs, the rain drove through cracks, and we reached home cold and damp. Eusty had a roaring fire and the tea set, and soon we were all comfortable around it, talking over the day.

'Dear me, what an interesting man Mr Beauchamp has developed into,' remarked Aunt Jane. 'Most of the young men are interesting until they begin to cackle with Sybylla and turn into perfect idiots.' Aunt Jane was disapproving of my disappearance all day, but Pa said I was as safe as in a church at the Royal.

I had received a letter from Old Harris in reply to my complaints of my woes. The sympathy in it rose to understanding and was as liberating as a new idea.

He stated that fowls would always peck at the wild swan that was hatched among them until it grew strong enough to escape. As to the excessive number of people who claimed that they had been caricatured, the more of these the greater the tribute to my gifts of characterisation: it was valuable evidence which should elate rather than depress. He went on to say that one should be magnanimous about misplaced censure as the day was swifly coming when it would be reversed. The future boast of my associates would be that they had known me. He implored me to remember that I wore the mantle of genius—a royal mantle which should never be lined with rancour. He said he hoped to see me in London whither he was soon returning. I would find my rightful place there. I was as out of my element in Possum Gully as a swan in the Sahara. 'Your wings, my brave girl,' he concluded, 'are fashioned for grand flight. Lift them up and soar, and if an old man who once knew the world overseas, to which you will soon gravitate, may venture a word of advice: think and wait, make no entanglements to cripple the power of long distance flight.'

He enclosed some English reviews. One of the two columns in length compared my gifts with those of several immortals. The printed word was irrefutable, though I could not show the reviews abroad or I should be accused of blowing my own horn.

It was a stimulating letter. I brought it to Pa in triumph. It had been quite a heady day. Pa was more excited than I. 'I knew, my girl! I knew!'

It seemed as if Possum Gully might not have the last word about me. Aunt Jane had that: 'It sounds as if poor Old Harris must be drinking more than ever.'

My balloon was pricked. Bang! BUNG! it went.

CHAPTER 10

Harold Beecham and Five-Bob Downs

'Harold' came out as he threatened after the Show, and quite settled down with us. My elders talked about him and stopped when I came near. It made the housework quite entertaining to receive a note every half hour or so. I got into the habit of replying. First I put on his table the long English review; then a whole page one from the philosopher of the *Squatters' Journal.*

'I don't know about this English Johnnie,' he said, 'but old Frogabollow in the Journal, I always wonder why they let him have so much space when it could be given to the latest prices. I must see what he says.'

This was daunting, so my next shot was the letter from the GREATEST AUSTRALIAN WRITER.

'I always thought that booze and rattiness and "pomes" went together,' was the response to this. 'So I must get your blooming little book and see what it is all about.'

'Haven't you read it?'

'Never read a book since I left school. I had a cook last year who used to sit and ready penny dreadfuls till the bread rose over the tub and fell on the floor.'

I did not know how to cope with this. I fell into a Government Dam of silence. Books were an excitement and joy to me. In teaching me manners Ma had laid down the rule, 'When you don't know what to say, say nothing.' I said nothing. I went on with my housework. I shuddered. If I missed a stroke anywhere it would be put down to my inclination to write. Other girls could border on being slatterns without attracting attention.

I suddenly felt unhappy and full of failure.

No one that I knew had ever seen a real live author. I had imagined them as having different qualities of soul and intellect. When I had found myself in print—a suffering, mistake-making, walk-about person—it resulted in a frightful drop in the stock of authors. I had thought critics to be above authors as school teachers are above scholars. This English one must have been drunk—like Old Harris. The contemptuous dismissal of his praise was supported by Mr Beauchamp's attitude, and at times men who worked on the *Penny Post* had stayed with us, and there were tales that they could have been on big Sydney papers but for drink.

'Do you think I should read your book?' Mr Beauchamp asked later.

'I wish you would never read it, but I can't make out why you are interested in me, if you haven't.'

'All the hubbub has brought you to my attention, like a filly that is advertised. I could not make out why Moongudgeonby was suddenly being called Five-Bob Downs, and found that it was because in a book written by some bit of a kid no bigger than a bee's knee, Five-Bob Downs was owned by Harold Beecham, so people have the cheek to call me that. Some of them have asked me when I am going to settle down with Sybylla Melvyn. The young fellows say I am a lucky devil, that they would have a shot for themselves only that I am the hero of your dreams. I took it as a bit of chyacking while I was in Queensland, but when I got back to Gool-Gool people buzzed like a swarm of bees. I thought it a rum thing that a girl could change the name of a place christened by the blacks hundreds of years ago. She must be a witch who could pull the wool over my eyes and have me tied up before I knew where I was, and I value my freedom.'

I began to feel worse than when Old Grayling's letter came.

'I never thought of you—never heard of you,' I gasped weakly.

'But Harold Beecham is the fellow that all the girls are wild to see, and all the men are envious of.'

'But your name is Henry Beauchamp,' I murmured, wishing I could hide for a year.

'But I was nearly christened Harold, and Beauchamp is pronounced Beecham.'

'Harold is my favourite name—Harold Earl of Kent, who fell at the Battle of Hastings with an arrow through his eye. A tragic thing to be conquered by an outsider. You have not the slightest resemblance to the Harold in the book. The name is a mere coincidence.' My voice would hardly come.

'Ha! Ha! A jolly coincidence. I know half-a-dozen young fellows who are pretending they are Harold Beecham without the name. When I found out you were Dick Melvyn's youngster I was more astonished than ever, and came along to take a look at you. As soon as I clapped an eye on you I decided that I was going to take up my option.'

'What option?'

'On you. You proposed to me. I accept with alacrity. I would not have thought an oldster like me had a chance, only you put it in my head. I always go for first-class things and leave the ordinary stuff to the rabble.'

All the shame I had hitherto felt rolled into one lump was an infant to what I felt now. I, who would rather have died than 'throw myself at a man', seemingly had done just that. Ma was quite correct. There was no end to the annoyance caused by that feraboraceous book. I turned sick all through to think what further embroglios might spring from it. More and more I understood Ma, and was sorry for what I had brought upon her.

'Please understand,' I pled. 'I never thought of you. The book is not real. The girl is only make-believe, and Harold Beecham a figment of imagination.'

'That's what is so nice,' he laughed. 'Make-believe and life are sometimes the same thing. You are Sybylla Melvyn, I am Harold Beecham, and not going to relinquish my advantage.'

What was I to do? I had a wild desire for flight, but he slipped into the doorway and was too big for me to pass. Was there anyone in all the world who would understand the mess I was in, or my agony of sensitiveness? I jammed my lips together to keep them steady, and sat down despairingly. Oh, why didn't he understand; and how I could have adored him if he had!

'I'd like to put you in my waistcoat and keep you safe,' he

said, not laughing any more. 'It suits me all to pieces to get into the show. I can give you so many things that you'll soon forget you ever wrote a book.'

'Please go away where you won't see me any more,' I said. 'I am terribly upset by what has happened. Good-night!'

He did not try to detain me. I went to my room. He slipped a note under my door before he went to bed: 'The only thing doubtful is my age, otherwise you have made me the proudest man in Australia.'

I lay awake all night shivering with distress and listening to the mopokes and willy wagtails. A strayed cow was as sleepless as myself, and told the world. A piffling wind sucked the blind against the window panes and teetered in the leaves of the trees. Pa snored and was chid by Ma. All these sounds measured the silence of the night which at length was terminated by the waking poultry, and I had to face the day and Harold Beecham. Fortunately he departed early to inspect stock, as he had grass to spare. On other days he attended the sales in Goulburn, which is a big centre. He returned incredible distances to spend the nights at Possum Gully. The surplus condition was knocked off those flying ponies.

Grandma took a hand presently. Possibly Aunt Jane had reported, though Aunt Jane was jolly good for an old codger, and carried on her combats with me single-handed without tittle-tatting. Grandma seemed to stamp over Ma and be as contemptuous of her as Ma is of me. It was disgraceful, she said, for a girl to be so much talked about as Sybylla was. What on earth could Ma be doing to allow it? She did not like to hear of me attracting Henry Beauchamp, a dirty old fellow who could cast his eye on married women, and who should have had a wife of his own long ago, seeing he had plenty to keep one.

Bang, bang, went romance under Grandma's touch!

She could not sleep at night for fear she would hear of me coming to harm. I was sick of this 'coming to harm' notion. According to it girls have always to be chaperoned or armed against men's ravening. My experience so far has contained no

336

hint of such unbuttonedness. Not one of my lovers ever put his hand on me except to my toe to toss me to horse back. As for a kiss, I should have fled in horror from one so unchaste as to suggest such a thing. In my code, a kiss could come only after definite engagement. Pa always said, 'It doesn't matter what a man says to you: words cannot hurt us if we have sense, but never allow a man to place his hand on you. Make him show his respect by keeping his distance.'

The men evidently knew this as well as Pa, and acted upon it scrupulously. They never disrespected me further than to beg me to marry them. Some of them offered in return to leave Australia to settle in South Africa or New Zealand to meet my desire for travel. City people, of course, were much more wicked than country ones. It is probably city men, I thought, who are sensual and coarse.

Grandma's suspicions roused even Ma's dander a little. She said as a girl it had always been annoying to her to be watched as if she were an incontinent drab who couldn't impose respect upon any man she ever met. During this attack of Grannie's, Ma was the least off my side I had ever known her. She said, however, if I intended to marry, I had better think of picking the best of the men who came along, as Pa was useless as a provider, and in a world arranged as this one was, the only boat to success for a woman is a rich man to dote on her and back her up. It was all very fine while I was young and saucy to be giggle-gaggling, but I would early find that a girl had small choice. It would be a miracle if there was someone at all acceptable. That is how Ma had found it.

Ma was not at all a slavish advocate of marriage. She said if women had the sense to organise themselves and refrain from marriage till they had won better conditions there wouldn't be so many wives wishing they had had some other chance to earn their living, nor so many spinsters either thankful they had escaped marriage or regretful that they had not known the fulfilment of love. Ma said also that many girls married out of mere curiosity, but quickly had too much of THAT.

Grandma wrote again that if Beauchamp was in earnest it would be a lucky disposal of me, Richard being such a failure and I so self-willed. Grandma was away back in the stages of thinking that it was natural for women to be quelled by marriage and the giving birth to as many children as God's will or a rabbit's example dictated. She and Father O'Toole were in the same boat in putting God's will and the rabbit's instinct on the one level, though Grannie was such a vigorous Protestant and Father O'Toole such a sealed Roman that either would have argued till he or she was blue without budging an inch, and have called the other a benighted bigot.

Aren't old people silly when you question their ideas, and yet they prate at us as if they were God Himself!

The bickering continued about me and Henry and other young men. When I came to think it over, I never heard Grannie say a good word of Ma, and yet Ma was the most beautiful and capable daughter a woman could have. Ma was passing on this piece of heredity. Perhaps, I began to think, you could not respect a thing you made yourself, or else they had such high standards that they concentrated on flaws and took excellences for granted. There were other mothers though who thought their children marvels because they were their own.

Grandma wanted to know had Beauchamp taken up permanent residence with us. If he was trifling with me, it was in rather a queer way. I had a hundred notes, most of them telling me what he was going to do with me when he married me. And he had had a long talk with Pa, who said not to worry me yet. I said I would not think of marrying until I was at least forty. Henry said no one would want to marry me then, and I said I would not want them to, so we would be quits.

He would laugh with unruffled good-humour. 'You're as good as Mrs Henry Beauchamp already. You cooked your own fish. I'm ready to spell my name Beecham to fit in—more sensible in any case. I'm willing to wait a year.'

I said I would not marry Adonis himself, until I was twenty-one, and he said he would wait three years, but not another day.

I murmured that sixty would be early enough to enter the field of bad health for women called marriage.

'What whims you have. Marriage is a sacred institution.'

'That's superstition you have foisted on to us just to clamp us down for your own amusement.'

However, upon finding that he and his station were connected with my book I felt responsible. This put much worry into my soul and took the fun out of parrying his advances. How I longed for someone to understand and help me. Old Harris might have understood well enough to decide if I must in honour submit to this 'entanglement', but he had gone to England and had not yet sent me his address. I played for time.

Into these days of surface entertainment and underground worry Old Grayling again barged like a mad bull. He was just as luny as our most aristocratic bull, who would put himself against fence posts or toss gates on his horns and tear up anything that came in his way, even his favourite heifers. At certain seasons we had to leave everything open until he calmed down.

Old Grayling came jolting and swaying up to the side gate, the black now considerably subdued, but incited to show off, as the flash young shearer pricks up his horse when he thinks the girls are looking. Pa and Henry went out to meet him. Grayling gave the reins to Pa and roared, 'I have come to see Sybylla. She avoids me. She does not answer my letters. I make her an honourable proposal of marriage. I'm prepared to give way to her in everything . . .'

I fled. Old Grayling caught sight of my dress as I dashed in the front gate and along the veranda to the spare bedroom. With a shout and surprising speed he leapt after me. He looked in the door, but I was under the bed, and he dived into the main house. I scrambled out the window, scattering Henry's brushes as I went. Old Grayling caught another glimpse of me from the back door. Pa was left in bewilderment with the horse.

The old toad suspected me of a repetition of tactics and tore to an unmentionable apartment to outwit me. I saw him leathering past from the shelter of the fowl house and sped once more to the consoling friendliness of the pigs. A motherly old sow enjoyed being scratched, and stood contentedly as a screen while I indulged her.

I could descry unusual motion at the house. Ma came out and about looking for me. Aunt Jane followed, then Pa and Henry. They had a colloquy, after which Pa went to the outhouse, knocked on the door and asked Mr Grayling if he were ill. He came out and began to rage. I could not hear it all because I had to huddle behind the sow. She thought I wanted a drink, and grunted so loudly that much of the argument was lost; also they went behind the fowl houses and that cut off their voices.

Ma came to the gate and called that tea was ready, and I saw Pa urging Old Grayling to come. He waved his arms like a wind mill and bellowed a little, but soon they went inside together.

Henry came from the kitchen calling softly to me and looking everywhere and saying, 'I know where you are.' Now and again he laughed to himself till he shook, which showed that he had no understanding of my feelings. It was coarse and thick-skinned to laugh at such a caricature of LOVE, when he himself was pretending to be in its thrall.

After a while Pa came looking for him, and when they disappeared inside, I said ta-ta to the pigs. Feeding time was approaching, and I meant to stay out all night or until Old Grayling left. I circled to the hayshed where I climbed near the roof and made a warm sweet-smelling nest. Baby mice squeaked, and a lizard visited me, and I must have been there two hours when Pa came for the horse. Old Grayling shook hands all round and drove away at a wild bat. I slid down, took every straw off me, crept around by the buggy shed and sheep yards, and reappeared as if I had come over the hill. Pa was feeding the pigs, who were squealing at being neglected, and he came to meet me.

Pa never said a flaying word to me in his life, no matter how debbil-debbil I may have been. 'I'm sorry you have been frightened, my girl,' he said.

I wasn't frightened. Thunderstorms, mad swaggies, bulls breaking out, fractious horses, bush fires—any of the things that frighten most girls—do not upset me, but things about which they exchange smutty confidences can sicken me all through and drop me in a cauldron of nerves. This was one of them.

Pa inquired how it had begun. I told him of the letter and how I had run away before and how Ma had scolded me for being remiss.

'But we never suspected. If you had confided in your mother all this could have been avoided.'

'Oh,' I said, shrivelling, 'it has disgusted me so that I'd hate Ma to say the wrong thing.'

'Your mother is a wonderful woman. I'll speak to her. You'll have to be wise and full of mercy in meeting all these situations.'

Aunt Jane was a boon as she kept Henry talking in the front garden while I plunged into preparations for dinner. Pa moved in and out of the kitchen bringing wood and filling the water cask, as a protection. During dinner I kept behind the flowers, and Henry never said a word to me, though I knew that his eyes were constantly on me.

Afterwards Ma helped me wash-up and sent Eusty to turn the horses out.

'You should have told me when Mr Grayling first wrote to you,' she said, but not in a disciplinary tone.

'Oh, I couldn't! You always blame me so, and I could not stand any more. Loathsome old toad, he makes me sick.' I burst into tears and hid in the pantry and left Ma to the work. She did it like a lamb.

'Come,' she said at length, 'no harm has been done. The poor old man is childish, and this has overtaken him. Old men are often like that.'

'Do old women go like that too?' I asked, overcome by a horrifying possibility.

'No. Old women are never as silly as old men. When he comes again, go into my room and I'll say you are not here for the day; and he will soon be himself again.'

341

Ma had never been so clement to me. She further acquiesced that I should retire without reappearing. As I lay awake I pondered another inconsistency. If old men being thus disgusting was so usual that Ma could be quite calm about it, why did men give themselves such airs about having all the brains and strength of mind? The more I thought, the more did old men seem like the God they had set up in their own image for women and children to worship.

CHAPTER 11

Not So Expurgated

Life is not all as black as ink, even in an unliterary career. After Pa and Ma came to my help concerning Old Grayling, things took on a different aspect.

Henry went away for the winter to look after property in Queensland. I did not agree to be definitely engaged, but could not be hoity-toity seeing how I had implicated him in my misadventure. I was in hopes that he would tire of me before long. He was content to wait for three years. He said it would be safer if I looked around to see if I found any one that I could like better than myself. If I did not he was sure that I would not find any one whom I liked better than *himself*. 'I don't want you to buy a pig in a poke,' he said and laughed. It was nice of him to ease up on the Harold Beecham and Five-Bob Downs embarrassment.

As I would not break my training and accept a present, he got around the rules by leaving me a dashing filly to ride, called Popinjay. He also gave me a diary as a keepsake, in which I was to write a list of those I met and everything I thought, to read to him when next we met.

Tell him all I thought! Well, what do you think?

More and more English criticisms arrived and frightened me by their approbation. A Melbourne editor printed extracts from the whole tribe to controvert those who held that I should have been whipped for writing such a bad advertisement of Australians and shut up in a strict school until I outgrew my misguidedness. Ma kept the paper on the sitting-room table, where it could be seen. Some of the critics compared me to Emily Brontë. Zola and Dickens were other names used in comparison. The more high-flown a critic the more cordially he welcomed me as an audacious child who spoke unaffectedly from the heart.

343

Paradoxically, it was the people who knew my types by heart who reviled me as a liar and hypocrite. Dear old fellow-residents of Wallaby Range, I can see after these scarifying years the pathos of their disapproval, when for the first time they saw their own reality in print. No doubt they longed for something of the beauty of life, even as I, though in a less passionate and rebellious degree: or they may have imagined that in fiction they would be transmogrified into cavaliers like those in the stories in the *Penny Post*. It was too dismantling to find themselves in their own old beards and coats, and conversations about the crops and droughts and pudding recipes and little Tommies' toe aches.

Nevertheless there was a new tide of complaints from those who blamed me for neglecting them. A curate lectured me as an ignoramus that I did not include him—an Oxford University graduate. I had missed my only chance to portray culture. Lordy, had I thought of doing him, he might have been punctured by my view of his stuffed magpie education and the Oxford impediment in his speech.

Other emissaries of the church came to denounce me to my face. Tales of those who tiraded behind my back were frequent—whether church wardens, local preachers, precentors, acolytes or other scribes and pharisees soon became a jumbled mass. We parted in a spirit of mutual unvanquishedness. They had every established institution on their side in one way or another, dependent upon whether they followed the Protestant or Roman Catholic recipe for endowing God with undesirable qualities, but I had Pa on my side and he assured me that TIME also was with me.

One gentle old Canon so impressed me that I thought him quite a gun. He was as thin as a lath which was appealing because the tickling Canon was balloony. This dear soul said when young himself, he had suffered torturing doubt and lonely seeking similar to mine. Patience and experience (how I hate patience, and there was Ma's panacea—EXPERIENCE!) would garden my soul and show the futility of seeking peace in extraneous things. We must cleanse our hearts and look within for truth and salvation.

I abhorred the deadliness of peace, and was hankering for joy.

The Salvation Army thumping tin cans and wearing ugly bonnets and roaring about being saved in such an unladylike way had too much of a corner on salvation to leave it any glamour.

One of the last to appear was the tickling Canon. Ma welcomed him and handed him the Melbourne paper, remarking that he might be interested to see what interest was taken in her daughter in England. Ma said she was surprised that he had been so dilatory—*dilatory* mind you, but Ma is no vassal—in coming to see Sybylla. No wonder the church was losing its influence when a young girl had to depend on the sympathy of other pastors than her own. She neatly mentioned the names of Father O'Toole and other educated odds and ends. I withdrew so as not to explode with pleased surprise. Fancy Ma!

The Canon was not at all haw-haw when I came in again. Softened by Ma's support, I sat as demurely as a mopoke. He congratulated me. I thanked him. After a while he recovered slightly and said, 'You can't expect me to agree with you *in toto*.' (I could not find this in the dictionary, but it sounded like Trilby's 'altogether' in ideas.) Ma invited the Canon to lunch, but he had promised to return to the Ollivers. Selah!

Other callers were tanned men all the way from the Cooper or the Paroo to bring me souvenirs or to shake the hand that had penned the book. Others wrote from Riverina and Out Back that they had met a man who had seen me. There were many whom I had never seen who gained notice by meeting me in places I had never been. Many others claimed relationship which did not exist. I was for ever hearing of cousins from Cape York to the Leeuwin—cousins in their own imagination. My real cousins, with a few exceptions, from Cape Otway to Charters Towers, maintained social superiority by deploring me as unworthy of the family progeniture. Inconsistently the people who had intended to turn their backs on me to illustrate my inferiority now reversed to attest their equality. The girls now said they did not mind how high I went, because I was not conceited and had never put on the slightest side. Pa, through EXPERIENCE, had predicted this.

The queerest characters thought they were my twin souls, and without having read my book. A far-flung tribulation of girls claimed me as their other self. People not near enough to feel caricatured loved my outburst because it was 'just like ourselves'. They thanked me for my pluck and ability. I had given them all a lead in letting-go in egotism, and they found it a boon. My shrieks of discontent necessarily being crude and unformulated, and my fellows of all ages and no attainments, so to speak, also being crude and unformulated, or having been crude and young and unformulated, found me an affinity. Egotism can conceive no higher compliment.

An all is egotism. The only people whose mainspring is not egotism are the dead, and perhaps idiots—the one class having ceased to have a mainspring and it having been omitted from the words of the others. Immediately people's egotism fails them, if they are not on the point of death from senile decay, they commit suicide. Egotism is the spirit of self which is designated human nature. The more human nature one has, the more egotism. Some people are not so readily fitted with the adjective of egotistical as others because they are not such pronounced types or are cunning in dissimulation. There are of course different brands of egotism. Some egotists are lovable and some not. The child is the perfect example of egotism, and the most lovable. One of the lovable kinds among adults is he with a high sensitiveness which can be used as a thermometer to gauge the worries and desires of his fellows' heads and hearts. Such are classified as sympathetic. The commonest, the least interesting, have their egotism interwoven with a delusion that their most banal experiences are unique. These are called bores. The intense egotism of another class is so charming that it is called personality, but all human manifestations are brewed from egotism—it is their major psychological content.

Leading people, some of them set aloft by money, hired vehicles in Goulburn and harried their horses in getting lost among the stumps of back tracks and bridle tracks, and found their way to call on us. One was an old gentleman of individuality in the

346

matter of grey toppers and leggings. He paid an investigatory visit to Pa on behalf of his brother philosophers, or windbags as they would have been called only they had money too. Pa and he had a long, mysterious conversation out near the beehives and quince trees.

Pa told us about it afterwards. Grey Topper wanted to know unmentionable and intimate things about my prenatal days. The Governor-General, who had literary leanings, was responsible for classifying me as a genius, so a genius I became. Grey Topper and his coterie had a theory that a genius arrived from a mother who had far from enjoyed surrendering to a satyr.

I knew of a satyr as the mythological beast. To apply this to Pa was productive of chortles. The dictionary divulged the words' fissiparations: 'A very lecherous person and a species of butterfly.'

Pa did not fit any of these. When other women were divulging the atrocities which appear to be a normal risk of marriage, Ma would always say, 'Thank God, I have never had to endure anything like that.' Ma would add that any woman who did, deserved it.

Ma disdained Grey Topper's theory, though her remarks confirmed rather than exploded it. She said 'she never seemed to come to the end of the foolishness of men, this à propos Grey Topper having time as well as the indelicacy to trot about prying into such matters. Ma added that it was only men's maniacal egotism and complacency that enabled them to wreak their will regardless of women's revulsion and weariness.

Ma seemed all right in her half of the recipe for genius. It must have been dear old Pa who had failed in the satyr business.

Old Grayling was unregenerate and his senility was incurable, so Pa and Ma decided to accept one of the many invitations that came for me at that time. Mrs P. Darius Crasterton was most pressing. The Rt. Hon. P. Darius had been Minister for Lands when Pa had been member for Gool-Gool. His widow assured Ma that she would chaperone me carefully and that I should see all the best people—the worth-while ones of weight in the country.

Pa recalled that the old man had made his fortune by rake-offs in the distribution of railway lines during his administration. Pa had lost his seat because he had resisted the swindle of taking the railway around by some big fellows' runs instead of through a farming district. Old Crasterton and one Sir James Hobnob later had had their way and grew rich and honoured, while Pa became poor and obscure. Pa said he did not suppose that the old woman could help her husband's misappropriation of public funds: I could see the world with her and learn to judge it.

What I would be able to pick up from people who 'really mattered', she said, would be an invaluable education to me with my 'very considerable but uncultivated natural gifts', and that what counted in cultivating good style were the 'contacts' which she would be able to give me.

She misspelled *litreature, privilidge* and *realy*, but not to spell correctly is sometimes considered a sign of genius and sometimes a lack of education. The thing was to find out when it was which. Ma had a struggle to find the railway fare, but there was a cheap excursion, and Mrs Crasterton said she would be pleased to give me some dresses in return for the pleasure it would be to have my fresh young company.

Ma warned me against putting myself under obligations. 'You'll be more self-respecting if you don't,' said she.

Pa said 'Hoh! the people who want you for your clothes are not worth knowing.'

'Nevertheless, I can't send the child away naked,' said Ma.

I craved a long dress, but Ma said that would involve more than she could afford. If I kept my hair down I was still a girl 'not out', staying with Mrs Crasterton, and it would be simpler for everyone. She made me a dress of white organdie. It had frills at the cuffs and two flounces, and tucks all over the bodice. Ma could sew better than anyone else, and cut out with a beautiful line. The dress was finished with a bow at the V of the sailor collar, and I had more ribbon to tie my pigtail in a bump on my neck, something like the bob-tailed draught horses at the

Show. I longed for a blue sash, but Ma said it would be useless expense and that only tall slender girls could wear sashes.

What did it matter about a sash when I was on the way to the station to go to Sydney, a cauldron of excitement about the holiday that was coming—my first visit to the city! I also dwelt upon the aristocratic address to which I was bound.

CHAPTER 12

The Denizens of Geebung Villa

Goulburn slid behind. I felt all crumbly and full of pangs that poor old Pa and Ma were not coming too, but they both had been to Sydney often in days gone by. I was bubbling with glee inside like a bottle of honey-mead. If the stopper had not been firmly tied I'd have effervesced right out in one high jet.

There was nothing joyful in the landscape. It was naturally barren and scraggly and dry, and now dotted with dead beasts. Those alive were so pitifully frail that it was painful to behold them. Milch cows being beaten in and out of bails and dusty yards, in such condition, was surely a cruel purgatory for animals. But the coastal belt approached with everything green and soft, and ferns and shrubs and flowers not to be seen inland. I ran out on the platform at each stop to see all I could. Liverpool, and after that it all seemed town. Strathfield and the roar of the city like a flood. Surging, exciting. It gave me tremors all over. The racket of the trains passing each other shocked like blows. Sydney was all around me. I was swamped by new feelings.

I was to be the guest of people who were somebody, I was to see all the sights and meet heaps and heaps of people, and work at nothing but pleasure from morning till night for a month!

I stood beside Pa's old Gladstone bag—my only luggage—and when most of the passengers had gone a large old lady came and claimed me with: 'This is my little girl, I know. I am Mrs Crasterton.' She gave me a friendly kiss and said, 'This is my brother.'

A man much her own general cut but younger, greeted me with a chummy nod and a flabby handshake. Mrs Crasterton was weirdly smart. She had 'kept her figure' with corset and belts as strong as patent wire strainers. The brother had a short figure, enlarged by a corpulency. He was instantly ruled out as an object of romance. Knights of the imagination are straight and slim, preferably tall and beautiful. Married men, however, have a false importance through their wives that one has to recognise; and in most cases it is impossible to conceive what elderly people ever saw in each other to admire.

I put the brother in the married class. He took a side-long squint at me like a judicial old cockatoo. His sister called him Gaddy, but he did not look it. He carried my port along the platform and put Mrs Crasterton and me in a cab and muttered, 'See you later.'

The first thing I noticed about Sydney streets was the rain rushing through them in muddy torrents and a tram with water spraying out of its rear to the derision of the bystanders. The bystanders took my eyes. There were so many. Except at a horse race or a funeral bystanders in the bush are scarce.

The noise and bustle were enchanting. A labyrinth of streets obscured my sense of direction. Such a lively change from the bush where there was an ache of quietude and every range and road was dulled by familiarity and where one could steer by the sun or stars when outside the usual run.

At Circular Quay, Mrs Crasterton puffed and I sprang out of the cab where Gaddy, who had arrived on a tram, was awaiting us. Cabs are contraptions designed to defeat all but the sturdiest horses, and the Sydney cab-men were not half so respectable-looking as those of Goulburn, but the ferry boat to North Sydney was a scrumptious dream.

My, the comforts and joys of the city compared with the bush! At Miller's Point, Gaddy dumped us in another cab, which he directed to Geebung Villa, Pannikin Point, and we went off full rip in the wind and rain without him. I craned my neck to see the magnificent rocks rising on one side of the street, covered with the loveliest ferns with little springs of water trickling amongst them. The bamboos waving over walls high above filled me with astonished delights—giants' wands with fairies' grace. Doves were mourning and sparrows were twittering everywhere.

On the other side were Aladdin glimpses of the Harbour. All too soon we had arrived.

My hostess paid the cabman. He was not satisfied. 'You ugly old buzzard, and two of you and luggage to boot; Had I knowed you were to be that mean, I'd have tipped yous both out in the mud.'

'Run inside, my dear,' said Mrs Crasterton.

'You old skin flint, you'd bile down fleas for their hides.'

'Run away, you'll be shocked,' repeated Mrs Crasterton, but it seemed cowardly to leave her. The language did not worry me. I had been audience to bullockies in action, to amateurs getting sheep across a creek, and to veterans training sheep puppies. Besides, I have never cultivated the pose that to hear of the common actualities of life would outrage me out of health. It is the being compelled to subscribe to cant and inconsistencies about them that I find so enervating.

A maid took my portmanteau. Mrs Crasterton told me to follow the maid while she followed me laying the blame of 'the growing insolence of the lower classes' on the unhealthy growth of the Labor Party, which she averred would be the ruin of the new Commonwealth. The rain pattered greyly on the bamboos and hibiscus, which shaded the side veranda, the cabby's voice came as a refrain as we entered the home of a dead statesman where I was to find culture and high congeniality.

Only once in a lifetime can anticipation hold such a quality of flattery towards a clique or a class as mine did at that moment.

'We are not having anyone in tonight,' said Mrs Crasterton when she came to my room. 'Show me your dresses, child.'

It was a trying moment. I showed the new dress that I was to wear in the evenings, and the other one for street wear. 'I must give you some dresses,' she murmured.

Shame invaded me. 'I would rather not,' I said shakily. 'I could just stay with you. I don't want to see smart people, and then it would not matter about my clothes.' My frugal wardrobe merely covered me and the demands of decency, and was in no sense decorative.

352

I was alone when there was a tap on the door, and there stood a beautiful young lady. 'I am Edmée Actem,' said she, with a most gorgeous smile. 'I'm a bush girl too, and staying here on purpose to meet you. I was born on a station up the country. I just love your book. It's ripping. You've said all the things we all think, but did not know how to express.'

Edmée had big bluish grey eyes that she rolled most arrestingly, and her hair was in chestnut curls on her forehead. Her dress showed off her figure in a SOCIETY manner. She was tall 'yet voluptuous', just like the heroines in *The Goulburn Evening Penny Post*, and she could languish and cast appealing glances. She looked as if she had all kinds of lovers—quondam, hopeless, distracted and those who would even try to be *clandestine*, and propose to her in *conservatories*, or find her monogrammed handkerchief in the *shrubberies*. Life must begin for me too on meeting her, so lovely and romantic—the very girl of my dreams.

She said she was dressing after dinner. 'But that is such a pretty dress, and oh, you are lovely!' burst from me.

She called it just an old rag that she kept for wet nights and when there was no company. Every man who met her must fall madly in love with her. She confirmed this as soon as I confessed apologetically that I had no evening dress. She said it did not matter in my case as I was only a little girl from the bush, but that she was so conspicuous for her fatal beauty that it was an effort to keep pace with it. She knew I would not misunderstand her, and it was a relief to speak from soul to soul without humbug.

I wished that I was so beautiful that men would love me to distraction, but she said I was not the type. I doted and gloated on her while she told me there and then in confidence some of the burdens of her fascination. Such luscious love affairs put my little experiences out of existence.

Right in Geebung Villa Edmée was having trouble. Derek was very troublesome, and would have been the boy of her dreams only that he was four years younger. Gaddy too was a silly old thing. I asked was that why he was called Gaddy, and she laughed and said he had been christened Gad. Derek was a spoiled darling only son, and Gaddy . . . Both lived at Geebung Villa.

I could hardly keep from laughing at the thought of Gad approaching such a beauty as Edmée. In a democracy where admirers abounded by the dozen a girl does not at first realise that a bachelor of any age can purchase a woman of any youth if he but have the wherewithal and determination. It takes time also for a girl to grasp that any old tramp of a man thinks that every woman is craving a man, even a thing like himself, which she wouldn't wipe her boots upon; when all the time her despair is not that she is without men importuning her, but that among the flock there is not one that she could consider with satisfaction, and that the one that she would desire might think her as undesirable as she found the ones who were plaguing her.

Edmée said she was hungry and dissatisfied in her soul, just as I was, and seeking for something other than a mere man. She craved an affinity. We were interrupted by the gong, and Edmée promised to tell me more anon.

The house seemed as big as the Royal Hotel as Edmée took me down with her. Gaddy was waiting to open the dining-room door for us, and wearing a dinner jacket. Mrs Crasterton was in evening dress, but well-covered in a big shawl and wrestling with a joint. I sat beside Gaddy. Edmée sat opposite. I was glad of that, as I could feast my eyes on her and I hoped that Gad would not mind my being in long sleeves and such a tiny V that it hardly showed any of my neck. Derek did not appear until after we had gone to the library for coffee.

Edmée retired to dress with Wheeler—Mrs Crasterton's personal maid—in attendance. Derek was being babied in the dining-room and elsewhere, I learned from Gaddy, who had charge of me in the library. Edmée and Derek were going to a ball at Lady Somebody's. This lady herself was chaperoning Edmée as Mrs Crasterton had a slight chill.

I longed to be helping Edmée to dress, tending her like an altar boy. The incense would have come from my admiration. Derek was all over the place calling to his mother and Gaddy, but I did not catch sight of him. In time he appeared 'with 'em all on', as Gaddy said. I did not let my eyes pop too much on beholding him. Here was the beau—the counterpart—of all the heroines embodied in Edmée. He carried a shining topper and snowy gloves, and was in a cloak sort of coat with wings—too swell for words.

He bowed to me from a distance, but charmingly, and smiled with the loveliest teeth. I felt myself beneath his interest and took care not to obtrude. His mother came in and sat near the fire.

'Is she never going to be ready?' he said impatiently, and after a while threw aside his cloak and I saw the perfection of his slimness in the becoming swallow tails. He cursed his tailor, though I thought he must be a virtuoso.

There was no sign of Edmée. Derek went to the piano in the drawing-room and, after half an hour, sent his mother to find out what was keeping 'that pestiferous creature'. He went into the hall as his mother returned, and complained about being saddled with such a confisticated bore as the ball in the first place, and Edmée as a Woman Friday in the second.

'Dekky darling, you mustn't talk so,' said his mother. 'Edmée has great influence with Sir George, and you must keep up these connections.'

'She always foists herself upon me,' grumbled Derek. 'Gaddy ought to take his turn. I'd just as soon have stayed at home and played cat's cradle with the infant prodigy.'

Derek sounded as if he were dissimulating his passion for Edmée. In another ten minutes she 'swept into the room'. Her hair was a *coiffure* in which was a pink rose. She was enveloped in a cloak of gold tissue and chiffon and lace. Derek remarked icily that the cab had been waiting an hour, but Edmée wasn't worried or hurried by that. She made lovely flirtatious eyes at Gaddy, kissed me and Mrs Crasterton and departed.

Mrs Crasterton disappeared to telephone. Gad played on the piano and showed me books and things, but my heart had gone out for the night with Edmée and Derek. If Derek would give me a few dancing lessons I was sure I could learn in an hour, but it was not natural for such an attractive young man to repair the social deficiencies of a little bush-whacker. The ridicule in his remark about the infant prodigy showed me my place. I longed for just one evening dress. Edmée's wet-night gown would have satisfied me, but Pa hadn't a penny to buy me one and I did not wish to be beholden to Mrs Crasterton. I did not sleep on going to bed. The day had been packed with experiences, the lights and voices of the Harbour were so alluring, and I thought much of a ball room with an orchestra playing gay waltzes and Edmée and Derek the 'cynosure of all eyes'.

I was up early. It seemed hours before breakfast. Geebung Villa had terraces to the water's edge, and they were rich with daphne and camellia bushes. The sun came up through the Heads and stole its way to the Quay, far over the bay. Each of the tiny waves turned to flame, and as the sun rose higher it left pearly tracks across the water. A month would not be long enough to imbibe such beauty, and I did not mind a bit that I had no dresses.

Gaddy found me and said that breakfast was nearly ready. He blew his nose like a trumpet and turned about and rattled both hands in his trousers' pockets, and looked as if he would displace his eyes, and then blurted out, 'See here, my sister is having a lot of people tonight. Don't you let 'em fuss you. Don't you listen to anything they tell you. You are better than the whole lot of 'em—just as you are.'

I was pleased about the people. I longed for people who would be interested in things that I was interested in, and people living in such circumstances and surroundings must surely be they. I did not expect them to worry me, and I certainly intended to listen to all they said. Why should Gaddy give such a queer warning?

Derek and Edmée were both absent from breakfast. Mrs Crasterton went up to Derek's room while Gad telephoned for a cab, and there was a fuss with a cup of coffee in the hall as Derek later bolted for the cab to race to his office. It was

entirely different behaviour from that of young men in the bush—
seemed a little *infra dig* for masculinity.

I had established such relations with Edmée that I went to
her room while she made her *toilette*. I was impatient to hear
of the ball. She and Derek had been the *cynosure*, just as I
thought. She was going to lunch with some girl friends at Potts
Point, and her dress congested me with superlatives. It was filmy
stuff such as worn by the heroines in the *Penny Post*, over a
bright colour that *shimmered*, and a lace petticoat. She lifted the
fluffy skirts around her ankles in open-work stockings, and she
had high-heeled shoes. She had a perfect figure as well as a
beautiful face. Her waist was small and her bosom full. She had
a spreading picture hat of pleated tulle and feathers, and what
she called a *brolly* to match. I revelled in her. She said she had
a hard bore of a day ahead of her—lunch and two afternoon
teas. There was a new man who was mad about her, of whom
I panted to hear, but she departed as soon as she was dressed.

Mrs Crasterton took me in hand for the day. She said I looked
so dainty and girlish, and the real bush maid in my little dresses
that it would be a pity to spoil the effect with sophisticated clothes;
ordinary girls needed clothes. We lunched at Geebung Villa in
solemn state. Mrs Crasterton said that I must guard against
any irreverence for things that mattered or I would not succeed
socially.

As a beginning she recited her pedigree. She had descended
from a Saxon king. We had a fine pedigree too, containing some
moated ruins in Chancery, but Pa always said that a pedigree
counted only in stock, as human beings had not sufficient knowledge in eugenics to make it count in themselves yet; that there
were too many people living on the reputation of a grandfather
while their own works would not bear examination. Pa also held
that it was not *descent* in human breed but *ascent* that counted.

Until initiated by Mrs Crasterton, I had not dreamed that
aristocraticness was locally of so much importance.

I knew we had many genuine ladies hidden in remote humpies,
while females of feraboracious manners and habits were installed

357

in the mansions of Potts Point, where dwells the nucleus of our aristocracy yet to be—or to be done away with.

I did not enjoy my lunch. It takes great cooking to equal Ma's. Mrs Crasterton directed my admiration to the antique candlesticks. The age of the cheese had more pungency. Judged by the normal longevity of cheese, it must have been of such antiquity as to have earned resurrection. It had become a living thing.

Everything hung fire until the evening when Mrs Crasterton was to be 'At Home' to her friends. We were to dress early, have dinner early, and await SOCIETY. Edmée informed me that Mrs Crasterton was truly of a fine family, though of course slightly inferior to the Actems.

Even in the bush each family I knew was sure of being a little superior to the others. Perhaps it is to obviate such an absence of classification that the society zoo in England is so strictly graded in steps, with a stud book, so that those listed cannot take more than their share of importance.

CHAPTER 13

Society

I put on my white dress and stole down. Gaddy was already there, and in swallow tails looked like an egg. I found out later that his nickname was 'The Egg'. Mrs Crasterton's head and train promised smartly for what was hidden in the big shawl. Edmée was in her little wet-night dress. There was no trace of Derek, but there was present a small insipid young man with big ears. He was unmistakably infatuated with Edmée. There was also a man about six-foot-two in a violent check suit and long faded walrus moustache.

Mrs Crasterton had apologized for him as a sort of cousin. She said relations were so huffy that she had to overlook his not being in evening dress, that he was leaving immediately after dinner. He talked in a self-important voice to Jemima, as he called her, and did not see me at all beyond a nod when introduced as 'a little girl'. His theory was that people of his class, that meant SOCIETY'S and Jemima's, should never touch politics except for what was in them. They should feather their nests and get out while the going was good.

When the meal was eaten Big Ears and Big Checks went to the smoking room with Gaddy. Edmée disappeared upstairs. Mrs Crasterton had still more telephoning to do, and told me to remain in the drawing-room, as Lady Hobnob was going to run in and see me on her way to a ball at Admiralty House. I must not delay her, as it was kind of her to come.

I wrote in my diary with a fountain pen sent to me by a commercial traveller at Broken Hill, until Gad seated himself nearby with an odour of wine and the stuffed look peculiar to men with short necks and long appetites. My soul did not go out to him. Mrs Crasterton came in for a moment and said that Edmée's admirer was not of an *old* family, and she pointed out a dog-eared ornament and named the howling swell from whom it had descended.

'Stow that old rubbish, Sis,' said Gad testily. 'The girl is as young as morning and as fresh as dawn. She doesn't want to concern herself with anything but being herself and not getting spoiled. Age is no recommendation of an article if a new thing would be an improvement. If we are here only to degenerate and breed rotters and find out that old things were better, the sooner we throw up the sponge the better.'

I discerned an unexpected ally.

Mrs Crasterton threw off her shawl to meet arrivals. I was abashed to be in close proximity. Her bosom was like two vast white puddings, her waist was sinfully compressed, she rocked on silly little heels, but she was as fashionable as Wheeler, the expert, could make her. Lady Hobnob was as big as Mrs Crasterton, but more flabby and spreading. She had her head wrapped in tulle with feathers that nodded precariously, but she was kind. I was sure she must be a muddler. (I had had a *méchante* idea that one bared one's arms and chest to extend one physical beauty and increase feminine attraction, but the startling exposure of four or five old ladies dispelled this notion. Evening dress must be an obligation of aristocraticness.) The very pronounced human form *au naturel* looks so very pronounced that it would be less of a shock to respectable way-backs to begin EVENING DRESS SOCIETY among slender people. However, the lessons in breeding that I had undergone that day starched my own, and without a blink I continued a when-you-don't-know-what-to-do-do-nothing stand.

Other ladies in grand dresses called for an hour on their way to the ball. They were surprised that I was such a child, and that I had nothing to say for myself. Some said what a pity it was that I would so soon be spoiled. Everyone asked for me, and Mrs Crasterton said, 'Here she is!' Many women kissed me: old gentlemen pinched or goggled and said kind or silly things. Then they settled to talk to Jemima and Gaddy about affairs of the day, and the gossip of Sydney. Some of them were judges, and some were barristers, and M.L.A.'s., and there was a Chancellor, but I don't know of what. Mrs Crasterton beamed and said it was like old times.

Presently Edmée made her entry. Everyone saw it. She stood for a few minutes in the doorway. She was in a pale green satin dress with a gored skirt with a train and a bodice fitting like a glove. It had no sleeves and was cut very low. Her bosom seemed to rise out of creamy foam. She had a cape of the same satin trimmed with ostrich feathers, and it slipped off in the most exciting way. She languished and distributed her glances. There was a rush from the gentlemen to attend her: but she was true to me. She drew me down beside her where I sat raptly drinking her in. How proud I was when she put her arm around me!

Henry Beauchamp wondered how I'd act when I met girls that could rival me. Here was one who blotted me out, and I was enchanted with her. There was no jealousy in me. I forgot even to be envious; forgot that I was in a plain white dress with all my bath-room charms hidden. I was sorry for Big Ears' hopeless passion for Edmée, and motioned him to come and sit on the other side of me on the couch on which we were sitting. In the crush that ensued around us, I slipped away without being missed. Behind a shoulder of the wall in the back of the long drawing-room I found Big Checks all by himself.

'Hullo!' he said. 'You sneakin' out of the ruck too?'

'Yes, I was only taking up space around Miss Actem. Isn't she lovely?'

'A rather upstanding filly. Been a bit too long in the stable. She hangs around here tryin' to bag old Gaddy. She'll bag young Derek if he doesn't keep his eyes skinned.'

What a poisonous old man! I knew him at once for a broken-down swell. The bush is full of such. Sometimes they are tramps, but other times they are tea-agents. There was a book-agent around Possum Gully, the image of this gentleman, checks, moustache and all. When there is a position as Stock Inspector their relatives use INFLUENCE to get it for them.

'I meant to go after dinner, but Jemima said something about a girl who writes, comin' tonight. I'd as soon have a performin' bear about the place as a woman who writes. The bear's performance would be more natural too.'

'Then why did you stay?'

'Thought I'd better see what the world is comin' to. Now that women are to have votes, life won't be worth livin' much longer.'

'Do you think that women should not have any brains?'

'Brains! A woman with brains is a monstrosity.'

I never can understand why men are so terrified of women having special talents. They have no consistency in argument. They are as sure as the Rock of Gibraltar that they have all the mental superiority and that women are weak-minded, feeble conies; then why do they get in such a mad-bull panic at any attempt on the part of women to express themselves? Men strut and blow about themselves all the time without shame. In the matter of women's brain power they organise conditions comparable to a foot race in which they have all the training and the proper shoes and little running pants, while women are taken out of the plough, so to speak, with harness and winkers still on them, and are lucky if they are allowed to start at scratch. Then men bellow that they have won the race, that women never could, it would be against NATURE if they did. Surely it is not brave to so fear fair play. No self-respecting woman could possibly *respect* men, no matter how strong an appetite she might have for them, but to be sorry for them, as some women pretend, is mawkish, and is carrying dissimulation too far.

Big Checks would put me on a level with a performing bear, and never know the alphabet of my language, but I could talk his pidgin while thinking about something else, so I indulged him on the subject of horses.

It was evident that he was a full bachelor. He lacked the mugginess of husbands and the air of false importance which they assume through the protection of their wives. Why women can be led astray by others' husbands or have any traffic with them I cannot conceive.

'I heard about this girl,' I said.

'By jove, do you know her! Tell me what she is like.'

He was greedily interested for that sort of bachelor which the women don't try to attract as compared with the sort that they do.

'I believe her book was meant as a joke, but people couldn't see it. Her relations say that she is a silly goat and that her book is just like her.'

'I knew it. No nice girl would write a book.'

'I wish I could write one—only of course a much better one than this girl has done.'

'Oh, no, my dear, don't be led astray by the false adulation and fuss about this minx. People come to look at her like a Punch and Judy show, but the kind of girl the world is in need of, the kind a man respects is one just like your pretty little self.'

Nevertheless he had not come to see her but the dreadful female who wrote.

'Me, pretty,' I scoffed. 'My mother doesn't say so.'

'Ah, you have a sensible mother. She wants to save you from conceit. You take it from me, and I've seen all the girls come out for the last twenty-five years, there's not many could hold a candle to you if you were properly tricked out. You have a face that grows on a man—something that would make him come back and look a second time; and no paint or artificiality.'

'Think how lovely Miss Actem is,' I said to end his embarrassing exaggeration.

'Pooh! Your figure and complexion run her into the Harbour, and her eyes . . .'

'They're glorious.'

'Go and look at your own. The way she ogles and throws hers about—I'm afraid, 'pon my word, that they'll drop out and I'll have to pick 'em up.'

No doubt he had been snubbed by Edmée for getting in the way of more interesting cavaliers. He babbled of how the world would be dished by female suffrage. Women were never meant to express themselves politically; they were born to sacrifice themselves—that was their glory and their crown: as soon as women began to assert themselves a nation declined.

I hung on secretly to my faith that the greatest nations would always be those where women were freest. The United States and the British Empire were the two countries where women could march about alone without being assailed by the men, and even BIG CHECKS and LOUDER CHECKS would agree that the English are the greatest race on earth, and themselves the most wonderful men.

Mrs Crasterton found me as she came through to give some order about the refreshments. 'Dear me, Obadiah,' she remarked, 'was it you that abducted the guest of the evening? Everyone wants to talk to you, Sybylla. You must not hide yourself.'

BIG CHECKS stood up and said, 'I can't wait any longer for this performin' bear.' He grunted as if he had said something smart and funny. 'I've enjoyed myself so much with you that she would spoil the taste in my mouth. Look here, don't you go worryin' because you haven't any brains, me dear: You're perfect as you are.'

'I don't worry for lack of brains,' I said demurely.

'That's right, you leave brains to this performin' bear with long teeth, and a thick waist, and about ten feet high.' He was again so pleased with his joke that I laughed at him, and he shook my hand very friendlily and went out by the hind door, took his cane and hat and let himself out.

Mrs Crasterton, Gaddy, Edmée and I were finally left before the dying fire.

'Well, my dear, you are a huge success,' Mrs Crasterton said to me. 'I hope your dear little head won't be turned by being the lion of the hour. Everyone has invited me to bring you to lunch or afternoon tea. People whom I had lost sight of since Papa died, came tonight, and smart people who have arisen since my young days have telephoned that they must meet you. Dear old Lady Hobnob is so taken with you that I am to take you to her big dinner tomorrow night and you are to spend the night with her. The literary people and artists are clamouring for you like the hungry lions at the zoo, but I don't approve of the bohemians: they have dangerous political views and are loose in their morals.'

It was not disguised from me that my good behaviour had been a surprise. I had not shown the shock of disappointment on finding that people who had enjoyed opportunities of education, travel, 'contact' and refinement, which had long been debarred me owing to indigence, were only like this. There weren't any but Derek and Edmée who took my eye, and I heard Gaddy having quite a row with his sister about Edmée.

I sat by my window looking on the city across the Harbour for a long time. It all seemed unreal. A myriad lights shone like misty jewels across the balmy water where the ferry boats flitted like floating fires. It was all so beautiful that I resented more tensely than ever that so much of my life had been cramped into the ugly environs of Possum Gully.

Edmée was up betimes next morning. I heard her talking to the others as I approached. 'I was in hopes she would be more the *enfant terrible*, but she is too correct to be entertaining.'

'Wait till she comes out of her shell,' said Gaddy.

'I like her affection, and she is not a troublesome guest,' said Mrs Crasterton. 'Professor Jonathan says she promises more genius than anyone in the Colonies today, and Lady Hill says she would take Professor Jonathan's word before anyone's. He is a really cultured Englishman, and it is a pleasure to hear him say ninety-nine.'

'Go on, Sis!' said Gaddy good-humouredly. 'He says nainty-nain.'

CHAPTER 14

Hi-tiddly-hi-ti-hi!

I was all on tip-toe for the dinner of Lady Hobnob. The Hobnobs were described by one of the English guests of the 'at home' night as able 'to do things rather well for the Colonies'. This meant that they had the money and EXPERIENCE to give dinners of many courses including decayed game and several kinds of wine served by the regulation number of imported flunkeys.

The whole toot was going to this dinner. We went a little early so that my host could have an additional word with me. He became noisy on finding that I was the daughter of good old Dick Melvyn, one-time Member for Gool-Gool, 'One of the straightest men who ever lived, but ideas ahead of the times, and no head for business.' So that was his idea of Pa's ideals. I let him do the shouting, and soon we went in to dinner.

There was a glare of bosoms above the table and much superfluous drapery lying around the chair legs underneath, and hardly one dish out of the long list of courses that was sweet and wholesome enough for my palate so it must have been a *recherché* meal.

I sat on old Sir Jimmy's left, a married woman had to have his right, but he grinned at me and talked to me most of the time. He declared that he never read a novel, but proclaimed that I was a ripping little girl and would soon settle down in marriage and leave scribbling to men or to those women who couldn't catch a man. Such pidgin exposed his attitude towards women. His small talk was small indeed, even when he enlarged it by discussing probabilities for the Melbourne Cup. So he was easy to humour, and we got on swimmingly until he began about his wines. He was a connoisseur, and prided himself on his cellar.

'Come, come! You must drink wine at my table,' said he, with pompous geniality.

366

'No thank you, Sir James.'

'You must, my dear. You must.'

'No thank you,' I said firmly.

'Have you principles against drinking wine?'

'No, but I don't like it, thank you.'

'Then you must learn to like it.'

Edmée was signalling for me to drink it, but my fighting blood was up. I had had to sink to his level about writers, which was most insulting to artistic intelligence and the rights of women. I would go no lower to please him, especially as I was feeling very resentful inside, and despising him as a swindler of public funds, who had thereby grown rich and important—with his gluttonous dinners and snifty servants!—while Pa's honesty had resulted in deprivation and failure.

'Now, now, I insist,' persisted Sir James.

Poor old Gaddy was red in the face. Derek was pretending not to hear.

I shook my head and looked modest, which further incited Sir James. 'Can you give me one good reason why you should not drink my wine?'

'Yes. If you came to see Pa and Ma and me we wouldn't have any wine because we could not afford it. Pa tried to do good for his fellows and lost his money. We could offer you nothing better than tea and coffee and if you did not like them we would be sorry but we would not pester you to drink them against your wish.'

Sir James patted me on the hand and said, 'Plucky little filly. If you were entered at Randwick you would run away from the field. I'll drink your health out of a damned feeding bottle. What I like in women or horses is mettle.'

Later in the drawing-room he sat beside me and said that while Lady Hobnob was away in Melbourne he would give a dinner specially for me with no damned married women present, so that I could have the place of honour. He smelt and looked as though he had drunk my share of the wine in addition to his own. Ill-bred old toad!

367

Why should one be plagued to drink alcohol but allowed to refuse coffee or tea without any buzz?

I did not look forward to Sir Jimmy's company when the guests left but he was in bed snoring ten minutes after the last good-night. Lady Hobnob said they were old campaigners and had such a heavy social round that they did their best to curtail late hours.

Breakfast was brought to my bed by a maid, but I dressed before eating. It seemed frowsy to eat in bed as if I were ill. The maid later took me to her ladyship's room where she was sitting up with the remains of a meal and many letters and papers scattered on her bed. This was an off day, by a miracle, and she was giving it to me because she had been moved by my book. She said that once she too had been a little girl in the bush who had thought that the great world would be wonderful.

'And now,' I glowed, 'You have met all the great people and have seen Queen Victoria as well as King Edward and Queen Alexandra.'

She had been home to both Jubilees as a Government guest and to the Coronation, and told me of the wonders of Buckingham Palace and Windsor Castle, but wound up 'It has been a long weary way, my dear, from the old bush track with the mopokes calling and the moon coming up over the back paddock, and you brought me home to my youth.'

I stayed to lunch with her alone. I liked her, though she suggested untidiness. She was a bit gone about the belt and straggly around the hem, and not above grubbiness in the lace at wrists and neck, and her hat was dowdy.

You should see Ma's belts, and her hems and her lace! She is always the pink of perfection (her own phrase) even when she is baking, or washing the blankets. From Ma I had gathered the idea that to be unkempt about hem or belt was the equivalent of being weak-minded, and Ma was emphatic that daintiness of person, especially when women were elderly, was indispensable.

I hate to have to mention anything so low, but it had a big influence on my attitude, so it must go in. I found that Hobnob House had BUGS. Yes, insects that are never mentioned except in soft pedal and with a nick-name B FLATS. The vegetables at lunch tasted of antique butter and there was a mouldy atmosphere in the top floors. No one as capable as Ma had been there. It appeared that Lady Hobnob specialised in big dinners for which caterers and waiters came in. There were lots of other things that would have made Ma and Grandma snort in Hobnob Villa and the other houses I saw later.

When we were at dinner at Geebung Villa after my return, Edmée took me to task for provincialism in refusing Sir James's wine, and Mrs Crasterton said I must guard against being tiresome and odd or showing any taint of socialism. Only Gaddy cheered me still.

'You had a case,' said he. 'You have a right to your own tastes and old Jimmy was rude. As for the crowd they'd dress in sugee bagging if some bigger swell took the lead.'

I sat silent and rather stubborn. I would have adduced the B FLATS only that Lady Hobnob had been so kind. I thought about them, however, and resisted SOCIETY pretensions. Pa and Ma had reared me exceptionally, plus which I had my own affliction of bringing reality to bear. After all, my paternal grandmother had been assured of her altitude above the hoi polloi of the 'beastly Cawlonies'; and a cockatoo's crest would have been an infant compared with the eyebrows of my maternal grandfather had Sydney society tried to dictate his right to tolerate it or to ignore it.

As I retreated upstairs I heard Gaddy again, 'If she weren't different from other girls she wouldn't be such a draw, and you would have to give her some new dresses. I never met another kid who would have the pluck to go among others all dressed to kill while she has nothing but the one school-girl dress of some kind of white rag.'

I was continually surprised by Gaddy's understanding: but ah, if Derek had only championed me! Gaddy put on no airs about literature and we both loved flowers, so we had an absorbing topic in common. He was responsible for the beauty of the terraced gardens and dug in them himself on Saturdays and Sunday mornings. He was something in a Government Department—a soft job, I was told, with a big screw that his brother-in-law had secured for him while in power.

Sunday. Mrs Crasterton asked Edmée and me to accompany her to church. Edmée laboured in a Sunday school while in Sydney. 'Horrible little brutes of kids!' she observed. 'I detest them, but it is good to keep in with the Church. Sometimes the most distinguished people from England have introductions that keep them tight in church circles. Besides, men say that a girl without religion is like a rose without perfume.'

This sort of yelp raised in me a devil of opposition and I decided to tell any man that began to admire me that I was a free-thinker.

My hostess appeared in a black satin gown and a resplendent yellow bonnet and a set of 'wonderfully old' jewellery, and carried a prayer book inscribed by the Bishop. I chose to stay at home with Gaddy. I did not feel well-dressed enough for church.

Gaddy read a yellow-back in French and I read the *Sunday Times*. In it I found a story about myself. Some writer under an *alias* said I had no idea of how to dress. She ridiculed my appearance among fashionable people in a dress suitable only for the house in the morning, and flat-heeled shoes and cotton stockings, and said that I had no cloak but a sort of jacket, and that my hands showed the effects of manual labour, and that I had no idea of how to exercise sexual charm. She also said that nothing could have excited more interest than my lack of a suitable wardrobe.

'What does exercising sexual charm mean?' I asked Gaddy.

He damned and exploded and said he had meant to burn that unholy rag, and that exercising charm meant rolling one's eye like Edmée did, and exposing the salt-cellars around the clavicles, and having a lot of damned rags on the floor where he was for ever tripping over 'em.

This SOCIETY REPORTER was a Mrs Thrumnoddy who had been at the Hobnobs' dinner, and considered herself the best-dressed woman in Sydney. 'Does she get money for writing like that about me?' I asked.

Gaddy said she certainly did, and was the wife of a rich broker. No wonder she could dress well!

'Gaddy,' I said, 'I could dress well if I had money, but the drought killed all our stock, and Pa is not a good business man. We haven't a thing really. I couldn't even have a sash for my dress, but my stockings are real good cashmere.' I began to cry.

'Never mind, ducky,' said he. 'Your little finger is worth all those old cats put together. Do let us get you some clothes. My sister owes it to you for all the social prominence you are bringing her.'

I shrank into my shell. A man offering me clothes filled me with shame, even though it was only fat old Gaddy, who seemed more like Humpty Dumpty than a man or a bachelor or even an uncle. I longed for pretty clothes but could bear up without them, what cut me so deeply was that a woman who had kissed me and made such a fuss over me could write about me like that in the paper for everyone to read, and that she could get money for writing thus while I could not get any for writing about her, though I needed it so dreadfully. I hate unfairness.

Gaddy said no more. He got books and read to me. His reading was feraboracious, but his kindness soothed like oil on a burn. As we were going in to lunch, he said that I was not to mind Mrs Thrumnoddy, that she was a petty parasite who had had the opportunity of her life in meeting me.

Even the Harbour with the white sails on it and the ferries all gay with clothes and busking men could not rescue Sunday from being a stale day. Young Mr Big Ears came home from church with Edmée and Mrs Crasterton. Gaddy said that he was a teacher in the Sunday School and that was why Edmée laboured in that vineyard.

Big Ears brought two boxes of chocolates, an enormous one, which he handed to me, and a tiny one which he handed to Edmée. When we were alone I said he had made a mistake, but Edmée said no, she had asked him to give me this as she hated chocolates, but Big Ears evidently thought it would look queer to leave her out altogether.

On Monday, Mrs Crasterton took me sightseeing. We looked at the shops and she gave me a little imitation gold brooch which delighted me, as I had no other. I dragged her everywhere from the Post Office Tower to a waxworks show. She was a kind victim, as she was old and heavy. I loved it all, though I was haunted by a sense of delinquency in doing anything but the wash on Monday. Monday with me had always been sacred to the laundry and Sunday's scraps, except when Christmas despotically fell on a Monday.

It was such a busy day that I had not time to brood on the writing woman's pricks, and when we got home there was a parcel awaiting me—the most wonderful necklace and bracelets, heavy and old-fashioned and valuable. They were from Big Ears. He said they had been his mother's so that he could not give them to me outright yet, but that he had heard me say that I loved bracelets and it would be a great honour to him if I wore these while in Sydney.

This looked like another kindness *grace à* Edmée. Big Ears had also left a note for Mrs Crasterton. As it was an off night he hoped she would be free and that he might take her and me to a concert to hear a budding Melba. Edmée said, 'By jove, I'm glad you are rescuing me from that screech owl, and I do hope Big Ears will soon come to a head so that I can get rid of him.'

Derek had a similar idea of Big Ears. When his mother said that Big Ears was interested in me because he too was a writer, Derek snorted uproariously. He was having dinner with us for the first night since my arrival.

'Dekky, don't be naughty. He wrote charming verses in my album. He is one of our minor poets.'

Already we had met no end of poets—the big fellows one at a time, that is if Mrs Crasterton thought them 'nice' enough to be exposed to my unsophistication. We had the damned little twinkling stars in constellations at tea to produce a stellary effect.

'Big Ears doesn't look like a poet,' I exclaimed. Messrs Lawson, Paterson, Brady, Quinn, Ogilvie and others set a high standard of physique which outclassed poor little Big Ears.

372

'Look like a poet! He looks like a greengrocer's assistant who—who teaches Sunday School,' ended Derek.

Gaddy had a stunning blue sash waiting for me. I longed to own it but had not been educated to receive things. Mine was the independence which loves to lavish gifts upon others but squirms at receiving them. The sash was so long and my middle inches so few that I had to put the sash twice around me, and then it covered me to the armpits, and the ends of the big bow fell to the hem of my skirt. The cook, who was a darling, had done up my little dress and it was all fresh and glistening. Gaddy said that the sash was no more than a box of chocolates, and with a laugh added, that I could at least borrow it while I was in Sydney if I wouldn't take it altogether. I consented to wear it until I could write and ask Ma if I could keep it.

CHAPTER 15

My True Friend

Being too young and too poor to make a formal début, I was an anomaly. Other youngsters as poor as I already had their shoulders to the working wheel; those of financial status were acquiring extra polish to enhance their value in the matrimonial market. I had not 'come out', but was a chicken that walked around inside its shell—a good simile, seeing my lack of an evening dress. I was treated like a visitor of thirty or fifty years of age. Without any fuss or feathers I was just tucked in at dinners and luncheons, and people called to see me by the score. Quite two-thirds were men and half of them over forty. It was rare that there was a youngster of my own youth amid the throng. A great many talked about nothing; others exclaimed, 'Oh, how interesting!' People were not described as pretty or clever or entertaining or queer but as *interesting*. I grew very sick of this description of myself, but had quickly perceived that it was wiser to think what I said than to say what I thought.

I met numerous men, each of whom had written 'that beautiful thing' or 'this beautiful thing', each thing according to some authority, being the best thing that had been done since Pope or Dryden or Keats, and the authors designated as the Australian Poe, or Burns or Milton. I was in an uncomfortable predicament owing to my ignorance of all this Australian genius, but I had no difficulty in getting the geniuses on to the subject of their own supremacy and thus hiding my own inferiority.

People asked silly questions about myself. I had brought this to pass by pronunciamentos upon the desirability of honesty in egotism. In this way I found a new angle in the workings of egotism. I did not mind what I said about myself as a subject impersonally, while I stood aloof like a scientist in his laboratory, but I resisted when outsiders tried to intrude behind my reserve. I developed much ingenuity in turning the tables.

One man persisted, 'Why, when you speak so frankly against humbug in egotism, why do I find you the most difficult, the most shrinking, little creature I ever met? Can you explain?'

I couldn't. I can't.

Perhaps there are two divisions of egotism, one the absorption in self as self, the other the analysis of self as part of a universal complex force, and I am an analyst rather than the normal egotist.

As one of those old professor birds, with less gift for obscurity than usual among the academic, has said, 'Criticism means self-consciousness, and self-consciousness means renewed activity on a higher plane. The reflective play of one age becomes the passion of another.'

There was an article about me in a paper that I had not previously known of, but it had a big circulation in Sydney by currying scandals about people of prominence. The Editor said that Sydney people showed their general degeneracy in running after each new thing as it was advertised. Sybylla Melvyn's dreadful book had been written in six weeks, and when he expressed his disapproval people said, 'Yes, but it was wonderful for a girl of sixteen.' Then he felt as Dr Johnson towards the *difficult* musical performance which he wished had been *impossible*. The Editor asserted that I had begun as a conceited and self-assertive hoyden and the foolish lionising of Sydney SOCIETY had confirmed and developed me into an obnoxious specimen.

This was interesting and did not hurt like Mrs Thrumnoddy's defection towards a fellow guest. I went to Gaddy. He spluttered. 'Did that man ever see me?' I inquired. Gaddy said no, that he was the real scum, that his jealousy in not being able to get within coo-ee of me had inspired this attack. I said if he had ever met or even seen me he would be entitled to his opinion however harsh or undiscerning, but as he hadn't, there was the rub, because before I had got into print, I had, like other innocents, depended upon the printed word, and another bulwark was going bung. The accusation that I advertised myself was particularly unwarranted. I had no acquaintance among newspaper people, and did not give so much as a backward glance to make myself conspicuous. My strenuous endeavour was to be as inconspicuous as possible.

'Is that Sydney SOCIETY I have been meeting?' I asked.

Gad said I could bet my sweet life it was; not only the nice old parliamentary people and the University professors but some of the real smart-setters among whom even riches would not always buy an entry. There was disillusionment in finding that I had to reef in my standards to be at home here. It was now that I felt the force of Pa's tenet that Ma was a wonderful woman. I did not come in contact with anyone of Ma's ability and appearance.

I had hours to put in while Wheeler dressed Mrs Crasterton, and I wrote in my diary or pondered discontentedly on the waste it was that Ma could not have a nice town house. It was a heinous thing for all Ma's administrative ability to be squeezed into a petty grind of one irreverent urchin, one rebellious girl and one gentle and easily-pleased man. Ma could have managed a grand hotel or some vast institution, and in the place unto which it had pleased God to mis-direct her she had but a poverty-restricted cubby. No doubt she had found the same luny obstructions to using her ability as I had run my head into with mine.

I was desperately in need of money. If I had had the means I should have been a recluse, but when you are poor you are helpless to build a barrier to keep people away. I stood it as quietly as I could. I told Mrs Crasterton that I had imposed upon her hospitality long enough, I would now like to go home.

She positively wailed that that would make a fool of her. All of Sydney that had not met me was clamouring to do so, including the Admiral; and some of these high official invitations were really commands. I was tired of high officials and longed for young people like Derek and Edmée. I sometimes played the piano while they practised new steps in the hall. If I could play tennis and dance, and have just one evening dress to show my

376

décolleté I was sure I could have some fun coloured by a little of the romance that swirled around Edmée. When I went swimming the girls always said that the more clothes I took off the prettier I grew. I wished that Derek would give me a lesson in dancing, but his hopeless passion for Edmée's fatal beauty so burdened him that he thought of me only to play the piano so that he could 'hold her in his arms'.

Mrs Greville de Vesey put the cap on my society rights regardless of the frock of 'some kind of white rag', and my cotton (cashmere) stockings. Her mother had been born on the station adjoining my mother's, and knew that Ma was as high as herself. Mrs de Vesey was the chic leader of the younger smart set. People were no longer surprised that I was so properly behaved, my mother being one of the lovely Misses Bossier of Caddagat, which is one of the few original stations entered in the *Landholders' Record*. The Melvyns too were among the earliest educated free men to take up stations in the Southern District. It was I who was entitled to look into other people's pretensions to being of the old squattocracy.

Mrs de Vesey said that banana-barrow and bottle-o commercialism did not yet rule SOCIETY in Sydney though it was going that way. I loved Zoë de Vesey. She reminded me of a cruiser cutting a clean high wave and sending barges and lesser craft scuttling to their lesser ways. With the Governor-General to announce that I was a genius, and Zoë to vouch for my antecedents, I was established. Zoë said that I need not be shy about imposing on Mrs Crasterton. Poor old soul had sunk into 'innocuous desuetude' following the death of her husband, and this was a happy revival for her. She was really of good family, and Gaddy was a bachelor whom all the girls tried to bag.

'Bag Gaddy!!'

'Gaddy is rich. Edmée Actem camps there every now and again, but he hasn't given in yet. He'd be a fine instrument for an ambitious woman.'

'He's silly about Edmée,' I said. 'But she cannot be bothered with him.'

Zoë laughed her short mocking laugh, 'You are taking Edmée at her own valuation.'

Zoë was almost young, not more than twenty-eight and I loved going to her house and talking to her.

My wearing the jewellery of Big Ears brought me fresh attention. He too was rich, though not of high aristocraticness. His father had made his money in mines. Big Ears had been sent to Cambridge to acquire gentility and was to go into Parliament to establish himself. People seemed to gather importance under Zoë's classification, though I had discerned nothing much in them when trying to place them by my own INEXPERIENCE. Her estimate of people was out of EXPERIENCE mixed with CONTACT. She summed them up by what they *did* and *had*. I could only measure them by what they *were*. When I saw Mrs Crasterton booming across a drawing-room I measured that she was of exactly the same proportions and human texture as Mrs McSwat, save that Mrs Crasterton had had some sort of a tilling and wore expensive stays, whereas Mrs McSwat's form was unconfined and her culture had camped out at Barney's Gap and subsisted on bully and damper. I saw that the brass buttons and uniforms of the Admiral's staff, which have a dangerous charm for the fair, were worn by boys of helplessly English posture and stilted speech. Some of them were clean cut and straight of limb, but I could see that there were any number of bullock drivers, shearers and boundary riders of my acquaintance in patched shirts and thrummy moles who matched them muscle for muscle and thew for thew.

Soon the people who had predicted that I would be ruined by adulation were croaking that there was something the matter with me as I was not impressed by anyone or anything, that I was very difficult, and laughed at the most important people and made friends of those of no substance, just because I liked them. I would never advance by such tactics.

At the end of my first ten days in SOCIETY my true friend hove above the horizon of my bantling career. Ma had warned me that those who flattered me would not be my true friends, they would want only to get something out of me. My true friends would correct me for my good. Mr Wilting so mangled the vanity I did not have, that there was no mistaking his good intentions.

He was a pugnacious old boy who did a lot of reviewing on the *Watchdog*, a paper not so long born, with the reputation of possessing the only literary acumen in the new Commonwealth. The sole reason that Mr Wilting was to be found in the crude wilds of the Antipodes was to better his health. This, I inferred, though exile for him was likely to be the making of Australian literature.

He orated from the hearthrug, standing. 'My dear child, I have read your book and discern in it germs of genius. If fostered and cultivated these may bear fruit in time.'

This was opposed to the point of view that marriage would take literary prankishness out of me.

'Of course you are very crude. Your workmanship does not exist. You must start from the a b c. I wish I could have the forming of your style. I don't know of anyone else in these beastly Cawlonies who wouldn't ruin you.'

'Do you think women *ever* could write?' I inquired in a very small voice.

'Madam,' said he, drawing his chest upwards and twirling his mustache, 'the immortal Sappho was a woman.'

'Yes, but Shakespeare is claimed as a man. Men always say there is no female Shakespeare.'

'Humph! You study the fellows who say that, and you'll see they are a long way from being Shakespeares themselves. Why shouldn't women have the same privilege?'

Good for the old boy! After that I did not care how he strutted. He had won my affection.

'You'll never do work that will live if you listen to your friends—*so-called* friends. They will gush over you and call you a genius. Don't listen to them; and as for the literary talent of Australia, there is none. Unfortunately the literary men of Sydney are neither *literary* nor *men*. Even your University professors are only third-rate fellows—men who could never rise out of the ruck if they remained in England, so they came out here where they can lord it in a tin-pot circle.'

Mr Wilting had stated that his health was the reason of his own exile.

'The wife of one of our Governors said there is no society in Australia,' I murmured.

'She was right. Neither is there any culture. Neither are there any *literati*. There is only a set of local cacklers unknown out of their own barn. You will quickly set in the same crude limitations unless you can gain a perspective. You must burst the bonds of your environment. In your childish ignorance you are over-awed by the tinkling horse-rhymes and bullock-driving jingles of these fellows. They are beneath consideration from a literary point of view. The crudeness of the average Australian is appalling—appalling! and his cocksureness prevents his improvement.'

In many a friendly bush home the more tender of the poems decried by this gentleman were copied by girls into their albums and were treasured as the only expression of familiar emotions and scenes, while the more rousing couplets were often on the lips of their brothers and gave a little colour to arid monotony as they ploughed, ring-barked, shore, milked and put up the heavy fences. Around the camp fires far out this gentleman could have heard the work of these poets he despised enlivening the bare nights of the unfurnished pioneer life. I plucked up courage to voice my conviction that in another generation or two these Australian ballads would be lauded as being as typically Colonial as Burns's were Scottish. I held that our poets were our folklore-ists, and worthy of all the affection we gave them. I ventured to suggest that perhaps the English mind, to its loss, did not extract the essence of Australianism.

Oh, my! what I brought upon myself! Mr Wilting said that what he feared was true. I had the Australian cocksureness, was so crudely self-opinionated that I could never improve. The only thing to save me would be immediate transplantation to England, where I would find my level before my mind became set.

'But,' I persisted, becoming possessed of a devil, as Ma used to say, 'why should everything English be our model just because it is English? Shouldn't we do something on our own hook?'

'*On our own hook?*' he repeated with a shudder. 'To quote some of your own doggerel-mongers,

> * '*But objects near the vision fill,*
> *When one forgets the things afar;*
> *A jam tin on the nearest hill*
> *When touched by sunlight seems a star.*'

'But that seems to be on your side,' I suggested.

'He has gropings. He's not quite so cocksure.'

I had met Mr Wilting's mentality before. Plenty of it had penetrated to Possum Gully. Such people's families found Australia a handy dumping-ground for their misfits and undesirables, but the silly dumpedees instead of having the spunk to help us natives do something *on our own hook* in Australianism, thought we should all imitate the English most lickspittlingly. Of course we are proud of our English heritage, than which, sad to say, there is no better. By that I mean that it is depressing that it is the best that man has achieved at present, but hang it all, one *is* a bit of a crawler not to be *something on one's own hook*. It's a jolly good phrase, and we must achieve something better than servile imitation to be worthy of England and Shakespeare.

Mr Wilting shook his head at me. Well he might, had he known what I really contained in the way of ideas: but with one part of myself I thought it most kind of him to stoop to me at all. At least he did not want to extirpate my idea of writing, he merely wanted to direct it and change its personality. I was grateful for this, but thought him rather a confisticated bore and an obsolete frump in his other strains. I ventured to ask if I could earn a few shillings like other people by writing articles. He said to

* '*Bulletin*' *Verse.*

be sure I could, I should write an article about my own views and send it to him. This filled me with hope.

Having eaten all the cakes and sandwiches which Mrs Crasterton had left me to dispense so that this culture-engendering CONTACT might be undiluted, he took up his hat and stick and said, 'You know nothing about love. Keep off the subject until you mature; though study will help you a little, and you'll need practice. I hope to see a great improvement in your love-making next book: it is very crude in this one, very crude indeed.'

'It's exactly the way men make love,' I maintained.

'That's the reason it's a failure as art—mere raw material—crude.' With this puzzling statement he clapped his hat crudely on his head, shook my hand and departed.

If I put down what really happened when men were spoony, why should that be crude? Well, at any rate I had had lots of practice in love—in being loved—since I had perpetrated that fake autobiography.

To escape Mrs Crasterton's sententiousness as to how much I should have learned from a man like that, and to begin on the article, I betook myself to my own room. Gaddy was sitting in his study with the door open as I passed, having just come home by cab. He often called me in to ask what measure I had taken of things. I threw away caution with him as I felt I could trust him. His fatness made him safe and kind, and he was always on my side.

'What kind of an old frogabollow is that?' I demanded.

'He's one of the geni-asses from HOME. They send us a good supply. They fill the vacancies left by our crude youngsters who go to put punch into the effete old world.'

Gad emphasised the word crude with a wink. 'The pressure of competition or tippling drives them out to us. We haven't the population to make an arena for our men of art or letters or other kinds of ability, so they go to the central market. This old chap is right in some things, but in others he's a decadent blitherer, and when our young fools try to reflect his point of view it quite breaks 'em up.'

I felt like hugging Gaddy, but refrained because he did not enjoy interruption in the middle of a discourse.

'I think, meself, there's something in imagining the greatness of an undeveloped country, but old Wilting measures greatness by the style of clubs and art galleries, and dismisses the menace of the slums as being inevitable for the lower orders.'

'He says Australia has no background.'

'And England has so much that she is a museum of what has been, while Australia is an experimental laboratory of what will be. I prefer foreground to background.'

'He says the lovemaking in my book is crude. Miss Elderberry and Mrs Swift said that too.'

'It's a fact, me dear. There is the same difference between your idea of love-making and the experience of those old war-horses as there is between an English breakfast and a French dinner. To gain the approval of those destriers you would need to have love made to you by none except those who should not approach you—other women's husbands for instance.'

'That would be disgusting. I wouldn't listen.'

Gaddy laughed till he cried, but I could not see why. 'You should be able to incite *amour* and extract the erotic excitement from it without running amok of the conventions or the tongues of those experienced in detecting smart love. You'll find plenty of fellows so skilled in lovemaking that they can put a double end on it, so that if you know how to give experienced en-couragement they are prepared to go the whole length; but if you are found to be of honest virtue they can take the down off the situation and leave you to feel that you had been the one in the wrong. Thank God you are crude, as crude as your lily and roses complexion that can bear the sun's crude morning glare, and crude may you remain as long as possible, is my prayer.'

CHAPTER 16

A Great Name in Australian Literature

From that date I began to have more practice in love, or perhaps it was merely experience.

The following morning I posted my article to Mr Wilting, then opened my mail. In it was a long letter from Big Ears. He told me that he loved me to distraction. Every day since I had come to town he had perched in a Moreton Bay fig in his grounds which overlooked our route to the ferry, to watch me go by. Would I, could I ever think of him? He would have patience for ten years if necessary. I was shocked. What would Edmée think—when she had been so kind to me! Fortunately she despised him, and was waiting for him to propose solely to dismiss him. With another section of myself I thought, Huh! if I put this down, Mr Wilting would say I know nothing of how men make love.

I hadn't time to think just then: the telephone rang and Mrs Crasterton called me. 'You had better hear the whole of this,' she said. 'I find you are a wise young thing and seem to know more than those who are trying to instruct you.'

She handed me the second ear piece. Zoë de Vesey was speaking.

Now it appears that Australia has one great literary man, or that one great literary man was a native of Australia? He had been many years in London, had gone HOME on the Press Association but in London had had the opportunity to turn into a real man of letters. He was now one of the most successful playwrights of the day. His plays had record runs in London. Here was a comet with two tails when compared with the LOCAL CACKLERS. He made pots of money, Zoë said, but his expensive tastes kept ahead of his income. He went everywhere and was a social lion. And this great god had expressed the wish to see little me during his visit to his native land.

He had been born on the Northern Tableland as I on the Southern, but he had gone to the University and had swum about in SOCIETY since a tadpole, whereas I had simply been entitled to do so, but had been kept on the cockatoo level because of indigence.

At the time of the Diamond Jubilee he had won a prize for an ode entitled, *Australia to England!*, and became known as the Australian Swinburne. However, he had quickly renounced all Australian crudities and had written a novel of London entitled *The Woman Who Wilted*, one of the greatest circulating library successes, which had earned him the title of the Australian Anthony Hope.

'He doesn't seem to be anything *on his own hook*', thinks I to myself.

On going to London he had not stressed his Australian origin but played the game on London lines. He had outdone the Londoners in Londonness through having more of England known in knowing Australia too. His comedies of duchesses and high ladies who knew all about extracting the erotic excitement from *amour*, as Gaddy put it, were the last word in being risque without being bannable. He was a SUCCESS. He must be just reeking with EXPERIENCE, thinks I, drinking in this titilating news.

He had had to fight for long years in London for recognition, and might never have won it only that he had got away as a war correspondent for the *Daily Thunderer* for a year with the Boers, and his articles had charmed everyone. He was a sizzling imperialist. Rhodes had condescended to him, Kipling patted him on the back, Barney Barnato nudged him in the ribs. He was on the way to a title and all that. What he needed to complete him was a wealthy and influential marriage. Only now could he afford to emphasise his Australian nativity and turn it to commercial account.

He had always kept in touch with the Press Association and while out was to do some articles on Australia from an imperial angle which would appear in *The Thunderer* and *The Argus*, or perhaps it was *The Age*—I can't tell these two apart. He was also connected with a leading publishing house, and if he saw anything worth picking up, was to pick it up. This gave him great importance among us poor LOCAL CACKLERS, of which I was the localest and least. If he could, without compromising his status and deteriorating his attainments, he would insert an Australian character or scene in his next comedy. His former set was jubilant about this. He was trumpeted as a good Australian. Zoë did not tell us all this on the telephone at that moment. This was pieced together later from different sources of information or misinformation.

What Zoë said, and the reason she said some of it was because she ranked Mr Goring Hardy very high as one who both *did* and *had*. She said that to meet him was a unique chance and would be an education for a little girl like me. He thought there was promise in my book, though he did not approve of its point of view. It was possible, Zoë said, that something might come to me through his interest, but she did not want the poor little thing to be hurt in any way. Goring was a fascinating fellow and he might take the imagination of a girl reared in seclusion. Too many strings had harped to his bow. Zoë's advice was that I should not be too accessible. 'He wants her to call at his office at Cunningham and Bucklers, but he must meet the poor little thing in the proper way.'

'I'll see to that,' said Mrs Crasterton.

'I want to have her here, but I haven't a spare hour this week,' said Zoë.

Mrs Crasterton turned to me. 'He must come to us. I shall let him see that you are a celebrity too.'

She telephoned to the Union Club for Mr Hardy to call her, and he did. He started by ordering that I should be sent to him—like a girl from a registry office seeking employment.

'He does feel his oats,' remarked Mrs Crasterton, aside. 'But my people were bishops and generals when his were mere market gardeners.'

'Oh, no,' she continued into the phone. 'I'm so sorry. I haven't time to go with her this week. We could try to wedge you in here though. So many people are craving for my little friend's time that the days are not long enough. Perhaps you could come to breakfast.'

At last he was so generous and condescending as to say he would come to dinner that very day if we would not mind his running away immediately after. He had to open an artist's show at five and was to be at an official gathering at Government House that evening. Mrs Crasterton said that would fit nicely as we too would be engaged until six and had an after-dinner engagement.

On that night Gaddy went to his Club. His sister asked him to support her, 'After all, Mr Hardy is a really distinguished man,' she observed.

'Don't lose your head,' Gaddy replied, 'he certainly has marketed himself like a politician, but when it comes to literary genius, we have five hundred poets, every blooming one boomed as the greatest, but some of the greatest have yet to be born.'

Derek, on the other hand, loudly lamented that he was not to be home for dinner. 'Hardy's a regular swell,' he said, 'not in the same street with the little unwashed "potes".'

Edmée was half through an elaborate *toilette* when we got home that evening, and poor Mrs Crasterton was taken with cramps and had to go to bed. Edmée unselfishly gave up her dinner engagement to dine at Geebung Villa.

'It's really an amazing condescension for Goring Hardy to come to see you,' she said. 'It must be because Zoë de Vesey's mother knew yours and it has become the thing to see you. He is run after right and left. Some panjandrum in the literary world in London has written out to him to find out what you are like, and if you could ever write anything else. You had better make the most of your furore while it lasts.'

A little later Mr Hardy telephoned that he found himself half-an-hour ahead of his schedule and would have a chat with me before dinner. 'Don't let him paralyse you,' Edmée said. 'Women throw themselves at him, especially the married ones . . . I think,' continued Edmée reflectively, 'it must be no end of sport to be safely married and then seek a little diversion.'

I sat tight in my room until the maid had a colloquy with Mrs Crasterton and then came to me. I stole down the back stairway, catching sight of my reflection in a mirror—like a doll in the white dress and Gad's big sash.

A tall figure in immaculate toggery—a dress-coat knight with silk on heel—rose from a couch and looked so hard at me that I was unable to withstand the battery of his glances. His whole face was indicative of keenness and might have been that of a money-lender, a bishop or any other manager of property and investments, instead of a poet and literary man.

The hard blue brightness of his eyes sent me firmly into my shell. He had light eyelashes that reminded me of our old white boar, whom I despised, as he did so precious little for his up-keep. Mr Hardy's bright stare was relentless, and not free from cruelty, though I felt that he gave me swift credit for all my good points—complexion, youth, silky shining hair, feminine lines. My inventory of men was equally comprehensive and penetrating.

In thinking of him in the years that have gone I know it was his unalloyed maleness that hurt me. He would appraise women in the light of the pleasure or service they could give him. He had no scrap of that understanding for which I was hungry. That perhaps is to be found only in men of more complexity, who have something of the mothers who bore them as well as of the fathers whose name they bear.

I could be 'simply ripping' to Mr Hardy if I let fly with one side of my disposition, and there was yet another that would also be tempting to him. A man who had sipped deeply of for-bidden women would like thoroughly untried soil, so I sat down primly in the full bloom of conventional innocence and waited for him to play first.

'Well, do you like Sydney?' he asked, quizzically.

'The Harbour is lovely,' I breathed ecstatically.

'Well, well! You really are as young as advertised,' he remarked.

'I expected you to be at least thirty, with knives in your socks. Celebrities are usually well on in years before they are known.'

He made remarks in the character of the fake autobiography, but that sent me as far into my shell as a winter snail, so he did a little putting to get me out again, staring with an expression of vivid interest and amusement. He was talking to one whom he estimated as without the defence of social *savoir faire*.

'How do you come to be putting up with the Old Campaigner? Is she going to see you through?'

'She is very kind to me,' I rebuked him.

'She's not a bad old bolster, but you needn't feel indebted to anyone for entertaining you. You ought to charge 'em. You've provided a lot of idle resourceless women with a new sensation.'

'More men than women have come to see me, and have given me luncheons and lunch parties,' I said, like a child.

'By jove! Have they? I seem to be behind the times. What stamp of callers does the Old Campaigner most encourage? Poets, I suppose. What would you think of a poet for a lover?'

'The Lord preserve me! Common men, when spoony, are sickly enough in poetic quotation.'

'Well done, little one! I believe you could sock the balls across the net like a champion if you liked. What about Gad—the old egg, we used to call him.'

'Gad is a dear,' I said staunchly. 'He is so kind to me.'

'I expect he can't help himself.' Mr Hardy laughed shortly, with a tantalising gleam in his brilliant eyes.

Edmée appeared in her grand pale green satin with the foamy cloak half-slipping from her shoulders, and made soft coo-ing explanations of poor dear Mrs Crasterton's indisposition. Mr Hardy instantaneously changed into a different man, with a face as grave as a judge's and which suddenly looked lined and old. He talked in a high tenor drawl and asked if he might telephone.

While he was out, Edmée remarked, 'You look all lighted up. Getting your heart cracked right at the jump?'

A little giddy, I said, 'He might fall in love with me. Other men have.' Roderic Quinn, Banjo Paterson, John Farrell,

Rolf Boldrewood, E. J. Brady, Sidney Jephcott, Henry Lawson, Victor Daley and others had all taken notice of me in some way— some had flattered me in verses and voices of many colours, two had even kissed me—in a fraternal fashion, I ween.

'You little softy! The idea of Goring Hardy falling in love with any woman for more than a week! I heard today from old friends that it was suggested by a high official that he had better take a trip to Australia. That explains why he would waste his time here in his prime. He was much too friendly with a certain titled lady—a relative of royalty, and the husband threatened to use him as co-respondent. That bird is not to be caught with chicken feed.'

We went in to dinner. Mr Hardy made orthodox remarks with orthodox politeness, that politeness called chivalry, which women are expected to accept in lieu of their rightful control of the race and the ordering of life with sanity and justice for their children.

Mr Hardy ignored me entirely. Edmée took it as a matter of course that he should. I was twittering internally to realise that little me from Possum Gully was in a SOCIETY scene at last. Here was a belle who drove men to distraction, palpitating her snowy bosom and twitching her shoulders so that no contour was wasted, and languishing and ogling in the exercise of sexual attraction on a man who had been clandestinely loved by a titled married lady (there were always *clandestine* affairs in the novels of lords and ladies I had read) and wearing silk socks. I had never before seen a man wearing silk socks. My own were cashmere, and Mrs Thrumnoddy earned money by describing them as cotton. Think of the EXPERIENCE I was imbibing in sophistication, in *savoir faire*—taking these two out of winding.

Mr Hardy did not seem in a hurry during dinner, and acceded to Edmée's invitation to coffee before running away. He said he had telephoned, and had a half-hour longer than he expected. In the drawing-room they continued to ignore me, but I some-times found those hard bright eyes on me in a stimulating way. Edmée gave him all sorts of gossip interesting to a homecomer.

I took refuge in a big album. Here were people who by their style of dress had been old when I was born. I forgot Edmée and Mr Hardy in wondering how many of these album people still lived, how many had gone into that awful silence, which I hate and resent.

Edmée was called to the telephone, and Mr Hardy surprised me by springing rather than walking to my side of the room.

'Tell me what you are thinking as you look at those old frumps.'

'They aren't frumps. I was thinking that once they were girls just like me, and wondering did they long for things as I do.'

'Don't worry about them; they all had their day. Take yours while you can. They weren't like you: they were ordinary.'

The camellia fell from his button-hole and I hastened to re-place it as Edmée returned. She laughed something about the white flower of a blameless life, and her glance had that flicker which saves her from being overlooked by the men who like women who are up in masculine sophistications, and condone them.

As Mr Hardy was bidding good-night to Edmée he said casually, 'I want your little friend to meet Cunningham the publisher tomorrow morning. I could send a cab for her.'

'She will be delighted to go; it is good of you to take an interest in her,' said Edmée without consulting me.

'Imagine him staying all that time—wasn't going to spare a moment at first—haw-haw, the great man!' said Edmée.

'But he went to telephone to get time immediately he saw you. Why don't you distract him?'

'What would be the use? A man of his tastes must marry money, and he's old enough in the horn to know it. But he's most fascinating.'

Edmée telephoned the friends, to whom she had been going, of her triumph. Mr Hardy had come for five minutes with the prodigy, but had stayed with her, and, as Mrs Crasterton was ill, she could not leave the ship, and so on. Well, it was lucky when people came and saw that I was nothing, that Edmée was on hand to save them from disappointment.

The parlour maid was admitting Big Ears, so I sped to my room and left him to Edmée. I felt sure that Mr Hardy had noticed my sash. I had not previously been noticed so intensely by sophistication, and found it thrilling. I sat down to enjoy my diary.

CHAPTER 17

I Didn't Say Anything

Mrs Crasterton recovered on the morrow, and in the afternoon Mr Hardy sent a cab for us and we went to meet him at the GREAT AUSTRALIAN PUBLISHER'S. People ran forward at sight of Mrs Crasterton, and one after another conducted us through the lovely book store. Oh, the books! We went up stairs, with books everywhere, and pictures of celebrities, and entered a new kind of room to me. There were more books and pictures, but also lovely easy chairs and two desks. Goring Hardy was at one, and a terribly polite man at the other. The publisher man was away in Melbourne.

The polite man chatted to Mrs Crasterton. Goring Hardy excused himself, something entailed cabling. Mrs Crasterton and the Polite Man continued a conversation on family matters while I gazed about me. Oh, the books! Mrs Crasterton had another engagement, and the Polite Man said she could leave the little lady in his charge, and he or Mr Hardy would send her home safely in a cab. Mr Hardy made many apologies and escorted Mrs Crasterton down stairs with most knightly tenderness, making jokes and yarning. When he returned he dived into his papers again without taking any notice of me. The Polite Man talked to me a while and then began to shut drawers, got his stick and hat, straightened his waistcoat in the way which suggests it would be more comfortable to bone this garment unaffectedly like a bodice. Then he whispered that Mr Hardy would soon be done, and departed. Mr Hardy, with his nose down, said that if anything urgent came in he would attend to it.

He continued quill driving until his colleague, with fussy goodbyes, had withdrawn, when he flung the pen across the room to the fireplace and erected a placard with
O U T
on it, and said in an impelling tone, 'Come!'

We went up a little stairway into a snuggery, which Mr Hardy said was old Cunningham's private lair.

'What do you think of that for a chair?' said he, backing me into a huge one while he sat across the arms so that I was imprisoned. 'Now, we'll enjoy ourselves.'

'About writing any more books,' I stammered, 'I've decided not to. I shall have to earn my living. We're poor.'

'We're not going to think about books today,' he laughed.

'I mustn't waste your time,' I said uneasily, trying to get out of the chair without touching him.

'I don't let anyone waste my time, little one. I've manoeuvred this opportunity to have a talk free from the idiots one meets at dinners and things, who want to make a tin-pot lion out of the most innocent of us.'

'I couldn't possibly waste your time,' I said again. I did not know how to cope with the grave breach of the conventions he was forcing upon me. I was so hurt about it that I was petrified.

'You must see these etchings,' he said in a manner surprising after the way he had ignored my waiting presence for more than an hour. 'Old Cunningham has some stunning prints from London, and you shall be the first to see them.'

He went down stairs and came back with a vast book. He dawdled over every picture, but they came to an end at last and I rose again, longing to escape and murmuring about trespassing upon his time. He inquired point blank, 'Don't you like being here with me? Do I bore you?'

BORED! It would have been thrilling but for the wound to my sense of propriety. He wouldn't do this to Edmée or any girl who knew the ropes, I felt.

He removed the sting by saying, 'I had practically to kidnap you. There is a howling pack after you and another after me, and this was our only chance of enjoying ourselves simply. Mrs Crasterton will know you are as safe as a church. I'll send for afternoon tea.'

I sat down, but with an uneasiness which was partly genuine shyness.

'You really are more unsophisticated than I could have believed,' he said, and entertained me delightfully all the afternoon. Oh, the books! I was a duck reared in a desert seeing a pond for the first time. I gained ease, Mr Hardy was now treating me delightfully. Time ran all too quickly, and I had to insist upon departure.

'It was lovely. Thank you for entertaining me.'

'Look here, we must take the law into our hands and escape to enjoy our own society, and keep it secret or we should soon be smoked out of cover. The rabble has no right to bore us to death.'

This was most flattering, and he took me home to Mrs Crasterton himself.

Edmée questioned me, but was not too persistent, as she was dressing for a ball to which Mrs Crasterton was chaperoning her, and from which my lack both of clothes and accomplishments shut me. I said that Mr Hardy had been too busy to bother much with me, that I had looked at a lot of books.

'But why did you stay so long?'

'I had to wait till he could bring me home.'

Gaddy was to look after me for the evening, for which I was grateful in view of the danger of Big Ears turning up on the way to the ball. Gad collected children's books, which seemed to me a peculiar hobby for an old bachelor. He read from them. I never had had any children's books. Ma thought them trash and I don't believe that Pa ever heard of them.

Gad and I got on famously till half past nine, when there was a ring. 'If it's Big Ears, don't leave me alone with him for a single moment,' I pled.

'I promise, but why, what earth . . . but it can wait.'

It was Big Ears. In response to Gad's interrogations he said that he was bored to the spine with the dance, and why had Gad not been there?

'Why, with the beauteous Edmée, that is strange, did someone cut you out?' grinned Gad.

'Why did you neglect your duty, were you lame?' demanded

Big Ears. 'Derek disappeared after the first dance and left her on my hands.'

'I understood that you would be after me with a gun if I did not give way,' said Gad.

'Yes, and you are so persistent that the lady is worn out.'

They both laughed. I listened in amazement to the workings of male vanity in saving face.

I excused myself and left Gad to the guest. He went early. One more night safely past. But I had a habit of running down to the sea wall to watch the sun rise over the Harbour, and Big Ears had found this out. There he was waiting for me next morning. He insisted upon bringing me up to the scratch. I would as soon have married a moon calf, whatever that may be, and thought it like his insufferability to be squawking after Edmée one week and trying to fool me the next, but I said I could not be so wicked as to drag him down to my level. 'I'm a free-thinker,' I said, piling it on a little. 'It is as bad for a woman to be without religion as a flower to be without perfume. That is the companion piece of love being for men a thing apart, but for women their whole existence.'

Big Ears was commended as a remarkable young man who not only taught in Sunday School, but carried on the custom of his father in reading family prayers each morning to his household. 'I would laugh out loud to see you reading prayers, you'd look so funny and young,' I added.

That should finish him, I thought, and raced up the terraces and into the house. Gad met me. 'Hey,' he began, 'what about Big Ears?'

'Gaddy, I can trust you like everything, can't I?'

'That's what I'm living for,' grinned he.

'Well, you see, Big Ears is trying to flirt with me, and it puts me in a fix as Edmée might think it was my fault. He is so dead gone on her.'

'Did the Actem tell you that?'

'Well, yes, but you'll treat it confidentially?'

'And that put you off Big Ears—well, well, I never thought

I'd be grateful to the Actem. I must give her a pair of gloves for this.'

I asked what he meant, but he only cackled and kept on saying, 'So she dished Big Ears by that, God bless m'soul, ha! ha!'

Mrs Crasterton came in and wanted to hear the joke, but Gaddy winked at me and dived into his paper. Mr Wilting's paper had come and my article was in it. I was painfully self-conscious about it, but Mrs Crasterton praised it kindly, and I was longing for the money. I telephoned to Mr Wilting to thank him and to ask how much I should be paid, hoping it would be enough for an evening dress.

'My dear little girl,' he said, 'you wouldn't get any money for that. I put it in out of my interest to keep you before the public.' My acute disappointment was equalled by the feeling that I had been vulgar and pushing in bringing myself to notice. How was I to make a few shillings for an evening dress? I had suffered the notice solely to that end.

I was called to the drawing-room to meet a young man who said he was a free lance, and by interviewing me could make a guinea. I said I nearly fainted each time I was mentioned in the papers, and was trying my very best to get out of sight and be forgotten, could he not interview some important person instead? He said he would be surer of the guinea if he wrote about me, and pled with me to be a good sport and help him. He was one of a number who had come with similar pleas and who were able to make a guinea by submitting me to the torture of fresh notice, but I couldn't make a penny anywhere. The few shillings Ma had given me in pocket money were running out because people bullied me for copies of my book—said I must present one to the public library and to this and that—and I had to buy these at Cunningham and Bucklers. I felt pecked to death for lack of a few pounds. Hopes of an evening gown receded.

Mrs Crasterton cut the interview short by calling me to the telephone. Sir James Hobnob wanted to speak to me. I found that it was Goring Hardy. 'Say,' he drawled, 'I enjoyed you so much yesterday that we must make a break for it again this afternoon. I'll ring the Old Campaigner again in a few minutes.' He left me to do my own prevaricating.

'What did he want?' asked Mrs Crasterton.

'He got rung off,' I said.

'There he is again now,' she said, going to the telephone. It was Mr Hardy saying that he was so sorry that he had been unable to give me any time yesterday—but these things can't be helped, you know. If Mrs Crasterton would spare me again this afternoon he would see that we were not disturbed and he would advise me as best he could concerning future work. I had everything to learn. 'Of course, of course,' agreed Mrs Crasterton. Today he invited me to his aunt's flat.

'Do I know your aunt?' inquired Mrs Crasterton.

It was established that they had served together on Committees. Aunt spoke to Mrs Crasterton on the telephone and said that she would be waiting for me at the wharf. Her flat was right in the city, which made it convenient for Goring.

Another ring was from Mrs Thrumnoddy. She ordered me to meet her that afternoon at the Australia, where she was having a few distinguished people, and made it plain that it was a distinguished honour for me to be asked. I said I had another engagement, but she said, 'Get out of it.' Mr Goring Hardy was to be with her, and a man like that had to be considered. It would do me good to meet him. Mrs Crasterton said that I could go to her from my other engagement. I begged Mrs Crasterton not to mention that I was seeing Mr Hardy, as it would take the wind out of Mrs Thrumnoddy's sails, and she would put it in the paper, and Mr Hardy would think I was a chatterer. Mrs Crasterton said she told Mrs Thrumnoddy only those things she wished to be reported. That settled that nicely.

Mr Hardy himself was waiting for me at the wharf, and we jumped into a cab and went straight to his aunt's flat. Aunt looked me over piercingly, but asked no questions. Mr Hardy spread out books and stationery in a workmanlike way and assumed his public shell towards me, which was brisk and ignoring. I dived into my rôle of girly-girly bushkin from Possum Gully. Presently Aunt came in hatted and with a hand portmanteau. She and Goring had a colloquy, from which I gathered that she was leaving for a week. She merely nodded good-day to me and went.

Mr Hardy made sure that we were locked against intrusion, and then acted like a boy leaving school. He whirled me around, tossed me on to the table and sat looking at me with a leaping light in his eyes. 'Now let us both come out of our shells. In spite of your cast-iron shyness there must be mines of things in you. You could not write as you do and just be the ordinary miss.'

'That is just writing,' I murmured.

'We cannot express passions and longings in an original and convincing way if they are not in us. It is your power of emotion that attracts me.'

'My Pa put that part in for fun.'

'Nonsense!' he said, and laughed. 'You have a puckish sense of humour.'

I said nothing, so he tried a different tack. 'Do you like pretty things?'

'Oh, yes!' I exclaimed with frank eagerness. 'But my blue sash is the only pretty or expensive thing I have ever had, except of course, horses.'

'What a dashed shame! You would be a beauty in a different sorty of way if you were properly tricked out. Let me plan a turn-out from sole to crown by some smart dress-maker—something to show your curves and pretty arms.'

In accordance with my upbringing it was an affront, almost an outrage to be offered clothes. Clothes could be offered with propriety only to a child or perhaps to a 'person', and we were not in the person class.

'Shall we take the colour of your eyes, your hair or your cheeks and work out a scheme? I'd just like to see the flutter you would cause if you were properly dressed.'

'Oh, please, my mother taught me not to accept presents from gentlemen.'

'Your mother was quite right, but I am different.'

'She told me that all the men would say that.'

He had a real good laugh; it was nice to hear him.

'Your mother made a good job of you, but it would be quite safe to take a little present from me. It wouldn't . . . '

'It wouldn't?'

'Yes, I wouldn't—hang it all, little one, you know what I mean.'

I gazed at him in owl-like fashion, which I suddenly found most effective.

'Oh, well,' he said at length. 'I must not expect you to run before you learn to walk in a new dimension. We must think out schemes for your future.'

He asked business-like questions about my means, and I told how poor we were and that I must earn my living and that I hated teaching and did not want to get married.

'Are you in love with anyone?' he demanded quite fiercely.

'Not one scrap. I never have been for a moment. I don't want ever to get married.'

'That's the best poem I've heard since I left London,' he laughed. 'You *can* write, you know.'

'Do you really think so?'

'There isn't anyone in Australia with your gifts today, but you must put them on the right rails for success. I can help you there if only we can have a little time to ourselves, without all the old cats miauling and ruining our game. You must get clear of the Old Campaigner for a start.'

'She is very kind; you could come there.'

'Faugh! Writers must have a retreat without anyone knowing where they are or what they are doing.'

He asked me my Sydney connections, which were Pa's old-time parliamentary colleagues, especially Mr Simms, the Minister for Education.

'We'll go and see him,' said he.

I reminded him of Mrs Thrumnoddy's tea at the Australia, where he was going, and that she had said I must go because he was to be there.

'Is that how she worked it on us? That woman would sell her skin—she hasn't any soul—to bag a social lion. Why should we go there when we can see each other here so much better?' He chuckled. So did I. 'Do you think that the Old Campaigner will split about where you are?'

'No. I asked her not to because Mrs Thrumnoddy put it in the paper that I had only cotton stockings—and they are cashmere.'

This made him hilarious and he put on his hat. 'Come, we'll rout out a few people in Macquarie Street. We must start your career.'

We had a friendly time in both Houses of Parliament. I was disappointed that our law makers were such common looking old men, but to be with Mr Hardy gave the visit glamour. Everybody made a fuss of him and seemed to think it just right for him to have me in tow. 'You'll teach her the ropes and see that she makes the most of her genius,' was the sort of thing they said. Mr Hardy acted as though I were a child he was indulging, but sometimes in his eye was a look which a woman knows for what it is without EXPERIENCE. I sat on the seat beside Sir Somebody in the Upper House, and we were given tea in the M.L.A. Place. Mr Simms had us wait while he spoke in debate, and then gave us coffee in his room. I had not seen him since I was a child, and it was a day full of debate, but he was cordial and said Mrs Simms would take me home to stay with her. Everybody thought Mr Hardy a great man, and that my career was on the way to glory under his guidance.

He accompanied me across in the ferry. (How I revelled in travelling on the ferries!) He saw me to the gates of Geebung Villa. 'We must have all the days we can together. I'll fix up something for tomorrow.'

Mrs Crasterton was quite fussy about my late appearance. She had returned a few minutes earlier to find that Mrs Thrumnoddy had called up three times during the afternoon. Mrs Crasterton was surprised to hear that I had not gone to the Australia. I said that Mr Hardy had not gone either, that he thought it was much more important to give me a lesson in style, and that we had been at the House of Parliament seeing my father's old friends.

Mrs Thrumnoddy rang again. She was angry to be flouted by a little country bumpkin. Mrs Crasterton said I had better make my own excuses. 'I'm so sorry,' I murmured into the 'phone, 'but I was detained by the Minister for Education in Debate, and I was frightened to go to your party in *cashmere* stockings. I knew if you had Mr Hardy I should not be missed, because he was at Parliament House while I was there, and everyone was so excited to see him that they did not notice me.'

Gaddy came in while I was saying this, and patted me on the back. I told him that Mr Wilting had not paid for my article, and Gaddy snorted, 'The old swine, he wants a kick in the pants. He was too tight to turn in any copy and filled his space with your article.'

There was a letter from Big Ears which thickened that plot. He said that it would be the aim of his life to turn me to spiritual things. If I would marry him, to show his tender regard, when he brought me home, prayers would be discontinued until I expressed a wish for them to be resumed. Would I meet him in the morning to give him my answer. He said he would be praying for me all night. I thought, ' "Bust him," he ought to join the Salvation Army.'

CHAPTER 18

A Game for Two

In the morning Mrs Crasterton was again called to the telephone by Sir James Hobnob, who asked for me. 'Dear me, poor old Sir James must be getting senile,' she remarked. 'Old men can be very silly about young girls. You must exercise common sense, my dear.'

It was Mr Hardy, chuckling. 'Say, I've arranged for you to lunch with Mrs Simms today, and we shall have all the afternoon together.'

He rang again in a few moments in *propria persona* and arranged the day with Mrs Crasterton. She was busy otherwise, and content to let me go. I went with bubbles of anticipation inflating me.

Lunch with Mrs Simms was mere morning tea, as that lady was overworked opening things like bazaars to aid poor babies or golf clubs for rich ladies, and she was glad to be done with me. She said she would see more of me at her house. Would I come tomorrow? She had a big family and many friends and constituents, and some of them were always at home. She lived at Burwood, and a tram would take me to her door. This meeting had been arranged by Mr Simms and Mr Hardy, and I was to be left at the publishers. Mrs Simms said I would be wise to strike while the iron was hot.

Mr Hardy was nearing the publishers as Mrs Simms deposited me on the pavement, and he saluted her very politely. She was in a hurry, and away swung the cab. Mr Hardy, without seeming to see me, eased me off into the crowd and strode along to his Aunt's flat.

'Hooray!' he exclaimed when we were safely immured. 'Another day free from the crowd.'

I said no word lest I should expose my inexperience. I was

a scientist with her first case, terrifically interested and as clear-headed as a cucumber. Mr Hardy was having lunch sent in, and was free until the evening.

'Dear me,' said he, sitting down and looking at me with his bright abashing gaze. 'I'm back among the tall trees again with their bloom filling the world like heaven, when I look at you. To think I was once as eager and sensitive as you, ready to worship at the feet of the great! I wouldn't give up an hour with you for a week with the best girls that Sydney can bring to the post.'

This would have been inebriating if real, but Ma's training was sticking to me splendidly. Was he going to 'lead me astray'? It would be interesting to observe the preliminary stages. I was deprived of evening dress and dancing, but this would be something. Mr Hardy was sympathetic about my cramped life, my desire to escape, but success, he said, had to be attacked from the jump and given no quarter. Could I stand up to the fray?

I had no more idea of what to do than a wild duck scared up from the reeds of its dam. Mr Hardy put in that day instructing me. I must get away to London as soon as possible, while I was young and interesting. There was nothing for a person of real gifts here. I would soon be ruined if I lingered among the *local cacklers*. He used the same term as Mr Wilting.

I timidly advanced my dream of there being an Australian soul *on its own hook*, and my desire to be part of its development. Phew! How severe Mr Hardy was with me. That was a wicked socialistic notion which would ruin me socially and artistically. One should stick to the right crowd.

I gathered that I was well in the right crowd for a start, that I was the intimate of people who ruled the social roost, whom others—with money and position—strove to cultivate in vain. Stiff-necked egotism invaded me, for I felt it difficult to even my wits and ideas to many of the people I met, and they had B FLATS, but I did not expose my INEXPERIENCE.

I brought up the idea in a different form. Wouldn't it be self-respecting for Australian literature to do something on its own

404

hook? This was on account of his dictum that the first thing to do was to comb the gumleaves out of my hair.

'This tosh of doing things on your own or Australia's hook, where did you get it? You want to use any hooks that come handy. The other fellows' when you get the chance: they'll use your hook if you don't look out—without saying thank you. The whole secret of success is to beat the Philistines at their own game.'

I just sat and looked mousey. Even a fool is counted wise if she holds her peace.

'As for that notion of the brotherhood of man that you have, and loving the unwashed, anything in that direction is sheer drivel, drivel! Propaganda is fatal to any artist.'

'What does propaganda mean?' I inquired. I knew the word only as a joke to couple with improper geese.

'Aw!' he said impatiently, 'it's any of those luny ideas about the underdogs being superior because they have nothing, and the theory that their betters should support them in a velvet cage.'

'I see. It's propaganda to advocate justice for the weak and helpless. What is it to uphold the rich?'

'Ha! Ha!' he chuckled. 'It's darned good busineess. It pays.'

'I see,' I repeated with a chill down my spine. 'When you propagand for the top dogs it's not propaganda: it's like praising God: and God must be praised all the time or you'll go to hell.'

Mr Hardy laughed, but rather grimly. 'See here, a man must take pride in his breed, and uphold the Empire.'

'Of course, but couldn't there be different ways of upholding it?'

'Now, don't spring any more of that socialist rot about the young men's dreams, and the old men being able to rest, or you're a goner as a writer. Editors would scent you a mile off. See here, the biggest literary success, the greatest artist today is the most rousing imperialist. Gad, if only I could write like Kipling!'

To succeed by his recipe I should have to deny what I honestly felt. I should have to keep my inner self hidden from Mr Hardy or it would be bruised and sore. What puzzled me was that my first attempt was praised for its sincerity, and yet every man who wanted to marry me or to help me in my career immediately set out to change me into something entirely different. Why not in the first place seek the writings and the girls that they wanted me to be like? There were plenty of them. No one would ever have heard of me had I not been different, but that difference was immediately to be erased.

I could not argue with Mr Hardy. My emotions made my thought go woozy when he dragooned me both for provincialism and drivelling sentiment about the under dog. It was, oh, so easy to fall back on being a girl. That was the only side of any woman Mr Hardy would really want except those to do his cooking and laundry and other things that could be done for him equally well by men, only that he would have to pay them more.

His aunt was away for some days, and Mr Hardy spent every one of them except Sunday with me alone. At the beginning it was a game of parry.

'Dear me,' he said on the second afternoon. 'It is a shame that you have no pretty things. You are meant for evening dress: you have all the lines, and flesh like pink wax. Let me see your arms.'

I was shocked by this suggestion, but he insisted upon unbuttoning the simple wrist-band and turning up the bishop sleeve.

'Good gracious! and you waste your breath in admiring Edmée Actem. Her arms are drum-sticks compared with yours. To think of the scarecrows with the salt cellars under their ears and necks like a plucked fowl that are thrust upon a fellow in society, while you are covered up like a nun.' He insisted that mine was the arm of an odalisque, with dainty bones and dimpled wrist and elbow.

'Any man who wasn't ossified would devour your arms,' he exclaimed, proceeding to act upon his word. Then he devoured my lips until I was almost unconscious.

This was magnificently startling and thrilling and quite unexpected, that is in intensity and extent. There was something else that was intoxicating: the lightning intuition that he would not have gone as far as those devouring kisses, had I imposed restraint, even the raising of a finger. I had not invited him, being too modest for that, but neither had I exactly disinvited him.

The old wives' tales of men that filter to the most secluded girl represent men of maniacal sexual greed. I knew the gruesome tales told by midwives who have to protect their patients. The denigrating knowledge of prostitution was also known to me; there were milder confidences but always of feminine weariness opposed to merciless demands. No one had ever suggested that there would be any sensitiveness among men, that some men, however few, would, like myself, be incapable of *amour* if they were unacceptable or unless many other things such as the loved one, the time, the place and response struck twelve together.

This was a revelation of another side of the lure of the Groves of Daphne. One felt as the Ancient Mariner when he was the first that ever burst into that silent sea, for all I had heard of this previously.

Ned Crispin, Arthur Masters, Billy Olliver and others had not laid a finger on me. Was that too, male sensitiveness? I had not speculated on this before. Were men sensitive only in the presence of virginity? Once the bar was down did they lose all respect? It did not seem that I could ever find a man with whom I could retain my self-respect in such a surrender.

Mr Hardy and I were at variance on my deeper and inner ideas, but in playing the most magic game known we were equally matched in this vein of sensitiveness. I was his quarry because of my inexperience, but he was equally mine in my thirst for knowledge.

I was so elated by the discovery that maidenly safety lay in my own hands that I planned some sorties on my own account. This arrangement of going to Mrs Simms acted admirably for liberty. It was another inebriating thing to discover that in a great city one could have adventures and no one the wiser. In the bush the very crows and magpies reported every movement. Little wonder that city people were wickeder than those in the bush, with opportunities and temptations so available.

I decided to go secretly to the *Bulletin* office. The *Bulletin* was a mine of fascination, but not considered nice for young girls or clergymen. I had a friend in its office, Mr A. G. Stephens. I was much more eager to know him than dozens of silly old Sir James Hobnobs and stuffy professors and ponderous parliamentarians, but Mr Stephens was regarded as a devil with horns. I asked was he a liar or a thief or a rake, and the reply always was, 'Oh, no, not that, but the man is *wrong-headed*.' By persistent cross-examination I elicited that he discussed sympathetically the works of men who promulgated abashing views on sex and sociology: someone named G. B. Shaw, in particular. I sounded Mr Hardy about him, and it was laughable to hear his execration of a real hog who would subvert society. As for my meeting 'that crowd', well, that would be to throw pearls of innocence before the swine of dangerous propaganda.

Nothing could now have stopped me from going to Mr Stephens, and I climbed to his office and spontaneously burst into affection for him in a fraternal and intellectual way. How generous he was! He took me to tea, he gave me books, wonderful new books for my own that I had not dreamed of possessing. He talked in a whimsical way with twinkles in his eyes, adding to my literary education in every paragraph.

He asked about my future work, and was it true that Mr Hardy had me in hand? 'Would you advise me to make a model of Mr Hardy?' It was as funny as a circus to hear his views of Mr Hardy. He did not exhibit the vehemence against Mr Hardy that Mr Hardy had against Mr Stephens, but was equally damning. I should not think of such a man at all. His work was thin and vicious, imitative; he had been unable to work in Australian material, so had decamped to London and there echoed a cheap kind of smartness. It would be suicidal for me to ape such a course. Hardy lacked literary or any other ideals.

If some fairy had offered me a gift I should have chosen to be able to draw, so I asked breathlessly for Norman Lindsay. He was young like myself, his drawings were more shocking than my book, and he was equally talked about. Mr Stephens shook his head. Norman would not be interested in me: I was not his type physically or mentally. He woud be contemptuous of me as a bread and butter miss. No coaxing would make him disgorge Norman, but he gave me a book illustrated by him.

Mr Stephens sent a messenger to Geebung Villa with the parcel of books, but I would not let the Norman Lindsay drawings out of my possession and departed on the adorable little King Street cable tram with them clasped to my bosom. I was to lunch with Zoë de Vesey at Potts Point, and I burst in with the drawings in triumph. Mr Hardy was also there for lunch. Zoë did not bag social lions: people knew they were in SOCIETY if she noticed them, and so sought her invitations. With opportunity they turned from lions into tame house cats for ever under her feet.

I gurgled inwardly to hear Mr Hardy fulminate about those drawings. He said to Greville de Vesey that it showed what kind of a swine the fellow was to give such things to a child like Sybylla. Zoë said, 'Nonsense! I am so glad, Sybylla, that Mr Stephens gave you those drawings. I must ask him to lunch. If I had a daughter I would much rather give her Lindsay's drawings than let her read that sloppy trash of the Greatest Australian Writer for Girls—it is enough to bemuse girls mentally and morally.'

Mr Hardy wanted to take the Lindsay book from me, but I put it safely on Zoë's bed. I was looking forward to showing the drawings to Great-aunt Jane.

After lunch I got Zoë aside and said as she knew all about SOCIETY and LIFE and LOVE would she tell me how the fascinating belles managed to refuse to marry men and retain them for QUONDAM LOVERS. I was ambitious for such possessions. 'That's the ABC. You must make each man feel that he has broken your heart, and but for some fluke you would have married him. That works like a charm, but of course it requires a little finesse.'

Four o'clock found Mr Hardy and me together again in the flat. He may have been as great a rake as reported, who thought no more of cracking a woman's heart than of shooting a partridge, a man of the London world, a society idol who had achieved money and réclame by comedies of sultry duchesses and adulterous clubmen—Piccadilly club-men—but with me he was an Australian and kept to Australian rules in the game.

'Such innocence! Such inconceivable innocence!' he would exclaim. 'I should like to take you away and shut you up somewhere so that your quaint childish purity would never be spoiled, and keep you for myself.'

I *was* innocent. I had only intuition to guide me, but suddenly woman's knowledge had come and I was ages old in rebellion, and I did not kindle because I felt that Mr Hardy looked on women as being created solely for the delight of men. I often chuckled to myself to picture how incredulous Zoë or Edmée would have been that Goring Hardy found me sufficient entertainment for hours together. Zoë would have thought me on the high road to having my unseasoned heart cracked. She would not have guessed that I was offsetting exploitation of unsophistication by turning *amour* inside out to see the wheels of passion go round.

A fool is counted wise if he holds his peace, can be made to work by a woman if she is young and her eyelashes are long. Whirlwinds of sophistication won't protect a man from gullibility in this respect. A woman has the advantage if she is equally matched in intelligence. To start, a man is an open book to her while she has depths that he does not suspect because some of them he will not concede to her. He insists that they are not natural for a woman, and it being impossible to fully cheat nature he only cheats himself.

Goring Hardy would sit in a big chair and pull me to his knee. Oh, Aunt Jane and Ma if only you had seen that I could sit there without danger to my virtue, because that issue lay in my own hands! Dangerous—perhaps. So was it to ride a rampant stallion in girl-girly skirts, but approximately safe with skill. I had come to like the kisses, but any further caress or familiarity waited on a release which I did not give. Automatically any infringement of my code would have sent me up and away startled and resentful, and Goring Hardy was sensitively aware of that.

As he revelled in my innocence I grew more and more unsophisticated before his eyes. This was easy because I was genuinely blindfolded by INEXPERIENCE. Simple silence or to hang my head when in doubt had the desired result. I sat muffled in modesty: there was no chink through which a breeze of illicit *amour* could make its way. He would ask me what I was thinking. I withheld that I was pondering the monotony of such procedure, which could lead to nothing but consummation, and that was out of the question to me. Then, would there come only monotony and satiety again? Disillusion. Must one become drunk to find rapture in *amour*, or remain without illusion? It appeared so from what evidence I could garner, and that was a fatiguing thought to me.

If, in trying to usurp the maternal rights of the race as well as their own, men have accentuated the simple eternal feminine until it is cloying and infernal, no less have they made over-virilised masculinity equally infernal, crude and repellent.

'Haven't you any feeling? Are you made of ice? Are you anything of a woman or are you only a spirit?' he would demand, kissing my arm. I watched the aforesaid wheels turning, my innocence outwardly intensifying, quietly, easily self-contained. My attitude and very tone of voice had been ingrafted by generations of conventionalised, continent mothers who had swallowed the prescriptions laid down for them by men instead of developing themselves in the exercise of natural law, and with nothing to ease their lot but the superstition that the impositions foisted upon them had been God's will.

He would sometimes lay out a fairy tale. I was to go to London and have a retreat where he and I would work. How baffled I felt by INEXPERIENCE. It bound me like a cocoon. I imagined how Edmée would revel in like case, how histrionically she would handle it. All Sydney would know that Goring Hardy had been madly in love with her, that he had kidnapped her and shut her up with him while hostesses had been expecting them and suffering the ruin of parties by their absence. Everyone would know that her heart too had been just a little touched, and she would achieve glamour.

Whereas I did not get the enjoyment to which I was entitled because I did not know how to handle the situation and feared that Goring Hardy was regarding me as he might have a chorus girl or a social inferior who would be on all fours by his patronage. However, when you don't know what to do, do nothing. If a young woman in her teens wishes to pile on innocence one of the surest recipes is to murmur something about MOTHER. I said I did not think my mother would let me go to London. That shooed him off those suggestions.

'I wish to God I could marry you,' he would say vehemently, 'but I can't afford to.' He would be imploring, heated and almost angry by turns at what he called my iciness.

'I cannot marry you, but by jove, how I wish I could,' he would repeat, speaking as if to marry me he would only have to ask. I might have succumbed if he had invited me inside a wedding ring, but I knew, young and inexperienced though I was, that it would never work, and no man living could have tempted me outside a wedding ring. I had been so reared that any other suggestion was so deadly an insult that it iced any emotion I might have had.

On one occasion when he repeated his refrain I murmured, 'Perhaps it would not make anyone happy to marry you. Someone told me you are a terrible flirt.'

'The Old Campaigner, I suppose,' he sneered.

'No, she thinks you a very distinguished man.'

'Then, who was it?'

'It's in the air, from all the society women; they say you are a rake.'

He flared into sentiments ignoble before an unsophisticated girl, so defenceless that he could say, 'I'm sorry I can't marry you,' to her face without fear of being snubbed.

He said women were a pack of cats, only that was a politer word than he used. I said nothing at all. When the first fury passed he said women had no call to talk about men, that a woman's whole aim in life was to chase some poor devil and trap him into having to slave for her for ever after.

I thought this cowardly inconsistency seeing that women were compelled to marry by nearly all other occupations being closed to them, and by the pressure of public opinion. Men want it both ways like a bully arranging a game.

Mr Hardy continued that there wasn't one woman of all the pack, who, if she had the chance without being found out, would not have taken a swifter gait than he had, and that it was typical of feminine treachery for them to betray him to me; but I thought it loyal on their part to warn me.

'What did you say to those low cats?' he demanded.

'Nothing at all. I thought I'd wait for your defence.'

At that he smiled wryly. 'If you were an ordinary girl, I could make a defence, but all the things that satisfy other girls, seem to lose their value when offered to you.'

So this was an example of an uncrude man making love. He had been an artist in beating up his game. It may have been demoralising to the game, but perhaps EXPERIENCE cannot be harvested without some demoralisation. AUNT'S holiday was nearly done and I had my worries, so I said plaintively, 'Are you sure that you couldn't marry me—aren't you rich enough at all?'

'It's quite out of the question, little one. We must both marry money. Love in a garret and sacrificing one's self for the lower orders is delirium tremens. The common people are not worth lifting and are the first to turn on those who waste their talents in trying to better the world.'

It seemed to me that it was not merely a matter of lifting the helpless, but that certain people could not find oil for the soul in them if they did not give ear to the still small voice of justice and fair play.

'Then I must go away and not see you any more for I don't want to be so terribly hurt that I can't bear it,' I murmured, applying Zoë's recipe, to which I clung dumbly, refusing to explain or to add or subtract a syllable.

And that was the end of that little bit of psychological research.

CHAPTER 19

In Need of a Friend

There was a dismal letter from home awaiting me at Geebung Villa. Pa's sciatica, Ma's rheumatism, the rain gauge and every sign combined could not bring rain to the Southern District. It was in a ghastly state. Even the curlews were puzzled and the new moon unreliable. The rabbits, however, flourished unabatingly. Pa had been laying phosphorus baits and had got too many whiffs and was not well. Ma said I was needed at home to look after things.

It was time for me to go in any case. Otherwise I should lose my excursion ticket, and we had no money for an extra fare. I wrote to catch the mail to Possum Gully, stating when I should be in Goulburn. I had two more days in Sydney.

There was also a letter from Big Ears telling me he was going over the Gap if I continued to spurn his undying love. This scared me stiff. There would be a dreadful scandal. I should be regarded as a murderer, and no one would have any sympathy for a girl so unsexed as to write books. I could not handle this alone. Mrs Crasterton would not quite understand. I longed for a friend. Edmée was no good in that respect except for me to admire. It was all on my side. Her vanity would be upset that Big Ears had transferred his aberration. She might blame me for being underhand. I shrank from Derek's ridicule. Zoë, I felt, would be a tower of strength, but she had gone to Brisbane for a holiday.

Dear old Gaddy! He would understand. He would not lecture me about the way I did not want to go. I was ashamed that I had not appreciated Gaddy until this moment. He had given the blue sash in such a way that I could accept it. He had 'shouted' all the plays and concerts that I had seen. Like Sister Anne on the parapet, or wherever she took up her stance, I had been looking for a knightly lover and had disregarded Gaddy because he had a double-chin and a girth like the mayor-and-corporation, and breathed so that I could always hear him if the conversation died down a little. He could not be idealised as a lover, but there had been more pestiferation than pleasure in lovers as known to me; and Gaddy's person was formed to buttress friendship. I was famishing for a friend. When all is said and done, friendship is the only trustworthy fabric of the affections. So-called LOVE is a delirious inhuman state of mind: when hot it substitutes indulgence for fair play; when cold it is cruel, but friendship is warmth in cold, firm ground in a bog.

'Gaddy, come into the garden with me, like Maud,' I pled. 'I love it and the Harbour so, but I'm not safe there without you.'

Gaddy always did what he was asked without fuss, and no one noticed how unselfish he was because he was fat and old. He waddled around the flower beds plucking me a masculine bouquet—a leafless mixture of bloom, short of stalks and tightly compressed, but it smelt of heaven.

I confessed my trouble with Big Ears, and Gaddy wanted to know could I not consider him. I said I'd rather earn my living as a nurse maid. 'Well, then,' said Gaddy, 'just don't bother about him.'

'But supposing he should commit suicide!'

'I'll tell Derek, he'll knock sense into him.'

This brought relief mixed with fear of Derek's ridicule. I then told Gaddy about the drought and Pa being ill, and that I had to go home. Gaddy said that that was no sort of a career for a girl like me. I said my literary career had entirely gone bung in Sydney. Gaddy wanted to know what this fellow Hardy had been doing to help me. 'Is he putting you in a play or what? A fellow like that doesn't waste his time without getting something out of it.'

'What do you mean?'

'Oh, a little bird told me that a certain AUNT was away.'

So it seemed there were crows and magpies in Sydney as well as in the bush. 'He wanted me to turn into someone that I am not, and go to London, but we have no money for that.'

Gaddy snorted and walked about a bit. 'It's a shame,' he said. 'You need a patron, who would let you be yourself, and then you would have a brilliant career. Or you should have some cushy job with plenty of cash and leisure; but those jobs are given to men with influence. It would never do to let women have them, or where would men get wives?' He said this with a grin which extracted the sting.

Things would be righted now that women had the vote, but it would not be in time to help me, and I had not the necessary education. Gaddy breathed around the drive a bit and then we sat on the sea wall and he said, 'There is a way that it could be settled as tight as a trivet.'

'Tell me how?' I demanded eagerly. Gaddy looked strange, even apoplectic, and his eyes bulged as if he were twisting his squint straight to look at me.

When a woman has warning she can obviate the conventional fable that a man stutters or mutters about loving her more than life or a good dinner, and which necessitates the companion fibs about being unworthy of his love combined with humble thanks for the honour he has offered her in the opportunity to be his wife, likewise drudge, echo, unfailing flatterer and so on. I had no warning from Gaddy. He said that I needed time and leisure to develop my kind of genius, and as he had plenty of money for the job, and loved me better than all the flash and selfish exploiters of my youth and beauty put together were capable of doing, what about solving my problem and making him as proud and happy as a pup with two tails by becoming Mrs Gad.

It was a disgracefully crude thing to have done, but I put my fingers in my ears and fled to my room. No firm ground anywhere. 'Oh, Gaddy, Gad!' I said in my grief. 'How could you betray me so? How could you?' To lean on FRIENDSHIP and find treacherous AMOUR in its sheep's wool! Old Grayling and Henry Beauchamp at Possum Gully, and Big Ears and Gaddy in Sydney. My career had certainly gone bung at both ends and in the middle. Kerplunk! Bang!

I sat in the dusk and suffered my plight. Mrs Crasterton might think that I had led her brother astray. I folded the blue sash and put it on Gaddy's desk and continued to sit in the dark. I had recently read an article about men with gooseberry eyes and big girths making splendid husbands, but that girls passed them over to throw themselves under the feet of the man who would make their lives a misery because he could grace a dress suit and top hat. Gad and Goring. Goring had none of Gad's unselfish generosity. Gaddy might even be noble, yet so powerful is appearance that the phrases of AMOUR would have GLAMOUR from Goring while Gaddy was so fat that his protestations could be nothing but fatuous. Such are the stupid tricks that NATURE plays. I wonder why.

It was Mrs Crasterton's At Home night. Wheeler coiffured the ladies. I heard Gaddy come in and dress across the corridor. Derek called to his mother, 'Who's coming tonight?'

She named three members of the Cabinet, a university professor of note, an editor, several society nonentities, and the Chief Justice.

'The usual rabble,' said Derek, 'but I might look in to see the Chief.' Derek was designed for something brilliant in the law.

'That will be nice, darling,' cooed his mother. I sat and shrank and shrank in the dark and wished I were back at Possum Gully. I was misplaced in SOCIETY. Think how Edmée carried off admirers! They all made a fool of me, but think how she made fools of them so that they were for ever muttering around town about her, and trying to make out that she pursued them.

I was worried about Big Ears, as no doubt Gaddy would now leave him on my hands.

Everybody went down. There was great asking where was I, and at length Mrs Crasterton came and turned on the light and found me. I felt a terrible fool. I said everything had gone wrong. Poor old Pa was not well, and the drought terrible, and it was wicked to be in Sydney enjoying myself while Ma had been struggling at home. I was as bad as a man who went on the spree. I said that I had written of my departure.

Mrs Crasterton was kind and consoling. I pled to go to bed,

out she said that would be no way to get the best out of the opportunities that Ma had let me have, that I must come down and put my worries aside. Only amateurs of life let their set-backs be known. 'I'll send Wheeler to tie the sash. She is an artist with bows.'

I said if I appeared in the sash again it would seem as if I went to bed in it. Mrs Crasterton said that helped my quaintness.

I had to go down to dinner. Gaddy ate a large meal. He did not seem to be abashed or upset, whereas my food stuck in my throat. 'The old toad, to spoil friendship,' I kept thinking to myself. 'The old toad!'

Derek was an exposition of style from his patent leather toes to his shining hair. He gurgled and chuckled and winked at me until I did not know which way to look. At least it seemed that Big Ears couldn't be in danger of *felo de se*.

Derek took me aside at the end of dinner and said that he had taken up my case with Big Ears. 'He must be given a penny and told to take his hurdy-gurdy to some other corner. We don't like the noise here.'

'You won't let him commit suicide?'

Derek laughed. 'People with his make of ears never die for love. They propose to all the girls and at last one takes them and they rear a big family and praise God.'

Mrs Crasterton here summoned him. The Chief Justice had come early to have a few words with me. Derek surprised me by presenting me to the lovely old man with a beautiful mop of white hair. 'They've all tried to spoil her, but she's full of wit and common sense and takes everyone out of winding. She's the richest thing I ever met. Her judgments of people would amuse you, Sir.'

Derek beamed upon me every now and again. Gaddy actually shone with feats of interestingness and attentiveness to all and sundry. A couple of lieutenants from the Flagship engaged Edmée's attention. They were so carried away by her that they wound up like a clock stopping when Mrs Crasterton tried to put them in circulation. She remarked afterwards that so many young Englishmen reminded her of underdone suet dumplings.

A cabled item in the evening papers was discussed. A certain nobleman was suing for divorce from his wife and naming as co-respondent an officer of the Guards. It was infatuation for this lady, said the quid nuncs, which had resulted in Goring Hardy coming to Australia and remaining so long. He would be now free to return to London. They speculated whether or not he would marry Lady Hartlepool when she should be free, whether he had been writing during his visit or if his time had been entirely wasted. 'Was there no Sydney young lady able to engage his fancy?' inquired Sir James Hobnob, making eyes at Edmée. She languished and got away splendidly with the suggestion that she had not exerted herself, that he was much, much too old for her.

'A fascinating chap,' brayed Sir James. 'A real man of the world, and a great name in Australian literature.'

'You bet,' said Derek. 'The only Australian literary name that cuts any figure on a cheque.'

To my consternation Big Ears was announced. He soon found his way to me and concentrated his gaze upon me until I thought I should go off into yelps of nervous laughter. The Lord be praised, Edmée came to the rescue. She needed someone to set against the naval boys, and Big Ears was the nearest insect.

'That's what I call a wind in your favour,' said Derek, as he slipped into a seat beside me. 'What's this about you leaving us so soon? I had planned all sorts of things for you next week.'

'I should have been here next week,' I murmured. Then he said I was the jolliest little chum who had been in the house for ages. 'All sorts of freaks impose on the Mater, but I have felt that perhaps she imposed on you, letting you carry all this social blither without any armour, so to speak.'

I had heard him making fun of my lack of wardrobe and my unsophisticatedness. 'I've felt that I was chasing you from home,' I said.

'I always go out as much as possible when Edmée comes to stay. She'd jolly well have me up for breach of promise, if I wasn't too slippery. I warn Gaddy to put nothing in writing. I'm

419

sick of her family too. It's all a fellow can do to put up with the breadth and antiquity of his own without having someone else's mouldy pedigree thrust down his throat with the breakfast bacon and dinner soup.'

'Oh, but I think Edmée is lovely.'

'So does she, but all but herself recover from the delusion in time. If she doesn't soon hook a fish she'll be *passée*. Let's tackle Big Ears together. I'll be best man if you like.'

This was too much of a finish on the day and I could not keep my lips from quivering. 'I'm sorry,' he said quickly. 'I'll take the beastly little green-grocer out the back and we'll give him the order of the turnip.'

He beckoned to Big Ears and extracted me quietly through the hind door and took us upstairs to his own snuggery. I said I wanted to return safely into his own hands the lovely jewellery that Big Ears had so kindly lent me, as I was going home.

'And I've just been telling her not to take any notice of you,' chirped Derek, 'that you are such a devil of a fellow with the girls, you have half-a-dozen on the string at once. Sybylla is as serious as a pest, so I hope you have not been flirting with her.'

Derek was an audacious wag. I left the situation to him. He represented me as too young and simple to be pestiferated with the confisticated boredom of marriage. 'Why, even I would not dare to flirt with Sybylla. I'm letting her mature unmolested. I love her as a sister, but no larks with such a clever young lady.' If only he had flirted with me just a little, how delightful it would have been. He was so full of fun that he amused everyone. People always helped him laugh, but anyone who attempted to laugh at him came a cropper.

'You wait till she comes to town a year hence,' advised Derek. 'And what's more, my beauty, you're going into training for our tennis tournament. I mean to make a champion of you.'

'A champion at paying all the loose ends of expenses,' murmured Big Ears.

'Well, you'll have your portrait painted for that as soon as you get a tummy to fill the middle of a canvas. When training, the first rule is that you must not think of a lady. Nothing so puts a man out of condition.'

'That's pugilists,' protested Big Ears.

'What will put the punch into pugilists is good enough to give a forehand wallop to your serving. Now, assure Sybylla that she mustn't have any spoony drivel for a whole year at least. You are as free as air. So is she. In a year's time, we shall see.'

I gave Big Ears his bracelets. He began to discuss the possibility of getting into a first-class game, and we three returned to the drawing-room together.

The people dribbled away rather early that night. The Editor stopped a moment on the doormat talking to Mrs Crasterton and promised to ring up in the morning.

Gad insisted upon my having a talk with him in his study as I went up to retire. I did not feel too easy, but did not know how to escape.

'Dear, dear,' said Gaddy, 'so you have returned the sash like a novelette. You take life too hard altogether. Cuss it, I don't think it will hurt either of us for you to keep that piece of rag. So my little bit of spoof scared you! I did not understand what an inexperienced child you are. I'm awfully sorry that I upset you, because I have no other feeling but one of friendship.'

Waves of shame swept all over me to find what a fool I had made of myself, but I was learning the technique of dissimulation hour by hour. If only I had kept my head and applied Zoë's recipe!

'Oh, Gaddy, I really thought for a moment that you were in earnest, because others have been, you know, or thought they were for an hour or two, and you were such a lovely friend that it was sad to have you turn spoony.'

'That's what we are always going to be, I hope—friends.'

On this note we separated, I with the sash in my hand.

I had a tortured sleepless night. I roamed into Edmée's room. She was sleeping as soundly as Mrs Crasterton, and as audibly. All the lovers raging for Edmée or misconstruing her actions did not agitate her. A beauty, no doubt, early grows accustomed to that sort of thing. I envied Edmée her royal self-satisfaction. She had been adulated all her life so that her ears caught only approval, while mine, supersensitive and directed to concentrate on shortcomings, accumulated and retained only wounds and let the plaudits go.

I was disturbed by the antics of Big Ears and by Derek's intervention; and Gad's case was more botched-up than happily erased. I could not be sure that he had been joking. Even had he been, the worry was merely transferred to my being the fool. Derek too added to my humiliation by emphasising his brother-liness. Did I appear to him as absurd as a figure of romance as Gaddy did to me? Could I have had just one evening dress and dancing lessons I could have had some fun among people of my own age.

I should be relieved to escape to Possum Gully and leave my measley little pig-dog career behind me in Sydney.

CHAPTER 20

It Might Not *Have Been*

I breakfasted early to escape the embarrassment of Gaddy's presence. I ran down to the sea wall and, to my surprise, saw Derek and Big Ears disporting themselves in the shark-proof enclosure. Derek's dazzling teeth appeared in a gay smile. He had evidently begun training—was really a friend in shouldering the job of curing Big Ears.

During the forenoon Mrs Crasterton, Mrs Simms and the Editor of the previous evening were in telephonic communication. Then Mrs Crasterton asked me how I would like to remain in Sydney and do the WOMAN'S LETTER on one of the big newspapers. The present writer under the alias of Lady Jane, was paid seven pounds a week, but of course I could only be offered half that as a beginning. Even so, it seemed an enormous amount of money to have each week. Little me who never had a penny, at any rate not five pounds spent on me in a whole year! It was a dazzling prospect until I picked it to pieces.

What would I have to write? I should have to lackey around to all the SOCIETY affairs and describe Lady Hobnob's dresses and Sir James's wonderful cellar—in short kow-tow to a lot of people who had not advanced my search for something better than Possum Gully. Quite the contrary: they were disappointing results of the opportunities for which I was avid. What was the present Lady Jane going to do? This was rather glozed over. She had been growing duller and duller. I would go around with her for a month to learn the ropes. But what would she do then? That was her problem, not mine, I was told. 'But she would hate me for taking her position from her!'

'My dear, you'll never be a success in society or the professions unless you are indifferent about hate or love. It's a sign of your own worth sometimes if you are hated by the right people.'

That scared me off entirely. How could I take another woman's livelihood from her? I would rather share what I had with her. It was described as a tragedy that I, with my talents, should return to feeding the pigs and milking the cows, and white-washing hearths and shining pot-lids—a poverty-stricken grind in a petty domesticity which I hated. Mrs Simms said that nevertheless she was glad that I did not attempt the journalistic job, which for women of any mental capacity was so devitalising—writing rot about recipes and ball-dresses and becoming a disheartened and frustrated hack. I was so young yet, there was time or literary talent to develop. Writing was not, as some vocations, dependent upon youth. And that was that.

The glorious escape from Possum Gully, or what was to have been a glorious escape, had ended in nothing but a wish to return to Possum Gully as an escape from the escape that was not glorious.

That was a painfully flat day. Mrs Crasterton had made arrangements exclusive of me, as for the past week I had been *on my own hook*. Edmée had gone to a garden party. I arranged my belongings ready for flight. Life seemed to have run aground. The Harbour was divine in the full day sun, brilliant blue but with a breath of haze like a veil, and little grey cow tracks all across it like sashes on the tides. The small waves whispered of the tides on the rocks covered with oyster shells and draped in seaweed with a grand sedgy odour. The gulls rocked about like paper boats at play. Out beyond the Heads the swelling Pacific towered high as a plain. Behind was the city so full of people, but nowhere in it had I found anyone to whom I could tell my perplexities with any hope of being understood or really helped. They would criticise and advise, but Ma and Great-aunt Jane had already furnished me with that kind of friendship and assistance.

I sat on the sea wall and looked down at the jetty at Pannikin Point. We always come home to Geebung Villa that way when we had no luggage needing a cab. Gaddy got off the ferry boat in company with a tall man. Gaddy added to the friction in my thoughts, so I stayed on the terrace with the camellias and watched the shipping. Presently he approached, calling me. When he appeared before me he flung out a leg and waltzed, an indulgence for aesthetic reasons improper to a corpulent man.

'Do you know who has put off his departure a whole day on purpose to see you—enough to give you swelled head, young woman. He heard about you on arrival, put in last night reading your book—guess who it is.'

'It couldn't be Renfrew Haddington!'

'The very man! My idea of a real man and a literary josser combined—very rare, for I largely agree with old Wilting about local cacklers.'

Here was the really truly GREATEST AUSTRALIAN POET, but when a man had so many other distinctions it was easy to overlook this trifling indigenous dementia. He was known as one of the really influential journalists on the Australian press. He had represented the *Melbourne Tribune* in the Boer War. His despatches had been so sound that they had also been snapped up by London and American journals. His book on the war was considered a masterpeice alike by those who thought the war ignoble and by the swashbucklers. He had been lecturing in the United States and was on his way home.

Gad reminded me of all this, but I was not excited. I was subdued by campaign bruises. EXPERIENCE was teaching me that people sought me for their own entertainment, not for mine, and that those supposed to be interesting were frequently less so than those reported to be otherwise.

I had to return to the house with Gad, feeling insignificant and crest-fallen, but I did not care. This was my last night in Sydney. Pa and Ma had not been in Sydney for more than ten years, and as far as I could see it might be all that before I could come again.

Mr Haddington came across the lawn to meet me as I kept behind Gaddy. He was tall and broad and brown, and there was something restful and enfolding about him so that I ceased to be driven to act any role whatsoever.

I drank of his understanding as I looked into his deep kind eyes, and gained assurance as he looked deeply back into mine. The world lit up with new possibilities. I was glad that Renfrew Haddington was alive and there holding me by the hand. I was refilled with the false hope of youth that happiness could come to me some day with shining face as a prince or knight and that a struggle to remain available for such an advent was worth while.

Manliness seemed to emanate from the man, with patience and strength as well as kindliness. He had bumpy features and iron grey hair, and no superfluous flesh. The eyes looked searchingly from cavernous sockets with an illumination of spirit which he could impart. Most men are so elemental that I suffocate in my antiquity of spirit by comparison, but Mr Haddington suddenly made me feel young and overcoming as if the awful things in life could be reformed. Here was a soul and mind in which one could take refuge.

I do not remember saying much to him, yet I felt that he knew a better self of me than consciously existed. He was departing on the Melbourne Express, and could not stay to dinner.

'Men will always seek you for your sympathy and understanding,' he said, as he held my hand in parting.

I was late down to dinner, and as I came in, Edmée was discussing the recent caller in her own style, and impressed upon me that I had been highly honoured. 'What do you think of him?' she asked for the third time.

'I like him better than any human being I ever met,' I said, just like that.

'The doll awakes from petrifaction,' laughed Edmée. 'We must get his son over from Melbourne. He must be as old as you.'

'I have never met Mrs Haddington,' remarked Mrs Crasterton.

'She's a remarkably fine woman,' said Gaddy. 'She needs to be to measure up to Haddington.'

I excused myself early. I wanted to write notes of good-bye to be posted on the morrow, but instead I sat recalling how Mr Haddington had looked as he stood talking to Gad on the

426

lawn in the light of the setting sun while I watched him from the drawing-room window curtains. I examined the inscription in the book he had given me. Magical that his hand had written there for me, the product of his own brain. If such a man was honoured because he wrote books, surely the attempt was not unvaliant for an ignorant girl. Surely none but piffling people thought that girls should not write. Renfrew Haddington would not think so. There must be numbers of similar men in the world. I had met few because I knew so few of all kinds, and humanity in the aggregate is so chock-a-block with culls.

When the household retired I continued to sit by my window looking at the twinkling lights of the city, lovely, alluring: they should have held something much nobler than I had met.

Why had Mr Haddington stirred me so? I couldn't be in love at first sight with a man old enough to be my father—that would be disgusting; but why should he be able to give a different meaning to life?

As many as a dozen old men have tried to probe if there was a real Harold Beecham to correspond to the hero in my book, and when I assure them that Harold Beecham was made out of imagination they still cling to their own notion. Many young men have told me that they *are* Harold Beecham or intend to be: girls ask is it true that Harold Beecham was drawn from their suitors because the suitors are claiming so to give themselves added weight and attraction. HAROLD BEECHAM! Pooh, he was the best I had been equipped to imagine at the time. Mr Haddington had given me an idea of something much better furnished. Now I could see what Mr Wilting and others meant when they said I had been too inexperienced to attempt a love scene. Mr Hardy at one end of the scale and Mr Haddington at the other had been a revelation.

I fell all night from spoke to spoke of a mental wheel:

His son is as old as you are.

His wife is a mighty fine woman.

I am the merest of women and the most special cannot marry where they list.

The one man of our dreams would be sure to rush into
    marriage early.
Nothing matters.
So what does it matter after all?
Pa always says it will be all the same in a hundred years.
A hundred days, a hundred months are a long dull stretch
    when taken piecemeal.
His wife is a remarkably fine woman.

This at any rate was something to be thankful for. If a man
with the power to so impress me had been such a driveller as
to yoke with a nincompoop or a 'tart', I should have felt disgraced.

The following night I fell from spoke to spoke of a different
wheel—that of the gallant steam engine which tugged the mails
and passengers from Sydney to Melbourne.

Despite an arid interior my last day in Sydney was a heavenly
specimen of weather—blue and gold—the Harbour lovelier than
a dream. Every garden in the roomy suburbs sprawling on the
city's ridges gave forth a wealth of roses and semi-tropic bloom.
The thoroughfares were decorated with comely young people
in white and gay colours. The city piles were outlined against
the effulgent sunset ocean of liquid gold as I returned to Geebung
Villa for the last time. The misty bays were a fairyland of twinkling lights as we crossed in the ferry and took a cab to Redfern.

Mrs Crasterton was horrified that I should be travelling second
class, but as in the matter of dresses she did not let it run to
her pocket. 'All those dreadful, coarse men,' she whispered. 'Are
you sure you will be safe with them? They look like working
men.'

That's what they were—station hands—and I felt as safe with
them as with a gum-tree. 'We won't be out of Sydney before
they will be doing everything for me.'

She gave me a final hug and thanked me for my visit, which
she said had brought so many old friends around her and so
many new ones that she was quite rejuvenated.

The men, who were shearers, disposed of my luggage and
gave me my choice of a seat, just as I expected, and I leaned

from the window to draw a breath from the luxuriant gardens of Strathfield, where the lights were putting out the starry evening.

The men talked of the drought and the terrible plight of the land immediately beyond the coastal belt, but the present hour was redeemed by moonlight. Moonlight is as lovely and as thrilling as a phantom. The silver glory etherealises the grimmest landscape. Soon it transformed the drought and filled the wide night universe with mystery and enchantment.

Scent of wattle drifted in from Liverpool onward. The good engine roared and tugged, shaking the tiny houses of fettlers beside the line, on, and on, through the potency of the wide and silent but echoing night. Not a month since I had left the bush, but EXPERIENCE had made it a cycle.

Otherwise I was taking nothing back from the city but a blue sash and the books given to me by Mr Stephens. I was clearly not a getter. Financially, I was as helpless as Pa. But my retreat was only a withdrawal. I would come again. I must start again from the beginning. I must stick to myself henceforth. I must go beyond Sydney. Few of the people I had met in Sydney had anything more in them basically than those around Possum Gully. The difference was in their having and doing, not in their *being*. There were greater worlds beyond Sydney. I should seek them. But henceforth I should not make holiday for others by exposing my intentions.

As the train pulled in to Bowral, Moss Vale and each little station I pondered on the people who at first predicted that my head would be turned by flattery and lionisation, and a little later had accused me of being abnormal or petrified because no one had been able to make any impression on me except through my affections.

Well, there wasn't a woman among them who could hold a candle to Ma, not in housekeeping, in diction, in reading or in anything to which she addressed her talents. Ma could have kept a big institution shining and well-oiled in every wheel, and yet she was stuck in the bush in a situation in which her capabilities were as wasted as a cannon fired off to quell a mosquito—pure squanderation of the cannon and unnecessarily flattening to the skeet.

Thus I went from spoke to spoke till Goulburn, where I left the train and went to the Commercial for the remainder of the night.

CHAPTER 21

Back on the Land

Eusty came to meet me with old Bandicoot and the buggy. Mr Blackshaw had come in with him to do a little business and save horse-flesh. The day was a horror. A western hurricane filled the world with wind gales, icy as winter, and fogged the air with dust. There had been no rain. There was no sign of spring.

I expected things to be rather desperate, remembering what they had been a month ago, and letters from home had had but one theme, but coming from the green coastal belt, the city warmth, brightness and beauty, where people daintily dressed rode on the comfortable trams and enjoyed every other convenience and entertainment of existence, the contrast was shocking. The bare cooked paddocks by the way filled me with a feeling of despair.

'It's a good thing you didn't stay away any longer or I reckon you would have had to walk home. Old Bandicoot is almost too poor to draw you,' remarked Eusty, giving the brave old friend an unnecessary flick of the whip and raising the dust from his long shabby coat from which his bones protruded.

Pa was about the same. 'Serve him right,' continued Eusty. 'He oughter learn not to be pokin' his nose so close into the baits. We can take a short cut through Burrawong, the gates ain't locked.'

Burrawong was one of the larger stations in which much of the good land of the district was locked. The cockies usually had to follow the main road, but since the drought the owners had opened one of their permanent waterholes so that the poorer settlers could cart water to their homesteads. They were to be seen with a cask and a dray bucketing water into troughs to a few staggering animals which had been watered thus since January, now eight months past.

In a hot dust storm the sun shows as a ball of blood, this

431

being a cold sirocco, it showed like a full moon. I shut my eyes against the whirling grit and wrapped my cape around me while Eusty urged poor old Bandicoot to keep toddling. In the paddocks of Burrawong, sheep skins lined the fence. The emaciated carcasses attracted flocks of black croakers and their dismal clamour filled the day.

'They've put on a couple of men to each paddock to skin the sheep as they die,' remarked Mr Blackshaw. 'They'll have their work cut out after this wind. It topples the jumbucks over and they ain't got strength to get up again. There were a few clouds knocking about yestiddy, but this wind has cooked their chances. Burrawong is about cooked, and so are we.'

'Like us,' chimed Eusty. 'Nearly all the cows pegged out while you were away. Old Roany and Nellie went first, and we have to lift up old Taralga twice a day; she can't hold out much longer.'

A dray passed loaded with wood and drawn by three horses. The tears came as I noted the condition of the animals. That morning they had been lifted on to their feet, and yet they struggled so gallantly for their incompetent masters—panting, trembling, staggering through their purgatory under lash and objurgation. My heart seemed to suffocate.

Eusty's voice was crisp with cheerfulness. Drought and debt had no power to dispirit him—it took a stomach-ache or something personal. 'What's making you so flaming down in the mug, Sybylla? It's us—who've been at home grafting away like fury while you were flying round among the toffs having a slashing time—that ought to hang our lip. Them city folks livin' on us people on the land!'

Bandicoot came to a dead stop opposite a man who was mending a gate. 'Hello! The old moke still alive and kicking,' he observed. 'Might get rain next month,' he continued hopefully. 'Pet of a day ain't it?'

'We're about drove off of the land,' said Mr Blackshaw. 'Well have to join the unemployed and get seven bob a day minimum.'

We dropped our passenger at the corner of his own fence and toiled on to our destination, Bandicoot's old coat sopping with the sweat of weakness.

'Put the poor old chap in the stable till he cools, and give him a handful of straw,' commanded Pa.

Ma adjured us to get inside quickly and close the door. She had cleared the dust away twice that day, and was now going to desist until the wind subsided. Home was a dreary spectacle. Four-footed friends had died of their sufferings in my absence. Only the hardiest plants in the garden survived. Everything had a dirty grey film irritating to the touch. Grit on the plates, grit between the teeth, grit on the pillow, grit in one's soul, ugh! An all-pervading smell of dust—ugh!

Dear old Pa was cheerful. He greeted me like a real friend and said we were better off than the people out West, whose homes were sometimes entirely buried in sand. He wanted to hear of everyone I had met, especially his former associates. When we were settled for the evening before the fire—one thing that the dust could not spoil—Pa, by eager questioning, had me telling of everyone I had met and what they said—with certain reservations.

'You saw Goring Hardy, did you have any talk with him?'

'Oh, yes, he was quite chatty, and advised me to go to London.'

'How did he suggest finding the means?' inquired Ma.

'He dropped the suggestion when I told him how we are situated.' I did not add, and after he had found my maidenly citadel invulnerable.

'You've had a great holiday,' interposed Aunt Jane. 'Times have changed since I was a girl. If I had acted as you have, flouting modesty and blaspheming God, I should have been locked up on bread and water instead of being flattered and entertained. I don't know what the world is coming to with vulgarity and immorality.'

'People will give you a little adulation, when it costs them nothing,' remarked Ma with withering actuality, and got out the darning.

Bung went my Sydney career. I was back on the land at Possum Gully.

The dust storm took three days to clear away, and left everything in a deplorable condition. It meant house-cleaning from end to end. I hated the coarse work after a taste of city luxury and conveniences, but I did not dare let my feelings escape me. The great adventure to Sydney had ended in débâcle. I sat amid the débris of hopes and expectations—only nebulous ones it is true, but all that I had had—and I had to grope my way out.

I produced the Lindsay drawings as a counter irritant. Ma dismissed them with one blast. She said that THAT was all that men cared for, but women soon had too much of it.

I left the book about just to see—well just to have the figures seen by Aunt Jane. Pa said that there was nothing immoral in the human body, that it was a work of NATURE. Aunt Jane agreed, but said that ******** **** * ***** ** God, but that delicacy should be maintained. She put on her specs and singled out an example. ***** *** Ma said Hhhh * *** ***** ******* ** ******* *****. I had not sufficient experience to refute such dicta. I hid the drawings at the bottom of a packing case.

No one mentioned Henry. He had not written to me lately, and was still away in Queensland. I hoped he had forgotten me, but should he have done so it would be one more nail in the coffin of AMOUR, another of Pan's 'Half told Tales'.*

So many kiss today, and die tomorrow:

And is remembrance sweet, or sweet and sorrow?

For some say only sweet; and sweet and bitter some . . .

Ah, who can end the tale, when all the dead are dumb!

As the days passed the mail brought a newspaper with Lady Jane's letter. She had a long paragraph about the departure of Mr Goring Hardy, Australia's greatest literary man. He had been in demand among smart hostesses, and there would be an ache in more than one heart, Lady Jane dared suggest, when his ship carried him away from his native shores. No Australian girl had

* *'Bulletin' Verse*

434

been able to interest him, but one beauty of the glorious eyes and velvety shoulders . . . Easy to discern this as Edmée. She was surely destined for a brilliant career matrimonially unless she was too ambitious and stayed too long in the stable, as Big Checks put it.

Lady Jane's letter kept me informed of those of her clients or victims whom I had met.

Aunt Jane asked me what I intended to do to help my parents. 'You met Big Ears, why didn't you improve your chances there? And what about Mrs Crasterton's brother?'

'I don't think anyone would want either of those,' I murmured.

'Hadn't Mrs Crasterton a son too?'

'Yes, but he's a terrible swell, wouldn't look at anything but a SOCIETY girl.'

As the dreadful hot months dragged by, killing more and more suffering animals and pet plants and trees, I read that Big Ears had become engaged to a top notch SOCIETY girl who was also a tennis enthusiast. He was a valuable property as represented by Lady Jane. Glamour oozed from her tales of him. Yet I had discerned nought but a creature that I would have wilted to acknowledge as my mate. I hoped that Aunt Jane would miss the news of his wedding.

I found pluck to inquire of Pa what had happened to Old Grayling.

'Pillaloo!' grinned Pa. 'He's kept in hobbles now. The flash buggy has disappeared.' His daughters had come to see Pa and Ma specially to apologise for the old man's dementia. Silly old toad had made such a noise that it was one of the jokes of the district by now!

Horrors!

Our stoical land suffered, and we and the animals with it. The year ran down to harvest, a poor pinched harvest, but sufficient for the few remaining animals. I received a cheque for my little book. The first instalment of three-pences had totted up to one hundred pounds. It was a lot of money to us. It saved us that year. There was also an editor on one of the big dailies who

435

encouraged me to write prose sketches, and by these I sometimes made twenty-five shillings a week. He was gentle and kind and kept watch with his blue pencil against any originality that would have got me into trouble. At first I nearly sank through the boards because of the sentences he cut out—always those I had prized as my own discoveries. That they were deleted showed that I must be lacking in good form, but intuition quickly taught me what was acceptable.

I was able to write these articles at odd moments, and struggled more diligently with housewifery to offset the delinquency of attempting to write. An author enjoyed no prestige in Possum Gully.

My rebellious discontent surged up more furiously than ever. I craved the pang and tang, the joys and struggles of life at the flood. I was willing to accept my share of tears and pains if I could have also some of the splendour and passion which were my temperamental right. Was all my power of emotion wrong?—something to be suppressed till it evaporated like youth itself—something ladled out to me for a span and passed on to another futile creature of an hour?

On being honest with myself I felt that any God set up, except by little Mr David, was contrary to a sane conception of a just and omnipotent God worth the name of Creator. The rubbish about self-will, and wrongs being rights in some foggy heaven could not stand against even little Jimmy Dripping common sense. The voice of the wind urges the soul to deeper conceptions of spiritual wisdom. The magic in the wide sunlight cancels the trivial church image of a God fashioned on the pattern of an unprepossessing old man. The contentment preached by pastors and masters to the less fortunate in goods and opportunities sounds like an impudent assumption of betterism by those who are often in the worse collection of parasites. Why should Ma's extraordinary skill and management, which enables her to excel a fashionable *couturière* and equal a *chef* and baker, be wasted, while poor old Lady Hobnob—to take one example—who cannot overcome B FLATS has a glorious mansion in a heavenly situation at Potts Point? Why should Pa, who had tried to help the struggling men by fearless and honest measures, have been robbed of his property while a vulgar old vulture like Sir James Hobnob, who had diverted to himself a fortune out of public funds, should have all the honours and be invited by the King to dine at Buckingham Palace and to sleep at Windsor Castle? I hated all the doctrines of Possum Gully and its want of works, but had given up saying so aloud.

About Easter there was a bobbery in Lady Jane's column. What do you guess? A SOCIETY WEDDING. A BEAUTY and a CON-FIRMED BACHELOR. Most notable wedding of the year. OLD FAMILIES, SOCIETY, all were marshalled. Shower bouquets, a dozen bridesmaids—a big galanty show.

I laughed to picture Gaddy in the middle of bridal flutter. What would he do with his corporation—ah, what . . .

No; I did not envy Edmée her bridegroom. Quite the reverse. Nevertheless, I did seem a petty failure with my hands showing more glaringly than ever the effects of coarse manual toil, and my feet still unacquainted with silk stockings, while there was Edmée in satin and orange blossoms filling the newspapers with her success. I envied her her suitability to success, her disregard of consistency, her obliviousness of personal detractors.

I could not complain of lack of opportunities. I wondered how many other women Goring Hardy had practically kid-napped for a week just for their company and nothing but kisses—ardent but respectable? Yet I had not improved the shin-ing hour.

I had fled from Gaddy in such a way that he had protected his vanity by pretending that his advances were spoof. In Big Ears, the catch of the previous season, I had discerned only a flap-eared weakling who stuttered prayers. He had offered to abrogate prayers until I was 'saved', but no, here I was back in Possum Gully and he not yet returned from a tour in Spain, and I had nought but a dream tho' it ne'er came true.

Bung! Bung! Pop! Pop! went all respect for romance. Edmée

could put Gaddy in the position of the romantic lover and affinity that she had gushed about. Gaddy, who had scoffed at Edmée, succumbed to her. Big Ears, who was going to commit suicide for love of me, forgot in a day. Marriage evidently was a piece of trading: one took the best animal procurable and got on with it. Ah, me! Oh, well!

I wrote things at odd times, things that I wanted to write, different from those I wrote to please the kind Editor, who was desirous of helping me with bread and butter. But nothing found favour with publishers or editors in Sydney or Melbourne. They said they expected something *different* from me. I gave thought to this, based upon their suggestions for acceptability. I deduced that I *was* different, and that they wanted me to be the same as all the others, to be one of the reigning school. Also they had stories from England. Their readers preferred English stories.

Well, so did I. I had had no notions about realistic Australianism until misdirected by old Harris. He had brought upon me all this trouble, this defeat. I wrote to ask him whither now?

I never had a reply. He was dead.

Any poor LOCAL CACKLERS who wrote to me and of which, with my OWN HOOK conceit, I was emphatically one, were assured that there was no hope for anyone in Australia. We must by hook or harpoon get away to THE BIG SMOKE.

For what does it matter if a scribe gain the encouragement of CRITICS and become the hope of the booksellers and circulating libraries that he will write a second best-seller, if the scribe himself does not gain enough profit either to earn the respect of those he lives among or to escape from them?

It was not that I did not hanker for the fleshpots of life, but that I was not constituted to accept the conditions which went with those offered to me. This depressed me acutely, for I was of a sociable nature and loved all that radiance and beauty of the world and life which is open only to those with means.

I had managed to alleviate my early unhappiness about God by discrediting the unpleasant representations of His vindictiveness with which religions abound, by crediting only what was beautiful and noble in conception and by eschewing prayer as a superstition. This helped to diminish God the tyrant, but I had not found God the refuge and helper. One of my elderly friends-by-correspondence was warning me against self-pity as a debilitating affliction and directing my mind towards philosophy, but philosophy is rather an arid diet when one is hungry for adventure and romance.

Thus went the days with empty heads and dusty feet.

Possum Gully fell back to normal after throwing me up. It grew poorer socially. The genial and conversable Father O'Toole was succeeded by a man with beetling brows and a brogue to match. Our R.C. friends invited us to his inauguration, at which he berated his flock and ordered them to have nothing to do with Protestants under penalty of purgatory. The Reverend peasant was doubtless ambitious for a bishopric, for it seems that in creeds or politics the less Christianity and reason and the more partisanship the surer the official rewards and honours for the protagonists.

Dear little Mr David had likewise departed. In his stead we had a visitation of English curates. Eusty said they talked like choking magpies, and many a time he had to be driven from the entertainment of mimicking them to his work. They seldom called. They preferred the richer fleshpots of Burrawong, venerated the owner as a 'squiah' and mistakenly relegated all cockies to those who should order themselves lowly and reverently to their 'bettahs'.

Billy Olliver had removed to a place near Inverell. From the day of the Show I had not seen him nor heard from him. Henry's consequence had evidently scared him from the course. Billy's friend, the teacher who had come in Old Harris's place, took me to task over Billy. He said it was a cruel thing to have broken Billy's heart—such a true honest fellow—no frill about him, but a thorough gentleman. How could I break his heart when he had never opened the question of love with me at all, how did Billy's spokesman know that it was not my heart that

439

had been trifled with? EXPERIENCE was showing me that this breaking of hearts and the hope of constancy in AMOUR were mirages like those encountered in the delirium of typhoid fever. I had to take refuge in dreams—dreams of the distant fields so green because they were far away.

CHAPTER 22

So to Speak!

Henry Beauchamp was nearly a year away in Queensland. The seasons there enabled him to take up the slack of his property pinched by drought in the Southern District. He came back overland, arriving first at Moongudgeonby, or Five-Bob Downs, as it had come to be known, as he said, over his head and under his nose, because of my pranks.

The warnings against his fickleness were contradicted by his actions, but the smut of certain allegations remained like the smoke from a railway engine when you get in a tunnel. Renewed business around Goulburn enabled him to spend a lot of time at Possum Gully.

We reopened our old battles, he being armoured in the dogma that it was NATURE for women to serve men and bring children into the world regardless of whether or not the world was a fit place to receive them. He said he could give me much more than I could ever make by writing. 'Marriage,' he insisted, 'gives a woman standing. If she gets hold of a fellow with any sort of a head on him she has lots more standing than sour old school teachers and these other old maids, on their own, can have.'

STANDING!

'You don't allow a woman any standing at all except by being the annexation of a man,' I said.

He laughed in his large healthy way. 'Well, I did not arrange the world.'

'Yes, but you could help rearrange it,' I flashed, though I knew that among all the billions of men in the world there were few so just and brave that they would attempt any rearrangement that would lessen their top-dog self-confidence and loot; and none of these except Pa had ever undergone a sojourn at Possum Gully.

'You'll have the vote when you are old enough. The rearranging of the world is in your own hands now; and I voted for woman suffrage.'

'There's a lot of evolution in that, and evolution like posterity will be rather late in doing anything for the current generation.'

'Oh, Lord, I can't make out how you can have so much rebellion in such a small soft frame.'

Many less stupid men than he would be surprised if they could see into the hearts of women who lie beside them so passively, or could hear what they say when the ogres of their bosom cannot hear.

'You'll find women more against your ideas than men.'

'That is because they think it will please men—merely a matter of business advertisement.'

'Ah,' he continued complacently. 'You are not meant to be one of those brainy old man-haters who would rather have a snake around than a child. You were meant for love and motherhood.'

'Man-haters,' I contended, 'are those who are game enough to object to the present state of affairs for their motherhood. One such woman has more power of deep loving than half-a-dozen of the namby-pamby over-sexed womanised things.'

'Look here,' I warn Henry over and over again, 'don't you risk me in the matrimonial basket. Throw your handkerchief on one of the dozens of girls and widows who would snatch it eagerly. The world is infested with women who will agree with you—little darlings without intelligence, and boastful of it, who have been trained to be afraid of the night and to screech at a mouse and all that sort of thing. I love being out alone in the night, and mice could sleep in my pocket without frightening me.'

If we are out riding when these discussions take place, he chews a few more gum leaves and says, 'Thank you, no. The dolls have no spirit. I'd sooner marry a cow. I'd run away from a doll in three weeks.'

He has the same mentality as Goring Hardy—take the world as it is and be comfortable and a success. Take me and set to

442

work to squash me into the groove of the noodles. The difference between Mr Hardy and Mr Beauchamp is in their interests, Henry's being those of a man on the land and the politics appertaining thereto, and Goring having the literary tastes and politics of the Londoner.

'After your first child,' Henry maintains, 'you'll settle down as steady as a church.'

My first child! Something to break my spirit and tether me to the domestic tread-mill! Had he known my dreams of a first child he would not have uttered that mistake.

Even so, a first child need not last for ever. It could contribute to the fulfilment of life if it were not followed by a dozen others. I claim the same right as all the Father O'Toole's to be a spiritual parent of my race rather than to submit to the ideal or to follow the example of the mother rabbit.

I repudiate the crawl theory that we should be servile to our parents or to God for the bare fact of a mean existence. Most people are satisfied with a world run in a wasteful insanitary fashion. I am not. They are unashamed that seventy-five per cent. of human beings are fit only for the scrap heap. I am not. They are thankful to thrive while others starve. I am not.

I rebel with all my lung force against sitting down under life as it is, and as for a first child being an instrument of enslavement, both for his own and his mother's sake, 'twere better he should never be.

The two greatest women in Australia are unmarried, and it would be a good plan for a few more to support them, to remain free to ventilate the state of marriage and motherhood and to reform its conditions.

'You just talk through your hat to be entertaining,' Henry continued after a while. 'You'll have to marry someone.'

'Why?'

'You could not endure to be despised as an old maid who could not get a man.'

At that I galloped right away from him leaving him a far speck on the glistening road that rises towards Lake George. I galloped until Popinjay was blown. Henry would not overtax Black-Dappled Grey to carry his sixteen stone at top speed. I reined-in on the crest from which far to the south can be seen the dreaming peaks of the mountains beyond the Murrumbidgee. Their beauty is a banner of spiritual strength raised for me to follow away from Possum Gully limitations.

Never in face of that wide brilliance of eternity stretched on space would I give in to mental decay and a dun dim routine calling for nothing beyond the endowment of a halfwit.

Despised for being an old maid, indeed! Why are men so disturbed by a woman who escapes their spoliation? Is her refusal to capitulate unendurable to masculine egotism, or is it a symptom of something more fundamental?

Why have men invented monogamy? All the laws, all the philosophies and religions of academic education, as well as organised fighting and politics, are men's inventions and are preserved by men as their special concern and business.

I chuckled into Popinjay's twitching ears to imagine the shock my ideas in this direction would be for grandmas of the tame hen order and for Celibate Fathers. Of all the people I knew perhaps only two or three would discuss my theories without hysteria, though bishops and great-aunts can accept harlots as necessary and count technical virgins as more worthy of honour. This was another thought which to utter would be madness, and which to suppress seems canting cowardice.

Henry came jogging up with his strong white teeth showing in a smile. 'What thought smote you to run away like that?' he demanded.

I diverted him with a bit of surface smartness. 'I was thinking that it must be difficult to sustain the fragrance and escape the frowsiness of marriage: singleness would be more aesthetic.'

'Is that all! Now tell me if you could order a man to fit your ideas, what would he be like?'

I did not reply that it would be one who could put his finger on some hidden spring in himself and in me and in grand fusion reveal the fullness of life.

444

'Come now, what's this fellow to be like?'

'At least he would not be afraid of freedom and the light of understanding for women as well as men. His mind would not prescribe asinine limitations for women as part of God's will. He would not take rabies at the idea of a world where there would be no hungry children, no unprovided old age, and he would be ashamed to have harlots at street corners awaiting his patronage and then come to clean girls and blither about LOVE.'

'Hooray! Tell me some more.'

'There are other things he wouldn't be that I have learned from old wives' gossip, but I cannot enumerate them without being indecent. So many old wives take all the sweetness out of life because life has taken all the joy and sweetness out of them: and lastly, no potting, panning and puddening for me for a set of noodles that might as well remain unborn for all that they attain.'

When Henry next caught up to me he said, 'You have two years more to get these notions off your chest. They are no end of fun.'

He refuses to release me until the 39–21 hour has arrived. As he will then be within a month of 40, and refuses to wait any longer because 39 will look so much better on the marriage certificate. I have not quite dismissed him because only in marriage can respectable women satisfy curiosity. The penalties for violating the social code are so painful that they are avoided by the sensitive with the care exercised against smashing over a precipice. Thrice free must be the innate wantons or the coarse who can plumb all heights and depths of curiosity and suck entertainment where they list unhampered by the agony of shame. The over-sensitive risk many chances of atrophying by the wayside.

Popinjay was restive for her foal, shut up at home, and grew so fractious that I had to relinquish argument and give myself fully to the delight of handling her as she reefed and plunged. At length I gave her her head at full gallop down the long steep incline, feeling sure that she could keep on her feet and I in my saddle on her round slippery back.

CHAPTER 23

There is England

My dear Editor has gone away out of the Colony—or State as
we call it since Federation. Perhaps he grew tired of taking himself
out of himself as well as myself out of me to find acceptance.
He has gone to a different kind of paper, and I am left without
a patron. It must be grand to be free to write what you like,
happier still to be so self-satisfied as to like what you write.

One amelioration is mine. I have lately received from the
stately publishing house of McMurwood a letter in character.
It is now time for my book to go into a final form and become
a CLASSIC. Surprise number 1: as I thought only Vergil, Homer,
Aristophanes and Co. were CLASSICS and that to couple the
word with a LOCAL CACKLER would be blasphemy or caricature. Surprise number 2: that I could have any say in a re-
issue. Could the book be stopped altogether? Through imaginary
characters being identified with real people I was accused of
belittling my connections, but if no more books were forthcoming
those in circulation would die of old age and disappear and we
could all sink to peace. In future I could have a *nom de plume*,
carefully guarded, so that my attempts could be taken on their
own demerits without the impetus of scandal. Conventional people
and I would not then suffer from a relationship uncongenial to
both parties and for which neither is responsible.

Messrs McMurwood met my wishes as if I were a real person—
an experience to give me back a shred of self-confidence. Honesty
and decency are basic necessities, but good manners are to the
sensibilities as cream and honey to the tongue. Certainly I can
withdraw the book. Would I care for a number of the remaining
copies for my own use? No, not one. And that was that. If only
I had known this after the first edition: but a number of LOCAL
CACKLERS had given me the benefit of their EXPERIENCE

446

with MSS bought and published on Australia's own publishing hook. They had been given ten or twenty pounds, and though the works in some instances sold as well or better than mine, the authors were not entitled to nor did they receive a penny beyond the first amount, nor were they allowed any control even in revising subsequent editions. There was a case where learning by another's EXPERIENCE resulted in knowledge as limiting as ignorance.

I am now twenty. The years have passed droughtily in a personal as well as a meteorological sense. I feel so terribly old. I have dried up in this barren gully while there are such glorious places elsewhere. If only I had a view of mountains or of the sea in storm, or in sun too calm for waves but glinting like the silver gum leaves in the noonday light, this would be to know wealth despite money poverty.

Only the trouble with God has abated. LIFE and LOVE and WORK insist increasingly. The need to submit to marriage or else find some other way of earning my living grows nearer, clearer, deadlier than before. Fortunately Henry Beauchamp has had to go to Queensland again to look after his property. It is a safe distance offering respite for the present.

The idea of marriage is going bung with me. Marriage is unnecessarily engulfing and too full of opportunities to experience GREY TOPPER'S receipt for producing genius.

Henry once said that he would be jealous of my writing if it took up my spare time when he needed me. In short, my brain-children would be proscribed. I am weary of Henry's indulgent but inflexible assumption that my ideas are mere vivacity or girlish coquetry, which motherhood will extirpate. I can discern under the padded glove of spooniness the fixed determination to bend me to prescribed femaleness. Ah, no, m'lord, the bait is not sufficiently enticing, nor does it entirely conceal the hook.

I have refuged in day-dreams, but one must have more than these on which to expend emotion: there must be some object of passion, personal or public. Mine is the beauty of the universe. And there is always England. England with her ancient historic beauty—tradition—the racial rooftree. I picture her cool green fields, her misty downs, her bare woods under the snow, her young leaves and soft flowers in spring. Her castles and cathedrals, her ivied towers, her brooks are as clear to my nostrils and closed eyes as the scents and features of Possum Gully. And there is London with its romantic fogs, its crowds and ceremonial pageants, Rotten Row and the Mall, the British Museum, the Mansion House, The Tower and Westminster. I know London much better than I do Sydney. Through song and story it has permeated every fibre of my mind since I could first scan a pictured page, while I have spent scarcely a month in but one corner of Sydney. London—THE BIG SMOKE—London, where our dreams come true.

England acclaimed my first homespun effort. England may welcome my second and third. I will arise and go to Mother England.

Lady Jane's column is devoted to escapees. Sculptors, writers, singers, actors, painters, educationists, politicians all depart inevitably. I have been going with them in imagination ever since I saw the Heads standing up there with the spray playing around their base and the Pacific beyond like a high blue plateau. It seems that only those remain who cannot get away, those who are tied to pots and pans by poverty and ignorance, by misfortune or incompetence.

The seasons have smiled once more. The chief reminder of the drought which killed the stock and bared the paddocks is that here and there a spot of richer green shows where in death some animal fertilised its pasture. The doubled value of remaining stock compensates for what was lost. Ridge and gully echo the cry of young things which replenish the earth.

The day is lovely in the atmosphere and ample draperies of November. Even Possum Gully, like a plain girl when happy, has a meed of beauty. The afternoon is hot and clear as though the sun were a box-wood fire. The flowers droop their heads in the fierce proud heat, lizards bask in the glare, the poultry spread their wings and pant in the shade, the cows lie in the reeds of the waterhole on the flat, the horses stand head to tail in pairs under the quince hedge rising above the orchard fence and stamp and switch the flies off themselves.

A tiny breeze goes flirting through the last of afternoon, the eschscholtzias furl their silken petals. I have ascended the hill behind which the sun departs and where a thousand times I have watched him gleam red as a fire between the trunks of the grey messmates and powdered brittle-gums. To the east, amid wild hop scrub and stringybarks, a bridle track threads its way to the crisp main road to Goulburn, and on and on to Sydney, where the sea tracks lead on to the WORLD.

The final gleam of the sun kisses the waterhole, the shadows grow long and dark, reversing their morning journey. The rumble of a train miles distant bears my heart on its rhythm of departure. The kookaburras are laughing themselves to sleep, chorus answering chorus—*coda—da capo—finale*. The gentle curlews lure me farther into the scrub, where I still can see the departing sun and the afterglow falling far away through a gap in the ranges on to one of the bright rich plains of an early holding.

The flaunting afterglow melts and passes, the evening star is bright and bold, and throws a spark in the dam of the back paddock at the fall of the she-oak ridge where the night birds call in unmolested scrubs and flap slowly from tree to tree. A tremor of nights run along the seeding grasses.

A wise old moon slowly chases the shadows westward once again and laps all in her silver enchantment. A thousand jewels flash above the dark shadows as she catches the eyes of the flock camped on the rise.

Beauty is abroad. Under her spell the voices of the great world call me. To them I give ear and go.

ENDNOTES

This introduction draws primarily on manuscript material from the Miles Franklin Papers in the Mitchell Library, State Library of New South Wales (ML. MSS. 364); her letters in this collection are reprinted with the permission of the Mitchell Library, State Library of New South Wales. The letters from Alex Montgomery to Miles Franklin of 18 April 1899, from Henry Lawson to Miles Franklin of early 1900, and from William Blackwood to J. B. Pinker of 29 January 1900 are also held in these papers. The extracts from the unpublished manuscript versions of *My Career Goes Bung* are also held in the Mitchell Library (ML. MSS. 364), and are reprinted with permission of the Permanent Trustee Company Ltd. Extracts from Henry Lawson's letters are taken from Colin Roderick (ed.), *Henry Lawson Letters 1890–1922* (Angus & Robertson, 1970). Some of the manuscript material quoted here has previously appeared in Verna Coleman, *Miles Franklin in America, Her Unknown (Brilliant) Career* (Angus & Robertson, 1981) and A. W. Barker, *Dear Robertson. Letters to an Australian Publisher* (Angus & Robertson, 1982), though my interpretation differs in some respects from that offered by these authors. For further information on Miles Franklin's later games with publishers and pseudonyms, see Val Kent, 'Alias Miles Franklin' in Carole Ferrier (ed.), *Gender, Politics and Fiction. Twentieth Century Australian Women's Novels* (University of Queensland Press, 1985).

OTHER TITLES IN THE
IMPRINT CLASSICS SERIES

ALIEN SON
Judah Waten

'As soon as they saw me they burst out laughing and pointed to my buttoned-up shoes and white silk socks. I was overcome with shame and ran back into the house where I removed my shoes and socks and threw them away. I would walk barefooted like the other boys.' With such a gesture a child can adapt himself to a new country and new people, even though for some time he may not 'know a word of what they were saying'. For the older generation, however, things may not be so easy. . .

Judah Waten's classic story of a Russian family settling in Australia in the years before the First World War is published here with an Introduction by David Carter.

'Alien Son is a real contribution to Australian literature. . . It even has some of the descriptive simplicity of Chekhov and Katherine Mansfield.'

Sydney Morning Herald

'This book pioneers a rich field for the fuller imaginative interpretation of Australian life. *Alien Son,* sympathetic, penetrating, shows us many possibilities. . .

The Australian

'In *Alien Son* the child, the parents are two additions to the short list of characters in Australian fiction who deserve permanent life in our imagination. . .They are fully, grubbily alive. Mr Waten's ruthlessly realistic picture of them is nevertheless wonderfully tender.'

The Age

WATERWAY

Eleanor Dark

This sparkling novel, set on the edge of Sydney harbour, follows a small group of people through the intricacies of a single day; a day that reaches its climax on the harbour when the ferry bound for Watson's Bay collides with a liner and sinks.

How will the accident change the life of Winifred, married to vindictive Arthur and in love with Ian? Will the events of the day alter the resentments of Jack Saunders or the vanities of Lorna Sellman? Is there any reason or morality when it comes to accident and death?

First published in 1938 when Eleanor Dark was at the heart of her powers, and reprinted here with an introduction by Drusilla Modjeska, *Waterway* is as brightly patterned as the harbour and as full of life as the people it describes.

INTIMATE STRANGERS

Katharine Susannah Prichard

Greg and Elodie have reached that point in a marriage when passion gives way to habit and the pleasures of a shared life become monotonous.

For Greg diversion is possible in discreet liaisons, but when temptation comes to Elodie, it threatens to overwhelm them both.

Set against the poiitical turmoil of the Depression, *Intimate Strangers* is a frank account of marital breakdown, and explores the choices a woman can make, and should make: as wife, mother and lover.

Intimate Strangers is published here with an introduction by Ric Throssell.

THE TIMELESS LAND

Eleanor Dark

First published in 1941, Eleanor Dark's classic novel of the early settlement of Australia is a story of hardship, cruelty and danger. Above all it is the story of conflict: between the Aborigines and the white settlers.

In this dramatic novel, introduced here by Humphrey McQueen, a large cast of characters, historical and fictional, black and white, convict and settler, brings alive those bitter years with moments of tenderness and conciliation amid the brutality and hostility. All the while, behind the veneer of British civilisation, lies the baffling presence of Australia, a timeless land that shares with England 'not even its seasons or its stars'.